NATIONAL GEOGRAPHIC
TRAVELER
New York

NATIONAL GEOGRAPHIC
TRAVELER
New York

Michael S. Durham

National Geographic
Washington, D.C.

Contents

How to use this guide 6–7   About the author 8
New York areas 47–226   Excursions 227–234   Travelwise 235–264
Index 265–269   Credits 270–271

History & culture 9
New York today 10–17
History of New York 18–29
The arts 30–43
Feature: Entrances 44–46

Lower Manhattan 47
Introduction & map 48–49
Lower Manhattan 50–65
Walk up Broadway 60–61
The neighborhoods 66–74
Walk: Cast iron in SoHo 72–73

The Villages 75
Introduction & map 76–77
A walk in Greenwich Village 80–81
Feature: A banner year for the arts 82–83

Midtown South 87
Introduction & map 88–89
Walk down Ladies' Mile 94–95

Midtown North 101
Introduction & map 102–103
Feature: The Great White Way 112–113
Skyscrapers walking tour 116–117

Upper East Side 131
Introduction & map 132–133
Feature: Silk stocking district 162–163

Central Park 167
Introduction & map 168–169

Upper West Side 173
Introduction & map 174–175
Walk from park to park 180–181

The Heights & Harlem 189
Introduction & map 190–191
The Heights 192–197
Harlem 198–202
Feature: Harlem Renaissance 200–201

The Outer Boroughs 203
Introduction & map 204–205
Brooklyn 206–214
Brooklyn Heights walk 206–207
Staten Island 215–218
The Bronx 219–222
Queens 223–226

Excursions 227
Introduction & map 228–229
Hudson River Valley 230–232
Long Island 233–234

Travelwise 235
Planning your trip 236
Getting around 236–237
Practical advice 237
Hotels & restaurants by area 238–255
Shopping in New York 256–260
Entertainment 261–264

Index 265–269
Credits 270–271

Page 1: Taxi in Times Square
Pages 2–3: Manhattan's sparkling skyline
Left: The Chrysler Building

How to use this guide

See back flap for keys to text and map symbols

The *National Geographic Traveler* brings you the best of New York in text, pictures, and maps. Divided into three sections, the guide begins with an overview of history and culture. Following are ten area chapters with featured sites chosen by the author for their particular interest and treated in depth. Each chapter opens with its own contents list for easy reference. A final chapter suggests possible excursions from the city.

A pictorial map introduces each area of the city, highlighting the featured sites and locating other places of interest. Walks, plotted on their own maps, suggest routes for discovering the most about an area. Features and sidebars offer intriguing detail on history, culture, or contemporary life.

The final section, Travelwise, lists essential information for the traveler—pre-trip planning, getting around, and survival—plus a selection of hotels and restaurants arranged by area, shops, and entertainment possibilities.

To the best of our knowledge, site information is accurate as of the press date. However, it's always advisable to call ahead whenever possible.

66

Color coding
Each area of the city is color coded for easy reference. Find the area you want on the map on the front flap, and look for the color flash at the top of the pages of the relevant chapter. Information in **Travelwise** is also color coded to each area.

South Street Seaport Museum & Marketplace
www.southstreetseaport museum.org
🅰 Map p. 48
✉ Fulton & South Sts.
🕓 Closed Mon. year-round, Mon.–Thurs. Nov.–March
💲 $$
🚇 Subway: 2, 3, 4, 5, J, Z, M to Fulton St.; A, C to Bwy/Nassau

Visitor information
Practical information is given in the side column next to each major site (see key to symbols on back flap). The map reference gives the page number where the site is shown on a map. Further details include the site's address, telephone number, days closed, entrance fee ranging from $ (under $5) to $$$$$ (over $25), and the nearest subway stop. Visitor information for smaller sites is provided in parentheses within the text.

TRAVELWISE

> **LOWER MANHATTAN** — Color-coded area name
>
> **HOTELS** — Category name
>
> 🏨 **MILLENNIUM HILTON** — Hotel name,
> **$$$$$** price range
>
> 55 CHURCH ST. — Address, telephone, & fax numbers
> TEL 212/693-2001
> FAX 212/571-2317
>
> Top-end corporate — Brief description of hotel
> destination with harbor views.
>
> 🛈 561 🚇 1 to Cortlandt — Hotel facilities & credit card details
> St.; C to World Trade Center
> 🅿 📺 ♿ All major cards
>
> **RESTAURANTS** — Category name
>
> 🍴 **CHANTERELLE** — Restaurant name & price range
> **$$$$**
> 2 HARRISON ST. — Address & telephone number
> TEL 212/966-6960
>
> Lovely, formal dining room — Brief description of restaurant
> with impeccable service, wines, and cheeses.
>
> 🍽 17 tables 🚇 1 to — Restaurant facilities & credit card details
> Franklin St. 🕓 Closed all
> day Sun., Mon. L ♿ All major cards

Hotel & restaurant prices
An explanation of the price ranges used in entries is given in the Hotels & Restaurants section beginning on p. 238.

AREA MAPS

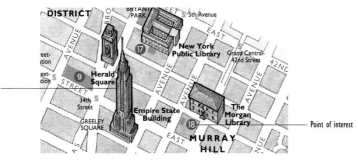

- A locator map accompanies each area map and shows the location of that area in the city.

WALKING TOURS

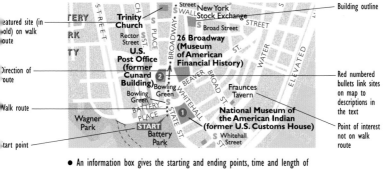

- An information box gives the starting and ending points, time and length of walk, and places not to miss along the route.

EXCURSION MAPS

- Towns and cities described in the Excursions chapter (pp. 227–34) are highlighted in yellow on the map. Other suggested places to visit are also highlighted and are shown with a red diamond symbol.

NATIONAL GEOGRAPHIC

TRAVELER
New York

About the author

Michael S. Durham, born and raised in New York City, now lives far from those streets in rural upstate New York. His continuing interest in the city is reflected in his writings, particularly the Mid-Atlantic volume of the *Smithsonian Guides to Historic America*. He has been an editor at the American Heritage Publishing Company and a correspondent, writer, and editor for *Life* magazine in both Paris and New York City.

His books include *Desert Between the Mountains* (Henry Holt, 1997); *Miracles of Mary* (HarperCollins, 1995); and *Powerful Days* (Stewart, Tabori & Chang, 1991), based on his coverage of the Civil Rights movement in the 1960s.

From experience he knows that New York City is not only a fine place to visit but a great place to live as well.

With contributions by:
Mary Ann Lynch, contributing editor and author of New York today
Lauren McGrath, compiler of Travelwise

History
& culture

New York today 10–17
History of New York 18–29
The arts 30–43

Times Square

New York today

NEW YORK CITY, THE FIRST DECADE OF THE 21ST CENTURY. THE GLEAMING Time Warner Center complex at Columbus Circle has opened a new gateway between Midtown and the Upper West Side, while farther up, Harlem pulses to the beat of an all-out economic renaissance. Throughout the boroughs, museums and neighborhoods add luster; and improvements along both the East River and the Hudson River are under-way—as well as a major transit hub at the World Trade Center site. The city's energetic retooling is all around.

A global nexus of creativity and commerce, the Big Apple is now more than ever the nation's heartbeat. Countless millions trace their ancestry to New York. People from all corners of the world keep coming, to seek a better life or realize a personal dream. Immigrants and itinerants, dreamers and schemers, students and professionals, these and more transplant themselves "beside the golden door." This dynamic cultural mix propels change and creativity, making the city endlessly fascinating.

The question is not who lives in New York City, but rather, who does not? Whether you are Old World Italian, Chinese, Jamaican, Greek, Arab, Slavic, or Iroquois Indian, you can find a neighborhood waiting for you, or you can start one up. In one sense, the essence of New York is its ever-changing population base, but there is tremendous stability within all that change. People come here with their traditions intact. They find niches in the workplace, settle, and assimilate, but they do not forget or discard their backgrounds.

Parades honoring ethnic groups are frequent, some large and loud, others intimate. The Puerto Rico Day Parade and St. Patrick's Day Parade sweep along Manhattan's broad avenues. But Italian processions, with saints carried aloft, wind through narrow neighborhood streets.

Time marches on, to the New York beat. The city is good at hanging onto what works, while rethinking or letting go of what does not. Sometimes it resurrects—witness Times Square, and the rebuilding of Lower Manhattan. Along Manhattan's far West Side, a defunct elevated railway known as the High Line is being rejuvenated as public space, just one of many community-driven rescues. With visitors (and residents) in mind, the city is

adding information kiosks and illustrated sig-nage. At the City Hall kiosk, programs are in cooperation with the Discovery Channel.

In SoHo, the East Village, the Lower East Side, and Harlem, growth is vertical, in new, tall buildings of modern design. And, like Russian nesting dolls, some neighborhoods enfold mini-ones—such as the popular shop-ping enclave of NoLita (north of Little Italy). The most supercharged areas thrive on a kind of post-postmodern New York City fusion—Chelsea's gritty western perimeter turned into gallery central; the Gansvoort (Meatpacking) District (between 15th & Gansvoort) become the province of the young, hip, and celebs—while during the day, workers hacking sides of beef coexist with haute couteur.

Midtown, the Museum of Modern Art is ensconced in its splendidly reimagined home. Farther afield, the renovated Unisphere in Queens gained national prominence with its high-tech lighting, and the new Yankee Stadium in the Bronx is targeted for comple-tion in 2009.

At times the city may seem to be a chaotic jumble of worn infrastructure, feuding politi-cians, gridlocked traffic from Macy's to the Holland Tunnel, and garbage piled up high during strikes. But whatever its problems or defeats, its victories are of such magnitude, its achievements so grand, its sheer human spec-tacle so astonishing, that nothing ever makes it stop. Newcomers continue to make New York their home, and many who visit are compelled to return. These kindred spirits have incorpo-rated its vibe, and discovered that New York City might really be the world's most unique

A gift of friendship from the French in 1886, the Statue of Liberty still shines in New York Harbor.

metropolis. It is without question the city that never sleeps, a place where at any time of day or night it is possible to find food, entertainment, drugstores, transportation, and architectural spectacle all around—and that's just for starters.

Maybe this is the kicker that separates a New Yorker from those who find the city is not for them: To survive in New York City, one must actually be aware of one's surroundings, ready to adapt, eager to excel, willing to be constantly tested in every possible way,

and—most importantly—in the know. About anything and everything. If New Yorkers are anything, they are "up to speed." In New York you can have a fascinating conversation with anyone you meet, from the street panhandler trying to sell you an original poem to the person seated next to you in the subway or Shea Stadium, from your waiter or—it goes without saying—your cab driver. And not only are they all in the know, but they know they are in the know, and they are strongly opinionated about what they know.

Times Square, ablaze with neon signs, lies at the heart of New York's theater district.

NEW YORK, NEW YORK

Who might be New York's power players today? Wall Street traders, yes. Celebrities, sometimes. Donald Trump, George Steinbrenner, Whoopi Goldberg, former President Bill Clinton, Mayor Michael Bloomberg, Martha Stewart—we can make a very long list. But the power players are also the subway conductor on your trip uptown to the zoo, the park ranger at Ellis Island who brings history to life, and the baker who makes those bagels that you seek out on your every trip to New York. Firemen, policemen, and emergency workers who put themselves in harm's way are power players as well.

Power players can be musicians, writers, actors, and artists, forging inspiring works. In *Gangs of New York* (2002), Martin Scorsese cinematically re-creates New York's bloody Draft Riots of 1863, dramatizing

their spark in the conflict between an Irish immigrant and a "nativist" American, and their followers. Remove the leaders and the story changes.

The point is that each and every resident has been, and is, vital to the New York mix, part of its incredible, unfolding destiny. Eight million people live in New York. It takes all of them to light up the metropolis to a voltage that casts its light upon the rest of the world. New Yorkers crammed together are the phenomenon that makes the city.

EATING OUT IN NEW YORK

No city in the country comes close to being New York's culinary equal. Nowhere can you find so many different things to eat and places to eat them. You can buy a hot pretzel—or a hot dog—from a street vendor. You can sit at a sushi bar and dine on raw fish. You can sample the cooking of some of the world's greatest chefs. New York has seafood and soul food— and Chinese, Japanese, Korean, and Thai restaurants galore. You can even have coffee in the Caffe Vivaldi where Woody Allen filmed

Balthazar, a popular SoHo dining spot, offers fine modern French food in a vibrant and upscale brasserie setting.

Bullets over Broadway. But smokers be warned: 2002 restrictions banned smoking completely in many cafés, restaurants, and bars.

New York's taste in food has been shaped by its immigrant population. Here, plain down-home American cooking is considered exotic, and the city's few genuine diners are chic. Many foods and drinks familiar to the rest of the country originated here. The recipe for the round doughy bagel, which is boiled, then baked, was a closely held secret in the Jewish community. In the 1960s the rest of the country discovered bagels, but somehow they still taste better in New York.

Vichysoisse, another all-American favorite with a French name, was invented at the now-extinct Ritz-Carlton Hotel. The egg cream is a blending of seltzer, chocolate syrup, and milk

(but no eggs or cream) known only in New York. On the other hand, the Reuben sandwich—a daunting combination of corned beef, swiss cheese, and sauerkraut (on New York rye, of course)—has a national following.

Delmonico's restaurant *(56 Beaver St.)* claims to have invented lobster Newburg and baked Alaska and gave its name to the Delmonico steak. It was America's first fine Parisian restaurant when it opened in 1831. The first restaurant to print its menu in French or allow women in the dining room, it is still at the downtown location it has occupied since 1891.

No culinary tour of New York would be complete without a meal in a delicatessen and a coffee shop. Here the food is hearty, the service brusque, and the amenities few. The delicatessen came with immigrants from Germany and central Europe. Some are strictly kosher and their specialties—pastrami, whitefish, matzo-ball soup—might be exotic to some palates, but their huge menus have something for every taste. Try Katz's Delicatessen or the celebrity-struck Stage Delicatessen.

Zabar's delicatessen and food shop on the Upper West Side serves up a stunning variety of comestibles.

Coffee shops, quick and inexpensive, offer delicatessen-like specialties—lox, cream cheese, and bagels—with ethnic touches depending on the owner (today probably a Greek). Each city neighborhood serves up delectable foods, from Brazilian and Cuban to Haitian and Vietnamese. Street festivals and markets offer chances to sample or just absorb the stimulating medley of sights and smells. In the "hot" neigh-borhoods, trendy restaurants open and close with lightning speed, though the many operated by Drew Nieporent in TriBeCa, including Nobu, seem longer lived. Excellent restaurants can also be found in such hotels as The Carlyle. Try Thomas Keller's Per Se at the Time Warner Center for an exquisitely imagined dining experience, served course after course…after course. The wait list can be months. ■

History of New York

IN 1998 NEW YORK CITY MARKED ITS "CENTENNIAL." COMPARED WITH THE
gusto the city brought to other recent anniversaries—the centennials of the Brooklyn
Bridge and the Statue of Liberty, for example—it was a lackluster affair. For one thing,
almost everyone realized that the city was much, much older. For another, what was
actually being commemorated was not a founding or a discovery, but the 100th anniversary of an administrative act: the incorporation of the city within its present boundaries.

The consolidation added the boroughs of
Brooklyn, the Bronx, Staten Island, and Queens
to Manhattan, greatly increasing the tax base; it
also increased the city's population from two
million to nearly three million, making Greater
New York in 1898 the second largest city in the
world—next only to London, with four million
people. But it has never been the city's size that

distinguishes it. It is the spirit that possesses the
city and its residents. New Yorkers dramatically
demonstrated their proud resilience in the
recovery after the terrorist attack on the World
Trade Center on Sept. 11, 2001.

**A 1664 map of New Amsterdam shows the
area that is today Lower Manhattan.**

t' Fort nieüw Amsterdam op de Manhata.

There are many other dates worthy of note. For example: 1609, when English explorer Henry Hudson passed Manhattan Island on his way up the river that now bears his name; 1625, when the first permanent settlement was established on Manhattan; 1639 (for Bronx residents), when a Dane, Johannes Bronck, settled just north of Manhattan. Anglophiles might celebrate 1674, the year the English took control of the city away from the Dutch, but patriots surely prefer November 25, 1783, when the British left New York City for good after the Revolutionary War. For more than a century, Evacuation Day, as it was called, was celebrated with enthusiasm in New York City.

Of course, Manhattan and the surrounding region was "discovered"—if that's the right word—by Paleo-Indians about 11,500 years ago. Their descendants were living in the region when Giovanni da Verrazano became the first European to sail into New York Harbor in 1524, a year the city's many Italians honor, although da Verrazano was sailing for France. Other groups relate to other dates. Africans came to New Amsterdam as slaves in 1626, the year Peter Minuit purchased the island of Manhattan from the Indians. There would not be a serious attempt to free them until 1799, when the state legislature passed the Gradual Emancipation Act. Jews might well honor the year 1654, when 23 Sephardic refugees from Brazil arrived in New York and formed Shearith Israel—the first Jewish congregation in the city and America.

DUTCH NEW AMSTERDAM

The first Europeans to spend any time on Manhattan Island were Adraien Block, a Dutch navigator, and his crew, who passed the winter of 1613 there after their ship burned offshore. Over the winter and with the help of Indians, Block built another ship and set sail for home. On the way out, Block sailed through the tricky strait in the East River that he named Hellegat (Hell's Gate) into the body of water he called Long Island Sound and on to Block Island, which he named for himself.

The same year, 1614, the colony called New Netherland was formed, with most of its activity centered up the Hudson River near Albany. In 1625, some Dutch families from elsewhere in the colony were ordered to Manhattan Island, and the next year their leader, Peter Minuit, purchased it from the Indians with trinkets, blankets, cloth, and metal goods said to be worth about $24. The Indians had no concept of property and could not have imagined they were selling their land rights. And though Minuit is remembered as one of history's great bargainers, some might say that $24 would not have been a bad price for an island that was—except for the southern tip where the settlers were eking out a miserable existence—mostly wilderness. The earliest view of New Amsterdam, the future New York City, by Joost Hartgers, based on drawings made in 1625–26, shows about 30 simple houses, a windmill, a fortification called Fort Amsterdam, and ships offshore.

Trade in beaver furs—to be made into

popular felt hats back in Holland—was the colony's one and only reason for existence. The number of pelts obtained from the Indians for export went from 7,520 in 1629 to almost 30,000 thirty years later. In 1628, when the first Dutch Reformed minister, Jonas Michaëlius, arrived from Holland, he was appalled by the ungodly state of the city's 270 residents, but the church he founded continues today as the Marble Collegiate Church *(29th St. at 5th Ave.)*.

As the colony grew, its devotion to business and easygoing ways attracted such religious dissenters as Anne Hutchinson. Driven from Puritan New England, she came to New York in 1642, only to be killed by Indians the next year. In 1644 the 11 slaves who had come with the first settlers were declared to be "half free." That is, they were free and could own land, but their children remained in bondage.

English Quakers, who arrived in New Netherland in 1657, were made less welcome by Governor Peter Stuyvesant. When Stuyvesant ordered Quaker John Bowne arrested in 1662, Bowne appealed to the Dutch West India Company, whose directors ordered Stuyvesant to stop. Religious persecution, they sensibly believed, was bad for business. In other ways, Stuyvesant was an effective admin-istrator: He encouraged trade, established a municipal government, and made and kept peace with the Indians. When threatened by the English presence, he built a wall stretching 2,340 feet, from the East River to the Hudson River, to protect New Amsterdam from inva-sion from the north.

ENGLISH NEW YORK

When the English came, however, they came from the sea. On August 26, 1664, Col. Richard Nicolls, acting on behalf of the king's brother, James, the Duke of York, landed 450 soldiers in Brooklyn and placed the remainder of his force aboard ships anchored strategical-ly around Manhattan. Stuyvesant, with a handful of soldiers, made a brave show of resisting, but leading citizens persuaded him to surrender. Nicolls became the first English governor, naming the town after his patron, but the settlement was to change hands once more. Warring with the French and the English in 1673, the Dutch took New York

back, then sued for peace the following year and returned it to England.

Under the English, New York shed its vestiges as a trading post and grew into a city, though not initially a prosperous one. British restrictions and ill-advised actions, such as paring away New Jersey as a separate colony, hindered commerce and growth. In 1683, under the new English governor, Thomas Dongan, a provincial assembly drew up a Charter of Liberties and Privileges, which included the freedom of religion and a right of self-government. By the time it reached England for approval, however, James, who as the Duke of York had charged Dongan with loosening the reins on New York, had become King James II. From his kingly perspective, the Charter of Liberties gave the colonists entirely too much liberty—so he nullified it.

The Glorious Revolution of 1688, which deposed the Roman Catholic King James, caused confusion about who was running New York. A German-born merchant and militia officer, Jacob Leisler, seized Fort George (Fort Amsterdam's English name) in May 1689, and proceeded to rule for most of the next two years. Leisler, an ardent member of the Dutch Reformed Church, ordered the arrest of "papists," dissolved the provincial assembly, and in 1690 attempted an unsuccessful invasion of Canada. When the new king, William III, sent a governor, Leisler was arrested for treason and hanged on May 16, 1691.

In 1734, another test of colonists' rights occurred when John Peter Zenger, publisher of the *New-York Weekly Journal*, was arrested and jailed for libeling the British governor, William Cosby, with merciless parodies and diatribes. At his trial, Zenger's lawyer, 80-year-old Andrew Hamilton, persuaded the jury that Zenger's articles were not libelous because they were true. It was a milestone case that established the principle of a free press in America. Hamilton told the jury: "The ques-tion before the court … is not of small or private concern. It is not the cause of a poor printer, nor of New York alone, which you are trying. No! It may in its consequences affect every freeman that lives under British govern-ment on the main of America! It is the best cause. It is the cause of liberty!"

The cause of liberty continued to be an

A deed signed by Peter Stuyvesant on May 15, 1664

undercurrent of this period, even infusing controversy into seemingly nonpartisan events like the founding of King's College (today's Columbia University) in 1754. After Britain emerged victorious from the French and Indian Wars, New Yorkers were rankled by having to support English troops headquartered in the city. To raise revenue for this purpose, Parliament passed the Sugar Act of 1764, which imposed strictly enforced duties on New York's molasses trade, and the Stamp Act of 1765, which required tax stamps for commercial transactions. In resistance, on October 7, 1765, New York convened a Stamp Act Congress in the city and sent a message to Parliament denying its right to tax the Colonies without their consent.

Mobs protesting the Stamp Act, led by the violently inclined Sons of Liberty, attacked the homes and property of British officials. When the Sons erected a liberty pole in the Fields (now City Hall Park), the redcoats cut it down, starting a sequence of semi-comic events that kept both sides busy putting up and cutting down liberty poles. Tension eased early in 1766, when Parliament repealed the Stamp Act and lowered duties on sugar and molasses. Suddenly King George III was a hero, and a statue lionizing the monarch as a Roman emperor was erected in Bowling Green.

The goodwill was short-lived. In 1767 Parliament's Townshend taxes on a variety of goods ignited more protests. Early in 1770, following a liberty pole incident, citizens and soldiers fought with bayonets, fists, and brickbats on a rise near John Street called Golden Hill, a clash that has been called by some the first blood of the Revolution. Then came the duties on tea, which led to the famous Boston Tea Party in December 1773 and the less well-remembered New York Tea Party, April 22, 1774. The New York tea dumping by Sons of Liberty dressed like Indians, as their Boston counterparts had been, took place before a cheering crowd.

In the two years that followed, there were lulls amid the tension as New Yorkers sorted out their loyalties in preparation for war. City merchants, believing prosperity depended on peace and stability, were reluctant to carry the conflict further. And New Yorkers were aware that their city would be a strategic prize and battleground in a war. George Washington, commander of the Continental Army, understood this, too, writing that British control of New York would "stop the intercourse between the northern and southern Colonies, upon which depends the Safety of America."

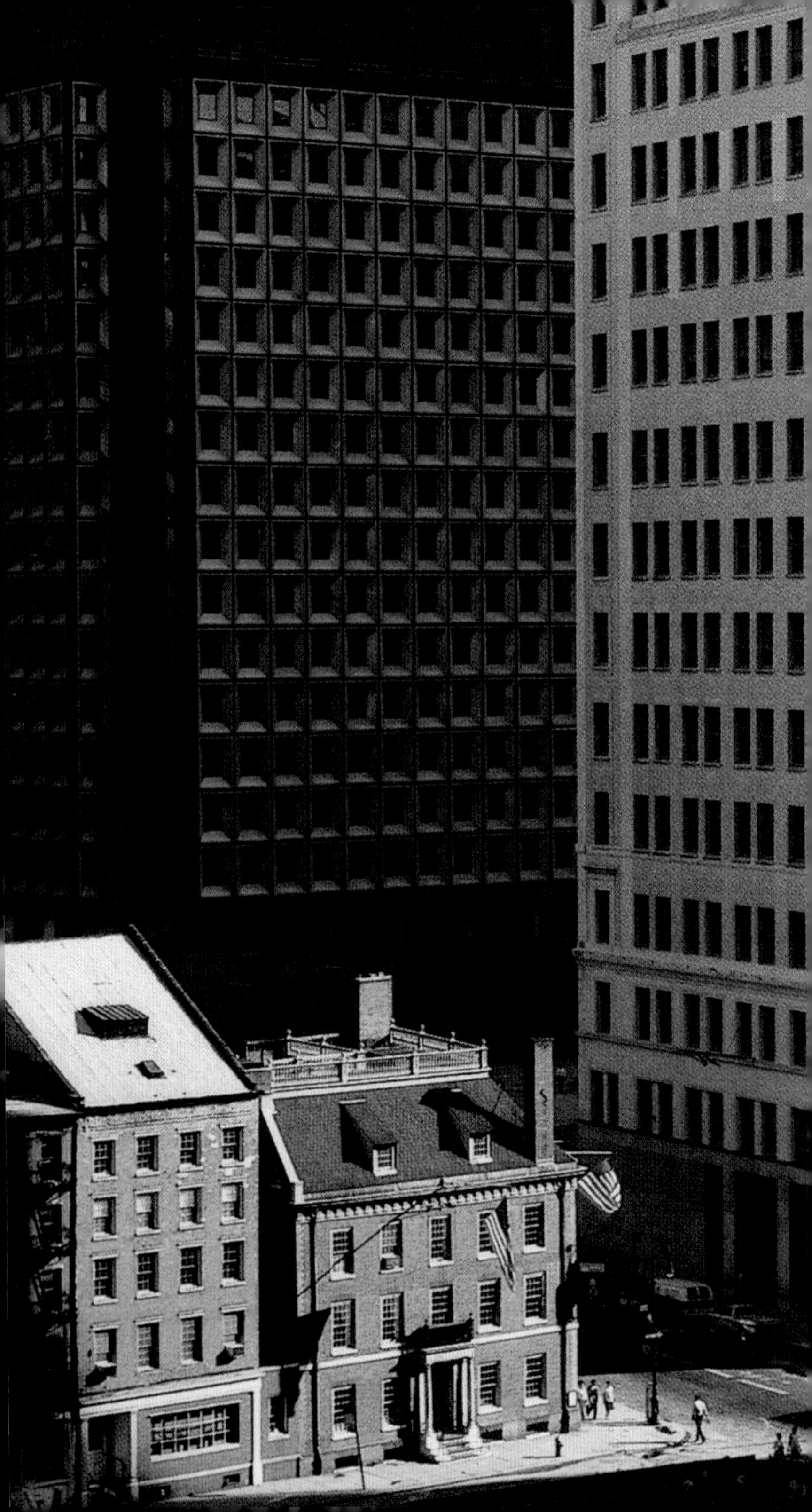

REVOLUTION

With war on the way, Washington moved to reinforce the city. When the Declaration of Independence reached the city on July 9, 1776, Washington had it read to his men. Once dismissed, they tore down the statue of George III in Bowling Green and melted it down to make bullets. By that time, New York was practically under siege. Nearly 500 British ships carrying 32,000 troops, commanded by Gen. William Howe, had arrived off New York and started disembarking soldiers on Staten Island.

On August 27, five days after Howe began moving men across the Narrows to Brooklyn, the British met the Americans defending Brooklyn Heights and, in the Battle of Long Island, drove them back to their entrenchment, taking some 1,000 prisoners in the process. Fortunately for the Americans, Howe hesitated. During the night of August 29–30, Washington ferried his entire force across the East River to Manhattan. Howe bided his time, waiting for an unsuccessful peace conference with the Americans on Staten Island to take place, before landing on Manhattan at Kip's Bay (near today's 34th Street) on September 15. When the green and outnumbered American troops broke ranks and fled, Washington in a rage tried to rally them and had to be pulled out of the line of enemy fire by an aide.

Although the Americans were in flight and divided between the northern and southern ends of the island, Howe did not press his advantage. Legend has it that Mrs. Robert Murray, a patriotic woman residing near present-day 34th Street and Park Avenue, intentionally delayed him with an invitation to tea. More likely, the visit took place while Howe was waiting for his forces to land on Manhattan. The delay allowed the Americans in the south to sneak up the west side to rejoin Washington. The next day they drove back the British at about 125th Street in a two-hour battle that boosted morale, though it was clear the Americans could not hold the city. On October 16, Washington withdrew from

Manhattan, leaving nearly 3,000 men to defend Fort Washington, which fell a month later.

The British occupied New York City for the rest of the war, from 1776 to 1783; during this time two serious fires destroyed some 600 buildings. Many Loyalists left at the outbreak of war, and during the frenzied summer of

Alexander Hamilton (1755–1804), influential shaper of an emerging New York

1783, some 60,000 more left the country through New York. The city became the holding pen for American prisoners of war, with many kept in appalling conditions on prison ships in the harbor, where an estimated 11,000 prisoners died—far exceeding the 6,824 Americans killed in battle throughout the country.

The tide turned in favor of the Americans after Lord Cornwallis surrendered at Yorktown, Virginia, in 1781. Still, New York City would not be liberated until after the Treaty of Paris, signed on September 3, 1783, ended the hostilities and recognized American independence. The British occupation ended with an orderly withdrawal on November 25, as Washington led his troops into the city. On the evening of December 4, Washington took leave of his officers in an emotional parting at Fraunces Tavern (see pp. 54, 55). He returned to be sworn in as the nation's first President in

Dwarfed by office buildings, Fraunces Tavern, now a museum and restaurant, evokes colonial days.

Hand-painted lithograph of an aerial view of Manhattan and Brooklyn by Léon-Auguste Asselineau (circa 1850)

1789. By that time, New York City was the capital of both New York State and the United States of America.

RECOVERY & RECOGNITION

Although New York would not be a capital city for long—the federal government moved to Philadelphia in 1790, the state to Albany in 1797—the city charged with characteristic energy into the 19th century. In a mere 30 years—from 1790, the year of the first federal census, to 1820—the city's population grew from 33,000 to 123,706, making it the largest city in the nation. This post-revolutionary period is the first from which many buildings survive. Castle Clinton (see p. 53) was built in preparation for the war with Great Britain in 1812. Commerce from the China and

California trades caused the rise of the South Street Seaport (see pp. 64–65). City Hall was completed in 1812. Federal Hall, built on the site where Washington was inaugurated, dates from 1842. Trinity Church, its steeple now dwarfed by skyscrapers, was completed in 1846.

This period also saw the rise of such institutions as the New York Stock Exchange, which began after the American Revolution but started trading in earnest after the War of 1812. As early as 1784, Alexander Hamilton helped found the Bank of New York, today one of the country's largest financial institutions (located at 48 Wall Street since 1797); later, as the country's first secretary of the treasury, Hamilton pursued policies that aided the growth of business and commerce in the city. (He died in the nation's most famous duel—with Aaron Burr on July 11, 1804.) Under Mayor and Governor DeWitt Clinton, New York became the country's leading commercial center when the 1825 opening of the Erie Canal connected the Great Lakes with the Hudson River and thus with the city.

COMMISSIONERS' PLAN OF 1811

In 1811 the city took steps to order its future growth by imposing a strict grid on the largely undeveloped region between 14th and 155th Streets. For a city that had grown haphazardly for almost three centuries, the Commissioners' Plan of 1811, as the grid was called, was remarkably forward looking.

A traditional ticker-tape parade—this one in 1969 marked the return of the first astronauts to land on the moon.

Running north and south were 12 numbered, widely spaced (920 feet in the interior of the island) avenues. The 155 cross streets stretching from the East to the Hudson Rivers were considerably closer together—200 feet. This purposeful configuration created long, rectangular blocks ideally suited, the planners believed, for "straight-sided and right-angled houses [which] are the most cheap to build, and the most convenient to live in."

Broadway, then called Bloomingdale Road, was the only thoroughfare allowed to cut across the grid. In doing so it created Manhattan's unusual triangular "squares"— Times Square, Herald Square, and the like. At the time, no one anticipated how fast the city would grow. Even the commissioners thought it would take time—"possibly centuries"—for the city to reach 155th Street.

The Commissioners' Plan, with its long, straight avenues and side streets, did accomplish its stated purposes of providing for the "free and abundant circulation of air" and controlling growth. Otherwise, it has been criticized for its monotony, for not providing enough parks, for requiring that much of the natural topography of Manhattan be leveled, and for the narrow side streets, which became a problem when the automobile came on the scene.

19TH-CENTURY SETBACKS: EPIDEMICS & WARS

There were setbacks along the way to preeminence. The yellow fever epidemic of 1798 took more than 2,000 lives. The Great Fire of 1835 destroyed more than 600 buildings in the heart of the city. The embargoes and blockades of the War of 1812 were hard on New York. When the British fleet threatened to invade in 1814, the city mobilized to strengthen its defenses and the mayor, DeWitt Clinton, announced he would prefer to "die in a ditch than tamely and cowardly surrender this delightful city." After the war, from which the city escaped unscathed, there were severe losses in the financial panics of 1837 and 1857.

New Yorkers were less militant during the Civil War, particularly merchants who had profited doing business with the Southern states. Although New Yorkers had responded to the initial call for troops, by the summer of 1863, when President Lincoln instituted the first draft, that fervor had dimmed. Immigrant Irish laborers were outraged by the draft, particularly the provision that allowed a man to buy an exemption for $300, a sum way beyond their means. In general, they felt that the Civil War was not their war.

July 11, the first day of the draft lottery, was quiet. But on July 13, when a second lottery was scheduled, the city exploded. A rampaging mob attacked police officers, wrecked draft offices, and ransacked the homes and offices of prominent Republicans and abolitionists. Then the violence turned against blacks: The Colored Orphan Asylum on Fifth Avenue at West 43rd Street was burned, and black men were brutally killed along Bleecker Street, then a black neighborhood. It took the combined efforts of police, politicians, Archbishop John Hughes, and five regiments of the Union Army to restore order. Over three days of

Helium-filled balloons in all shapes and sizes float high above Macy's Thanksgiving Day Parade.

rioting, some 105 people were killed and immense amounts of property destroyed in what is considered the most violent urban riot ever to occur in the country.

AFTER THE CIVIL WAR

The city boomed in the post-Civil War era, in spite of a city government, increasingly controlled by "Boss" Tweed and his Tammany Hall henchmen, which took municipal corruption and inefficiency to dazzling new heights. The addition of such enduring institutions as the American Museum of Natural History (1869), the Metropolitan Museum of Art (1870), and, in 1891, Carnegie Hall and the New York Botanical Garden gave the city the cultural

dominance it had always longed for. The dedi-cation of the Statue of Liberty in 1886 came in the midst of one of the greatest migrations in history. Of an estimated 23 million Europeans who came to America between 1880 and 1919, 17 million were processed through New York. Most of these settled in the city.

The city would never look the same after

its first skyscraper, the Tower Building, was erected on lower Broadway between 1888 and 1889. This ushered in one of the most remarkable building booms in history, which lasted until the onset of the Great Depression of the 1930s. Characteristically—in a city that has often torn down as easily as it builds—the Tower Building did not last past 1913. But many steel-framed buildings from that era still stand: the triangular Flatiron Building; the 1904 New York Times Building, which marked the beginnings of Times Square; the grandiose Woolworth Building; and two art deco masterpieces, the Chrysler and Empire State buildings, each a symbol of the city.

Like all great cities, New York is subject to cycles, the ebb and flow of time and change. New Yorkers cannot count on continuity; the city changes even as words about it are written or read. No one could have predicted that one morning hijacked planes would crash into the Twin Towers. The city and nation reeled. Just over a year later, New York won the national bid as the U.S. candidate for the 2012 Games. Though it was not selected, simply winning the bid was a victory.

At the start of the 21st century, the sparkle at the center of the city is as intense as ever. Two cherished public spaces, the New York Public Library and Grand Central Terminal, have been restored; the Museum of Modern Art is glori-ously expanded; the Hayden Planetarium enjoys its major face-lift. No urban rejuvenation has been more spectacular than that of Times Square. For decades somewhat depressed and dangerous, it now pulses with high-tech signs, new shops, and glamorous, restored theaters.

In Times Square, as throughout the city and its history, economics and commerce have been the driving forces for change. All great cities are subject to cycles. Those that endure, like New York City, do so through imagination, courage, and readiness to adapt, without sacrificing their essential nature. In the words of essayist E. B. White, written in 1949: "New York is nothing like Paris; it is nothing like London; and it is not Spokane multiplied by sixty, or Detroit by four."

New York is, and always will be, outstand-ingly New York. ■

Celebrating the Feast of San Gennaro in Little Italy

The arts

NEW YORK CAN FAIRLY BE CONSIDERED THE ART CENTER OF THE entire world. Why? Is it the artists who live here? Or the city's lively galleries and museums? Is it because the money, patrons, and collectors are here? Or critics and commentators? Is it because New York itself—wild, diverse, unpredictable—nurtures creativity and is such a good subject for art? All of these factors and undoubtedly more—those intangibles of place, spirit, and tradition—have contributed to New York's preeminence in the arts.

ART

In colonial times, portraiture occupied such successful New York artists as Gerardus Duyckinck (1723–1797). New York–born Abraham Delanoy (1742–1795) studied portraiture with Benjamin West in London, and, on returning to the city, painted members of the Livingston, Beekman, and Stuyvesant families. In the early republic, Robert Fulton and Samuel F. B. Morse were both accomplished painters before they turned to other pursuits—steamboats and the telegraph—that made them famous. John Vanderlyn returned from Paris to do a panoramic painting of Versailles, which he displayed in a rotunda in City Hall Park; it now hangs in the Metropolitan Museum of Art.

The Hudson River school, led by Thomas Cole and Asher B. Durand, believed it could capture the country's divine essence in glorious landscapes. Two of its members, John Frederick Kensett and Thomas Worthington Whittredge, were among the founders of the Metropolitan Museum of Art in 1870, a time when no work by an American artist was considered museumworthy.

Throughout the 19th century, New York artists banded together—and contentiously disbanded. In 1825 Morse and other younger artists rebelled against the conservative American Academy of Fine Arts and its president, historical painter John Trumbull, to found the National Academy of Design (see p. 151), now on Fifth Avenue. When the National Academy became stodgy, younger artists such as John La Farge and Albert Pinkham Ryder founded the American Society of Artists in 1877. This organization helped establish the Art Students League, the distinguished art school where Robert Henri, William Merritt Chase, and Thomas Hart

Benton taught and had as pupils George Bellows, Rockwell Kent, and Edward Hopper. The school still operates from its 1892 building (*215 West 57th St.*).

A group of New York–based impressionists known as the Ten also broke away from the National Academy of Design and set up their own gallery in 1898. Early in the 20th century, a different group, called the Eight, declared independence, and in 1908 put on a famous exhibit at the Macbeth Gallery: the paintings of William Glackens, George Luks, Everett Shinn, and John Sloan included realistic scenes of New York. The Macbeth Gallery show spawned the popular Exhibition of Independent Artists in 1910 and, in 1913, the Armory Show (see pp. 82–83), which exhibited the work of younger New York artists such as Stuart Davis, Marsden Hartley, John Marin, Joseph Stella (known for his evocation of Coney Island and the Brooklyn Bridge), and Edward Hopper, whose vision of New York is lonely, alienated, and melancholy.

Photographer Alfred Stieglitz was another influential figure of the era. In his gallery at 291 Fifth Avenue, he exhibited John Marin, Max Weber, and others, and during the 1920s and '30s he promoted the work of Arthur Dove, Charles Demuth, and Georgia O'Keeffe, whom he married in 1924. To gain attention for their work, other New York painters formed the American Abstract Artists in 1936. Its members—among them Mark Rothko, Willem de Kooning, Robert Motherwell, and Jackson Pollock—went on to experiment with a form of art that grew into the New York school, also called action painting, but best

The spiraling interior of the Solomon R. Guggenheim Museum, Frank Lloyd Wright's only New York building

known as abstract expressionism. Starting in the mid-1960s, abstract art veered in new, realistic directions with Robert Rauschenberg and Jasper Johns. This led into pop art and the works of Roy Lichtenstein, Andy Warhol, and James Rosenquist, with their vivid use of advertising and popular images. Most of these artists used New York as a subject, but as a group, the action painters expressed the city best, and none better than Jackson Pollock. His wild canvases—with paint slopped directly on canvas to pull beauty out of chaos—could serve as a painterly metaphor for New York City as a whole.

CLASSICAL MUSIC

Talent from abroad has always bolstered the New York music scene. In 1833 Lorenzo Da Ponte, librettist for Mozart's *Don Giovanni* and a New Yorker since 1805, founded the Italian Opera House, one in a succession of halls that followed the city as it moved uptown. In 1850, P. T. Barnum brought the Swedish soprano Jenny Lind to New York to perform at Castle Clinton. Antonin Dvořák was music director of the National Conservatory of Music on East 17th Street from 1892 to 1895; Tchaikovsky conducted at the opening of Carnegie Hall in 1891. Kurt Masur was director of a symphony orchestra in Leipzig before he took over the New York Philharmonic in 1991.

Wealthy New Yorkers have patronized the musical arts, sometimes as a path to social status. In 1825, John Jacob Astor, a music shop owner before he became one of the richest men in America, arranged the production of Rossini's *Il Barbiere di Siviglia,* the first full-length Italian opera performed in the city. The original 3,700-seat Metropolitan Opera House at Broadway and 39th Street was founded in 1883 by wealthy New Yorkers who were denied boxes at the Academy of Music (built in 1854) on 14th Street. In 1891, Carnegie Hall on West 57th Street opened. Built by Andrew Carnegie, it became home to one of the world's greatest orchestras, the New York Philharmonic, founded in 1842. Although other halls were built, the Metropolitan and Carnegie Hall reigned supreme until 1961, when Lincoln Center for the Performing Arts (see pp. 176–78), opened on the Upper West Side.

Robert Moses, the city's master planner, had chosen the site in the 1950s as part of a slum-clearance program.

In the mid-19th century, diarist George Templeton Strong noted that he could attend a concert most nights of the year. Had he lived today, it would have been several concerts every night. Classical music pervades the city; it is performed in large halls and in intimate spaces—museums, schools, churches—and unique venues such as Symphony Space, a converted movie theater at Broadway and 95th Street, or outdoors at Lincoln Center. You can hear a musician scratching out a Beethoven sonata on the street or listen to the New York Philharmonic perform under "the stars" (rarely visible in the city) in Central Park.

THEATER

"The Broadway theater is dead!" "Long live the Broadway theater!" Variations of these two cries have been heard, together and separately, ever since there has been theater in New York City. And yet the Broadway theater persists, even thrives, much changed over the years but still with us nonetheless. Of all the institutions identified with New York, the theater is perhaps the most prominent. "To see a show" is the main reason many people come to the city. And to act in the theater, or to write for it, or to play some other role connected with it, is still a dream that brings many young people to New York.

The theater has always been a fragile institution, vulnerable to all sorts of pressures, such as the American Revolution, the Great Depression, and World War II. Motion pictures (especially "talkies"), radio and television, the spread of regional theater, and the current phenomenon known as home entertainment have all caused doomsayers to predict the New York theater's demise. Financially, the theater always seems to be on shaky footing. Today's cost of staging a production runs into millions of dollars, and as a result a single ticket can cost more than $100.

The dearth of serious or innovative new plays on Broadway is another recurring complaint, but the fact is that theaters elsewhere fill the gap. Ever since the 1950s, when Tennessee Williams's *Summer and Smoke* opened at the Circle in the Square Theatre in Greenwich

Frequent outdoor concerts and plays in Central Park are major summertime events.

Village, the alternative theater known as Off Broadway has often debuted plays that wind up on Broadway. Off Broadway dates from 1951, when producer/director Theodore Mann and director Jose Quintero founded the Circle in the Square as a nonprofit theater. Jason Robards, George C. Scott, and Geraldine Page all began their careers there. In 1971 the theater moved to larger premises at 1633 Broadway between 49th & 50th Sts. As Off Broadway theater became more mainstream, another phenomenon, Off-off Broadway, burgeoned in the turbulent 1960s as a testing ground for experimental theater. Playwright Sam Shepard is one of several who first had works performed at the Caffe Cino, a coffeehouse on Cornelia Street, where Off-off Broadway supposedly started in 1958.

The theater has been a cultural force in New York City since the mid-18th century;

the first known professional production was *Richard III,* staged in 1750 by an English company at a Nassau Street theater. The versatile William Dunlap—manager, producer, playwright—was the city's leading impresario in the beginning of the 19th century. He ran the dominant Park Theater on Park Row, importing popular actors from England. From Lower Manhattan, the city's theater district moved to lower Broadway and then, in the 1870s, to Union Square. There vaudeville got its start at Tony Pastor's New 14th Street Theater, and grand opera was performed at the Academy of Music. By 1900, the final shift to Longacre Square, as Times Square was originally called, had taken place.

The legitimate theater thrived in the 1920s. Eugene O'Neill and other American dramatists—Maxwell Anderson and Robert E. Sherwood, among them—were produced reg-

Monty Python's *Spamalot* won the 2005 Tony Award for Best Musical.

ularly on Broadway. The American musical began its shift from gaudy revue to more dramatic and serious forms such as *Show Boat,* Jerome Kern's and Oscar Hammerstein II's 1927 hit. Today, lavish productions such as *The Lion King* attract new family audiences. Broadway theater thrives.

The restoration of venerated buildings introduced a new magic to Broadway. Even more remarkable has been the biggest Off Broadway theater redevelopment in the city's history, along 42nd Street's western stretch. Where intimate rundown theaters once stood a new 39-story residential tower houses the

Theater Row complex *(410-412 W. 42nd St.)*, with five new theaters under one roof. The 12-million-dollar Little Shubert Theater at No. 422 stages larger productions.

WRITERS & NEW YORK

New York is a rich backdrop for literature. In 1791, Susanna Rowson published *Charlotte Temple, a Tale of Truth*, a lurid novel about a fallen woman. Edgar Allan Poe was inspired by a New York murder to write *The Mystery of Marie Roget* (1845). After coming to New York in 1866, Horatio Alger wrote inspirational novels chronicling the rise of street urchins to success through hard work. In *Leaves of Grass* (1855), poet Walt Whitman celebrated the city as "the no more beyond of the western world." In the 1950s, Jack Kerouac and the Beats made poetry out of city life. About Times Square, Allen Ginsberg wrote, "There all the apocalyptic hipsters in New York eventually stopped, fascinated by the timeless room." Today, resident authors Caleb Carr *(The Angel of Darkness)*, Grace Paley *(Enormous Changes at the Last Moment),* and Stanley Crouch *(Adventures in the Skin Trade)* often make the city their subject matter.

Walt Whitman (1819–1892) sang the praises of Manhattan and the Brooklyn Bridge.

New York has given other writers the perspective to write brilliantly about where they came from. For Willa Cather, 40 years a New Yorker, it was the Nebraska of her childhood. Thomas Wolfe described his youth in North Carolina in the semiautobiographical novel he wrote in New York, *Look Homeward, Angel* (1929).

Washington Irving was one of the first city-born writers. His satirical *Knickerbocker's History of New York* was published in 1809. Herman Melville was born at 6 Pearl Street in 1819. He left to go to sea and returned to write such works as *Typee.* Novelist Henry James used his grandmother's Greenwich Village house as the setting for his 1881 novel *Washington Square.* His neighbor Edith Wharton wrote *The Age of Innocence* (1920) about the city's elite. Novelist Nathanael West

was born Nathan Weinstein in 1903 on East 81st Street. Brooklyn-raised Norman Mailer is still a prominent New York literary figure.

Harlem has produced such important writers as James Baldwin, who wrote about black New York in his 1953 novel, *Go Tell It on the Mountain.* Although they were born elsewhere, Richard Wright, Ralph Ellison, and Langston Hughes drew on their Harlem experience in their writings. In the 1920s, the movement known as the Harlem Renaissance (see pp. 200–201) attracted black writers from all over the country, including Zora Neale Hurston, author of *Their Eyes Were Watching God* (1937).

New York writers have always gathered in literary groups, clubs, salons, or in association with publications. In the 1820s, Irving was a leader of the Knickerbockers, gentlemen who wrote "for no other earthly purpose but to please ourselves." A few years later, James Fenimore Cooper founded the Bread and Cheese Club. Herman Melville gravitated toward the Young Americans, dedicated to encouraging a national literature. At the turn of the 20th century, Greenwich Village was a hotbed of literary activity, centered around the *New Masses* and other journals, theater groups, and salons. While some Village writers struggled, others, like Mark Twain, lived in patrician comfort in a town house near Washington Square.

In the 1920s, critics, editors, and intellectuals became recognizable figures on the literary scene—names such as Mark Van Doren, Lionel Trilling, Malcolm Cowley, and Brooklyn-born Alfred Kazin. The Algonquin Round Table was a lunch group of writers and artists that met during the 1920s at the Algonquin Hotel. Its members—among them Dorothy Parker, *New Yorker* editor Harold Ross, and drama critic Alexander Woolcott—were known for witty barbs and quips. In the East Village today, St. Mark's Poetry Project, long identified with such writers as Ed Sander and Ann Waldman, fosters poetry as performance. A community of writers is also alive today in New York via television talk shows and on the worldwide web, where one can engage in an online dialogue with a writer.

Even with the advent of the digital age and new ways to publish and market online, New York's foothold as the center of the world's publishing industry is certain. This is the place the industry began. The publishing houses, editors, agents, lawyers, reading venues, groups that give awards, media that publicize them—all the elements encircling the process of writing are entrenched here to stay. As for writers, the next Philip Roth or Tom Wolfe (both New Yorkers, by the way) will sooner or later make the trek to this mecca, hoping for a deal—over lunch at the Four Seasons uptown, or over drinks at Da Silvano in Greenwich Village. To be followed, of course, by appearances on the morning shows, "Live from New York!" Indeed.

NEW YORK IN SONG, FILM, & TELEVISION

Question: What do "Take the A Train," *Taxi Driver*, and *Seinfeld* have in common? Answer: They are by New Yorkers, about New York, and products of New York's creative industries—popular music, film, and television. "A Train" is a jazz composition by the great Harlem musician Duke Ellington. *Taxi Driver* is a quintessential New York movie, directed by New Yorker Martin Scorsese, starring a New York actor, Robert De Niro, and filmed on the city's mean streets (the title of yet another Scorsese film). *Seinfeld* was a phenomenally successful 1990s situation comedy that featured a collection of self-absorbed characters found only in New York.

Anyone wandering around New York will encounter, sooner or later, a street blocked by a crew in the process of making a film, television episode, or commercial. There will be cameras, trailers, lights, dozens of busy people, and occasionally a star or two. Both film and television started in New York City; they shifted to Hollywood, but have never really abandoned the city. The film industry, in particular, has a number of producers and directors who, by choice, do most of their work in New York, among them Scorsese, Sidney Lumet, Spike Lee, and Woody Allen. In Allen's films, the anxiety level of the neurotic characters rises whenever the plot requires them to leave Manhattan.

From the turn of the 20th century, when filmmakers associated with Thomas Edison started in the city, to World War I, New York was the moviemaking center of the country. Even in 1920, as the industry began moving to Hollywood, Famous Players–Lasky Productions, the production company that would become Paramount, opened Astoria Studios in Queens and continued to produce features there until 1937. The studio was taken over by the military during World War II and closed in the 1960s. In 1975 it reopened; Bob Fosse's *All That Jazz* (1979) and Woody Allen's *Radio Days* (1987) were among the features made there. In 1988 the Museum of the Moving Image (see p. 225), which documents New York's film history, took over part of the facilities.

Television also came of age in New York City. In 1927, an image of then Secretary of Commerce Herbert Hoover was beamed from the AT&T labs in New York to a receiver in Washington, D.C. The first CBS broadcast, in 1931, featured New York Mayor Jimmy Walker and composer George Gershwin. By the late 1940s, New York had four networks and about two-thirds of the nation's television sets. In the early 1950s, situation comedies such as *I Love Lucy* and *The Honeymooners* were all New York produced. Soon afterward, the entertainment end of the business shifted to the West Coast.

Still, New York remains a force in television. The network news is produced here, and such shows as *60 Minutes*, *Saturday Night Live*, and David Letterman's *Late Show* rely on a biting brand of humor that has its roots in New York. *Seinfeld* was so New York oriented that it still brings out-of-towners to the Upper West Side in search of Tom's restaurant, where the characters hung out; while such police and legal dramas as *NYPD Blue* and *Law & Order* present a grittier side of city life.

Hundreds of songs have featured the city since "New York, Oh What a Charming City." This and other 19th-century ditties were products of Tin Pan Alley—the country's songwriting capital—which moved from Union Square, to West 28th Street, to Times Square. Many songs, such as "New York, New York," written by Betty Comden, Adolph Green, and Leonard Bernstein, celebrate the city, and some are geographically specific: Bob Dylan's 1965 "Positively 4th Street," for example. Hank Williams, Jr. wrote the comically ironic "I Hate New York" in 1983, while other contemporary writers are socially conscious, such as Lou Reed, whose "Halloween Parade," has an AIDS theme. But of all New York songs and singers, Frank Sinatra belting out "New York, New York" is a universal favorite, and its oft-quoted line, "If I can make it there, I'll make it anywhere," is the heart of the New York City frame of mind.

ARCHITECTURE

Architecturally, New York is a proud but restless city. It is the city's nature to build, tear down, and build again, though in recent years preservation efforts have increased—and for good reason. New York today has only a handful of buildings left from the colonial era. Most are remotely located in the outer boroughs—at Historic Richmond Town on Staten Island, for example.

Buildings from the years after independence are better represented, with many surviving examples of the row house and its cousin, the brownstone, New Jersey sandstone over a brick frame. Those years also saw the construction of the Astor House (1836)—forerunner of the modern hotel—and A. T. Stewart (1846), the department store. The Gothic Revival style in church architecture was introduced with the completion of the third Trinity Church (see p. 57) in 1846.

In 1857, Richard M. Hunt, Leopold Eidlitz, and Richard Upjohn and his son, Richard M., and others founded the American Institute of Architects to put the practice of architecture on a professional footing. Cast-iron buildings were introduced in the city around 1850 by the inventive James Bogardus, and the world's first passenger elevator—the innovation that would make the city's later skyward growth possible—began its vertical journey in the Haughwout Building in 1857.

In the post-Civil War years, the luxury apartment was introduced as a living alternative for the wealthy. One of the first was Richard Morris Hunt's Stuyvesant, constructed on East 18th Street in 1869. On the Upper West Side, the still fashionable Dakota Apartments were completed in 1884. For the poor, there was the tenement with windowless flats, a housing type preserved today in the Lower East Side Tenement Museum (see p. 69). The postwar years also saw the construction of magnificent beaux arts public buildings—the Metropolitan Museum of Art, the New York Public Library, Audubon Terrace, and the Brooklyn Museum. And during this time, the millionaires' freestanding mansions on Fifth Avenue were built, including James B. Duke's 1912 mansion at Fifth Avenue and 78th Street, designed by Julian Abele, one of the city's first African-American architects.

SKYLINE TRANSFORMED

Then came the skyscraper, a word coined in the 1890s to describe an iron-framed building on which masonry was hung like a "curtain." The skyscraper, which transformed the city's skyline into one of the world's wonders, was born in Chicago but came to full flower in New York. In 1889 architect Bradford Gilbert built New York's first skyscraper, the Tower Building, a structure so thin and tall that New Yorkers thought it would blow over. In the ensuing race to build the world's tallest building, early recordholders included architect H. H. Richardson's Park Row Building (1897, 30 stories), Ernest Flagg's Singer Tower (1908, 47 stories), Napoleon LeBrun's Metropolitan Life Insurance Tower (1909, 50 stories), and Cass Gilbert's Woolworth Building (1913, 60 stories).

D. H. Burnham's triangular, 21-story Flatiron Building, when built in 1901–1903 the tallest building north of the financial district, remains a favorite with the public. The 1915 Equitable Building on lower Broadway blocked out so much sunlight that the city changed the zoning regulations to require setbacks—creating the so-called wedding-cake profile—on tall buildings. The race for height culminated in 1930 with the art deco Chrysler and the Empire State buildings; the latter, with 102 stories, was the city's record holder until eclipsed by the World Trade Center's twin towers in the 1970s. Both towers were demolished in the terrorist attack of Sept. 11, 2001.

After World War II, form rather than height became the prime architectural concern. The unadorned, boxy international style is reflected in the UN Secretariat Building, Lever House, and the bronze-clad Seagram

Noted for its gleaming stainless-steel spire, the Chrysler Building was for a few months in 1930 the world's tallest building.

Citicorp Center's sloping pinnacle rises above older rectilinear Midtown buildings.

Building, the last designed by Ludwig Mies van der Rohe, whose work is considered the epitome of the international style. Philip Johnson's AT&T Building (1984, now the Sony Building) brought postmodernism to New York City. Other landmarks of modern architecture are Frank Lloyd Wright's Guggenheim (1959), Marcel Breuer's Whitney Museum of American Art (1966), and the Citicorp Center (1978)—with its slanted roof a distinctive addition to the city's skyline.

The heyday of the skyscrapers may be over, but New York continues to both redesign existing structures and build anew. One can also expect future major construction on the city's east and west sides as more waterfront areas are reclaimed and improved. The 15-story Jacob K. Javits Convention Center (see p. 97), designed for the city by I. M. Pei, is already an established landmark against the West Side skyline. Opened in 1986 and busy ever since, the center features an elaborate glass-paned modern facade and Galleria River Pavilion (added in 1989), with outdoor terraces overlooking the Hudson River. These are popular for fashion and movie shoots.

Columbus Circle has been transformed by Time Warner Center, its new business/entertainment complex. The redesign and enlargement of the Museum of Modern Art has created it anew, and construction around 42nd Street has completed several entertainment complexes, theater renovations, and impressive architectural light structures. And never one to let go of the past—witness the remarkable transformation of Times Square—the city has plans for a major renovation that will move some of the train service out of Penn Station into the U.S. Post Office, a structure strongly reminiscent of the grandeur of the old Penn Station that was demolished (see below). Although buildings may disappear in the city, they are never forgotten, and often they live on—their grace and spirit echoed in creations blending old and new. And thus the city grows and endures.

PRESERVING & TEARING DOWN NEW YORK

Imbued with what Walt Whitman called "the pull-down-and-build-over-again spirit," early New Yorkers were not concerned about historic preservation. Particularly on Manhattan. Land is too scarce and valuable there to permit sentimentality over something as ephemeral as an old building.

So New York has done a lot of tearing down. The hope always is, of course, that the replacement will be better than what is lost. Sometimes that happens. In 1899–1900, the 45-foot-high granite walls around the reservoir at Fifth Avenue and 42nd Street—a sterling example of "Egyptian architecture"—were torn down to make way for the New York Public Library, one of the city's most beloved buildings.

The demolition of the majestic first Waldorf-Astoria Hotel is unlamented today because it made way for the incomparable Empire State Building. There was grumbling in 1939 when opulent brownstone residences

One of the New York Public Library's famous stone lions dresses up for the winter holidays.

on West 53rd Street were torn down to make way for the Museum of Modern Art, but that international-style building became a landmark in its own right—a worthwhile trade-off by anyone's standards.

There are certain buildings whose demise New Yorkers now regret. Ernest Flagg's great Singer Tower, at 47 stories, is now remembered as the tallest building ever demolished. The Brokaw mansions that once stood at

Fifth Avenue and 79th Street were emblems of wealth that are irreplaceable today. One loss that shocked New York was the demolition in 1963–64 of Pennsylvania Station, a "monumental act of vandalism," as the *New York Times* called it.

HISTORIC PRESERVATION
Penn Station's demolition marked the beginning of the historic preservation movement in

The Brooklyn Bridge, opened in 1883, crosses the East River to the financial district at the southern tip of Manhattan.

New York City. In 1965, the city created the Landmarks Preservation Commission to identify and protect landmark buildings and districts—and public interiors and scenic vistas—based on aesthetic, cultural, architectural, and historic criteria. Brooklyn Heights was one of the first neighborhoods to gain landmark status as a historic district. Today there are over 1,000 individual landmarks, 9 scenic landmarks, and 82 historic districts, encompassing nearly 21,000 buildings.

There have been several tests of the commission's considerable powers. When it rejected proposals to build a 54-story office tower over Grand Central Terminal or to squeeze in one adjacent to St. Bartholomew's Church on Park Avenue, opponents' appeals went to the Supreme Court. In both cases, the court upheld the landmark legislation and the city's right to protect its architectural heritage.

In other battles, the Edgar Rice mansion at the corner of 89th Street and Riverside Drive, owned by a Jewish religious school, was saved after a battle involving charges of discrimination. Even Park Avenue's first glass tower, the Lever House, only 30 years old at the time, had to be landmarked to save it from destruction. There have also been compromises: One allowed the New York Palace Hotel to be tacked onto the rear of the Villard Houses on Madison Avenue.

And there have been defeats. There is no way, ever, to replace such New York fixtures as Luchow's, the ornate German restaurant on 14th Street, or the low-slung art deco Airlines Terminal Building at 42nd Street and Park Avenue South, or the Hotel Biltmore on Madison Avenue, or the crenelated 71st Regiment Armory on East 34th Street, or ….

Today's preservationist forces might have saved some of those monuments; going forward, the new civic vigilance—which saved Grand Central Terminal and rescued Times Square's historic theaters—bodes well for the future of New York's architectural treasures. ∎

Entrances

Fly in or drive in, take a car, bus, train, ocean liner, or ferry, ride a bike or walk the Brooklyn Bridge: Any way you reach New York is dramatic. The city's exuberant etching of the skyline is exhilarating. By day the Chrysler Building gleams, and by night, lights of bridges, traffic, and skyscrapers cut the darkness. Fighting commuter traffic or rushing shoulder to shoulder with thousands in Grand Central Terminal, the excitement builds. You are entering the Big Apple.

TUNNELS

It is impossible to drive into Manhattan without negotiating a bridge or a tunnel. For those being taken somewhere by bus or taxi, it helps to understand where you are going. The Holland and Lincoln Tunnels, on the west side, go under the Hudson to New Jersey. The Brooklyn-Battery and Queens-Midtown Tunnels, on the east side, lead to the boroughs.

New York City has made important contributions to the evolution of tunnels. When the Holland Tunnel opened in 1927, it was the city's first vehicular tunnel and the world's longest. Its ventilation system was an engineering triumph. The 1950 Brooklyn-Battery Tunnel, at 9,117 feet, is North America's longest continuous vehicular tunnel. The Lincoln Tunnel, built between 1937 and 1957, is, at 40 million vehicles a year, the world's busiest tunnel. The Queens-Midtown Tunnel, stretching a mere 6,300 feet, holds no titles, but is a frequent route to La Guardia and Kennedy airports.

BRIDGES

To drivers, the tunnels can be terrifying, but the bridges are distracting. Some of them are beautiful; form and function marry so well in their spans that motorists can find it difficult to keep their eyes on the road. The beauty of the city's major spans is best appreciated from above, maybe from a circling plane or a skyscraper's observation deck. Here you will certainly hear the question, "Which bridge is that?"

The primary bridges, from Manhattan's tip and going uptown, are the Brooklyn Bridge, the Manhattan Bridge, the Williamsburg Bridge, the Queensboro Bridge, and the Triborough Bridge (125th Street). High on the west side, the George Washington Bridge connects to New Jersey.

The age of the great New York bridges began with the opening of the Brooklyn Bridge in 1883, joining Manhattan to what was then one of the world's largest cities. Measuring some 3,580 feet, with a central span of 1,595.5 feet between the two massive stone towers, the bridge was for years the world's longest, and it was the world's first steel suspension bridge.

In 1867 a steel suspension bridge was a radical idea, but this was John Augustus Roebling's plan. When the German-born engineer died, his son, Washington Roebling, saw the project through. Washington was crippled by the bends while working underwater in 1872, but he supervised the construction from a distance, using a telescope and passing instructions through his wife.

Today, the Brooklyn Bridge is still a marvel and a symbol of the city. Walk across the pedestrian walkway for a close-up view of the structure and harbor views; looking uptown, you will see the main bridges. On the Brooklyn side, the riverfront promenade provides spectacular views of lower Manhattan.

The city today has 2,027 bridges, 76 of which cross water. New York's first bridge, the King's Bridge, was built by Frederick Philipse across Spuyten Duvil Creek between Manhattan and the Bronx in 1693 and lasted until 1917. The city's oldest surviving bridge is High Bridge, constructed between 1837 and 1848 to carry water into Manhattan via the Croton Aqueduct system. The 1964 Verrazano Narrows Bridge between Staten Island and Brooklyn provides a spectacular starting point for the New York City Marathon. It is also the last bridge designed by the city's master bridge-builder, Swiss-born Othmar H. Ammann, whose other projects include the George Washington Bridge (1931), the Triborough Bridge (1936), the Bronx-Whitestone Bridge (1939), and the Throgs Neck Bridge (1961). The stately Queensboro

Top: The Brooklyn Bridge's architectural grace   Bottom: The Acela Express, North America's first high-speed passenger train, at Penn Station

Bridge will always be identified with F. Scott Fitzgerald's evocative words in *The Great Gatsby*: "The city seen from the Queensboro Bridge is always the city seen for the first time, in its first wild promise of all the mystery and the beauty in the world."

NEW YORK HARBOR

Go out into New York Harbor any way you can: There is no better view of New York than from its beckoning waters. Odds are slim that you will arrive in Manhattan as the immigrants did, crowding the rail of a ship to watch the city rise gradually from the horizon. But once you are on the water, the excitement will build, whether you are on a Circle Line cruise around Manhattan, a ferry, or a speedboat thrill ride; whether passing the Statue of Liberty or en route to Ellis Island—where millions of immigrants first touched American soil.

The Dutch settlers were quick to recognize the virtues of New York Harbor. It was wide, close to open ocean, and deep, providing easy passage around the island. This natural harbor became a magnet for commercial enterprise, beginning with the trade in furs. Peter Stuyvesant built the first wharf on the East River in 1648. The American Revolution, the War of 1812, the steamship, the industrial revolution, and the 1912 completion of the Ambrose Channel—which allowed ocean liner access from the East River—all contributed to the growth of the Port of New York. For the first 50 years of the 20th century, it was the world's busiest port.

Today, container ships go to facilities in Brooklyn and New Jersey, and the era of the transatlantic ocean liners is over. Nonetheless, the harbor remains a precious resource. Parts have been imaginatively restored, such as the South Street Seaport Museum (see pp. 64–65) near Manhattan's tip. This "living" historic district on the site of the original Port of New York includes 18th- and 19th-century buildings and a marina. Along the Hudson is Chelsea Piers, once a port of call and now a sports-entertainment complex at the beautifully restored piers 59 to 62. The *Titanic* was en route here when it sank in 1912.

Revitalization under way includes a state-legislated 325-million-dollar waterfront park, along the Hudson from Battery Park City to 59th Street; and plans for revamping the East River waterfront from Governors Island to Randalls Island, including areas along Manhattan, Brooklyn, and Queens.

AIRPORTS

You can dream about steaming into New York Harbor aboard a passenger liner, but if you are coming from any distance, you will probably fly. From a plane you get a view of the city in its entirety; it brings home the fact that New York is a city of islands and waterways. You can reach New York via three major airports: La Guardia handles domestic carriers; John F. Kennedy (JFK) International and New Jersey's Newark are gateways for overseas flights.

Through the 1930s, Newark was the only airport serving the city. This so galled New York's feisty mayor, Fiorello La Guardia, that he once refused to get off a plane at Newark because his ticket read "New York." The city got the point. Shortly thereafter, in December 1939, La Guardia Airport in north-central Queens opened.

John F. Kennedy International Airport opened in 1948 on Jamaica Bay, 15 miles from Manhattan. Then the largest airport in the world, it was named Idlewild until 1963. At JFK, airlines were allowed to design their own terminals, a decision that brought leading architects into airport design and produced such notable buildings as Eero Saarinen's TWA Terminal A (1956–1962), a winged masterpiece of curved concrete and glass, intended, in Saarinen's words, "to interpret the sensation of flying."

New York has played an important role in the history of flight. As early as 1830, 30,000 people watched a hot-air balloon launch from Castle Clinton. It flew an astounding 30 miles. The first international air races, sponsored by the *New York Herald*, were held in New York in 1907. In 1927, Charles Lindbergh left from Roosevelt Field on Long Island on his transatlantic flight. By then, important names in flight—Curtiss, Wright, Fairchild, and Sikorsky—had made New York and Long Island a center for airplane manufacturing. In the modern era, commercial jet service began in New York City in 1958; Pan Am inaugurated the first jumbo jet service from JFK in 1969. ∎

Start near the harbor and follow the city's growth north, from where George Washington was sworn in as president, through the fast-paced financial district, to the ever-changing ethnic and artsy neighborhoods.

Lower Manhattan

Introduction & map **48–49**
Statue of Liberty National
    Monument **50–51**
Ellis Island National Monument **52**
Manhattan's historic tip **53–55**
National Museum of the
    American Indian **56**
Trinity Church **57**
New York Stock Exchange **58**
Federal Hall **59**
Walk up Broadway **60–61**
City Hall & beyond **62–63**
South Street Seaport Museum
    & Marketplace **64–65**
The neighborhoods **66–71**
Walk: Cast iron in SoHo **72–73**
Museums off the beaten track **74**
Hotels & restaurants **238–241**

The stern face of Liberty

Lower Manhattan

FROM ANYWHERE ELSE IN Manhattan, go south, to the heart of Lower Manhattan. For it is here that you start to understand the changes the city has undergone: from fortification to thriving colony to seat of government to place of entry for immigrants to busy seaport to what it is today—the financial nerve center of the world, and since 9/11, a place of pilgrimage.

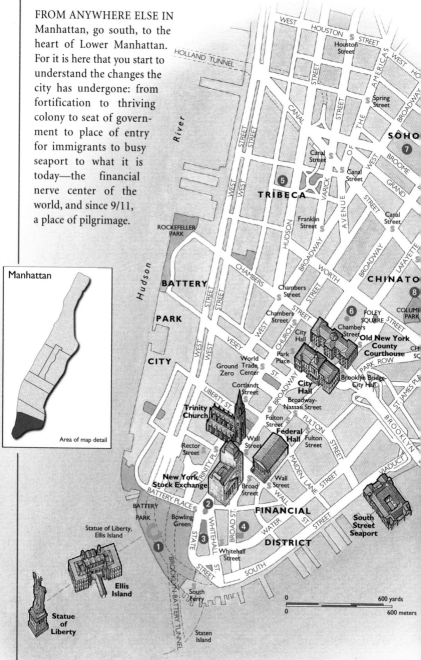

Manhattan

Area of map detail

WEST HOUSTON STREET
Houston Street
HOLLAND TUNNEL
CANAL STREET
River
Spring Street
SOHO 7
Canal Street
TRIBECA 5
Canal Street
VARICK STREET
THE AVENUE OF THE AMERICAS
WEST BROADWAY
BROADWAY
GRAND
Franklin Street
Canal Street
ROCKEFELLER PARK
Hudson River
CHAMBERS
HUDSON
BROADWAY
WORTH
CHINATO
LAFAYETTE STREET
BATTERY
Chambers Street
COLUMB PARK
Chambers Street
PARK
CHURCH STREET
City Hall
FOLEY SQUARE 6
Chambers Street
Old New York County Courthouse
CH SQ
CITY
VESEY
World Trade Center
Park Place
PARK ROW
Ground Zero
Brooklyn Bridge-City Hall
Cortlandt Street
City Hall
JAMES PL
BROADWAY
Broadway-Nassau Street
BROOKLYN
LIBERTY ST.
Trinity Church
Fulton Street
Federal Hall
VIADUCT
Rector Street
Wall Street
Fulton Street
FULTON
TRINITY PL.
New York Stock Exchange
Wall Street
MAIDEN LANE STREET
BATTERY PLACE
Broad Street
WALL ST.
South Street Seaport
BATTERY PARK
2
FINANCIAL
WATER STREET
Bowling Green
WHITEHALL
BROAD ST.
STATE STREET
3
4
Statue of Liberty, Ellis Island
Whitehall Street
DISTRICT
SOUTH
BROOKLYN-BATTERY TUNNEL
1
South Ferry
Ellis Island
Staten Island
Statue of Liberty

0   600 yards
0   600 meters

A 2.2-billion-dollar bird-like transit hub will be the first permanent structure to arise at Ground Zero. Nearby, the proposed Freedom Tower will rise to 1,362 feet, the height of the old World Trade Center South Tower. The surrounding 45-acre memorial grounds will include "Reflecting Absence," two reflecting pools. Completion dates are 2009–2010.

Visitors can watch progress streetside or from West Street, where the overall West Side and downtown development is exhilarating. Those starting a downtown visit near the harbor will find a modern-day immigrant experience with family and school groups and sightseers from far and wide and a carnival-like atmosphere of vendors and performers. The federal-style James Watson House *(7 State St. bet. Pearl and Whitehall Sts.)* stands proudly nearby, dwarfed by skyscrapers. The lone survivor of the elegant houses that were once all around, it is now the Rectory of the Shrine of St. Elizabeth Ann Seton (1774–1821), canonized in 1975 as the first American-born saint.

Some may feel drawn to a historic walk up Broadway, guided by Heritage Trail markers and signage. Others will head to the Battery for tickets to Liberty Island or Ellis Island (see pp. 50–52) or the always-free Staten Island Ferry.

The lively neighborhoods of Lower Manhattan from the Brooklyn Bridge north to Houston Street—Chinatown, Little Italy, the Lower East Side, SoHo, and TriBeCa—are evocative of earlier times and foreign ways. Traditionally this is where immigrants lived and worked, but now these areas are as likely to be inhabited by American-born artists or stockbrokers. At the turn of the 20th century, about three-quarters of the residents of the Lower East Side were Jewish; today Hispanics and Asians make up the majority of the population in this neighborhood south of Houston Street and east of the Bowery.

Boutiques, galleries, bars, and young entrepreneurs contemporize the flavor here. Even Orchard Street, New York's old-time shopping district, where immigrants shopped at pushcarts and small stores, is changing. Clothes and bargains still clog the sidewalks, but adjacent cafés and trendy shops add zest to the vibrant street life, and a high-rise hotel is a sign of others to come. ■

LOWER MANHATTAN

❶ Castle Clinton ❷ Bowling Green ❸ U.S. Custom House ❹ Fraunces Tavern ❺ TriBeCa ❻ African Burial Ground ❼ SoHo ❽ Chinatown ❾ Shearith Israel Graveyard ❿ Little Italy ⓫ St. Patrick's Old Cathedral ⓬ Lower East Side Tenement Museum ⓭ Lower East Side

Statue of Liberty National Monument

Statue of Liberty National Monument
www.nps.gov/stli

- Map p. 48
- Liberty Island, New York Harbor
- 212/363-3200
- $$ (Tickets at Castle Clinton)
- Subway: 1 to South Ferry; 4,5 to Bowling Green
- Ferry leaves Battery Park every 30 mins.

Note: The statue's crown and torch are closed

View from the torch

Statue of Liberty National Monument

BECAUSE SHE IS LOCATED FAR OUT IN UPPER NEW YORK BAY, the Statue of Liberty is rarely seen by many New Yorkers. Perhaps for that reason, even the most jaded have never tired of her. Nor have the words of Emma Lazarus's famous poem—"Give me your tired, your poor, your huddled masses yearning to breathe free"—which are inscribed on a bronze tablet on the base, lost their power. The Statue of Liberty, dedicated in 1886, was a gift to America from the people of France to celebrate the alliance of the two nations in achieving the independence of the United States of America.

Sculptor Frédéric Bartholdi modeled the statue on the ancient wonder, the Colossus of Rhodes. The statue's torch symbolizes enlightenment; her seven-pointed headdress denotes the continents.

She holds a tablet representing the Declaration of Independence. Lady Liberty is 151 feet tall, weighs 225 tons, and has a 35-foot waistline. Her index finger is eight feet long.

French engineer Gustave Eiffel,

who built Paris's Eiffel Tower between 1887 and 1889, devised a way to hang 88 tons of thin copper sheeting on an iron frame so that the statue is flexible enough to withstand high winds. Paris-trained Richard Morris Hunt designed the base and pedestal that lifts the statue 165 feet off the ground. The unveiling took place amid great fanfare on October 28, 1886. In one of the many accounts of Lady Liberty since, Russian writer Maksim Gorky tells of his entrance into New York Harbor: "Who's that?" a Polish girl asks softly, staring in wonder at the Statue of Liberty. "The American god," someone replies.

The statue was extensively restored in 1986 for its centenary. Visitors have access to the pedestal observation deck, promenade, museum, and the immediate Fort Wood area. ■

Once called Bedloe's Island, Liberty Island was the choice of sculptor Frédéric Bartholdi for the site of the statue.

Ellis Island
National Monument

SOME 100 MILLION AMERICANS AND MANY FROM OTHER countries have ancestors who passed through Ellis Island as immigrants. If you are one of them, or even if you are not, a visit to the restored processing center, Ellis Island National Monument, is a moving experience. It begins with a ferry ride, a small-scale simulation of those immigrant landings long ago. Inside, stand in the Great Registry—a room 200 feet long, 100 feet wide, and 56 feet high—and imagine the lines of anxious arrivals waiting to be processed. One-third of the 16 million who arrived here between 1892 and 1924 ventured no farther than New York.

**Ellis Island
National
Monument**
www.nps.gov/elis

🏛 Map p. 48
✉ New York Harbor
☎ 212/269-5755
💲 $$ (includes ferry)
🚇 Subway: 1 to South
   Ferry; 4,5 to
   Bowling Green
⛴ Ferry leaves Battery
   Park every 30 mins.

The island is named for Samuel Ellis, who purchased it in 1785. Over the years it grew, with landfill, from 3 to more than 27 acres. In 1892, the federal government

1900. During 1907, its busiest year, 1,285,349 immigrants entered the country through Ellis Island; 75 percent of them were from Italy, Russia, and Austria-Hungary, and the rest from northern Europe and countries all over the world, including China, Japan, Canada, and Mexico.

In 1924 Congress set strict quotas on immigration. From then on, the numbers passing through dwindled. The facility closed in 1954, a 160-million-dollar restoration began in 1984, and the Ellis Island Museum of Immigration opened in 1990. Exhibits on three floors re-create the experience of the immigrants on Ellis Island and celebrate their contribution to America. Follow their journey through the entry inspections and health checks, see the dormitory and dining hall, and hear the voices of immigrants telling their stories. The Wall of Honor outside is engraved with the names of thousands of immigrants; relatives can still add a name to the wall. On the island's south side are 29 medical buildings, untouched and deteriorating— listed by the National Trust for Historic Preservation as some of the nation's most endangered historic places. ■

**The Great
Registry, where
anxious immi-
grants were
once processed**

opened an immigration processing facility on the island. After it burned in 1897, it was replaced with the existing huge French Renaissance–style building of brick and limestone, which opened in

Manhattan's historic tip

BATTERY PARK IS A 21-ACRE SWATH OF GREENERY—AND a place of refuge for the financial district's many office workers—at the southernmost tip of Manhattan Island. It is dotted with memorials honoring, among others, early Dutch and Jewish settlers, the Coast Guard, and the explorer Giovanni da Verrazano, who first sighted the Battery's shore. To the north of it, the winding streets of the oldest part of the city disappear into canyons of skyscrapers. To the south, open water beckons. You can smell salt water and feel the pull of one of the most famous harbors in the world.

The Battery's principal building, **Castle Clinton,** is Manhattan's only existing fort. The circular structure was actually on an island 100 yards offshore when it was built in the days leading up to the War of 1812 with Great Britain. It took successive landfills to create the terrain that is Battery Park today. The fortification was named for DeWitt Clinton, a famous New York figure who, as mayor, was responsible for reinforcing the harbor defenses.

Castle Clinton, whose 28 guns never fired at an enemy, has had a varied history. In 1823 it was renamed Castle Garden and converted into an entertainment arena. From 1855 to 1890 (before Ellis Island opened) it was the city's immigration center. Luis Sanguino's statue "The Immigrants" (1973) pays tribute to the 7.7 million new arrivals who passed through Castle Clinton. In 1896 the building was transformed into the New York Aquarium, and so it remained until 1940. After a battle over its fate, Castle Clinton was restored in the 1970s and opened as a historic site with a small museum. Concerts and events are held here in the summer.

Castle Clinton

www.nps.gov/cacl

- Map p. 48
- Battery Park
- 212/344-7220
- Subway: 4, 5 to Bowling Green; 1 to South Ferry

Castle Clinton in Battery Park is a reminder that Lower Manhattan began as a walled fortress.

A bull in bronze, sculptured by Arturo Di Modica, is a symbol of a Wall Street stock market on its way up.

The 1907 Cass Gilbert–designed **U.S. Custom House** (*corner of Broad & Wall Sts.*) stands on the site of Fort Amsterdam (later Fort George), built by the Dutch in 1625. The highlight of the monumental exterior is Daniel Chester French's "The Four Continents," four allegorical sculpture groupings, each dominated by a female figure. Asia appears serene; America radiates vigor; Europe is regal; and Africa slumbers. The **National Museum of the American Indian** (see p. 56) is located within.

Just north of the National Museum of the American Indian is tiny **Bowling Green,** with benches and a picturesque fountain. Once used for cattle, this became the city's first public park in 1733, when it was rented to

Washington's farewell

On December 4, 1783, following the nation's victory over the British, Gen. George Washington gave a farewell dinner at Fraunces Tavern (see opposite) for his officers. The general was unusually eloquent on this emotional occasion: "With a heart full of love and gratitude I now take my leave of you. I most devoutly wish that your latter days may be as prosperous and happy as your former ones have been glorious and honorable." ■

Rector Street is a tribute to the rectors of Trinity Church. Beaver Street was at one time rich in beaver pelts, while Pearl Street once marked the shore and was named for the gleam of shells. Battery Park is named after the gun battery the British mounted there in the 1700s to defend the harbor.

Entering the historic block that includes **Fraunces Tavern** is a time warp back to colonial times. The tavern dates from 1719 and is today one of the financial district's better and more atmospheric restaurants. Samuel Fraunces, a West Indian who, tradition says, was black, purchased the brick building in 1763 and opened it as a tavern. It was saved for patriotic reasons—George Washington dined here (see box p. 54)—and, miraculously, the whole block has survived.

After deteriorating throughout the 19th century, Fraunces Tavern was reconstructed in 1907 in authentic Georgian style. Only the west brick wall is from the original building. It opened in 1910 as a restaurant and museum, which includes the Long Room, a re-creation of the site of Washington's farewell speech, and the Clinton Room, decorated with federal furnishings and 1834 wallpaper.

FRAUNCES TAVERN HISTORIC DISTRICT

Today the block by the tavern—bounded by Pearl, Broad, and Water Streets, and Coenties Slip—is a designated historic district with a number of early 19th-century buildings in the federal and Greek Revival styles. Coenties Slip, once a wharf created by landfill, is now landlocked. The adjacent plaza *(55 Water St.)* holds the **New York Vietnam Veterans Memorial,** a 14-foot-high rectangular glass prism, commemorating those who died in the war. ∎

three citizens for lawn bowling, at the yearly rent of one peppercorn. In 1770, the British erected a gilded statue of George III on the green. Revolutionary patriots later pulled it down and, legend has it, melted it into ammunition.

An unusual attraction north of Bowling Green is the massive bronze bull statue. The gift of a city sculptor, it arrived unexpectedly at the New York Stock Exchange one evening in the 1980s. It was later moved and it has become a favorite picture-taking spot.

Wherever you wander, note the history preserved in street names: Wall Street takes its name from the wooden barricade the Dutch erected in 1653 to protect the colony's northern flank. Bowling Green was actually used for lawn bowling.

Fraunces Tavern Museum

www.frauncestavernmuseum.org

🗺 Map p. 48

✉ 54 Pearl St.

☎ 212/425-1778

💲 $

🚇 4, 5 to Bowling Green; 1 to South Ferry

National Museum of the American Indian

National Museum of the American Indian: The George Gustav Heye Center

www.americanindian.si.edu

- Map p. 48
- 1 Bowling Green
- 212/514-3700
- Subway: 4, 5 to Bowling Green; 1 to South Ferry; R,W to Whitehall

ONE MILLION ARTIFACTS COLLECTED BY WEALTHY NEW Yorker George Gustav Heye (1874–1957) during his journeys throughout the Americas form the cornerstone of this fascinating museum.

Displayed on a rotating basis in the sprawling beaux arts U.S. Custom House, the artifacts represent significant Native American places, from the American Southwest to Hawaii, Canada, and South and

Above: A museum cultural interpreter demonstrates traditional weaving techniques. Right: A Seminole chintz "long shirt," circa 1840

Central America. They include stone and wood carvings from the Pacific Northwest; feather bonnets and quilled hides from the North American plains; Navajo weavings; ceramics from Costa Rica, central Mexico, and Peru; Mayan carved jade; featherwork from the Amazon; and the list goes on. One current exhibit focuses on contemporary Native American artists, including Rick Bartow, Joe Feddersen, Harry Fonseca, Jaune Quick-to-See-Smith, and Kay WalkingStick. Another details the history of the Native American cowboy through clothing, saddles, blankets, hunting tools, and colorful powwow regalia.

Since it opened in 1994, the museum has become a popular attraction—3.7 million visitors through 2002. It comes under the auspices of the Smithsonian Institution, which opened an impressive adjunct museum in 2004 in Washington, D.C. ■

Trinity Church

IN ITS 300 YEARS AT THE HEAD OF WALL STREET, Trinity Church has earned a prominent place in the life of the financial community. A good time to visit this lovely Episcopal church is during the week at midday, when—during services or concerts or on strolls through the historic graveyard—you can join Wall Streeters as they shake off the tensions of their fast-moving jobs.

Trinity is a very wealthy church, thanks to a land grant from Queen Anne in 1705 that gave it a huge chunk of Manhattan Island. The present building is actually the third church on the site. The first, completed in 1698, burned in the Great Fire of 1776. It was rebuilt in 1787. Two years later a service was held honoring George Washington's inauguration as President. After this building was razed, Richard Upjohn designed the present church in the Gothic Revival style, using New Jersey brownstone.

The 280-foot steeple was, until the 1860s, the highest point in the city and a landmark for ships at sea. Richard Morris Hunt designed the three sculptured bronze doors as a memorial to a wealthy parishioner, John Jacob Astor.

The church's museum displays newspapers, burial records, maps, and other documents and artifacts. The graveyard contains the remains of many prominent New Yorkers, among them Alexander Hamilton (see pp. 23 and 25) and Robert Fulton, developer of the steamboat. ■

Trinity Church

www.trinitywallstreet.org

🅰 Map p. 48

✉ Broadway at Wall St.

☎ 212/602-0800; concert information 212/602-9632

Trinity Church Museum

☎ 212/602-0872

🕐 Closed p.m. Sun.

💲 Donation

🚇 Subway: 2, 3 to Wall St.; 1 to Rector St.; 4, 5 to Wall St.

After a bell is rung to open trading, the floor of the stock exchange is abuzz with the buying and selling of shares.

New York Stock Exchange

AT THE NEW YORK STOCK EXCHANGE (NYSE), PANDEMONI-um reigns; people are invariably astonished that the business of trading securities, despite the mass of tickers, computers, and monitors, is still conducted by traders waving arms and shouting orders. It wasn't always this disorderly. In the early days members were assigned chairs. Today's traders are too busy to sit down, but a membership is still called a seat on the exchange.

New York Stock Exchange
www.nyse.com
🅰 Map p. 48
✉ 20 Broad St.
☎ 212/656-3000 (information)
🚇 Subway: 2, 3, 4, 5 to Wall St.; J, M, Z to Broad St.

Note: The Interactive Center is closed indefinitely.

The NYSE is the world's largest equities marketplace, home to nearly 2,800 companies valued at about 15 trillion dollars in global market capitalization. It is, in short, the center of the global economy. No one could have imagined such magnitude when, in 1792, 24 investors gathered under a buttonwood tree. There, at Wall and William Streets, they agreed to buy and sell stocks and bonds only among themselves.

In 1903 the institution moved into its current two-million-dollar

neoclassic building. The pediment sculpture, grandly titled "Integrity Protecting the Works of Man," was designed by J. Q. A. Ward. Although the exchange is now strictly regulated, "integrity" has not always universally applied.

Low points include the crash of October 1929 and the conviction and imprisonment of its president, Richard Whitney, in 1938 for bilking customers.

The NYSE is now permanently closed to visitors. ∎

Federal Hall

From its pedestal, Federal Hall's statue of George Washington gazes at the columned facade of the New York Stock Exchange.

FEDERAL HALL, POSSIBLY THE CITY'S FIRST GREEK REVIVAL building, stands at the heart of the busiest financial district in the world. Every business day, hordes of Wall Streeters stream past a location rich in colonial history. The financiers probably know that the statue in front is George Washington, but many of them—even those who spend their lunch hours lounging on the steps—may not realize that this is where he took the oath as the country's first President.

The present Federal Hall, erected in 1842, was designed by Ithiel Town and Alexander Jackson Davis. Eight Doric columns, 32 feet high, line the front and rear, on Pine Street. The statue of Washington, sculptured in 1883 by John Quincy Adams Ward, shows him lifting his hand from a Bible. Federal Hall housed the U.S. Customs Service for 20 years. It became a national monument in 1955, and currently is undergoing extensive renovation to repair damage from the World Trade Center attack. Visiting hours will be affected.

Nearby, the Bank of Manhattan Building, now the **Trump Building** (40 Wall St.), at 927 feet was the world's tallest from 1929 until the Chrysler Building surpassed it in 1930. First National City Bank Building, now **Citibank,** at No. 55 was built in 1840; it took 40 teams of oxen to haul its 16 Ionic granite columns up Wall Street. It was remodeled and enlarged in 1907. ∎

Federal Hall National Monument

www.nps.gov/feha

- 🗺 Map p. 48
- ✉ 26 Wall St.
- ☎ 212/825-6888
- 🕐 Closed Sat.–Sun.
- 🚇 Subway: 2, 3, 4, 5 to Wall St.

Walk up Broadway

If you would rather avoid fast-paced crowds, try this tour on a weekend, when the streets are quieter. It begins at the foot of Broadway, near Battery Park, going from the financial district to City Hall, convenient to shopping and restaurants.

Your stroll begins in front of the **National Museum of the American Indian** (see p. 56) ❶; be sure to take a peek inside. Then proceed to the Renaissance-style **Cunard Building** ❷ by Benjamin Morris, located at 25 Broadway. Constructed in 1921 as the Cunard Line's New York headquarters, it now houses a post office. You can buy stamps in the Great Hall, one of the city's best interior spaces. This room is where tickets for the *Titanic, Lusitania,* and other famous ocean liners were sold; its murals and decorated domed ceiling were based on Raphael's Villa Madama in Rome. Across from Bowling Green on Broadway is the **Museum of American Financial History** (see p. 74). Continue up Broadway. The building at No. 26, designed by Carrère and Hastings, has a pyramidlike tower; it was once the Standard Oil Building.

Just north of **Trinity Church** (see p. 57) and the head of Wall Street, the hulking 1915 **Equitable Building** ❸ (*120 Broadway*) rises straight up for 40 stories. The protests of critics who feared that such buildings would make the city a sunless canyon led to zoning laws in 1916 requiring setbacks (in which upper stories are stepped back to allow more light to reach street level). Just beyond the Equitable Building, the sleek **Marine Midland Building** ❹ (*140 Broadway*), built in 1967 by Skidmore, Owings & Merrill, has one of Lower Manhattan's nicer plazas, set off by Isamu Noguchi's red cube sculpture (1973). Turn right on Liberty Street.

Ahead, the **Federal Reserve Bank** ❺ (*33 Liberty St., tel 212/720-6130 for free tours with advance reservation*), in the style of a Renaissance palace, holds the cash reserves of many banks plus gold bullion from countries throughout the world. The four-story Vermont marble building at No. 65, fronted by Ionic columns, was built in 1901 for the Chamber of Commerce of the State of New York. The organization was founded by 20 city merchants meeting at Fraunces Tavern in 1768. Turn left on Nassau Street, then right on John Street. The austere **John Street United Methodist Church** ❻ (*44 John St., tel 212/269-0014*), built in 1841, replaced the 1768 Wesley Chapel, the first Methodist church in the United States. An early sexton was a slave who purchased his freedom from the chapel's trustees. He later founded the country's first black Methodist church.

Turn left on William Street. On the southwest corner of Fulton Street is the site of writer Washington Irving's birthplace (*131 William St.*). Turn left on Fulton, and right on Broadway. **St. Paul's Chapel** and its churchyard ❼ (*tel 212/602-0874*), between Fulton and Vesey Streets, has been in continuous use since it opened in 1766 as an adjunct of Trinity Church. George Washington worshiped here; his pew is marked by a plaque. The chapel is now a memorial to victims of the Sept. 11, 2001, terrorist attack. It houses "The Unwavering Spirit," a permanent exhibition.

Just beyond St. Paul's, at the Ground Zero site, construction of the Freedom Tower, public memorial, and major transit hub (with a terminal as large as Grand Central's) will be ongoing through 2009–2010.

Proceed up Broadway. No. 233, between Park Place and Barclay Street, is the 60-story **Woolworth Building** ❽. Topped by a

---

Ⓜ Map inside front cover
► National Museum of the American Indian
↔ 1.25 miles
⊕ 2.5 hours
► City Hall, City Hall Park

NOT TO BE MISSED
- Cunard Building
- Federal Reserve Bank
- Woolworth Building

golden crown, it was the world's tallest from 1913 until 1929, when the tower at 40 Wall Street outdid it. Its architect, Cass Gilbert, described it as a steel frame covered with masonry and terra-cotta. The building's lobby—decorated with murals, a vaulted, mosaic-studded ceiling, and a stained-glass skylight—includes a whimsical statue of F. W. Woolworth, founder of the five-and-ten chain that bears his name. Cut across City Hall Park to **City Hall** (see p. 62) to end the tour. You can go back to Broadway or swing over to **South Street Seaport** (see pp. 64–65) for refreshments or more sight-seeing. ∎

The Gothic beauty of the Woolworth Building made it an instant landmark in 1913.

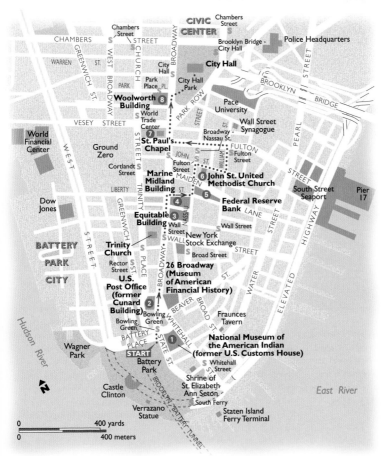

City Hall & beyond

CITY HALL PARK, ONCE A DUTCH COW PASTURE AND NOW pleasantly landscaped, surrounds the magnificent, federal-style City Hall. Frederick MacMonnies' bronze statue of patriot Nathan Hale on the green is a reminder that Americans once protested British rule here. For a liberating experience, stroll across the street to the imposing Brooklyn Bridge, with its wide wooden walkways and bike paths, and spectacular views north and south.

City Hall

🅼 Map p. 48

✉ City Hall Park

☎ 212/788-2170

🕐 Closed Sat.–Sun. Tour reservations required.

🚉 Subway: 4, 5, 6 to Brooklyn Bridge; 2, 3 to Park Place

City Hall's soaring rotunda, reached by twin spiral staircases, is the centerpiece of the 1812 building.

Even if you are a stranger to New York, chances are you will recognize City Hall. It is on these steps that the mayor greets visiting heroes and dignitaries and hands over the keys to the city, a scene captured countless times in news footage. City Hall has also been the center of numerous celebrations and demonstrations. Here is where ticker-tape parades up Broadway from the Battery generally end, a tradition that started spontaneously in 1886 when office workers threw ticker tape out of windows during a parade celebrating the dedication of the Statue of Liberty. Although City Hall is congenially sited in the middle of City Hall Park, you might wonder why its architects, John McComb, Jr., and Joseph Francois Mangin, faced the building south. Answer: When City Hall was built in 1812, no one thought the city would extend much farther north.

Venture inside, where you will see in the lobby a bronze copy of a statue of George Washington, done from life by the French sculptor Jean-Antoine Houdon.

The **Governor's Room,** once used by the governor on visits to the city, is now a museum with George Washington's writing table on display. The painting collection includes a portrait of Washington on Evacuation Day 1783, by John Trumbull, a leading historical painter, as well as works by John Wesley Jarvis, who painted the

heroes of the War of 1812; Samuel F. B. Morse, inventor of the telegraph, whose painting of Lafayette was done during the marquis's triumphal return to this country in 1824; and George Catlin, later known for Western paintings, who did the portrait of DeWitt Clinton.

Northeast of City Hall, near Park Row, which borders the park, J. Q. A. Ward's statue of Horace Greeley shows the publisher seated with an open newspaper over his right knee. For years Park Row was the center of Manhattan's newspaper publishing. For the day's news and tours, and interpretive displays, visit the NYC Heritage Tourism Center at the park's tip *(between Vesey & Barclay Sts.).*

OTHER SIGHTS

Nearby at 31 Chambers Street is the **Surrogate's Court** or Hall of Records. Completed in 1911, this beaux arts building is adorned with sculpture. Philip Martiny did the facade carvings, including a row of city mayors below the Chambers Street cornice, and the two groupings flanking the main entrance, "New York in Its Infancy" and "New York in Revolutionary Times." The wedding-cake tower of the 1914 **Municipal Building** *(Centre and Chambers Sts.)* is topped by Adolph Weinman's 25-foot-tall copper statue, "Civic Fame," the

largest statue in Manhattan.

Head two blocks north on Elk Street to reach the **African Burial Ground** *(Duane and Elk Sts.)*. Human remains dug up in 1991 by workers excavating at Broadway and Duane turned out to have come from a five-acre graveyard, where upward of 20,000 African Americans were buried between 1712 and 1794. The find drew attention to the large number of African slaves and freedmen in the city in the 18th century. Slave revolts in 1714 and 1741 were brutally suppressed, the leaders executed and then presumably buried here. ■

A fountain spouts in City Hall Park, in existence since 1730 as the Common. City Hall appears through the trees, and the Municipal Building rises to the right.

Tweed Courthouse

At the north end of City Hall Park is a three-story marble courthouse that is often confused for City Hall. Today the building, officially named the Old New York County Courthouse, is held in high esteem, and its interiors are among the finest of middle 19th-century New York. But when it was finished in 1878, the assessments were not so generous, and it was known as the Tweed Courthouse after the man who went down in history as a corrupt politician. One account described the building as "a gloomy meandering mess of unattractive rooms." The unfavorable review probably reflected the public's frustration, as the courthouse had taken 20 years to build and cost almost 13 million dollars, 50 times the original estimate. Two-thirds of that amount is believed to have been diverted into the sizable pockets of William M. "Boss" Tweed and his cronies. ■

South Street Seaport Museum & Marketplace

South Street Seaport Museum & Marketplace

www.southstreetseaport museum.org

🗺 Map p. 48

✉ Fulton & South Sts.

🕐 Closed Mon. year-round, Mon.–Thurs. Nov.–March

💲 $$

🚇 Subway: 2, 3, 4, 5, J, Z, M to Fulton St.; A, C to Bwy/Nassau

Visitor center

✉ Pier 16

☎ 212/748-8600 (main); 212/732-7678 (events)

This tall ship is part of the fleet on display at Piers 15 and 16.

FOR A TRIP BACK TO THE DAYS WHEN NEW YORK HARBOR was the world's busiest port, visit the 11-square-block historic district around the East River at South and Fulton Streets. Here is the South Street Seaport Museum & Marketplace, a restoration of the early 19th-century waterfront. Developed in the 1980s, the seaport offers a mix of history and entertainment—plus a burgeoning neighborhood vitality, as residents move into newly renovated buildings.

Titanic Memorial Lighthouse at the intersection of Pearl, Water, and Fulton Streets marks your introduction to the seaport. Do not let crowds obscure the fact that the seaport surrounding the market is an outstanding maritime museum, in and among important 18th- and 19th-century buildings.

The seaport divides into two areas ahead of you, with F. D. R. Drive perpendicular to Fulton Street in between. West of the drive, in front of the lighthouse, are complexes of joined buildings. These house the seaport's museums, exhibits, offices, and small

stores. East of F. D. R. Drive is the pier, where there are historic ships and where tickets for harbor excursions can be purchased. **Pier 17** also has a multilevel shopping center, including a food court. For spectacular river and Brooklyn Bridge views, go to the area outside the food court where there are complimentary lounges.

EXPLORING THE SEAPORT

From Water Street, head for the piers via the main Fulton Street corridor, which is lined with shops and restaurants. The 12-building complex on the right side is historic Schermerhorn Row. Here you can stop for visitor information at 12 Fulton Street. This is also the entrance to the main gallery.

Schermerhorn Row dates from 1812 and comprises 12 federal-style brick buildings. Walking around the building brings you to John Street. This was once Burling Slip, a water entrance for ships from China that unloaded their wares into the countinghouse of the **A. A. Low Building** *(171 John St.)*. The building (now containing offices) was constructed in 1850 by a trader whose ships dominated the mid-century China trade. Turning back to the harbor, near the intersection of South and Fulton Streets, Pier 16 and the historic ships await. Here tickets for attractions and harbor cruises are

available at the Visitor Center and various outdoor booths.

The buildings at Fulton and Water Streets contain four interesting places. **Bowne & Co. Stationers** *(211 Water St., tel 212/ 748-8651)* is a working restoration of a 19th-century printing shop. Ship models and ocean liner memorabilia are on display at the **Walter Lord Gallery** *(209 Water St., tel 212/748-8667)*, and the **Melville Gallery** *(213 Water St., tel 212/748-8649)* has visual art exhibits. The **Museum Library** above the Melville Gallery is open by appointment.

Be sure to wander **Piers 15** and **16.** Outings include Circle Line tours, a speedboat thrill ride, and even seasonal tugboat rides *(information, tel 212/748-8786)*. The piers' fleet includes the **Ambrose** (1908), a lightship that marked the entrance to New York Harbor; the **Peking,** a 1911 four-masted ship built in Germany; and the **Pioneer** (1885), a former cargo schooner popular for its twilight sails. ∎

Eateries and shops fill the three-story Pier 17 building, a 1983 addition to the seaport's complex.

The Fulton Fish Market and beyond

Since Dutch colonial times, New York's store and restaurant owners have bought their fish at the Fulton market. The 170-year-old market was named for Robert Fulton, developer of the steamboat. From 1814 he ran a Manhattan-to-Brooklyn ferry from the market site. The market is scheduled to move to the Bronx—at the Seaport, exhibits with fishing paraphernalia, signage, photographs, and an actual stall keep its story alive.

Meanwhile, the seaport is a focus of the East River Waterfront Plan, which includes a playground at Burling Slip, a plaza and a pool at Peck Slip, the rebuilding of Pier 15, and opening up access to the river with walkways and a waterfront esplanade. ∎

The neighborhoods

MOST IMMIGRANTS HISTORICALLY BEGAN THEIR NEW
American lives in the neighborhoods. Today these areas strive for balance as gentrification and high-rises introduce change.

**Museum of
Chinese in the
Americas**
www.moca-nyc.org
✉ 70 Mulberry St.
   at Bayard St.
☎ 212/619-4785
⊕ Closed Mon.
$ $
🚇 Subway: B, D, Q to
   Grand St.; J, M, N, R,
   Z, 6 to Canal St.

**Opposite: On
Chinatown's busy
Mott Street, signs
are in English and
Cantonese—and
tourists mix
with residents.**

CHINATOWN

For the center of old Chinatown,
head for Mott and Pell Streets
below Canal Street. New York's first
Chinese settlement developed in
the mid-1870s along Mott Street,
and today the area is filled with
restaurants, cafés, curio and
antique shops, and bookstores. Try
one of the many fine restaurants
and then explore.

There are daily masses in
Cantonese and English at the 1801
**Church of the Transfigura-
tion** *(25 Mott St., tel 212/962-
5157).* The church was built for
English Lutherans, sold to an Irish
Roman Catholic congregation in
1853, and attracted an Italian
community before becoming
primarily Chinese.

The most visible symbols of
Chinatown are the Chinese shop
signs and the pagoda-style roofs
that top anything from banks to
telephone booths. At 41 Mott
Street stands the only wooden
pagoda roof left in Chinatown.
The **Eastern States Buddhist
Temple** *(64 Mott St., tel 212/966-
6229)* is filled with candles and offerings to more than a hundred gold
Buddhas, while the small **Museum
of Chinese in the Americas**
holds fascinating exhibits.

You may seek out enclaves
such as Doyers Street, once a
dead-end alley known as the
Bloody Angle, where warring
tongs ambushed one another.
Confucius Plaza at Chatham
Square is graced by a bronze statue
of the ancient philosopher.

The most colorful event is the
five-week-long Lunar New Year

Festival, kicked off with a mammoth celebration on the official
New Year's Day in January or
February (varies each year).

Chinatown today has expanded
into Little Italy. Canal Street, once
the division between Chinatown
and Little Italy, has a bustling sidewalk market and Chinese groceries
stocked with curious roots, herbs,
and vegetables. West on Canal closer to Broadway, shops teem with
Chinese souvenirs and fashions as
well as knock-off designer clothes
and perfumes. All of Chinatown is
fun to shop.

Historic sites

The **Edward Mooney House**
(circa 1785–89), at 18 Bowery,
recalls an era when the area was
known for its fine residences.
Stanford White designed the
Bowery Savings Bank (1895), now
the Greenpoint Bank at 130 Bowery
in the classical style of a Roman
temple. **St. James Roman
Catholic Church** *(32 James St.)*
is the city's second oldest Roman
Catholic church. Nearby, the **First
Shearith Israel Graveyard**
(55–57 St. James Place) is the burial
ground of the first Jewish congregation in North America, formed in
1654 by Sephardim from Brazil.

LITTLE ITALY

Mulberry Street north of Canal is
the pulse of what remains of Little
Italy. Here are good Italian restaurants, cafés, delis, shops, and legendary Mafia sites. You might start
off with a cappuccino and a treat
on Mulberry or at **Ferrara's** *(195
Grand St.),* a hundred-year-old

Shoppers browse the informal displays along Orchard Street on the Lower East Side.

pastry shop just around the corner.

Little Italy's annual gala is the Feast of San Gennaro, held for ten days around September 19. A statue is paraded through the streets and there are food stalls, music, and dancing, with activity centered around the courtyard of the **Church of the Most Precious Blood** (*109 Mulberry St.*). Mulberry Street is also connected to organized crime. Before being jailed, mobster boss John Gotti frequented the Ravenite Social Club at No. 247. Gangster Joey Gallo was shot to death in 1972 while celebrating his birthday at No. 129, Umberto's Clam House.

Some historic sites have little original connection with Italian residents. Gothic **St. Patrick's Old Cathedral** (*263 Mulberry St., tel 212/226-8075*) is one of the city's oldest churches (1815), largely rebuilt after a fire in the 1860s. Its first congregation was Irish; a smaller Italian congregation developed in the 1880s. The **Stephen Van Rensselaer House** (*149 Mulberry St.*), with its brickwork front, gambrel roof, and dormer windows, was built about 1816. The baroque-style 1909 New York City Police Headquarters (*1 Police Plaza*), once a proud symbol of the city's modern police force, was converted into luxury apartments in the 1980s.

LOWER EAST SIDE

Street names are all that remain of the Lower East Side's rural, colonial past. Orchard Street ran through

appalling—tiny, windowless rooms, without electricity or plumbing. Some 10,000 people are estimated to have lived in the building until it was condemned in 1935. Visitors can see immigrants' apartments and educational displays, as well as pick up informative pamphlets. The small shop sells gifts and books on immigrant life.

The **Henry Street Settlement** *(265 Henry St., tel 212/766-9200)* was founded in 1893 by Lillian Wald, a German Jew from Rochester, New York. It offers a range of social services and arts programs to offset urban poverty. The settlement owns three landmark buildings: Federal-style Nos. 263 and 265 were built in 1827; No. 267, a Greek Revival building, in 1900. The Buddhist temple at No. 152 was until 1990 a social center for retired rabbis.

The recently restored **Eldridge Street Synagogue** belies the belief that the entire Lower East Side was impoverished. Completed in 1887, the Moorish Revival building cost $100,000, a stupendous sum at the time.

As the population changed, synagogues took over churches. The 1826 **Bialystoker Synagogue** *(7–13 Bialystoker Pl., tel 212/475-0165)* was built in 1826

Lower East Side Tenement Museum
www.tenement.org
✉ 97 Orchard St.
Museum Visitor Center
✉ 108 Orchard St.
☎ 212/431-0233
🕐 Closed Mon.
💲 $$$
🚇 Subway: F to Delancey St.; B, D to Grand St.; J, M, Z to Essex St.

Eldridge Street Synagogue
✉ 12–16 Eldridge St. at Canal St.
☎ 212/219-0888
🚇 Subway: B, D to Grand St.

fruit trees. The Bowery, a principal north–south thoroughfare, once led to Peter Stuyvesant's bouwerie, or farm. Some of the city's finest houses were on the Bowery, but once the immigrants arrived—Irish in the 1830s, then Germans and, in the 1880s, thousands of Eastern European Jews, Poles, Italians, Romanians, Russians, and Greeks—the Lower East Side became a place of tenements and slums. How that has changed with escalating rents!

To travel back in time, visit the **Lower East Side Tenement Museum,** in a preserved and restored tenement building. Purchased by the museum in 1988, the six-story brownstone was built in 1863 before there were housing laws. Living conditions were

A brightly painted mural adorns a Lower East Side building front off Delancey Street.

as the Willett Street Methodist Episcopal Church and it became a synagogue in 1905. The **Forward Building** (*173 E. Broadway*), a ten-story classical revival structure that now houses a Chinese church, was completed in 1912 for the *Jewish Daily Forward,* a widely read Yiddish newspaper. The building is decorated with flaming torches, symbols of the socialist causes the paper supported. Nearby, the Educational Alliance at No. 197 was founded in 1897 to ease the process of Americanization. Comedian Eddie Cantor, sculptor Chaim Gross, and broadcasting pioneer David Sarnoff studied here; they are just a few of the talented people from the neighborhood.

Traditional Jewish shops bring former residents back to the "old neighborhood" for religious items—and especially for food. The **Essex Street Market,** filled with a vibrant mix of food merchants, originally housed push-cart peddlers. At Streit's Matzoh Company (*150 Rivington St.*), you can watch the freshly baked unleavened bread slide from conveyor belts. Also here are Guss' Pickles (*35 Essex St.*), Kossar's Bialys (*367 Grand*), and Katz's, the popular delicatessen (*205 E. Houston St.*). Meg Ryan's memorable moment in the 1989 film *When Harry Met Sally* was filmed at Katz's, and yes, the food is that good.

SOHO & TRIBECA
SoHo, an acronym for "South of Houston (Street)," lies between Houston and Canal Streets, West Broadway, and Lafayette Street. Famous for its concentration of

fine cast-iron buildings (see pp. 72–73), its main thoroughfare, West Broadway, is lined with specialty shops, antiques stores, trendy restaurants, and galleries—though many have relocated to Chelsea or Midtown.

In the 1970s SoHo's lofts and low rents attracted young artists. As the area was "discovered," rents soared, and artists sought affordable space elsewhere. Many moved to an industrial section between Canal and Chambers Streets.

The area acquired a chic new name, TriBeCa ("triangle below Canal"), and the SoHo phenomenon repeated itself, with building conversions and an influx of shops, galleries, restaurants, and nightclubs.

Into the 1990s, the transformation of TriBeCa picked up speed, led by Robert De Niro's 1989 renovation of a warehouse into the TriBeCa Film Center and the TriBeCa Grill *(375 Greenwich, tel 212/941-3900)*. From Sixth Avenue to Hudson Street there are now upscale furniture stores, unusual shops, and restaurants in all price ranges, from Drew Nieporent's establishments to Bubby's *(120 Hudson)*, where brunch is an institution. The TriBeCa Grand Hotel *(2 Avenue of the Americas, tel 212/519-6600)* caters to the entertainment industry, and celebrities frequent the public lounge. The TriBeCa Film Festival, established in 2002, is a heralded annual event. As the neighborhood's transformation continues, it guards its architectural treasures, including the federal-style Harrison Street Houses *(25–41 Harrison St.)*. ■

Outside an Italian restaurant in SoHo, tables spill onto the narrow sidewalk.

Walk: Cast iron in SoHo

This walk takes you through SoHo's historic cast-iron district. It begins in the heart of SoHo on West Broadway, goes south, then briefly touches on Canal Street before swinging back north on Broadway, ending on West Houston. Along the way you will see some of the country's most outstanding examples of the cast-iron style, which were pre-fabricated in factories, then shipped to the building site and bolted onto the structures. The result was highly ornate architecture with the appearance of stone carving.

Start on West Broadway, between Prince and Spring Streets. You can pick up a free gallery guide at any gallery nearby and head west on Prince Street for a coffeehouse treat. Then it's on to 429 West Broadway, the **Nancy Hoffman Gallery** ➊ *(tel 212/966-6676)* for contemporary art. One of the first on the SoHo art scene in the 1970s, this is one of the few majors not to have relocated. Across the street No. 420 was home to the famed Leo Castelli Gallery until 1999. Just before you enter the cast-iron district, stop by **Cipriani Downtown** *(376 W. Broadway, tel 212/343-0999)*, a French bistro offering cozy tables indoor or out, with heated lamps for winter.

Turn left (east) at Broome Street. The building at No. 489 was built in 1873, as indicated by the date on it. The brick-and-brownstone building at No. 484 is not cast iron, but it has lovely gargoyles and facade decorations. Turn right (south) on Wooster Street to No. 33, the **Performing Garage** *(tel 212/966-9796)*, home of the avant-garde Wooster Group of actors. Founding members Kate Valk and Willem Dafoe still appear here. Staying on Wooster, cross Grand Street. Look back at the Grecian-style Nos. 72 and 74 and 68–70 Grand Street, designed by George da Cunha. Go south a short block to Canal Street, where you turn left. Artists may want to visit **Pearl Paint** *(308 Canal St., tel 212/431-7932)*, just across the street, the world's largest discount art supplier. Otherwise, turn left from Canal Street onto Greene Street, heading uptown.

This is SoHo's premier cast-iron district, with an unbroken expanse of ten buildings, No. 8 through Nos. 32–34. Mostly Italianate, these are by some of cast iron's best architects. Isaac F. Duckworth designed the imposing, Empire-style building at Nos. 28–30. Known as the **Queen of Greene Street** ➋ its mansard roof is a fitting crown. The true cast-iron king, however, is the ubiquitous Henry Fernbach, who designed most of this block, including Nos. 60, 62, 67, 69, 71, 75, 77, and 81. Note the many variations in the exterior staircases, columns, and windows, with the repetitive identical elements that suggest their origin in a cast-iron mold. One of the most extravagant structures, also by Duckworth, and aptly dubbed the **King of Greene Street** ➌, is Nos. 72–76, with stacked porches supported by Corinthian pillars—five stories high.

Turn right (east) on Spring Street, then right (south) on Mercer. If you need a break, Bar 89 at No. 89 has a skylight view of the surrounding buildings. Turn left (east) on Broome Street. Vaux and Withers, designers of the Jefferson Market Courthouse (see p. 80), designed No. 488 in 1872. Turn left (north) on Broadway. The 1857 **Haughwout Building** ➍ *(488 Broadway at Broome St.)* is the oldest and best preserved cast-iron building in the city, and the first to have a passenger elevator, designed and installed by Elisha Otis. John P. Gaynor designed the building, known for its harmonious arches, for a china and glass business.

On the left, between Broome and Spring Streets, 521–523 Broadway is all that remains of the larger, elegant thousand-bed St. Nicholas Hotel (1854), which closed in the 1870s. Alfred Zucker built 555 Broadway in 1889 for wholesaler Charles Rouss, a real-life Horatio Alger story. A sign on the construction site read: "He who builds, owns, and will occupy this marvel of brick, iron, and granite, thirteen years ago walked these streets penniless and $50,000 in debt." The dark green structure at 561 Broadway is known as the **Little Singer Building** ⑤, designed in 1903 by Ernest Flagg for the Singer Manufacturing Company. Note the terra-cotta facade, intricate wrought-iron balconies, and windows. The building is often cited as a precursor to the glass-curtain walls of 1950s skyscrapers. No. 560 ⑥ houses the several top-notch galleries, including Janet Borden and Staley Wise.

At Prince Street, bibliophiles will want to turn right and then a quick left to 126 Crosby Street, **Housing Works Used Book Café** *(tel 212/334-3324)*, where you can browse and snack. Then retrace your steps and head north on Broadway to the crossroads at Houston Street. Across the way at 610 Broadway rises a seven-story modern office building by architect Christian Amolsch. West along Houston, the new structures at Nos. 19–35 and No. 55, by H. Thomas O'Hara, represent the "gateway to SoHo." The **Angelika** *(18 W. Houston St., tel 212/995-2000)*, one of the city's best independent cinemas, has a public café where you can relax. ■

- Map inside front cover
- ➤ West Broadway
- 1.1 miles
- 1.5 hours
- ➤ Angelika Film Center

NOT TO BE MISSED

- Queen of Greene Street
- King of Greene Street
- Haughwout Building
- Little Singer Building

WEST HOUSTON ST.
Angelika Film Center
Broadway - Lafayette St.
Housing Works Used Book Café
New York Earth Room
PRINCE STREET
Prince Street
Nancy Hoffman Gallery
START
"Little" Singer Building
560 Broadway
SOHO
Cipriani Downtown
SPRING STREET
Former St Nicholas Hotel
OK Harris
King of Greene St.
Haughwout Building
BROADWAY
CROSBY
BROOME STREET
WEST
Performing Garage
GREENE
MERCER
GRAND STREET
Queen of Greene Street
WOOSTER
CANAL STREET
Pearl Paint
Canal Street
200 yards
200 meters

Renovated cast-iron-fronted buildings along Greene Street

The Museum of Jewish Heritage, near the former site of the World Trade Center

Museums off the beaten track

THE DRAWING CENTER

Founded to promote drawing as an art, the center's excellent contemporary and historical exhibits feature everyone from Picasso to contemporary cartoonists and street artists.
✉ 35 Wooster St. ☎ 212/219-2166 🕐 Closed Sun. 🚇 Subway: A, C, E to Canal St.; N, R to Prince St.

MUSEUM OF AMERICAN FINANCIAL HISTORY

This display is based on the personal collection of founder John E. Herzog. The collection includes an 1880 stock ticker invented by Thomas Edison.
✉ 26 Broadway ☎ 212/908-4110 🕐 Closed Sun.–Mon. 🚇 Subway: 1 to Rector St.; 4, 5 to Bowling Green

MUSEUM OF JEWISH HERITAGE

A living memorial to the Holocaust, the museum opened in 1997, with a new wing dedicated in 2003.
✉ 36 Battery Place, Battery Park City ☎ 646/437-4200 🕐 Closed Sat. & Jewish holidays 💲 $$ 🚇 Subway: 1 to South Ferry; 4, 5 to Bowling Green

NEW YORK CITY FIRE MUSEUM

This rich collection of historic fire-fighting equipment and memorabilia, housed in a former fire station in SoHo, includes fire engines dating back to 1765.
✉ 278 Spring St. between Hudson and Varick Sts. ☎ 212/691-1303 🕐 Closed Mon. 💲 $ 🚇 Subway: 1 to Houston St.; C, E to Spring St.

NEW YORK UNEARTHED

This center at South Street Seaport preserves and exhibits archaeological objects dug up as the city expanded. A glassed-in laboratory area lets you see archaeologists analyze artifacts.
✉ 17 State St. opposite Battery Park ☎ 212/748-8753 🕐 By appointment only 🚇 Subway: 1 to South Ferry; 4, 5 to Bowling Green ∎

The streets are refreshingly narrow; the buildings are quaint and low-rise. Greenwich Village and its East Village neighbor have been home to New York's finest families, its immigrants, and some of America's best artists and writers.

The Villages

Introduction & map **76–77**
Washington Square Park **78–79**
A walk in Greenwich Village **80–81**
New York University **84**
Astor Place **85**
East Village **86**
Hotels & restaurants **241–243**

Old Glory on an Astor Place building in the East Village

The Villages

GREENWICH VILLAGE IS ONE OF NEW YORK'S MOST LEGENDARY neighborhoods. Centered around and west of Washington Square Park, it extends from Houston Street north to 14th Street and from Broadway west to the Hudson River. Today it is often called the West Village to distinguish it from its neighbor, the vibrant East Village (east of Broadway), which until the 1950s was viewed as part of the Lower East Side.

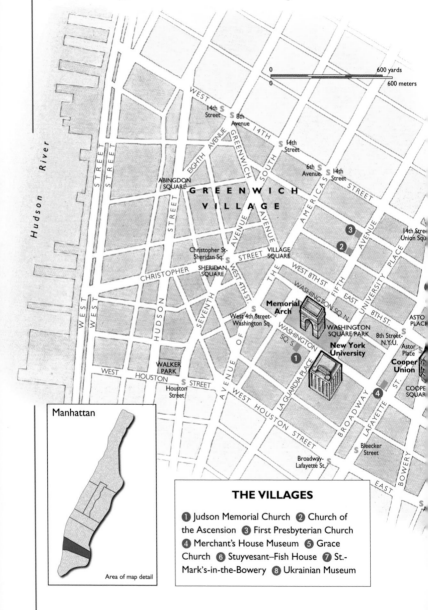

THE VILLAGES

❶ Judson Memorial Church ❷ Church of the Ascension ❸ First Presbyterian Church ❹ Merchant's House Museum ❺ Grace Church ❻ Stuyvesant–Fish House ❼ St.-Mark's-in-the-Bowery ❽ Ukrainian Museum

The West Village's reputation as a haven for free-thinkers, free-lovers, artists, poets, writers, rebels, and revolutionaries dates back to the turn of the 20th century; and that reputation applies now equally to the East Village. Even the street plan of the West Village is bohemian—the diagonal streets defy the grid plan imposed on the rest of the city starting at 14th Street. West Village streets follow divisions that once marked farms and are lined with low-rise houses and green courtyards from an earlier era.

Today, in addition to poets and artists, you will find students, skateboarders, matrons pushing baby carriages, and men playing chess in Washington Square in the West Village or Tompkins Square in the East Village, along with that unfortunate fixture of urban life, the drug dealer. Washington Square is well protected by the New York city police, and Tompkins Square, renovated and free of squatters, is one of the city's most community-oriented parks.

Nothing keeps away visitors and new residents able to pay the ever-soaring rents. The West Village is unique and alluring, an attraction for New Yorkers from all over the city and tourists from all over the world. Drawn by the Italian groceries, antique stores, and outdoor art shows, they seek the past in coffeehouses, bars, and streets where the now famous once hung out. Bob Dylan sang his folk songs in the '60s in Washington Square. Writers haunt the White Horse Tavern, an 1880s saloon at the corner of Hudson and West 11th Streets. Here the Welsh poet Dylan Thomas had his final drink. In the East Village, there is McSorley's Old Ale House on East Seventh Street, founded in 1854 and dedicated to "Good Ale, Raw Onions, and No Ladies" (until 1970 when women were finally admitted). At CBGB's on the Bowery, American punk was born, and the new Bowery Poetry Club (308 Bowery, tel 212/614-0505) hosts open mics, readings, and events.

EARLY VILLAGE

Long before settlement, Canarsee Indians used the marshy area of what would become Greenwich Village for hunting and fishing. When the Dutch arrived, they grew tobacco along Minetta Brook, and the area became the best tobacco plantation in the colony. In 1644 slaves who had been given partial freedom by the West India Company settled near Minetta Lane, which would later become part of the Underground Railroad. When the English took over, the section became Greenwich, meaning Green Village. As the city spread northward, the West Village attracted well-to-do New Yorkers fleeing yellow fever and cholera epidemics in the 1820s. Among the 19th-century residents was Henry James, who used his grandmother's house at 18 Washington Square North (now demolished) as the setting for his novel *Washington Square* (1881). The immigrants, intellectuals, writers, and struggling artists who gave Greenwich Village its reputation began to arrive at the end of the 19th century. ■

Washington Square Park

Washington Square Park on a rare quiet day during a snowstorm. Washington Arch dominates the square, a nexus point for the NYU and Greenwich Village communities.

WASHINGTON SQUARE PARK WAS CLOSED TO TRAFFIC IN the 1960s, turning it into one of the city's great gathering places—for students, performers, dog walkers, tourists, and, to keep an eye on things, police. The focal point is the landmark 86-foot-tall Washington Arch, which was designed by Stanford White and dedicated in 1895, six years after the city enthusiastically observed the centennial of Washington's presidential inauguration.

The city used the eight-acre parcel of land as a potter's field, public gallows, and parade ground before redesigning it in 1826 as Washington Square Park. With it came fashionable town houses, including the 12 exquisite Greek Revival brick houses (1831–33) known as "the Row" on Washington Square North.

Although the Row and northern environs housed writers and artists—Edith Wharton, Willa Cather, John Dos Passos, and Mark

1841 Gothic Revival **Church of the Ascension** *(10th St. & 5th Ave., tel 212/254-8620).* The stained glass and altar mural are by John La Farge. The 1846 **First Presbyterian Church** *(12 W. 12th St., tel 212/675-6150)* has a tower that is based on one at Oxford's Magdalen College.

Across from the arch, however, in the direction of Bleecker Street, the atmosphere becomes more ethnic and earthy. **Judson Memorial Church** (1892) is to this day known for its political activism. This Romanesque basilica has stained-glass windows by John La Farge and a marble relief by Augustus Saint-Gaudens. The church's social/political mission was to bring together the square's aristocratic northern residents with the immigrants moving into the south.

Struggling writers and artists moved into the Village along with the immigrants. Mrs. Blanchard's boardinghouse at 61 Washington Square South became famous as the "House of Genius": From the 1890s it was home to writers Stephen Crane, Theodore Dreiser, and Frank Norris. Nearby, at 139 MacDougal Street, Provincetown Playhouse was founded in 1917, where the works of Eugene O'Neill were produced. The radical writer John Reed (1887–1920), resident at 42 Washington Square South between 1911 and 1912, celebrated the Village as a place where "nobody questions your morals, and nobody asks for the rent."

Nowadays the situation has changed: No one's rent remains delinquent long. The Village is among the city's most sought-after addresses, home to such writers as Stanley Crouch and Grace Paley and actors Willem DaFoe and Nicole Kidman. ■

Judson Memorial Church

▲ Map p. 76

✉ 55 Washington Square South

☎ 212/477-0351

Twain, among others—there was never anything bohemian about his neighborhood. The writer Djuna Barnes described the difference between the north and south sides of Washington Square in early 20th-century terms: "satin and motorcars on this side, squalor and pushcarts on that." Even today, the square separates two very different neighborhoods. Along the northern side, near the arch, the streets are quiet, tree-lined, and patrician. Two churches a short distance north of the arch on Fifth Avenue continue the sense of restraint. At West Tenth Street, Richard Upjohn designed the

A walk in Greenwich Village

This 90-minute walk in the West Village historic district wends its way through quiet residential areas, charming nooks and enclaves, and busy thoroughfares.

Begin at Sixth Avenue and Ninth Street, by the landmark **Jefferson Market Courthouse Library** ❶. Its name derives from a market named for President Thomas Jefferson that opened on the site in 1833. The present redbrick Gothic structure (1877) was designed by Calvert Vaux, one of the designers of Central Park, and Frederick Withers. In the 1960s, crusading Villagers, including poet e. e. cummings, saved the structure from demolition.

Go left on West Tenth Street to tiny **Patchin Place** ❷, a cul-de-sac of ten brick houses from 1848, originally built to house waiters from the nearby Hotel Brevoort. Cummings lived at No. 4 for 40 years until his death in 1962, and was regularly visited by luminaries including Ezra Pound and T. S.

Eliot; author Djuna Barnes lived at No. 5 until her death at age 90 in 1982.

Turn left on Greenwich Avenue, right on Christopher Street, and left again on **Gay Street** ❸. This short curving street is a perfect introduction to the irregular street pattern in the Village, which refused to adopt the grid plan imposed on the city north of 14th Street. Once an alley, Gay Street became famous as the birthplace of *My Sister Eileen* (1938), a book about life in zany Greenwich Village. The author, Ruth McKenney, was a young woman from Ohio who lived here with her sister, a struggling actress, at 14 Gay Street.

Turn left on Waverly Place. Edgar Allan Poe, master of the macabre, lived for a time at No. 137. When he had a cold, he simply walked down the street for treatment—to

George Segal's sculptured gay couples in Christopher Park

- 🅜 Map inside front cover
- ▶ Sixth Avenue and Ninth Street
- ↔ 1.5 miles
- ⏱ 1.5 hours
- ▶ Sixth Avenue or Bleecker Street

NOT TO BE MISSED
- Gay Street
- Sheridan Square

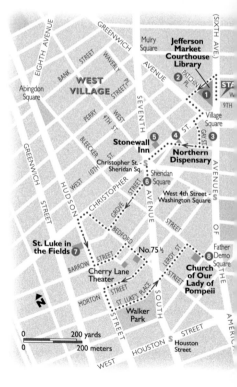

The picturesque streets of Greenwich Village are rewarding to wander.

follow his path, turn back, walking west on Waverly Place. The triangular building just ahead is the 1827 **Northern Dispensary** ④, where the city provided Poe and others with free medical care.

Turn left on Stonewall Place (part of Christopher Street), named after the **Stonewall Inn** ⑤, where the gay liberation movement began on June 27, 1969. The present Stonewall bar occupies part of the space of the original inn *(53 Christopher St.),* and plaques on the wall inside detail the events of 1969. Christopher Park, across from the bar, has a George Segal sculpture of gay couples.

Ahead is Seventh Avenue. This area is known as **Sheridan Square** ⑥, and it is a pulse of Village life today, as in the past. Early in her career, Barbra Streisand appeared at the Duplex cabaret *(61 Christopher St. at 7th Ave. South, tel 212/255-5438).* The Village Vanguard *(178 7th Ave. South, tel 212/255-4037)* has been preeminent among jazz clubs since 1935.

Go south on Seventh Avenue and turn right on Grove Street. Revolutionary-era writer Thomas Paine lived for a time at No. 59, where an 1839 building now houses Marie's Crisis *(tel 212/243-9323),* a sing-along bar.

Continue to Bedford Street and turn right to No. 102, Twin Peaks. In 1926 financier Otto Kahn remodeled the building after one in Nuremberg, as an inspirational home for artists. Continue to Christopher Street and turn left, then left on Hudson Street to No. 485, **St. Luke in the Fields** ⑦ (restored 1981). Around the corner is a peaceful garden path with benches open to the public.

Turn left on Barrow and then right on Bedford Street (or meander onto Commerce Street to see the 1924 Cherry Lane Theater, one of the first Off Broadway theaters). Don't miss **Chumley's** *(86 Bedford St.),* a signless 1873 building. This speakeasy from the 1920s is lined with old book jackets from its writer patrons. Note the "secret" back exit.

Return to Bedford Street, walking left (east). Actor John Barrymore lived at 75½ Bedford around 1915, and poet Edna St. Vincent Millay from 1923–24. Just 9.5 feet wide, this is the city's narrowest house.

Turn right on Morton Street, left on Hudson Street, and left onto St. Luke's Place, with its fine 1850s brownstones. New York's popular mayor Jimmy Walker lived at No. 6 from 1886 to 1934. Resident writers here included Theodore Dreiser (No. 16) and Marianne Moore (No. 14).

Cross Seventh Avenue to Leroy Street; Jimmy Walker was born at No. 100. This returns you to Bleecker Street, the Village's main street, where there are shops and restaurants from one end to another.

Benches await you at Bleecker Street and Sixth Avenue in **Father Demo Square** ⑧, named for a priest of the 1926 **Church of Our Lady of Pompeii** *(Carmine & Bleecker Sts.),* which has lovely murals.

If you have leftover energy, cross Sixth Avenue and continue down Bleecker Street to the heart of the legendary coffeehouse district, and pilgrimage on to the Bitter End at No. 147 *(tel 212/673-7030),* famous as a springboard for such comics and musicians as Woody Allen, Bob Dylan, and many more. ∎

A banner year for the arts

In 1913, the Village—and its artists and intellectuals—came to the attention of the outside world. A building on West Eighth Street, once the Village's best shopping street, is a link with that 20th-century heyday. Then, 8 West Eighth Street housed the gallery and residence of Gertrude Vanderbilt Whitney, one of modern American art's most influential patrons. It was in salons such as hers, and another hosted by the wealthy and well-connected Mabel Dodge Luhan, that Village artists and intellectuals gathered. Out of these salons came plans for two extraordinary events: the 1913 Armory Show, critical in the recognition of American art; and the Paterson Strike Pageant, a theatrical extravaganza staged by the Villagers to support striking silk factory workers in Paterson, New Jersey.

THE 1913 ARMORY SHOW

Greenwich Village had been the center of artistic activity for decades and it was out of the tradition of artists gathering to share ideas that the Armory Show grew. In the 1840s, Herman Melville and Edgar Allan Poe were among those frequenting a salon at 116 Waverly Place. In 1858 a wealthy businessman commissioned Richard Morris Hunt to build an artists' studio building on West Tenth Street, which had 25 studios grouped around a large central exhibition space. Tenants of the Tenth Street Studio Building included architect Hunt himself and painters John La Farge, Winslow Homer, Frederic Church, and Albert Bierstadt, whose collection of American Indian objects was an added public attraction.

By the early 20th century, artistic gatherings in the Village became more avant garde and radical. Whitney herself was an accomplished but conventional sculptor, but as a patron and collector, she was dedicated to modernism. The 1913 Armory Show that she helped sponsor was held at the 69th Regiment Armory at 25th Street and Lexington Avenue. Featuring more than 300 artists and drawing 70,000 people, this was the single most important art exhibition ever held in America. Disturbingly abstract pieces like Marcel Duchamp's "Nude Descending a Staircase" were ridiculed in the press—one critic called the show "a toss-up between madness and humbug"—but the exhibition had an immediate and lasting impact, altering America's assumptions about what art ought to be.

After the show, Whitney expanded her Eighth Street studio into exhibition space and an artists' club. In 1929 she offered to give her collection of modern American art to the Metropolitan Museum of Art. When her offer was refused, she established her own museum, the Whitney Museum of American Art, in four town houses at 8–14 West Eighth Street. This was the first museum in the world devoted to American art, and the origin of today's Whitney Museum (see pp. 164–65).

THE PATERSON STRIKE PAGEANT

Mabel Dodge Luhan's salon at 23 Fifth Avenue was another influential Village institution. Luhan was a hostess, not an artist or intellectual, who had mastered the art of bringing creative people together. Regulars included radicals Emma Goldman and John Reed, photographer Alfred Stieglitz, and birth-control advocate Margaret Sanger. It was at a Luhan soirée that Village intellectuals first learned of violence against workers striking at the silk factories in Paterson, New Jersey. The result of the meeting was an extraordinary pageant, staged on June 7, 1913, at Madison Square Garden: More than a thousand of the strikers reenacted scenes from the confrontation.

Luhan supported the Paterson Strike Pageant production financially; Reed wrote and directed it, and painter John Sloan, a member of the so-called Ashcan school, did the scenery. Performed on a 200-foot-long stage, the pageant was attended by 15,000 people. Although it lost money, it encouraged radical and experimental theater in New York. Afterward, Reed and Luhan became lovers and she nursed him through a bout with diphtheria, but eventually he moved on. Her autobiography revealed that Village artistic life was not without heartache. She wrote: "That I have so many pages to write signifies, solely, that I was unlucky in love." ∎

Left: A dramatic poster advertising the Paterson Strike Pageant. Below left: The re-enactment of the Paterson Strike. Below right: A banner outside the Armory for the 1913 modern art show.

New York University

New York University

www.nyu.edu

🅰 Map p. 76

✉ Washington Square

☎ 212/998-1212

🚇 Subway: A, B, C, D, E, F to W. 4th St.– Washington Sq.

The NYU bookstore lies on Washington Place, off the east side of Washington Square Park.

WASHINGTON SQUARE IS THE NERVE CENTER OF NEW York University (NYU); its library, law school, and administrative buildings line the park, and its students are visible all around. The rest of NYU, the largest private university in the country, is scattered throughout the city. Founded in 1831 as the University of the City of New York, NYU was intended as a nonsectarian alternative to Columbia University. It is a cauldron of creativity.

Although its early buildings are gone, signs of their history are scattered about. In 1833 stonecutters rioted, protesting the use of prison labor in the construction of the university's first building. A memorial to the event is in Washington Square. In 1835 the Gothic Revival University Building (demolished in 1894) opened on Washington Square East. Among those who taught and worked in its tower were architect Richard Morris Hunt, artist Winslow Homer, poet Walt Whitman, and Samuel F. B. Morse —who demonstrated his new invention, the telegraph, there. Part of the tower is on display at Gould Plaza on West Fourth Street. The University Building itself appears in Morse's painting "An Allegorical Landscape Showing the University."

The university moved to the Bronx in the 1890s, but retained a presence in Washington Square. In 1911 its community witnessed a horrific event. On the site where the Brown Building now stands, 146 young women died in a fire at the Triangle Shirtwaist Company. The city's worst factory fire, it led to the creation of workplace safety laws.

In 1973, NYU sold the Bronx campus to the city and returned to Washington Square. Among its buildings there now are the 1972 Bobst Library *(Washington Sq. S.);* Tisch Hall *(40 W. 4th St.);* Andre and Bella Meyer Hall *(4 Washington Pl.);* and the exotic Hagop Kevorkian Center for Near Eastern Studies *(50 Washington Sq. S.).* A number of 19th-century converted stables stand on **Washington Mews,** the charming alleyway north of Washington Square North. The **Grey Art Gallery** *(100 Washington Sq. E., tel 212/998-6780)* specializes in modern and contemporary art. ∎

Astor Place

ASTOR PLACE IS AT THE CENTER OF A LIVELY STUDENT-filled neighborhood formed by the junction of exotic St. Mark's Place, businesslike Fourth Avenue, the once-derelict Bowery, and the architecturally distinguished Lafayette Street.

Historically, Astor Place is identified with the 1849 Astor Place riots that happened where an opera house stood on the plaza. When English actor William Macready was hired over Irish-American actor Edwin Forrest to play Hamlet, more than 10,000 Irish Americans gathered in protest. Police fired on the crowd, killing and wounding many. Today many know the area as the home of the Italianate redbrick building housing the highly respected Cooper Union for the Advancement of Science and Art, commonly called **Cooper Union.**

Founded in 1857–59 by Peter Cooper to provide a free higher education for worthy sons and daughters of the poor, Cooper Union is still tuition free. Every President since has spoken here. Cooper, who built the country's first steam locomotive, was a self-taught entrepreneur and reform-minded politician. His statue, by Augustus Saint-Gaudens, stands at the school's entrance.

Astor Library opened in 1854 as the city's first free library, with a bequest from John Jacob Astor. It is now **The Public Theater,** founded by Joseph Papp, the dynamic late producer who, in 1965, persuaded the city to convert the building into theaters. Excellent plays and films are regularly scheduled. Also worthy of note is the 1886 **De Vinne Press Building** *(393–399 Lafayette St.),* built in the Romanesque Revival style, and **Colonnade Row** at Nos. 428–434, four houses remaining from a row of nine 1833 marble-fronted Greek Revival residences. ∎

Cooper Union
www.cooperunion.edu
✉ 41 Cooper Sq.
☎ 212/353-4100
🚇 Subway: 6 to Astor Place

The Public Theater
www.publictheater.org
✉ 425 Lafayette St.
☎ 212/260-2400
🚇 Subway: 6 to Astor Pl.; N, R to 8th St.

"Right makes might"

On the snowy evening of February 27, 1860, 1,500 people packed Cooper Union to hear Abraham Lincoln, soon to be a presidential candidate, speak about slavery. Arguing that the Constitution gave the federal government power to control slavery in the federal territories, he closed with these now-famous words: "Let us have faith that right makes might, and in that faith, let us, to the end, dare to do our duty as we understand it." ∎

The Cooper Union Building lies just south of Astor Place. In the 19th century it was the first free college in the United States.

East Village

Merchant's House Museum

www.merchantshouse.com

◪ Map p. 76

✉ 29 E. 4th St.

☎ 212/777-1089

🕐 Open noon–5 p.m. Thurs.–Mon.

💲 $$

🚇 Subway: 6 to Astor Place; N, R to 8th St.

Ukrainian Museum

www.ukrainianmuseum.org

◪ Map p. 77

✉ 222 E. 6th St. (between 2nd and 3rd Aves.)

☎ 212/228-0110

🕐 Open Wed.–Sun. 11:30 to 5 p.m.;

💲 $$

🚇 Subway: R, W to 8th St.; 6 to Astor Place

Tompkins Square Park hosts the annual Howl Festival, featuring East Village art.

ONCE PART OF THE ETHNIC LOWER EAST SIDE, THE EAST Village has attracted artists, musicians, writers, and political activists since the 1960s. Large numbers of immigrants still live here as well. Explore the many bookstores, record stores, and specialty shops. Eateries—from two-table storefronts to Jewish delis, Polish coffee shops, an entire street of Indian restaurants (East Sixth Street), and atmospheric gourmet restaurants—reflect the area's zesty ethnic mix.

At the East Village's heart is Tompkins Square Park, named for Daniel Tompkins (1774–1825), a governor of New York. Dutch governor Peter Stuyvesant is buried behind **St. Mark's-in-the-Bowery** (E. 10th St. at 2nd Ave., tel 212/674-6377) and some say his ghost walks the grounds, tapping his wooden leg. The church is a center of activism and the arts, featuring contemporary dance and weekly readings (Danspace, tel 212/674-8112).

Across from the church is a classic federal-style structure, the 1803 **Stuyvesant-Fish House** (21 Stuyvesant St., not open to the public). Architect James Renwick built the 1861 Italianate town houses here (Nos. 23–35) and at 114–28 East Tenth Street, comprising Renwick Triangle. South of the church, Janis Joplin, the Doors, and others appeared at Bill Graham's now extinct psychedelic Fillmore East (2nd Ave. at 6th St.).

West of St. Mark's is an 1846 Renwick Gothic Revival masterpiece, the Episcopal **Grace Church** (802 Broadway and E. 10th St., tel 212/254-2000). The interior has exquisite stained glass and a mosaic floor. North of Grace Church is a must for bibliophiles, the **Strand Book Store** (828 Broadway, tel 212/473-1452), "home of 18 miles of books" and bargains galore.

The **Merchant's House Museum** dates from 1832 and provides an authentic look into 19th-century life. In 2005, the **Ukrainian Museum** opened its new nine-million-dollar, 25,000-sq.-ft. building, now housing its extensive collections and exhibitions on all things Ukrainian. ∎

Midtown South has many faces: quiet enclaves such as Gramercy Park; libraries of unsurpassed riches; one of the city's busiest shopping districts; a building shaped like an iron; and two of New York's favorite skyscrapers.

Midtown South

Introduction & map **88–89**
Chelsea **90–91**
Gramercy Park **92–93**
Walk down Ladies' Mile **94–95**
Empire State Building **96**
Herald Square **97**
The Morgan Library &
Murray Hill **98–99**
New York Public Library **100**
Hotels & restaurants **243–245**

The unusual geometry of the Flatiron Building

Midtown South

THE DIFFERENCES BETWEEN MIDTOWN SOUTH AND THE CITY'S TRUE CENTER farther north are ones of pace, style, and age. Whereas Midtown North aggressively races through the day, its southern neighbor has pockets of tranquility along with areas of frenzied activity. Midtown South has quiet enclaves where the bustle of a modern city hardly penetrates. But it also has Herald Square, home to Macy's, and the Garment District, where traffic and crowds are among the densest anywhere in the city.

Midtown South's buildings are older than the more famous skyscrapers uptown, but they are no less significant or beautiful. In its 19th-century heyday, Midtown South was the center of the city, boasting everything that its uptown neighbor has today: the best hotels, restaurants, theaters, opera houses, department stores, and the opulent residences of the rich and powerful.

The New York Public Library was erected in 1898–1922 on the site of an 1842 walled reservoir that was part of the 41-mile-long Croton Aqueduct. Madison Square Garden, the city's famous sports arena, is still a Midtown South fixture. The first "Garden" (1879) was located in a converted railroad depot on the east side of Madison Square Park, near 23rd Street.

Stanford White's elaborate replacement opened on the same site in 1892. A nude statue of the goddess Diana atop its tower was controversial in a city still in the throes of Victorian prudery. White himself was anything but a prude; his fast lifestyle caught up with him in 1906, when a jealous husband shot and killed him in the building's roof garden. When the Garden moved uptown in 1925, the building was demolished.

In the 19th century, Midtown South became the center of the city's clothing factories. From its beginnings on the Lower East Side, the garment industry moved first to the Madison Square area around 23rd Street, then to the West 30s, the now famous Garment District. Here even today a pedestrian's way might be blocked by racks of clothes moving through the streets. A 1984 bronze statue—Judith Weller's "The Garment Worker," a man at a sewing machine—honors the Jewish immigrants who helped build the industry. The Fashion Institute of Technology (7th Ave.

at 27th St., tel 212/217-7999), a training ground for the trade, hosts frequent fashion exhibits and operates a museum with over four million textile swatches in its collection.

The past two decades have seen renewal in the region. Stores, restaurants, nightclubs, and businesses such as advertising agencies and publishing companies are reoccupying buildings abandoned by similar businesses almost a century before. The area around the Flatiron Building is now known as the Photography

MIDTOWN SOUTH

❶ Jacob K. Javits Convention Center ❷ General Theological Society ❸ St. Peter's Episcopal Church ❹ Church of the Holy Apostles ❺ General Post Office ❻ Madison Square Garden ❼ Holy Communion Church ❽ New Amsterdam Theater ❾ Macy's ❿ Flatiron Building ⓫ Worth Monument ⓬ Museum of Sex ⓭ T. Roosevelt Birthplace ⓮ Con Edison H.Q. ⓯ N.Y. State Supreme Court ⓰ N.Y. Life Insurance Co. ⓱ American Radiator Building ⓲ Church of the Incarnation ⓳ Daily News Building

District: Photographers converted lofts to studios and labs and art stores followed. The neighborhoods above 14th Street continue to change, as rents skyrocket Uptown and Downtown and the demand for "affordable" housing grows. ■

Manhattan

Area of map detail

Chelsea

CHELSEA, ALONG THE WEST SIDE FROM 14TH STREET TO 30th Street, has blossomed into the city's most dynamic neighborhood. Now home to more than 190 art galleries plus trendy shops and restaurants, it retains its past aura in 19th-century row houses and well-preserved churches. The former Ladies' Mile emporiums along Sixth Avenue bustle with new stores, while on Eighth Avenue high-tech companies occupy buildings long vacant.

St. Peter's Episcopal Church

The innovative **Dia Center for the Arts** *(tel 212/989-5566)* opened its 40,000-square-foot exhibition facility at 548 West 22nd Street *(bet. 10th and 11th Aves.)* in 1987, leading the way for droves of galleries to follow. At Dia you can see modern art that is too big to be shown elsewhere. Next door, the new **Chelsea Art Museum** *(556 W. 22nd St.)* shows postwar European art.

Prominent in Chelsea's banquet of art venues, the **Rubin Museum** *(150 W. 17th St., tel 212/620-5000,*

Dia Center for the Arts
www.diacenter.org
✉ 548 W. 22nd St.
☎ 212/989-5566
🕐 Closed a.m. & Mon.–Tues.
$ $
🚇 Subway: C, E to 8th Ave. & 23rd St.; 1 to 7th Ave. & 23rd St.

$) is the first museum in the Western Hemisphere dedicated to Himalayan art. Six floors of lovingly curated art are installed around a central spiral staircase. More intimate is the **John Stevenson Gallery** *(338 W. 23rd St., bet. 8th and 9th Aves., tel 212/352-0070)*, which showcases fine-art photography and art in a lovely townhouse setting. Heating up the mix is the **Museum of Sex** *(233 5th Ave. at 27th St., tel 212/689-6337, $)*, the country's first major cultural institution devoted to human sexuality.

CHELSEA HISTORIC DISTRICT

Chelsea was originally Dutch—Jacob Somerindyck owned a farm here that English army captain Thomas Clarke bought in 1750 for his retirement and named Chelsea, after London's Chelsea Royal Hospital. His grandson, the versatile professor and writer Clement Clarke Moore, became Chelsea's first developer. Moore is best remembered for his children's classic, "A Visit from St. Nicholas," popularly known as "The Night Before Christmas."

Moore donated a square block of land on Ninth Avenue at Chelsea Square for the **General Theological Seminary,** the oldest Episcopal seminary in the country, where he taught biblical languages. The interior courtyard is ringed by buildings, including the West Building (1836), the city's oldest example of Gothic Revival style.

Across from the seminary, **Cushman Row** *(406–418 W. 20th St.)* comprises seven Greek Revival houses, some adorned with window wreaths and pineapples on the stair posts as signs of hospitality. They were built in 1839–1840 for merchant and developer Don Alonso Cushman, who also built the four Italianate buildings (1858–1860) on the street's north side (Nos. 355–361). Nearby the **James N. Wells Row** of narrow Italianate houses *(400–412 W. 22nd St.)* is named after another prominent developer of this era. The 1835 Greek Revival mansion at No. 414 was Wells's home.

AN AREA OF CHURCHES

Clement Clarke Moore was also a founder of **St. Peter's Episcopal Church** *(346 W. 20th St. at 8th Ave.)*, a trio of buildings erected in 1836–38. The rectory is the city's oldest Greek Revival building. Its 1790 iron fence came from St. Paul's Chapel on lower Broadway.

Richard M. Upjohn, son of Trinity Church's architect, designed the outstanding **Church of the Holy Communion** *(49 W. 20th St. at 6th Ave.)* in 1846. Together, the Upjohns designed the transepts for the **Church of the Holy Apostles** *(9th Ave. at 28th St.)* in 1858. The church itself, with its unusual spire of bronze and slate, was built in 1848 by Minard Lafever. John and William Jay Bolton, the first stained-glass makers in the U.S., created the windows. Before the Civil War, the church was an abolitionist center and a stop on the Underground Railroad.

CHELSEA HOTEL

Distinguished by its ornate iron balconies, the Chelsea Hotel *(222 W. 23rd St. between 7th and 8th Aves.)* was built in 1884 as a cooperative apartment, but soon became a hotel catering to the literati. Plaques on the facade honor distinguished guests, from Mark Twain to Tennessee Williams. ■

General Theological Seminary

www.gts.edu

 175 9th Ave.

☎ 212/243-5150

🕐 Open 12 p.m. to 3 p.m. Mon.–Fri.; 11 a.m. to 3 p.m. Sat.

🚇 Subway: 1, C, or E to 23rd St.

Above: A venerable city landmark, the Chelsea Hotel has a history rich in legend, literature, and scandal.

Left: Brownstone town houses were built from an inexpensive form of sandstone in the mid-1800s.

Gramercy Park in winter

Gramercy Park

GRAMERCY PARK IS THE CITY'S ONLY PRIVATE PARK—AND, for that reason alone, one of the city's most desirable addresses. The park is surrounded by a tasteful but formidable iron fence, and unless you live in the immediate vicinity or know someone who does, you will not be able to go in. The rule restricting the use of the park to residents, who have keys to the locked gate, was relaxed only once—when troops were bivouacked there during the Draft Riots of 1863 (see p. 26). Today, it is often used for film shoots, such as Martin Scorsese's *Age of Innocence*.

The name was originally Dutch, Krom Moerajse, meaning "little crooked swamp," which the English, somehow, anglicized to Gramercy. In 1822, Samuel Ruggles purchased and drained the swamp, laid out the park, and sold lots. Early residents included lawyer and diarist George Templeton Strong and James Harper, a publisher and New York City mayor (1844–45), whose home at 4 Gramercy Park West

still has the traditional outdoor lampposts that marked it as the mayor's residence.

WRITERS OF RENOWN
One of the city's first cooperative apartment buildings, the 1883 Gramercy *(34 Gramercy Park E.)*, has housed such prominent figures as playwright DuBose Heyward and the late actors James Cagney and Margaret "Wicked Witch of the West" Hamilton.

On the south side of the park, 144 East 20th Street was built in 1860 as a Quaker meetinghouse and now serves as a synagogue. At the corner of Irving Place, the 1845 brick building at 19 Gramercy Park South was owned in the 1880s by financier Stuyvesant Fish; more recently the house was home to actor John Barrymore and, later, the colorful public relations genius Ben Sonnenberg.

Actor Edwin Booth (see sidebar below) gave his home at 16 Gramercy Park South to the **Players' Club;** Stanford White remodeled the 1845 brownstone in 1888. Next door, Calvert Vaux built No. 15 in 1884 for Samuel Tilden, a former New York governor. Fearful of populist revolt, Tilden had an underground escape tunnel dug to 19th Street. The restored brownstone is now the **National Arts Club,** where literary events often take place.

The **Gramercy Park Historic District** extends several blocks in each direction beyond the park itself. Developer Ruggles named the six-block-long street between the park and 14th Street Irving Place, after his friend, writer Washington Irving. The gesture led to the misconception that Irving lived on the street; however, he did visit his nephew who lived at 45 Irving Place. In the early 20th century, the house was the home of the society interior decorator Elsie de Wolfe, who was famous for the mix of high society and bohemia at her salons and her open relationship with her lover, the literary agent Bessie Marbury. Another well-known Gramercy Park figure, William Sydney Porter (pen name: O. Henry) did much of his writing and drinking at Healy's (today called Pete's Tavern) at Irving and 18th Street, where—in the second booth from the right—he supposedly penned his most famous short story, "The Gift of the Magi."

West of Gramercy Park, the **Theodore Roosevelt Birthplace National Historic Site** is a careful replica—right down to the slate shingles on the mansard roof—of the original 1845 building, which was demolished in 1916. Roosevelt was born here in 1858 and lived in the house until 1872; he later recalled the "gloomy respectability" of the building's library. Operated now by the National Park Service and open to the public, the birthplace was rebuilt in 1923 by Theodate Pope Riddle, the country's first woman architect. ■

National Arts Club
www.thenationalarts
club.org
✉ 15 Gramercy
    Park S.
☎ 212/475-3424
🚇 Subway: 6 to
    23rd St.

Theodore Roosevelt Birthplace N.H.S.
🗺 Map p. 89
✉ 28 E. 20th St.
☎ 212/260-1616
🕐 Closed Sun.–Mon.
💲 $
🚇 Subway: 6, N, or
    R to 23rd St.

The melancholy thespian

Inside locked Gramercy Park, but visible through the fence, stands a bronze statue of Edwin Booth (1833–1893), the most famous American actor of his day. In April 1865, he received unwanted notoriety when his actor brother John Wilkes Booth assassinated President Abraham Lincoln in Washington, D.C., and died trying to elude capture. After the assassination, Edwin retired temporarily, then built his own theater to stage his own productions. In 1888 he founded the Players' Club for actors at 16 Gramercy Park South. Twenty-five years after his death, the club commissioned the statue of Booth, a small, lithe figure, as Hamlet, a role at which he excelled—perhaps because the prince's melancholy matched his own after his brother's murderous deed. ■

Walk down Ladies' Mile

In the relatively short distance covered by this walking tour—which spans two pleasant parks, Madison Square on the north and Union Square on the south—you will see a neighborhood in the process of reestablishing its original image on a walk that will take about an hour, depending on stops.

In the 1870s, so many of the city's fashionable retailers were located along this stretch that it became known as Ladies' Mile. The stores moved northward, but many neglected buildings survived and today they are being renovated and reinhabited. Businesses have returned, bringing with them bars and restaurants. The Ladies' Mile Historic District also includes Fashion Row on Sixth Avenue, a cluster of late 19th-century structures centered between 18th and 19th Streets.

Start at the north of **Madison Square Park** ❶ near East 26th Street. When Madison Square opened in 1847, it was already home to the city's first organized baseball team, the Knickerbockers. The park contains excellent sculpture, notably the 1881 "Admiral Farragut Monument" by Augustus Saint-Gaudens, with a base by Stanford White.

Three eminent skyscrapers abut the park. Cass Gilbert designed the block-long neo-Gothic **New York Life Insurance Company Building** ❷ (*51 Madison Ave. between E. 26th and E. 27th Sts.*) in 1928. Another massive building is at the north corner of East 25th Street and Madison Avenue, the 1900 beaux arts **Appellate Division** of the **Supreme Court.** The interior is sumptuously decorated with stained glass and murals, the exterior by statuary, including "Justice" by Daniel Chester French. Napoleon LeBrun's tower for the huge art deco **Metropolitan Life Insurance Company Building** ❸ (*1 Madison Ave. between E. 23rd and E. 24th Sts.*) was built in 1932. Walk south to Fifth Avenue and East 23rd Street to see architect Daniel Burnham's 20-story **Flatiron Building** ❹ (1902); it was called Burnham's Folly by those who feared high winds would blow it over. The Flatiron was the city's tallest building until it was dwarfed by the Metropolitan Life Tower (*Madison Ave. at 24th St.*).

Head downtown (south) on Broadway to **901 Broadway** (*at E. 20th St.*), an Empire-style cast-iron building that was, until 1914,

the Lord & Taylor Store. One block south, there are three more impressive 19th-century survivors. The Queen Anne–style 1884 building at 889–891 Broadway was once a retail outlet of the Gorham Manufacturing Company, an American silver manufacturer. The **Arnold Constable Dry Goods Store** (*881–887 Broadway at E. 19th St.*) is an 1869 building; its cast-iron extension up to Fifth Avenue has an impressive mansard roof. On the southeast corner of East 19th Street, **884 Broadway** once housed W. & J. Sloane, purveyors of rugs, curtains, and fabric. Note the striking cast-iron storefront and carved columns.

Continue south about three blocks to **Union Square** ❺, renovated in 1986 and now a popular park and shopping area. To the north, at 33 East 17th Street, the **Century Building** (1881), faced with red brick and whitestone, housed *Century* magazine, an illustrated publication devoted to the reunification of the country after the Civil War. It is now a Barnes & Noble megabookstore. No. 31 Union Square West, at East 16th Street, is the original 1903 Bank of Metropolis building, designed by Bruce Price, an innovative architect of skyscrapers; the **Coffee Shop** (*29 Union Sq. W.*) is a trendy restaurant. On the square's east side (*Park Avenue S.*), the imposing Greek temple was built in 1907 as the Union Square Savings Bank. Try Zen Palate (*at 16th St.*) for tasty vegetarian fare.

When Union Square opened as a park in 1831, it was at ground level; it was later raised to accommodate the subway tracks beneath it. From the Civil War until recent times, the park was a stump for political orators. Today Union Square holds a year-round **Green Market** (*Mon., Wed., & Sat.*), where farmers sell a range of fresh produce, including home-

Opposite: For nearly a century the elegant and unmistakable Flatiron Building has attracted attention.

made cheeses, ciders, baked goods, and flowers. The park's impressive statuary includes heroic statues of Abraham Lincoln, the Marquis de Lafayette, and George Washington.

If you are hungry, there are good places to eat on all sides of the Square and going north along Park Avenue South, which begins at the east side of Union Square. Or you can stroll down Broadway toward New York University. For shopping, there are stores all around and discount merchants along 14th Street heading west. ■

- Map inside front cover
- ▶ Madison Square Park
- ↔ 0.5 mile
- ⊕ 1 hour
- ▶ Union Square

NOT TO BE MISSED
- Flatiron Building
- Metropolitan Life Insurance Company Building

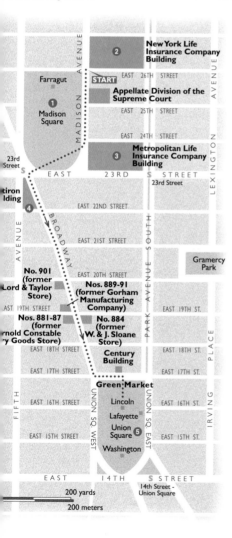

Empire State Building

Empire State Building

www.esbnyc.com

Map p. 89

350 5th Ave.

212/736-3100

$$

Subway: B, D, F, Q,
N, R to 34th St.

THE TALLEST IN THE WORLD FOR MORE THAN 40 YEARS, the Empire State Building will always be the quintessential skyscraper. From most places in Manhattan you will see it. As a destination, it draws many visitors night and day. A high-speed elevator whisks you to the 86th-floor outdoor observation deck. The view from the top, uptown and down, is matchless and essential to understanding Manhattan's lay of the land. Building attractions include the Guinness Exhibition of World Records, and Skyride, a motion-flight simulated tour of the city in a theater that moves.

Visible night and day, the Empire State is no longer a chic address, but still one of the world's great buildings.

Work on the new building proceeded at unprecedented pace, with an average of four and a half stories added every week; in one ten-day spurt, the project's 3,500 workers completed 14 stories. The Empire State Building opened on May 1, 1931, ahead of schedule and five million dollars under its 50-million-dollar budget. It was a hit with tourists from the start, but during the Depression about half of the two-million-plus square feet of floor space was unrented, hence its nickname, the Empty State Building. In 1945 a U.S. Air Force B-25 crashed into the 78th and 79th floors, without harming the building's structural integrity.

The 102-story building is 1,250 feet tall. Its 6,400 windows are designed to project beyond the limestone surface, thereby avoiding the mottled look that marred other skyscrapers. The five-story base covers two acres along Fifth Avenue between 33rd and 34th Streets. The metal-and-glass tower on top, 16 stories tall, was intended as a mooring mast for dirigibles but was only used twice. Some said the mast detracted from the essential beauty of the building, but that was before a giant ape used it as a perch in the classic 1933 film *King Kong*. Today the top is illuminated in different colors to celebrate holidays and special occasions. During the spring and fall migrations, the tower lights are turned off so as not to confuse large flocks of birds.

The Empire State Building lost its title as the world's tallest building in the 1970s. But that has not diminished its grace, its popularity, or its place in the consciousness. As a critic once said in its praise, "That it is the world's tallest building is purely incidental." ■

Herald Square

IN 1904, WHEN SONGWRITER GEORGE M. COHAN WROTE "remember me to Herald Square," it was the merchandising center of the city. Most of the original stores have disappeared, but the area— where Broadway and Sixth Avenue cross at 34th Street—retains a grimy vitality and attracts the masses and popular retail shops.

Traffic rushes by the front of Macy's, the venerated department store on West 34th Street.

Macy's opened here in 1902; still the world's largest department store, it has endeared itself to millions with its annual Thanksgiving Day Parade extravaganza.

The square is named for the *New York Herald*, headquartered here in a Renaissance-style building from 1894 to 1921. All that remains of the building is the ornamental clock. On the hour, two bronze bell ringers, nicknamed Stuff and Guff, appear and strike the bell with mallets.

To the west, **Madison Square Garden** (familiarly, the "Garden") stands on the site of the former Pennsylvania Station. Today's **Penn Station,** serving long-distance Amtrak trains and commuter trains to Long Island and New Jersey, is housed underground. The Garden itself, home to the New York Knicks and New York Rangers, is a major arena for sports, concerts, trade shows, and performing arts events.

At 2 Penn Plaza, the entrance to the present Penn terminal, are two Adolph A. Weinman sculptures from the 1910 Penn Station: a ten-foot-high statue of a railroad president, and two large granite eagles from the cornice. The present Penn Station is meant for grander quarters. Senator Daniel Patrick Moynihan spearheaded the 1990s effort to move the terminal into the monumental **General Post Office,** on the west side of Eighth Avenue between 31st and 33rd Streets. McKim, Mead & White designed the building in 1913 to visually blend with the old Penn Station's grander entrance across the avenue.

Farther west, on 11th Avenue between 34th and 39th Streets, is the **Jacob K. Javits Convention Center,** a huge, modernistic, all-glass pavilion designed by I. M. Pei and named for New York's longtime Republican senator. ■

Macy's
- Map p. 89
- 151 W. 34th St.
- ☎ 212/695-4400
- Subway: N, R, B, D, F, Q to 34th St.

Madison Square Garden
- Map p. 89
- 2 Pennsylvania Plaza
- ☎ 212/465-6741 for information and daily tours
- $$–$$$$$
- Subway: A, C, E, 1, 2, 3 to 34th St.

Jacob K. Javits Convention Center
www.javitscenter.com
- Map p. 88
- 655 W. 34th St.
- ☎ 212/216-2000
- Subway: A, C, E to 34th St.

Note: In 2006 the Morgan Library reopened after its three-year expansion/renovation project.

The Morgan Library & Murray Hill

NAMED FOR QUAKERS ROBERT AND MARY MURRAY, WHO owned an estate here in colonial times, the Murray Hill neighborhood extends, north to south, from 40th to 34th Street and east to west, from Third to Madison Avenues. Although it intrudes on Manhattan's busy Midtown, its tree-lined side streets are reminiscent of a more tranquil era when some of the city's richest and most socially prominent people lived here. Among them was financier John Pierpont Morgan (1837–1913), one of the world's richest men in a time when there were few restraints on making money.

THE MORGAN LIBRARY

J. P. Morgan was also a leading collector of the Gilded Age. His library, quipped its first director, "contains everything but the original tablets of the Ten Commandments." Contemporaries were divided on Morgan's connoisseurship, but today the Morgan Library (originally called the Pierpont Morgan Library) is recognized as one of the world's great collections. Visit it with reverence and wander amid the artistic and literary treasures on view in this marble palace. There is also a delightful café and gift shop well worth exploring.

Morgan began collecting books and manuscripts, such as the *Mainz Psalter* of 1465, and expanded to sculpture, Renaissance painting, old master drawings, and music manuscripts. When his collection grew too large for his mansion, Morgan commissioned Charles McKim to design the one-story, neoclassic building on East 36th Street.

The library was built, in classical fashion, from marble blocks put together without mortar. Adolph A. Weinman created the sculptured panels on the exterior representing the arts and other disciplines; Edward Clark Potter's lions at the entrance are forerunners of those he made for the New York Public Library. The interior consisted of the Rotunda at the entrance, the book-lined East Room, the North Room (an office), and Morgan's study, called the West Room. A biographer described Morgan during the panic of 1907, sitting here calmly "in a red plush armchair by the fire with a Madonna and Child by Pinturicchio looking down over his shoulder."

The collection

Morgan's son opened the library to the public in 1924. Four years later, Morgan's home at the corner of 36th Street and Madison Avenue was torn down and replaced by an annex, which became the entrance to the library. Hans Memling's "Portrait of a Man with a Pink" (circa 1475), perhaps the most famous painting in the collection, is displayed on the red damask walls of the West Room. One of three Gutenberg Bibles Morgan acquired is on display in the East Room. This room, with its spectacular domed ceiling and stone fireplace, is lined with three tiers of bookcases.

The collection continues to expand through acquisitions: in 1992, a signed copy of Lincoln's Emancipation Proclamation and other American historical documents; in 1998, the Carter Burden Collection of American literature, with more than 80,000 volumes dating from 1870, valued at eight to ten million dollars. In 1988, the library purchased Morgan House, the 45-room home of Morgan's son (*37th St. and Madison Ave.*), which was renovated as the education center and bookstore. A garden court connects the library and Morgan House.

AROUND MURRAY HILL

A tip of the hat to the wealthy Mr. Morgan is the luxurious hotel, **Morgans** (see p. 243), well worth seeing. Nearby, **De Lamar Mansion** (No. 233), now the Polish Consulate, was built in 1905 for a Dutch-born businessman. At Nos. 205 and 209 (at 35th Street), the 1864 **Church of the Incarnation** (1906) and its rectory contains stained-glass windows by William Morris, Louis Comfort Tiffany, and John La Farge and sculpture by Daniel Chester French and Augustus Saint-Gaudens.

A block east on Park Avenue, No. 57 was designed by Philadelphia architect Horace Trumbauer, with sculptured friezes, for socialite Adelaide L. T. Douglas. The 1911 building now houses the Guatemalan Consulate General and related offices. No. 23, the former Advertising Club, now apartments, is another McKim, Mead & White structure designed as a millionaire's mansion. Between Lexington and Third Avenues, Murray Hill's eastern border, lies **Sniffen Court** (*150–158 E. 36th St.*), the city's smallest historic district. This intriguing mews of ten brick carriage houses dates from the 1850s. ∎

Morgan Library

www.morganlibrary.org

🅰 Map p. 89
✉ 29 E. 36th St. at Madison Ave.
☎ 212/685-0610
🚇 Subway: 6 to 33rd St.

Church of the Incarnation

www.churchoftheincarnation.org

🅰 Map p. 89
✉ 209 Madison Ave.
☎ 212/689-6350
🕐 Open Sun.–Wed. & Fri. 11:30 a.m.– 2 p.m.
🚇 Subway: 6 to 33rd St.

New York Public Library

New York Public Library Humanities and Social Sciences Library

www.nypl.org

- ⓜ Map p. 89
- ✉ 5th Ave. & 42nd St.
- ☎ 212/930-0830 for exhibits & events
- 🕐 Closed Mon.; some areas closed Sun.
- Ⓢ Subway: B, D, F, V to 42nd St.; 4, 5, 6 to Grand Central; 7 to 5th Ave.

The library's Rose Main Reading Room was renovated in 1998.

GUARDED BY EDWARD CLARK POTTER'S SCULPTURED LIONS "Patience" and "Fortitude," the New York Public Library is one of the world's great cultural institutions. Founded in 1895, it grew out of the consolidation of two private libraries, those of millionaire John Jacob Astor and real estate heir James Lenox. There are now 85 branch libraries throughout the boroughs.

The New York Public Library opened in 1911 on the site of the old Croton Reservoir. The broad steps and terraces leading up to its grand exterior entrance, framed by Corinthian columns, have become a favorite gathering place for New Yorkers. The library is widely considered the greatest example of beaux arts design in the country. What's more, it works. In an enlightened move, librarians themselves assisted the architects Carrère & Hastings in designing a building that was not only beautiful but also functional. The behind-the-scenes system for moving its more than nine million books is still state of the art. The library's collection includes some 21 million other items, among them priceless manuscripts, recordings, periodicals, historical maps, prints, photographs, and family histories. Regular, changing exhibitions are drawn from these.

Rooms throughout display elegant design and clever use of natural light. The Rose Main Reading Room, lined by windows adjoining interior courtyards, is two blocks long, with chandeliers and a magnificent wood-paneled ceiling. The skylit Bartos Forum and the Periodicals Rooms with murals by Richard Haas are also superb, and the gift shop/bookstore has many unusual items.

Stretching behind the library to Sixth Avenue, **Bryant Park** is named for poet and editor William Cullen Bryant (1794–1878); beautifully restored in the 1990s, there are public benches and a fine indoor-outdoor restaurant, Bryant Park Grill (*25 W. 40th St., tel 212/840-6500*). To the south, the 1924 **American Radiator Building** (*40 W. 40th St.*), faced with black brick and gold terracotta, was Raymond Hood's first New York skyscraper. ■

The library holds one of the most precious documents of Americana in existence, Christopher Columbus's 1493 letter describing how "in thirty-three days I passed from the Canary Islands to the Indies." ■

From the East River to the Hudson, from Times Square to Rockefeller Center, this is the city's must-see area. Almost everything is nearby— restaurants, music, theater, art, enduring architecture, and much that is ephemeral.

Midtown North

Introduction & map 102–103
Grand Central Terminal & along
   42nd Street 104–105
Chrysler Building 106
United Nations Plaza 107
Times Square 108–111
43rd & 44th Streets 111
Broadway theaters 114–115
Skyscrapers walking tour 116–117
Rockefeller Center 118–119
St. Patrick's Cathedral 120
Fifth Avenue today 121
Museum of Modern Art 122–127
American Folk Art Museum 128
More Midtown sites 129–130
Hotels & restaurants 245–251

The statue of Atlas at Rockefeller Center

Midtown North

THE ENTRANCE COURT TO ROCKEFELLER CENTER'S INTERNATIONAL building features a massive statue of Atlas supporting on his broad shoulders an open sphere representing the world. The four-story statue is impossible to miss. To many, it is a symbol of Midtown North, that slice of Manhattan running river to river between 42nd and 59th Streets. This nerve center for business, culture, and entertainment has abundant office buildings and theaters, a most venerable concert hall, and landmark structures such as the Chrysler Building, as well as museums, art galleries, synagogues, churches, hotels, and restaurants. Grand Central Terminal has long welcomed visitors from all over the country, and the United Nations Plaza hosts the entire world.

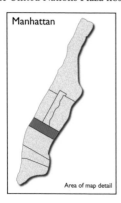

You can even live here, and New Yorkers pay a great deal of money to do so. Beekman Place and Sutton Place, on and near the East River, are among the city's most expensive addresses. Supermarkets are in short supply but sustenance can be found at such a variety of restaurants, cigar bars, delicatessens, and upscale stores— Bloomingdale's among them—that no one with money need ever go hungry. Another exclusive area is Central Park South along 59th Street, Midtown's northern edge. Rents are more affordable to the west along the Hudson, where the changing working-class neighborhood Hell's Kitchen is becoming known as Clinton.

No places better illustrate the diversity found in Midtown North than two focal points: frenetic Times Square in the 40s (where Broadway and Seventh Avenue cross) and staid Rockefeller Center in the 50s (between Fifth and Sixth Avenues). In Times Square you will be assaulted by traffic, noise, pedestrians, and the constant presence, night or day, of its gigantic animated signs. Rockefeller Center, though bustling, is quite different, the atmosphere proper and restrained. Its buildings and well-kept open spaces radiate a conviction that all is well with the world.

Midtown North was created as the wealthy elite led the city northward. Fifth Avenue was chosen as the site for St. Patrick's Cathedral in 1848 by a bishop who wanted to put his

Roman Catholic congregation on an equal footing with the Protestant establishment. In 1926 the Metropolitan Opera selected a nearby area for its new home. When the plan floundered, one of its key investors, John D. Rockefeller, Jr., instead built one of the world's great urban centers. Park Avenue developed into prime residential property—and later a business district—after 1903, when the New York Central decided to put the railroad tracks serving Grand Central below ground.

Midtown's southern boundary, 42nd Street, was designated a major crosstown street in the city's 1811 grid plan. Still, the *New York Times*'s decision in 1904 to move to its western part was considered daring. Then called Longacre Square, it was a red-light district with stables and shops

---

MIDTOWN NORTH

① Former McGraw-Hill Building ② Lyceum
③ International Center of Photography
④ Columbus Circle ⑤ Carnegie Hall
⑥ Algonquin Hotel ⑦ Chanin Building
⑧ American Folk Art Museum ⑨ Grand
Army Plaza ⑩ Trump Tower ⑪ Sony
Building ⑫ Citicorp Center ⑬ Waldorf-
Astoria ⑭ News Building

---

catering to the carriage trade. *Times* publisher Alfred Ochs persuaded the city to run the subway there, ensuring development. The newspaper's building became Times Tower, the area Times Square. A decade later, the *Times* moved to its present home on West 43rd Street and Times Tower became One Times Square: The name was there to stay.

As the theater district developed in the area in the early 1900s, Times Square also became home to the "Great White Way." Once and forever the area became a defining part of Midtown North and one of the most popular of all city destinations. ■

Grand Central Terminal & along 42nd Street

STAND ON THE BALCONY ON GRAND CENTRAL TERMINAL'S Vanderbilt Avenue side and enjoy the view of the Main Concourse; witness the ebb and flow of New York, timed to the rhythm of the daily rush hours. Grand Central Terminal is the gateway to the city, used by 150,000 commuters a day and thousands of pedestrians.

Grand Central Terminal

🏛 Map p. 103

✉ 42nd St. & Park Ave.

☎ 212/532-4900, 212/490-6650 (Oyster Bar)

🚇 Subway: 4, 5, 6, 7, S to Grand Central

The terminal opened in 1913. Warren Whitney designed the beaux arts facade facing south on 42nd Street. Atop the entrance is a clock topped by the figure of Mercury, whom sculptor Jules-Felix Coutan described as "the god of speed, of traffic, and of the trans-mission of intelligence." The firm of Reed & Stem, architects, made the station work by devising a rail system that brings trains in on two levels.

As part of a 196-million-dollar, nine-year restoration, the East Waiting Room was completed in 1992, followed by an impressive overhaul of the Main Concourse. This immense space—measuring 120 feet by 175 feet with arched windows soaring 75 feet on either end—has a floor of Tennessee marble and 125-foot-high vaulted ceilings, which are painted to resemble the constellations. Between the two levels is the **Oyster Bar,** famous for its oyster stew and its ceiling of Guastavino tiles, which was restored after a fire in 1966.

ALONG 42ND STREET

The following are a few sights to help orient you as you visit 42nd Street.

The former **McGraw-Hill Building** (*330 W. 42nd St.*) is a 1930 avant-garde skyscraper by architect Raymond Hood. You can visit its art deco lobby, which is green like the exterior terra-cotta tiles, hence the building's nickname,

"The Jolly Green Giant." Across the street is the **Holy Cross Church** (*tel 212/246-4732*), an 1870 Byzantine-style building and the parish church of Father Francis P. Duffy, chaplain of the Fighting 69th in World War I. Duffy Square (see p. 108) is named for him.

Past the renovated theaters (see pp. 114–15) is the former

Knickerbocker Hotel *(1466 Broadway at 42nd St.).* Built in 1906 by John Jacob Astor, the hotel's Maxfield Parrish mural now hangs in the King Cole Bar in the St. Regis Hotel. In 1924 George Gershwin's "Rhapsody in Blue" premiered at a concert hall across from the New York Public Library. Next door, the contoured **W. R. Grace Building** *(43 W. 42nd St.)* is a rarity in a city where horizontal and vertical lines are the architectural norm. Cross Fifth Avenue and walk about three blocks to the **Whitney at Altria,** a satellite of the Whitney Museum of American Art (see pp. 164–65). The enclosed sculpture court makes a relaxing stop. Pass Grand Central Terminal, then continue to the **Chanin Building,** at No. 122. This 56-story, 1929 skyscraper was the first in the area; the interior bronze art deco grillwork is by Rene Chambellan, whose sculptures also grace Radio City Music Hall. Across Lexington is the **Chrysler Building** (see p. 106), and across Third Avenue, the art deco **Daily News Building** *(220 E. 42nd St.),* home until 1995 of the city's first tabloid, and another 1930 Raymond Hood classic. The building is the fictional *Daily Planet* in the *Superman* movies. Cross to the **Ford Foundation Building** at No. 320, a 1967 glass box enclosing a public plaza and atrium. Reachable by steps near First Avenue is Tudor City, a Tudor-Gothic self-contained community. ■

Whitney Museum of American Art at Altria

www.whitney.org

✉ 120 Park Ave. at 42nd St.

☎ 917/663-2453

🕐 Closed Sat.–Sun.

🚇 Subway: 4, 5, 6, 7, S to Grand Central

Grand Central, a landmark building with a practical purpose

Chrysler Building

THE ART DECO CHRYSLER BUILDING IS THE FAVORITE skyscraper for many New Yorkers and visitors alike. A historic landmark since 1971, it was built for automobile magnate

Walter P. Chrysler, who wanted a corporate headquarters that reflected the glory of America's automotive industry.

To this end, architect William Van Alen adorned the facade with symbols such as wheels and radiator caps, adding stainless steel gargoyles that resemble Chrysler hood ornaments. The stainless steel pinnacle, called the vertex, is an art deco version of a radiator grill. The lavish granite and marble lobby, with its Edward Trumbull ceiling mural, was once a Chrysler showroom.

From the start, artists were taken with the building. Georgia O'Keeffe rendered it as a painting, and a famous photograph by Margaret Bourke-White shows her perched on a gargoyle high above the city. ∎

Chrysler Building

 Map p. 103

✉ Lexington Ave. at 42nd St.

☎ 212/682-3070

🚇 Subway: 4, 5, 6, 7, S to Grand Central

A block away from Grand Central Terminal, the Chrysler Building's famous spire dominates the night sky.

Ever higher

In the late 1920s an architect had only to announce a new skyscraper and he made the front page. In this charged atmosphere, the competition between the Chrysler Building's architect, William Van Alen, and his rival, H. Craig Severance, whose Bank of Manhattan building at 40 Wall Street was going up at the same time, was much in the news. Van Alen started at 56 floors, then, to top Severance, went to 65. Severance countered by adding a tower and, looking like a sure winner, finished at 71 stories. Van Alen, however, had secretly assembled a 185-foot steel spire within the Chrysler Building's fire shaft. At his signal, he recalled, "the spire gradually emerged like a butterfly from its cocoon." The Chrysler Building won, with a height of 1,048 feet. Opened in 1930, it was also briefly the world's tallest building, surpassing the Eiffel Tower. But Van Alen's triumph was short lived; a few months later the Empire State Building opened. However, the Chrysler Building remains a jazz age masterpiece, and its spire, lit since 1978, a distinctive skyline presence night and day. ∎

United Nations Plaza

N 1946 THE YEAR-OLD UNITED NATIONS ORGANIZATION decided to locate its headquarters in the United States. Although other cities were in the running, it was a John D. Rockefeller gift of 8.5 million dollars, for the purchase of an 18-acre plot on the East River, that made New York the chosen site.

The entrance is lined with flags of the 191 member nations. At the heart of the complex is the 39-story **Secretariat Building,** designed by France's Le Corbusier. Stretching north is the **General Assembly,** with its concave roof and central dome. The **Conference Building,** where the Security Council meets, extends east, over F. D. R. Drive. Guided tours leave from the General Assembly lobby, and there is a gift center and postal counter selling unique stamps.

Artwork donated by member nations is throughout. On the grounds, Barbara Hepworth's bronze monolith rises from a fountain at the entrance; see also Yugoslavian Antun Augustincic's statue "Peace" and the Japanese

Peace Bell. Inside the Secretariat Building's Dag Hammarskjöld Memorial Chapel you can see Marc Chagall's stained-glass windows.

Construction on the plaza began in 1947, in what was then an area of tenements, slaughterhouses, and breweries. The library is a 1963 addition. Other buildings surrounding the plaza include the office-hotel complex and UNICEF Building. Steps at 43rd Street lead to **Ralph Bunche Park,** dedicated to the African-American UN delegate and Nobel Peace Prize laureate. Upon its Isaiah Wall are engraved the words "They shall beat their swords into plowshares," fitting for this area, a symbol of world peace and freedom. ∎

United Nations Plaza

www.un.org/tours

🅰 Map p. 103

✉ 1st Ave. & 46th St.

☎ 212/963-8687

💲 $$ (tours)

🚇 Subway: 4, 5, 6, 7, S to Grand Central

The General Assembly of the UN can accommodate representatives of the 191 member nations.

Times Square

STAND AT FATHER DUFFY SQUARE BETWEEN 46TH AND 47TH Streets, to the north of Times Square. Traffic and pedestrians sweep by as Broadway and Seventh Avenue intersect: This is the Crossroads of the World. Night or day, gigantic neon signs blaze their messages. Here are theaters, Restaurant Row on 46th Street, and buildings that are destinations unto themselves. Such splendor is the gateway to the city's newest extravaganza, new 42nd Street. This legendary strip between Eighth Avenue and Broadway continues to amaze, with its attractions and mesmerizing signage.

Times Square Visitors Center

www.timessquare.org

✉ 7th Ave. between 46th and 47th Sts.

☎ 212/869-1890

🚇 Subway: 1, 2 3, 7, N, R, S to 42nd St.—Times Square

TKTS

✉ Broadway at W. 47th St.

☎ 212/221-0013

🚇 Subway: 1, 2 3, 7, N, R, S to 42nd St.—Times Square

Opposite:
Times Square forms where Broadway and Seventh Avenue cross.

Times Square today is a very different place from the tawdry tenderloin it had become by 1989. Buildings have sprouted, including one on **Duffy Square** designed especially for electric billboards. The new building at Four Times Square, housing the Condé Nast offices of *Vogue, Vanity Fair*, and the *New Yorker*, has been nicknamed the "citadel of chic." Just a few years ago, the thought of a *Vogue* editor in Times Square would have been inconceivable.

A decade ago, 42nd Street between Seventh and Eighth Avenues, known as the "deuce," was somewhat dangerous, a place of hustlers, deteriorating second-run X-rated movie theaters, peep shows, and sex shops. Times Square had become a blot on the city's image and a place to steer clear of. Today it is clean, policed, and visitor friendly. Commuters, tourists, and school groups on class trips to New York are much in evidence, as are sightseeing New Yorkers, proud to see this neighborhood reclaimed.

Before leaving Duffy Square, give your regards to the statues of actor-producer George M. Cohan and Father Francis P. Duffy, chaplain of the 69th Regiment during World War I and pastor of Holy Cross Parish, then get your bearings. With the TKTS discount ticket booth behind you (where you can purchase same-day discounted

theater tickets), the Times Square Information Center is left (east) of Duffy Square. Located in the landmark **Embassy Theater,** the first U.S. theater to show newsreels, it offers many tourist services and tickets. The tower straight ahead (south) of Duffy Square is One Times Square, where the glittering ball drops on New Year's Eve. Remember that between 45th and 42nd Streets, both Broadway and Seventh Avenue have Broadway addresses. East at 43rd and Broadway, the seven-story-high **Market Site Tower** dominates the corner, illuminating the area 24 hours a day. It houses a state-of-the-art digital broadcast studio transmitting 175 live market updates from major networks: CNN, CNBC, BBC, and more. You may forget the occupants, but not the high-tech electronic display wrapping the cylindrical building with up-to-the-minute NASDAQ information. To immerse yourself in a family interactive amusement center, walk south to **Broadway City** *(241 W. 42nd St., bet. 7th and 8th Aves.).*

LANDMARK BUILDINGS

You can also seek out landmarks. The theaters (see pp. 114–115) are architectural gems. The 1931 **Brill Building** *(1619 Broadway at 49th St.)* was known as Tin Pan Alley when it was the center of America's popular music industry. For an old-

At the stroke of midnight

It was the opening of the Times Tower on New Year's Eve 1904 that first brought the crowds into Times Square. Marked by fireworks, the celebration was reported in the newspaper: "The instant the first flash on the Times Tower showed, a great shout went up, and an ear-splitting blast was sounded from the horns of the myriad merrymakers on the streets below." Thus the *Times* unwittingly gave birth to a tradition that continued after it moved out of the building in 1913. Today, half a million people pack Times Square on New Year's Eve, to watch a lighted ball begin its countdown fall one minute before midnight. Millions more watch the spectacle on television. ■

fashioned, well-stocked music store, visit **Colony Records** *(1619 Broadway, tel 212/265-2050)*. At street level the **Paramount Building** *(1505 Broadway)*, a 1926 landmark with setbacks, towers, and clocks, once housed the Paramount Theater. An opulent movie palace of the day, it is also remembered for a 1944 concert when bobby soxers, as teenage girls were then called, went into a frenzy over Frank Sinatra.

Experience "hotel as theater" at the **Paramount Hotel** *(235 W. 46th St., tel 212/764-5500)*. A light tableau animates the sweeping lobby staircase, the Paramount Bar is trendy, and the Mezzanine Restaurant offers Latin-inspired cuisine. Downstairs is where Billy Rose had his famed Diamond Horseshoe. It is much in tune with Rose's rule for the shows he staged there in the 1940s: "No subtlety allowed." Less ostentatious is **Sardi's** *(234 W. 44th St., tel 212/221-8440)*, a theatrical restaurant and landmark. Opened in 1921, it is famous for the caricatures of celebrities on its walls and for the low-priced "actor's menu" it offers to members of Actors' Equity.

There have been casualties of changing tastes and times. Nathan's, specializing in the hot dog made famous at Coney Island, is gone. The atin Quarter, with its chorus line, osed long ago. The original Lindy's Mindy's" in Damon Runyon's ort stories) of cheesecake fame so shut its doors. Also gone are ubert's Museum, a long-lived imes Square institution featuring eaks; Dr. Heckler's Flea Circus; rev- ations on sex from "The French cademy of Medicine, Paris"; and ansvestite bars and streetwalkers. ome might argue that renewal has washed away Times Square's distinctive character, but even naysayers have begun to welcome a renaissance long overdue, a boon to tourism and the city economy, and a catalyst to revitalization elsewhere. An earlier renewal plan fortunately found no funding—it would have turned the area into a staid office district. Instead, in new Times Square the pulse of New York beats at its most vital. ■

43rd & 44th Streets

or a break from high-pressured mes Square, sample West 43rd d 44th Streets (between Fifth and xth Avenues), streets of almost ppressive dignity—whose build- gs hold some wonderful interiors.

Start with the 1902 **Algonquin** **Iotel** (see p. 245), famed home of e literary Round Table. This 1920s oup included Dorothy Parker, obert Benchley, and other writers d artists whose clever conversa- on set the standard for jazz age phistication. The venerable Oak oom, Blue Bar, and Rose Room— o longer rose—are open for din- g and periodic cabaret shows. The bby, delightful for tea, remains nteel: Ring a bell for the waiter. elebrity spotting is better across e street at the 1898 **Royalton** **otel** (see p. 246), renovated in 88 by Philippe Starck. Nearby, a aque identifies the building that used the *New Yorker,* whose fices *(25 W. 43rd St.)* also opened to here. Visit for free the **ossman Collection of Locks** the building housing the General ciety Library. The 400-piece col- ction of locks, keys, and tools is ite unique.

Exclusive associations occupy her turn-of-the-20th-century ildings. The limestone-clad 1895

Bar Association of the City of New York Building runs through the block and has two addresses *(42 W. 44th St., 37 W. 43rd St.)*. More fanciful is the 1899 **New York Yacht Club** *(37 W. 44th St., tel 212/382-1000),* home of the America's Cup from 1857 to 1983. Its beaux arts window bays have a nautical air. Architects McKim, Mead & White designed the 1894 brick-faced **Harvard Club** *(27 W. 44th St.)* as well as the 1891 Italianate-style building for the **Century Association** *(7 W. 43rd St.),* a men's dining club. ■

Mossman Collection of Locks

www.generalsociety.org

✉ 20 W. 44th St.

☎ 212/840-1840
(call beforehand)

🕐 Closed Sat.–Sun.

🚇 Subway: B, D, F, V
to 42nd St.

The imposing entrance of the Royalton Hotel, renovated by fashionable designer Philippe Starck

The Great White Way

Good news! The Great White Way is alight as never before—electric signs blazing, blinking, and crowding each other as they vie like noisy children for our attention.

O. J. Gude, whose company did many of the early Times Square signs, coined the term "The Great White Way" around the turn of the century. This referred to Broadway's appearance when lit up by signs, which at the time used only white lightbulbs. Gude believed that electric signage was art. He was also the first to understand its effectiveness: "Everybody must read them, and absorb them, and absorb the advertiser's lesson willingly or unwillingly." In another era, poet Ezra Pound saw them as "our poetry, for we have pulled the stars down to our will."

Gude and Pound were right: This kind of advertising surpasses mere communication. Here in Times Square developed a distinctly urban popular art form, one that wedded beauty, communication, architecture, and technology. Times Square's premier signmaker today is Artkraft Strauss. Look at any major sign and you can see their "signature," the name Artkraft along the bottom. To view the Great White Way, start at Times Square's southern perimeter, by the subway entrance on 42nd Street and Seventh Avenue, and look north to Broadway's main stem. Across from you, the latest fabulous sign will wrap the corner (look for the signature); to your left the marquees of the newly restored theaters fan out toward the multiplex cinemas. Cross 42nd Street and look back toward the subway station and crowded streets. Streaming, biking, horse-drawn crowds create their own energy field. The vibe is contagious. Proceed uptown, choosing your favorite signs. At Duffy Square, the stacked signs soar skyward. A recent favorite here was an electronic delight: the cap lifted off a 42-foot-tall Coke bottle and its contents disappeared through a straw.

The first electric sign was an 1898 advertisement for Coney Island, erected at 38th Street and Broadway. The 1904 move of the *New York Times* created Times Square, where electric signage would come into full flower. In 1910 the *Times* introduced its popular news ribbon for the Jim Jeffries–Jack Johnson fight in Nevada. This blow-by-blow account ran along the outside of Times Tower, the words rendered by 15,000 bulbs flashing 72,000 times a second. The technique is used today, in digital ribbons known as zippers.

A 1916 change in zoning regulations removed size restrictions, and in 1917, Wrigley Spearmint Gum erected what it claimed was the world's largest electric sign. Eighty feet tall and two hundred feet long, the ad featured animated spear-thrusting elves. In the 1920s, neon lighting brought color to the Great White Way, whose name was not to change. Everyone with memories of Times Square recalls specific signs. Many cite the Pepsi-Cola extravaganza of the 1950s, an immense waterfall flanked by huge Pepsi bottles. Someone calculated that it would have taken 7,812

New technology, including digital imaging, has made the advertising signs of Times Square brighter than ever.

gallons of Pepsi to fill the bottles. Artkraft Strauss did the Pepsi sign and such other landmarks as the Camel man who blew gigantic smoke rings, one every 20 seconds. The source of the smoke: Con Edison steam.

The fifties have been called the heyday of the Great White Way, but with redevelopment under way—and many signs of even grander scale in the works—that title may be lost, or two heydays acknowledged, for there are differences. Today, colors are brighter, more intrusive. Many of the signs advertise foreign imports. Although today's signs are spectacular, the contrast between past and present creates a certain nostalgia for the old days. On assignment to photograph Times Square, Jack Pierson deliberately made his pictures blurry: "I still like to believe that the signs say 'Franks One Nickel' not 'Casio' or 'TDK'—so, if they're out of focus, I've got my New York Dream." ∎

Broadway theaters

Broadway theater information

☎ 888/Broadway
(888/276-23929)

IF YOU HAVE HEARD THAT THE BROADWAY THEATER IS dead, don't believe it. In one recent year, 11,890,000 people paid $666,000,000 for theater tickets and had a choice of more productions—close to 40—than at any other time in recent memory. Since 1880, "Broadway" has been a term for large-scale theater that opens in New York City and often travels elsewhere; but since 1929, when movies took over many theaters, most plays have opened not on Broadway but nearby, on the narrow streets off Times Square.

1903 beaux arts masterpiece. Note the graceful marquee, ornate columns, and theatrical masks across the entablature on the grandiose facade. Two blocks away, Marlon Brando debuted in *A Streetcar Named Desire* in 1947 at the **Barrymore** *(243 W. 47th St., tel 212/239-6200, telecharge.com)*.

Although the architecture of many theaters is a show in itself, the wonder is what happens on stage. The boards echo with great performances, from the early Barrymores to Christopher Plummer playing Barrymore in 1997 to unknowns creating a success in the musical smash *Rent*. The best way to savor Broadway is to buy a ticket and go. You might find yourself in a Moorish palace inside the **Martin Beck Theater** *(302 W. 45th St.)* or amid plasterwork seemingly from the Renaissance at the Shubert or gazing at a French garden dance above the proscenium arch of the **Cort** *(138 W. 48th St.)*, whose exterior, by the way, was based on Marie-Antoinette's Petit Trianon at Versailles. You can also tour some theaters, such as the sumptuously renovated **New Amsterdam,** which one reviewer called "walking into a dream."

The Ethel Barrymore Theater has hosted some of Broadway's biggest shows and stars since it opened in 1928.

You can still step back into the past wandering these streets. Begin with the **Belasco Theater** *(111 W. 44th St.)* and walk west to the theaters along "Rodgers & Hammerstein Row," from the **Shubert** *(225 W. 44th St.)* to the **Broadhurst,** the **Majestic,** the **Helen Hayes,** and the **St. James.** Farther along is the **Actors Studio** *(432 W. 44th St., tel 212/757-0870, closed Sat.–Sun.),* founded by Elia Kazan in 1947. Here director Lee Strasberg taught his students, including Marlon Brando, Marilyn Monroe, and Al Pacino.

Starring on the next block is the **Lyceum** *(149–157 W. 45th St.),* a

New Amsterdam

✉ 214 W. 42nd St.
☎ 212/282-2900 or 212/307-4100 (Ticketmaster) for show tickets
🚇 Subway: N, R, S, 1, 2, 3, 7 to Times Sq.

PRESERVATION

A 1980s decision to give most of Times Square's legitimate theaters the status of historic landmarks was an important step in saving

hem. Unfortunately, five venerable heaters, the Bijou, the Astor, and he original Helen Hayes among hem, had already been destroyed. Preservationists turned their ttention to the nine 42nd Street heaters west of Times Square, decayed almost to the point of uin or converted to "grind houses," howing pornographic movies nd "adult" fare. Disney's 1995 ommitment of eight million dollars o restore the New Amsterdam hanged the area's fate. Now the nonprofit Times Square Business mprovement District guides the plan that is rescuing the theaters and evitalizing the area.

The stunning renovation of the New Amsterdam set the standard to follow. The original theater was the height of opulence, with promenades and a roof garden. From 1913 to 1927, the Zeigfeld Follies were produced here. Today the theater has been returned to use in all its art nouveau splendor; it opened with *The Lion King*, theater the whole family can enjoy.

So stand in line at TKTS (see p. 108) at Father Duffy Square, mingle with the crowds to get your discount seats (cash only), and feel the excitement build until you are in your seat. As the lights go down, let Broadway theater sweep you off your feet. ■

The beautifully renovated New Amsterdam theater has featured *The Lion King* since 1997.

Skyscrapers walking tour

This zigzag tour passes buildings pivotal in the city's architectural history. It begins with the baroque-towered Helmsley Building straddling Park Avenue, crosses Park Avenue a number of times, and ends with the art deco Fuller Building on Madison Avenue.

Built in 1929 as the New York Central Building—to house the railroad company—the **Helmsley Building** ❶ *(230 Park Ave. between E. 45th and E. 46th Sts.)* is stunning inside, and its white-towered outline impressive. Unfortunately, in 1963 the Pan Am (now Met Life) Building went up, blocking any clear view of it. Continue north three blocks to 301 Park Avenue, the famed art deco **Waldorf-Astoria Hotel.** Its twin 625-foot towers are residences for the rich and famous. The hotel is a favorite of royalty and presidents alike and far grander than the

original Waldorf. Visit its luxurious art deco marble-columned lobby, filled with bronze and rich mahogany. A highlight is "The Wheel of Life" (1931), a 148,000-piece tile mosaic depicting the drama of human existence, by French artist Louis Rigal.

Turn left (west) on East 50th Street, crossing Park Avenue, and go right at Madison Avenue to the **Villard Houses** *(Nos. 451–455)*, with the **Helmsley Palace Hotel** rising behind. Built for railroad tycoon Henry Villard, beginning in 1883, the Villard Houses are six brownstones joined to look like a single Renaissance palace. The complex was saved from demolition in the 1980s by incorporating the east wing into the Helmsley Palace Hotel lobby. The north wing now houses the Municipal Art Society and the Urban Center Galleries. You can stop for tea beneath the gilded ceiling in the Helmsley Palace Gold Room.

Take a right at 51st Street and right at Park Avenue for **St. Bartholomew's Church** ❷. This 1919 Byzantine-style Episcopal church exemplifies the city's movement north; the congregation was formerly located on Madison Avenue and East 44th Street. The Stanford White porch, with carvings by Phillip Martiny and Daniel Chester French, came from the earlier church. Go left (east) on East 50th Street to Lexington Avenue and turn left. The art deco **General Electric Building** ❸ *(570 Lexington Ave.)*, built in 1931 as the RCA Victor Building, was sheathed in brick and terra-cotta to complement St. Bartholomew's next door.

Go left at East 51st Street and right to 370 Park Avenue, the **Racquet and Tennis Club**, built in 1919. This members-only male bastion by McKim, Mead & White is a copy of an Italian Renaissance palazzo. Across the street rises the 1958 bronze-glass-and-steel **Seagram Building** ❹ *(375 Park Ave.)*. It is the city's only building by the great German-born American architect Mies van der Rohe. The design of the slab set back on a plaza became widely imitated. A block north at 390 Park Avenue, the landmark 1952 **Lever House** was the city's first glass slab office building. Turn right at East 54th Street to **Citicorp Center** ❺ (1978), an aluminum-clad cantilevered tower. Its chisel-shaped top is a modern reference point on the skyline. Inside are stores and St. Peter's Lutheran Church. On the corner of 55th Street and Lexington Avenue is the city's oldest continuously used synagogue, the onion-domed **Central Synagogue** ❻ *(123 E. 55th St., tel 212/838-5122, ext. 219)*. Dating from 1872, it was restored following a 1998 fire.

Go left on East 55th Street two blocks and right to Philip Johnson's 1984 **Sony Building** ❼ *(550 Madison Ave.)*, the first postmodern skyscraper. Inside visit the **Sony Wonder Technology Lab** *(tel 212/833-*

- ⊞ Map inside front cover
- ▶ Helmsley Bldg., Park Ave.
- ↔ 1.2 miles
- ⊕ About 1 hour
- ▶ Fuller Bldg., Madison Ave.

NOT TO BE MISSED

- General Electric Building
- Seagram Building
- Citicorp Center
- Sony Building
- Fuller Building

8100, closed Mon.), a hands-on technology entertainment museum. A personalized voice chip lets you use the interactive games. Farther along, the green granite 1983 **IBM Building** ⑧ (590 Madison Ave.) has an atrium for rest and refreshment amid soothing bamboo trees. The final stop is the art deco **Fuller Building** ⑨ (41 E. 57th St. at Madison Ave.), built in 1929. Note the Elie Nadelman sculpture, "Construction Workers," above the entrance. Inside are excellent galleries, including Howard Greenberg. ■

Opposite: The art deco Waldorf-Astoria
Right: The Sony Building

Rockefeller Center

ROCKEFELLER CENTER—WITH ITS WALKWAYS, SUNKEN plaza, gardens, outdoor sculpture, and architecturally related art deco buildings—has been copied but never surpassed. Bounded by Fifth and Sixth Avenues and 48th and 51st Streets, this 19-building city within a city is arguably the most successful urban development ever

Radio City
Music Hall
www.radiocity.com
▲ Map p. 103
✉ 1260 6th Ave.
☎ 212/247-4777
$ $$
🚇 Subway: B, D, F, V
   to 47th–50th
   Sts.–Rockefeller
   Center

Note: One-hour Stage Door
Tours Mon.–Sun.,
11 a.m. to 3 p.m.
(212/465-6100).

As a visitor, a good place to start is **Radio City Music Hall,** where the high-kicking, 36-member dance team, the Rockettes, still performs at Christmas and Easter shows and where top singers perform throughout the year. Here you stand at the edge of the original 14 buildings that comprised the center when it opened in 1940; five buildings west of Sixth Avenue were added after 1945. For a detailed guide to the complex, go to the **General Electric (GE) Building** at 30 Rockefeller Plaza. Headquarters for NBC is here, and outside *(between W. 49th and W. 50th Sts.),* the morning *Today Show* with Katie Couric and Matt Lauer films live. Watch it through the glass-enclosed set and maybe you will see yourself on TV. In the center of the complex is a flag-lined sunken plaza. Here you can skate outdoors in winter, or in summer dine at American Festival Café, which takes over the rink. Past the rink is the sloping Promenade, where the lighting of an immense Christmas tree is the focus every holiday season. Sit by the floral displays and sculpture in the Channel Gardens and then wander onto Fifth Avenue, but be sure and turn back for another look.

The elegant **Rainbow Room** (see p. 248) atop 30 Rockefeller Plaza is treasured for its revolving floor, cocktails, and spectacular views. Here you can dance to a live Big Band orchestra, or enjoy the spirited crowd at the

Opposite: The lighting of the immense Rockefeller Center tree is a highlight of the New York holiday season.

Piano Bar in the Rainbow Grill Room. In good or bad weather you can explore the many shops and eateries in the complex's underground concourse.

Although Mitsubishi now owns the controlling interest in Rockefeller Center, it was John D. Rockefeller who developed it. The site was originally intended as a home for the Metropolitan Opera, but when the stock market crashed the Met reneged. In late 1929 Rockefeller announced a plan for a commercial complex to house the new radio and television industry. When the Radio Corporation of America (RCA) moved into the building, the entire complex became known as Radio City, a name that soon gave way to Rockefeller Center. The name of the adjacent Radio City Music Hall stuck. It remains, with 6,200 seats, the country's largest theater, and it is a link with a time when RCA, RKO, and NBC were primary tenants. Rockefeller Center now houses publishing and communications organizations.

Not part of the complex but nearby are two historic streets. "Swing Street," 52nd Street between Fifth and Sixth Avenues, was the world center of jazz in the 1930s. All that remains of that era is the brownstone housing the swank **21 Club** restaurant *(21 W. 52nd St., tel 212/582-7200).* Still vital as a district is "Diamond Row," along 47th Street; the diamond cutters who formed it were European Jews fleeing Nazism. ■

St. Patrick's Cathedral

ST. PATRICK'S IS HUGE—AT 332 FEET LONG AND 174 FEET wide, it is among the world's largest cathedrals. Offering quiet refuge in busy Midtown, it is in constant use for weddings and other events, while its entrance steps are the ideal platform from which to watch the parade of pedestrians.

St. Patrick's Cathedral

⬛ Map p. 103
✉ 5th Ave. & 50th St.
☎ 212/753-2261
🚇 Subway: B, D, F, V to 47th–50th Sts.– Rockefeller Center; E, V to 53rd St.

St. Patrick's Gothic spires stand out among Fifth Avenue's modern highrises.

Its architecture is timeless; James Renwick, Jr., modeled it on the Gothic cathedral in Cologne, Germany, borrowing elements from others in Europe. The spires were finished in 1888; at 330 feet tall, they towered above the city until the 1930s, when skyscrapers appeared. Renwick's original east front was replaced in 1906 by the Lady Chapel, designed by Charles Matthews. The three sets of bronze doors on Fifth Avenue are a 1949 addition. Elizabeth Ann Seton, the first American-born saint, is among the saints of New York depicted on the central doors; inside is a shrine to her, with a bronze statue.

Go inside—visitors are expected to respectfully wander to view the interior. The central nave can seat 2,500 people. It is 108 feet high and 48 feet wide. Be sure to visit the Lady Chapel Cathedral honoring the Blessed Virgin, where there is a marble Pietà (1906, by William O. Partridge). Unlike most Gothic cathedrals, there are no flying buttresses, but above the altar is a 57-foot bronze baldachin. Note, too, the entryway, especially magnificent when light streams in through the 26-foot-wide Rose Window above the Great Organ over the Great Bronze Doors.

Archbishop John Hughes announced plans for the church in 1858. His successor, Archbishop John McCloskey, opened the church on May 25th, 1879. The 1.9-million dollar cathedral is dedicated to the patron saint of Ireland. ∎

Fifth Avenue today

MIDTOWN FIFTH AVENUE BEARS LITTLE RESEMBLANCE today to its residential past as Millionaires' Row. Still, there are signs of that history among all that is new. Architecturally, the stretch covered here features Grand Army Plaza, St. Patrick's Cathedral, Rockefeller Center, and other historic buildings.

The aristocrat of toy stores, **F.A.O. Schwartz** (*767 5th Ave.*) is the place to pick up an Eloise book or toy: The six-year-old fictional character of Kay Thompson's series lived nearby at the Plaza Hotel. **Tiffany & Co.** (*727 5th Ave.*) originated on lower Broadway, but the glitter of gems remains the same, and there are a few affordable purchases, so look inside.

Experience the Donald Trump aesthetic of glamour, glitz, and sparkling brass—plus shopping and a waterfall—at the bronze-colored **Trump Tower** (*725 5th Ave., tel 212/832-2000*); you ride crisscrossed escalators up the mirror-lined atrium to the retail floors. On opposite corners at 55th Street are two fine hotels, the **Peninsula New York,** a 1905 beaux arts landmark, and the 1904 **St. Regis**, built by John Jacob Astor. Visit its King Cole Bar and Lounge to see the Maxfield Parrish mural of the merry old soul. For city views, try the Pen Top Bar and Terrace atop the Peninsula.

In 1917 **Cartier** (*653 5th Ave.*) converted two turn-of-the-20th-century mansions into its jewelry emporium, while the design company **Versace** occupies a house built in 1902–05 by George W. Vanderbilt (*647 5th Ave.*). **Saks Fifth Avenue** (*611 5th Ave.*) has occupied its landmark Renaissance-style building since it was built in 1922. The 1927 **Fred F. French Building** (*551 5th Ave.*), with its multicolored faience, is a classic example of setback architecture, and its exotic lobby is a treat. ■

Above: Cartier—gift wrapped for Christmas
Below: Alternative transport outside Tiffany's

Museum of Modern Art

Museum of Modern Art

www.moma.org

⬛ Map p. 103

✉ 11 W. 53rd St. between 5th & 6th Aves.

☎ 212/708-9400

⬧ Closed Tues., Thanksgiving Day, and Christmas Day

$ $$$. Advance admission tickets are available from Ticketmaster at 212/220-0505 or www.ticketweb.org

🚇 Subway: E, V to 5th Ave.–53rd. St.; B, D, F, V to 47th–50th St.– Rockefeller Center

WHEN THE MUSEUM OF MODERN ART (MOMA) CLOSED for reconstruction in 2002, it was attracting more than 1.6 million visitors annually. Its 2005 transformation into "one of the most exquisite works of architecture to rise in this city in at least a generation" *(New York Times)* heightened enthusiasm worldwide for this already-favorite cultural destination. In a masterful move, architect Yoshio Taniguchi positioned the Abby Aldrich Rockefeller Sculpture Garden as the very heart of the museum, framed by a new gallery building and the towering cityscape. Visitors first view the garden through glass curtain walls. Enlarged from its original 1953 design by Philip A. Johnson, it has been transformed into a majestic gathering place, with bi-level seating, seasonal plantings, reflecting pools, and space to wander. It is both a welcoming prelude to exploring the bustling museum and a retreat for later on.

From Cezanne to Chuck Close, from the earliest daguerreotypes to interactive video and electronic displays, MoMA has it all—as well as spaces and galleries designed to match the type and scale of works displayed. These range from the lower-level refurbished Titus Theaters, where screenings are held, to the expansive, skylit galleries for temporary exhibitions on the top (6th) floor.

From its beginnings in 1929, the museum's guiding principle was to move beyond the narrow definition of art, which included painting, sculpture, and drawing, to embrace all the visual fields. MoMA was a pioneer in the fields of architecture and graphic, industrial, and textile designs. It collected and exhibited photographs long before other major museums and was early to

collect and preserve significant films. Since then its holdings have steadily increased, and its physical structure has been redefined and renovated to keep pace. This has included adding a variety of dining options: two cafés and The Modern, the museum's new fine-dining restaurant and bar, with a patio on the garden. A separate street-level entrance on West 53rd Street allows guests to partake after museum hours. For shopping, visitors can choose among a wide range of items in all prices at two shops in the museum. The MoMA Design Store, across from the museum on West 53rd Street specializes in objects licensed from the collection, from jewelry and scarves to glassware and small furniture.

THE COLLECTION

MoMA's permanent collection includes more than 150,000 paintings, sculptures, drawings, prints, photographs, design objects, and architectural drawings and models. There are, in addition, some 22,000 films, videos, and media works; 300,000 books, periodicals, and artists' books; the museum Archives with 2,500 linear feet of historical documentation; and a photographic archive of tens of thousands of photographs.

MUSEUM HIGHLIGHTS

The new MoMA that opened in 2005 has nearly doubled in size and added 40,000 square feet in exhibition space. It is now able to present the most extensive display of its collection ever, including many previously unexhibited works. On view are selections from each of the museum's six curatorial departments: Film and Media; Prints and Illustrated Books; Architecture and Design; Drawings; Photography; and Painting and Sculpture. Among these offerings are some of the museum's best-loved works, including Vincent van Gogh's "The Starry Night" and Pablo Picasso's "Les Demoiselles d'Avignon."

FILM & MEDIA

Works from this international collection are shown in two areas of the

Monet's triptych "Water Lilies" graces MoMA's main gallery at the newly renovated and reopened museum.

Note:
Lines for admission and the checkroom are often long, so travel light for your museum visit. All items larger than 11 x 14 in (28 x 35.5 cm) must be checked. Luggage may not be accepted.

One of Sol LeWitt's "Wall Drawings." The American artist has created over 1,000 unique but similarly titled pieces since his career began in the 1960s.

museum. The two movie theaters on the lower level have daily programs selected from the museum's 20,000 moving-image works. These cover more than a century, from the days of Thomas Edison to the present. The Media Gallery on the second floor has both installations and electronic media.

PRINTS & ILLUSTRATED BOOKS

These are on the second floor (along with the Contemporary Galleries, Media Gallery, and Café 2), drawn from a collection of more than 50,000 prints and illustrated books from the 1880s to the present. Among highlights are the Edvard Munch print "Madonna" (1895–1902) and a 1913 illustrated book combining art by Sonia Delauney-Terks and poetry by Cendrars. In the latter, cascading colors flow down one side of each page and poetry down the other. The artists called their creation "the first simultaneous book."

ARCHITECTURE & DESIGN

With exhibits on the third floor, this diverse collection provides an extensive overview of modernism. The architecture collection documents buildings and contains more than 60 models and 1,000 drawings, plus the large **Ludwig Mies van der Rohe Archive.** The design collection has more than 3,000 objects, ranging from appliances, furniture, and classic cars to textiles, silicon chips, typography, and posters: Rody Grauman's "85 Lamps Lighting Fixture" (1992), Christopher Dresser's fanciful red-and-black "Watering Can" (painted tin-iron, circa 1896), and Ludwig Mies van der Rohe's perspective drawing for a 1921 crystal tower, "Friedrichstrasse Skuscraper" brilliantly illustrate the synthesis of architecture and design.

DRAWINGS

The third floor holds selections from this collection's more than 7,000 works on paper, including those done in pencil, ink, and charcoal, plus watercolors, collages, gouaches, and mixed-media pieces. Highlights include works by such artists as Georges-Pierre Seurat, Paul Klee, Egon Schiele, and Dieter

Roth. Juan Miró's "The Beautiful Bird Revealing the Unknown to a Pair of Lovers" (1940) is an obsessively meticulous drawing with a nature theme, from his Constellation series. In contrast is a classic Georgia O'Keeffe work (and a bequest of the artist): "An Orchid" (1941), a fluid, sensual, green-and-white orchid.

PHOTOGRAPHY

MoMA's collection of more than 25,000 photographs, from 1840 to the present, is one of the world's most important. The museum began collecting in 1930 and established the photography department under Beaumont Newhall in 1940. In 1955, Edward Steichen, then chairman, curated the seminal "Family of Man" exhibit, raising awareness of photography as an art form. MoMA's third-floor galleries contain works from William Henry Fox Talbot and others at the dawn of the medium as well as later celebrated photographers Julia Margaret Cameron, Alfred Stieglitz, Man Ray, Imogen Cunningham, Manuel Alvarez Bravo, Diane Arbus,

and more. In the contemporary arena, a landmark acquisition was the purchase of Cindy Sherman's black-and-white "Untitled Film Stills" series; Andreas Gursky's one-man show (1999) and Lee Friedlander's 2005 retrospective drew large crowds. MoMA's annual curated exhibit "New Photography" can be counted on for outstanding new talent, such as Sam Taylor-Wood in the 1997–98 show (online at the MoMA site); using a rotating camera that records close to 360 degrees in five seconds, she created large-scale color panoramas blending aspects of motion and still photographs.

PAINTING & SCULPTURE

Works from this collection, shown on floors four and five, are likely to elicit the greatest collective response, for so many of them are iconic, often-published masterworks—only here you see the real thing. Containing some 3,200 works from the late 19th century to the present, MoMA's modern painting and sculpture collection is the world's largest and most inclusive. Perhaps

A large atrium dominates MoMA's new interior. Architect Yoshio Taniguchi's goal for the new museum was to "create an ideal environment for art and people through the imaginative and disciplined use of light, materials, and space."

Picasso's "Les Demoiselles d'Avignon" (1907) is among the thousands of works on display at MoMA. Exhibition space increased by nearly 50 percent with the 2005 renovation.

you will be fortunate enough to see its earliest work, Paul Cezanne's Postimpressionist painting "The Bather" (circa 1885). From the recent period, 1980s and later, artists include James Rosenquist, Susan Rothenberg, Cai Guo Quiang, Chris Ofili, Richard Serra, and others.

To enter more deeply into the world of painting, choose some works for comparison. Paul Gauguin's depiction of a Polynesian goddess in "The Seed of the Areoi" (oil on burlap, 1892); Frida Kahlo's "Self-Portrait with Cropped Hair" (oil on canvas, 1940); and Andy Warhol's rendition of a goddess of popular culture, "Gold Marilyn Monroe" (silkscreen ink on synthetic polymer paint on canvas, 1962) can spark fascinating discussions on the painterly canonization of women. Comparing two sculptures, Marcel DuChamp's "Bicycle Wheel" (1951) and Chris Burden's "Medusa's Head" (1980), raises fundamental questions about artmaking and influence. Both sculptures use altered common objects and rely on a conceptual premise and absurdist

visual surprise. "Medusa's Head" does not feature twine or snakes or a predictable component for the hair but, instead, model railroad track and seven scale model trains. And DuChamp's "Bicycle Wheel," his first Readymade, is not simply a bicycle wheel mounted upside down on a kitchen stool.

Floors four and five are replete with other equally wondrous works, of Claude Monet, Pablo Picasso, Piet Mondrian, Jackson Pollack, Constantin Brancusi, Alexander Calder, Joseph Cornell, and Eva Hesse, to name just a few. You may prefer to find your favorite work and stay with it for a time. Allow at least one piece to work its magic on you. Perennial favorites are Henri Rousseau's "The Sleeping Giant" (1897), Henri Matisse's "Dance 1" (1909), Marc Chagall's "Birthday" (1915), and Alberto Giacometti's "The Palace at 4 a.m." (1932).

On the fifth floor, you can also stop in at the Terrace Café and, season permitting, look down on the garden as you sip your drink or cocktail on the terrace. Back on the first floor, the garden and its many sculptures are still there for your return, and so is Auguste Rodin's "Monument to Balzac" (1898, cast 1954), presiding spirit of the lobby. A café is here as well.

HISTORY

The idea for the museum was conceived in the winter of 1928–29 when Abby Rockefeller, the wife of John D. Rockefeller, Jr., and Lillie P. Bliss met in Cairo, Egypt. They decided that America must have a museum devoted to modern art and sculpture, works other museums refused to exhibit. Mary Quinn Sullivan became the third partner in the enterprise.

The "ladies," as they were called, enlisted the aid of A. Conger Goodyear, a museum trustee and collector who had shocked the art world by spending $5,000 for a Picasso, and art historian Paul J. Sachs. Soon the museum opened in a small gallery on the 12th floor of the Heckscher Building *(750 5th Ave. at 57th St.)* with a brilliant 27-year-old art scholar, Alfred H. Barr, Jr., as its director. Barr shaped the museum during its formative years and insisted on expanding the museum's horizons to include all the visual arts.

In 1932 the museum moved into a town house at its current location on West 53rd Street. In 1936, MoMA commissioned architect Edward Durell Stone and Philip Goodwin, a museum trustee, to design a new building for its West 53rd Street site. The new museum, which opened in 1939, was fronted by a sheath of glass and marble and was one of the country's first examples of the international style. The museum doubled in size in 1984, when Cesar Pelli designed an addition, a garden hall, and two wings in a condominium tower.

Although the latest redefinition of the museum is its most extensive to date, it is unlikely it will be the last. What is certain, however, is that MoMA consistently offers a wealth of riches in a stimulating environment. As you leave, pick up pertinent brochures (including material on the research resources and study centers), plus schedules and flyers on the many workshops, lectures, films, and special events. You may also consider planning a trip to MoMA's affiliate, P.S.1, devoted to the advancement of contemporary art. It is housed in a 100-year-old Romanesque Revival school building in Long Island City, where it has mounted some of the most provocative visual-arts exhibits of the past quarter-century (see page 224). ■

Greenery and quiet pools complement the artwork in the Abby Aldrich Rockefeller Sculpture Garden.

The American Folk Art Museum's glimmering new facade

American Folk Art Museum

American Folk Art Museum: Midtown

www.folkartmuseum.org

- 🅰 Map p. 103
- ✉ 45 W. 53rd St.
- ☎ 212/265-1040
- 🕐 Closed Mon.
- 💲 $$
- 🚇 Subway: E, V to 5th Ave./53rd St.

Upper West Side:

- ✉ 2 Lincoln Square & Columbus Circle, bet. 65th and 66th Sts.
- ☎ 212/595-9533
- 🕐 Closed Mon.
- 🚇 Subway: 1 to 66th St.—Columbus Circle

SELF-TAUGHT FOLK ARTISTS HAVE SPENT LIFETIMES building castles out of old bottles or creating remarkable paintings, sculptures, or other fine artworks. The American Folk Art Museum has amassed 4,500 of these objects in the past 45 years. In 2001 it moved to its new 22-million-dollar, eight-story building on West 53rd Street—its original home when the museum was founded in 1961. The intimate Upper West Side satellite, the Eva and Morris Feld Gallery, shows collection highlights, along with its key exhibit, the 9/11 Tribute Quilt.

Since the museum was chartered, there has been considerable discussion about what constitutes folk art. The museum takes a broad view, showcasing decorative pieces that serve a practical purpose—quilts, trade signs, gravestones, and the like; religious and patriotic items; and household objects, such as carved cookie boards or painted tin. It also includes work by individual artists, including Grandma Moses.

Clad in textured bronze alloy panels, the new modernist structure housing the museum's fascinating collection itself becomes a kind of magical entity, catching and reflecting sunlight. Inside, art is displayed throughout, in public areas, along the stairways, and in intimate niches. Wood floors add warmth to visitors

move between levels. Greeting visitors as they enter is "Girl in Red Dress with Cat and Dog" (1834–36), an icon of American folk art.

The tremendous variety of artworks on exhibit are arranged in provocative juxtapositions: a Freemason's Masonic Plaque alongside "Les Amis," a contemporary work using Masonic symbols by Haitian artist Seneque Obin. Two utilitarian works express differing creative sensibilities: a gorgeously embroidered early crewel bedcover (Anonymous), and a whimsical iron chair, "The Comfort of Moses and the Ten Commandments" (1988) by Richard Dial. A visit to the uptown satellite, where admission is free, offers equally fascinating exhibits and a good gift shop. ■

More Midtown sites

Among Midtown North's many museums, two corporate standouts are at 51st Street: the **UBS Art Gallery** (1285 6th Ave., tel 212/713-2885, closed Sat.–Sun.), which has changing exhibits, and the **AXA Gallery** (787 7th Ave., tel 212/554-4818, closed Sun.). See the murals in AXA's atrium, including Roy Lichtenstein's huge "Mural with Blue Brushstroke."

INTERNATIONAL CENTER OF PHOTOGRAPHY (ICP)

This unique institution is the largest photography museum-school in the world and the only museum in New York dedicated solely to photography. Formerly housed in a mansion on Fifth Avenue's Museum Mile, in 2001 it relocated to its present campus. Here changing exhibitions are installed, many drawn from the museum's 60,000 original prints spanning the history of photography. Across the street is the new state-of-the-art school facility.

The museum entry opens onto a large airy space. Here is the museum shop, filled with everything from hard-to-find books to Holga plastic cameras. Ahead the spacious gallery area begins, continuing downstairs. An elevator or a wide stairwell reaches the second floor, where there are more galleries plus a café. At least three shows are usually on display on the museum's two floors.

Recent concurrent exhibits included "Andre Kertesz," "Modernist Photography," and "El Salvador, Work of Thirty Photographers." Retrospectives have showcased artists such as Imogen Cunningham, Man Ray, Annie Leibowitz, David Hockney, and more.

Cornell Capa, the former *Life* magazine photographer who founded the ICP in 1974, did so to present and preserve all aspects of photography—from photojournalism to the avant garde, from master photographers to emerging talents. Education is vital to this mission. Toward this end, ICP also sponsors monthly lectures and symposia and more than 500 courses a year, taught by leading photographers.

✉ 1133 Ave. of the Americas (at 43rd St.) ☎ 212/857-0000 or 800/688-8171 (mail order) ⏱ Closed Mon. 💲 $$ 🚇 Subway: B, D, F to 42nd St.–5th Ave.

INTREPID SEA-AIR-SPACE MUSEUM

This unique museum is moored at a Hudson River dock on the west side of Manhattan. The *Intrepid* is a decommissioned aircraft carrier that fought in World War II and the Korean and Vietnam Wars. Saved from the scrap heap in 1978, it opened as a museum of naval aviation history in 1982.

✉ Pier 86, One Intrepid Sq., W. 46th St. and 12th Ave. 💲 $$$ ☎ 212/245-0072 🚇 Subway: A, C, E to 42nd St.

JAPAN SOCIETY GALLERY

In addition to its own small collection of 20th-century woodblock prints by Shiko Munamata, the gallery exhibits art from other institutions. Founded in 1907, the society opened the gallery here in 1971. Its small lobby garden, with a pool and bamboo trees, provides a peaceful retreat from the hustle and bustle of midtown Manhattan.

✉ 333 E. 47th St. ☎ 212/832-1155 ⏱ Closed Mon. 💲 $$ 🚇 Subway: E, V to Lexington Ave.; B, 6 to 51st St.

MUSEUM OF ARTS & DESIGN

This appealing museum features works that blur the line between craft and art—from decorative arts to traditional crafts such as quilts to cutting-edge conceptual constructs. Expect the unusual in interdisciplinary pieces that blend performance and technology, or sculpture and graphic arts. In 2007 the museum moves to its new ten-story home at 2 Columbus Circle. Designed by Edward Durell Stone and opened in 1964, the rectangular concave structure was built as an art museum: double rows of round holes at its edges let in diffused natural light, for viewing the art inside. This landmark sat abandoned since 1998; the museum's occupancy restores it to its original purpose, with interior renovation replacing misuse and neglect.

✉ 40 W. 53rd St. ☎ 212/956-3535 💲 $$ 🚇 Subway: E, V to 5th Ave./53rd St.; B, D, F to 47th/50th Sts.–Rockefeller Center

MUSEUM OF TELEVISION & RADIO

Along with exhibits, vintage props, screening rooms, and memorabilia, this venue provides listening stations, computers for accessing your favorite television or radio episode, and workshops for both children and adults. Worth watching for are the excellent programs year-round in the onsite theaters, many with celebrity guests. Recent hits were "Cassavetes," a three-month festival of the famed actor/director's television career; and a visit with the cast of the long-running hit series *Law and Order*.

✉ 25 W. 52nd St. ☎ 212/621-6600
🕐 Closed Mon. 💲 \$\$ 🚇 Subway: E, V to 5th Ave./53rd St.; B, D, F, V to 47th/50th Sts.–Rockefeller Center

PLAZA HOTEL

Gracing Grand Army Plaza near Fifth Avenue is the revered Plaza Hotel, a French château of immense proportions, designed in 1907 by Henry Hardenbergh. The Plaza has long been a celebrity magnet—F. Scott Fitzgerald lived here, Marilyn Monroe visited in her New York years, and *North by Northwest, Breakfast at Tiffany's*, and other screen classics filmed onsite. Drinks in the Palm Court or dinner in the Oak Room offer the ambience of old New York (see page 246). To the north stands Augustus Saint-Gaudens's last major work (built 1892–1902): a gilded monument to Civil War general William Tecumseh Sherman.

✉ 768 Fifth Ave. (at Central Park South)
🚇 Subway: R, N, W to 5th Ave.; F to 57th St.; 4, 5, 6 to 57th Sts.

ROSE MUSEUM AT CARNEGIE HALL

Even if you cannot take in a concert, stopping in at this admission-free museum on the second floor places you inside Andrew Carnegie's famed concert hall, opened in 1891. Tchaikovsky was among the first to conduct here; since then, every major figure in classical music as well as the celebrated in jazz, pop, and rock have performed. The museum holds fascinating material, music, and even instruments, such as Benny Goodman's clarinet and Toscanini's baton. Unimaginable as it may seem now, when Lincoln Center opened in 1962, Carnegie Hall was scheduled for demolition. It was saved by the efforts of violinist Isaac Stern.

✉ 154 W. 57th St., at 7th Ave. ☎ 212/903-9629 🚇 Subway: N, R to 57th St.

TURTLE BAY HISTORIC DISTRICT

This delightful enclave of brownstones near the UN has been home to literati and luminaries, from Max Perkins and E. B.White to Katherine Hepburn and Stephen Sondheim. White's *The Second Tree from the Corner* immortalizes a tree in Turtle Bay Gardens, a large communal garden in the Italianate style, built in the 1920s. Visitors strolling are welcome.

✉ 224 E. 47th St. bet. 2nd & 3rd Aves.
☎ Turtle Bay Association, 212/751-5465, www.turtlebay-nyc.org ■

Beyond a carpet of tulips stands the grande dame of New York hotels, the Plaza.

The Upper East Side is the most exclusive part of town, bar none. The elegant avenues and tranquil side streets are the haunts of the very rich. On Fifth Avenue, great fortunes, great architecture, and great art find one another.

Upper East Side

Introduction & map 132–133
Frick Collection 134–135
Metropolitan Museum of Art 136–147
The Guggenheim 148–150
National Academy of Design 151
Cooper-Hewitt National Design Museum 152–153
Jewish Museum 154–155
Museum of the City of New York 156–157
Neue Galerie New York 158
El Museo del Barrio 159
More stops along Upper Fifth Avenue 160
In & around the Upper East Side 161
Whitney Museum of American Art 164–165
More places to visit 166
Hotels & restaurants 251–253

The interior dome of the Guggenheim Museum

Upper East Side

THE THREE MAGIC WORDS, "UPPER EAST SIDE," CONJURE UP AN IMAGE OF wealth and upper-class privilege that accurately reflects part but not all, of this large section of Manhattan between Central Park and the East River. Certainly only the wealthy can afford to live on Fifth or Park Avenues. These magnificent thoroughfares are noted for such rarified sights as uniformed doormen hailing cabs for apartment house residents, exquisitely dressed matrons walking exquisitely groomed dogs, and small children and their nannies on outings to Central Park. Such sights alone are enough to make a visit to the Upper East Side worthwhile.

Once there, you can savor life as the upper crust lives it. A visit to the Metropolitan Museum of Art, for example, can be enhanced by taking tea at Fifth Avenue's Stanhope Hotel—or on Madison Avenue, at the Carlyle or the Westbury Hotel. Many of Fifth Avenue's museums are housed in millionaires' mansions; inside you can absorb the ambience of wealth as well as the art treasures on view. Or go to the galleries, most on or near Madison Avenue, where the rich indulge their mostly conservative tastes. Two of the most prestigious, the Hirschl & Adler Galleries and the Knoedler Gallery, established in 1836, are housed in landmark residences on East 70th Street that were built for wealthy New Yorkers early in the 20th century.

But the Upper East Side is not all upper-class extravagance and ostentation. The avenues farther east—Lexington, Third, Second, and beyond—are today home to the middle class as well as the young and upwardly mobile, people to whom the term "yuppie" was first applied. Here the restaurants and bars are lively and trendy; even the literati enjoy mingling and being seen at Elaine's restaurant (1703 2nd Ave., between 88th and 89th Sts., tel 212/534-8103).

In an earlier incarnation, this part of the Upper East Side was the teeming home to immigrants. In 1878–79, elevated train lines (Els) were built along Second and Third Avenues, blocking out sunlight and bombarding the nearby tenements with noise. The first immigrants came from Germany, Ireland, and Bohemia. German Yorkville, its heart at 86th Street between Lexington and Second Avenues, was a thriving center of German culture that dwindled away after the tracks of the Third Avenue El were torn down in 1956. Today the Heidelberg (1648 2nd Ave. between 85th and 86th Sts., tel 212/628-2332) is one of the few German restaurants surviving in an area where German cuisine was once commonplace.

SPANISH HARLEM

The Upper East Side, at least from 96th Street north, is also a center of Latin American culture. These lively, overcrowded, and impoverished streets have almost nothing in common with the elegant avenues and side streets farther south. Called El Barrio or Spanish Harlem, the neighborhood was largely Italian until Puerto Ricans and other Latin Americans began settling there in great numbers after World War II. Museum Row's northernmost museum, El Museo del Barrio (see p. 159) embodies the culture of teeming Spanish Harlem. Its dynamic collection proves that there is more to the Upper East Side than wealth and its abundant trappings.

HISTORIC DISTRICTS

The historic buildings of the Upper East Side—mostly residences of one sort or another—are preserved in several historic districts. Among the hundreds of important buildings are early apartment houses, such as 998 Fifth Avenue (1912), which became, in form and function, the ideal to which other apartment houses aspired. On a much smaller scale is the Henderson Place Historic District, on a cul-de-sac off 86th Street, between East End and York Avenues, consisting of 24 relatively modest Queen Anne row houses built in 1881. ■

EAST DRIVE

GRAND ARMY PLAZA

Manhattan

Area of map detail

0   600 yards
0   600 meters

El Museo del Barrio

Museum of the City of New York

103rd Street

Jewish Museum

Cooper-Hewitt National Design Museum

96th Street

National Academy of Design and School of Fine Arts

CARNEGIE HILL

The Guggenheim

Metropolitan Museum of Art

86th Street

⑤

④

YORKVILLE

⑦

⑧

CARL SCHURZ PARK

79th Street

Museum ...ican Art

77th Street

UPPER EAST SIDE

The Frick Collection

JOHN JAY PARK

68th Street-Hunter College

③

LENOX HILL

63RD STREET

②

⑥

QUEENSBORO BRIDGE

East River

FRANKLIN D. ROOSEVELT DRIVE

CENTRAL PARK

EAST DRIVE

FIFTH AVENUE

MADISON AVENUE

PARK AVENUE

LEXINGTON AVENUE

THIRD AVENUE

SECOND AVENUE

FIRST AVENUE

YORK AVENUE

UPPER EAST SIDE

① New York Academy of Sciences
② Bloomingdale's ③ Seventh
Regiment Armory ④ New York
Society Library ⑤ Neue Galerie
New York ⑥ Mount Vernon Hotel
Museum ⑦ Church of the Holy
Trinity ⑧ Gracie Mansion

Frick Collection

Frick Collection

www.frick.org

🅰 Map p. 133

✉ 1 E. 70th St.

☎ 212/288-0700

🕐 Closed Mon. &
a.m. Sun.

💲 $$$

🚇 Subway: 6 to
68th St.

Note: Children under ten
are not admitted,
and those under
16 must be
accompanied by
an adult.

**The Frick's
largest room,
the skylit West
Gallery, combines
old masters and
the ambience of
a classic New
York mansion.**

A VISIT TO THE FRICK COLLECTION IS A TRIP BACK TO THE Gilded Age, when millionaires competed to build mansions along elegant Fifth Avenue and fill them with art treasures. Housed in the former residence of industrialist Henry Clay Frick (1849–1919), the collection has welcomed visitors from around the world since its celebrated opening as a museum and library in 1935.

In contrast to the monumental character of some of the city's museums, the Frick is just the right size for a serene immersion in the arts in a refined setting. Furnishings and artworks are arranged as though the Fricks were still in residence, without regard to chronology or period. A free acoustical guide (in six languages) and a brochure with a floor plan guide you through the collection's 19 rooms. A small shop is outside the Reception Hall, and across from it is the entrance to a downstairs gallery for changing exhibits.

The main collection is on the first floor. The **Boucher Room** just off the East Vestibule is unforgettable—cloying to some—

adorned with a series of decorative panels entitled "The Arts and Sciences," depicting cherublike children engaged in various adult activities. Created by François Boucher (1750–52) for Madame de Pompadour, the artworks once graced **Mrs. Frick's bedroom** upstairs, reached by the grand staircase off the vestibule. Portraiture by Hogarth and Reynolds and others line the walls of the **Dining Room**, which also holds the fine "Mall in St James Park" (1783) social landscape by Thomas Gainsborough.

The highlight of the **Fragonard Room** is the light-hearted 18th-century series of paintings, "The Progress of Love," by Jean-Honoré Fragonard. The austere **Living Hall** is dominated by masterworks including "Portrait of a Man in a Red Cap" by Titian (circa 1488–1576), "St. Jerome" by El Greco (1541–1614), and "Portrait of Sir Thomas More" (1527) by Hans Holbein the Younger. The Living Hall's furniture is by French cabinetmaker André-Charles Boulle. Beyond is the wood-paneled **Library,** where one of Gilbert Stuart's many portraits of George Washington is a lone American classic amid European masterpieces.

Be sure not to miss the offerings in the halls. A portrait by Ingres, "Comtesse d'Haussonville" (1845) in the **North Hall** is among the most popular works in the collection. Dutch artist Johannes Vermeer's "Officer and Laughing Girl" (circa 1655–1660) hangs in the **South Hall.** Adjacent to the halls is the Garden Court; save this for last.

Visitors take a breath as they enter the **West Gallery;** it is long, high, and skylit, very unlike what has preceded. A gallery of this sort characterized 19th-century upper-class homes. Here is a formidable grouping not to be missed: Rembrandt's portrait of himself as an older gentleman (1658) plus important works by Vermeer, Van Dyck, Hals, Velázquez, and more.

The **Enamel Room** at one end is intimate, replete with French Limoges enamels, including the exquisite "Seven Sorrows of the Virgin" (1500–1550). Frick acquired most of these from the estate of J. P. Morgan. The **Oval Room,** formerly Frick's office, has large portraits by Van Dyck and Gainsborough and a life-size Houdon sculpture of Diana. In the **East Gallery,** a pair of Whistlers handsomely frame the doorway, and Claude Lorrin's "Sermon on the Mount" (1656) is on the far wall.

Johannes Vermeer's "Officer and Laughing Girl" (circa 1655–1660)

Proceed to the enclosed **Garden Court,** with a pool, greenery, benches, portrait busts, and a charming bronze angel by Jean Barbet, with the year 1475 engraved on its left wing. In this soothing place you may reflect upon all you have seen and decide what to revisit.

FRICK FAMILY LEGACY

Frick, a self-made man, was criticized at an early age as being "a little too enthusiastic about pictures." Starting in coal mines, he was a millionaire by age 30. By 40 he was president of Carnegie Steel. He moved to New York in 1900, partly to protect his collection from the polluted Pittsburgh air. Philanthropically inclined, he built his mansion with the idea of eventually turning it into a museum open to the public. In 1920, Frick's daughter opened the **Frick Art Reference Library** *(10 E. 71st St.),* with 750,000 photographs and 174,000 books and catalogs. Today the library is a research center and a photoarchive. ∎

Metropolitan Museum of Art

THE METROPOLITAN MUSEUM OF ART IS THE LARGEST museum in the Western Hemisphere. Its collection, some two million items, is not only broad—the entire world, from antiquity to the present—but deep with holdings so large in a number of areas that some collections might be considered museums unto themselves. The best way to approach this vast repository is to understand the museum's arrangement and select a limited number of areas to see during your visit. Those who do not, usually come away feeling overwhelmed.

The museum itself is a very large structure. Study it from the Fifth Avenue side before you go in. Large hanging banners announce important temporary exhibits. You might decide to choose one of these, but if you plan to stay longer, orient yourself to the building and identify basic locations for some of the most popular collections. Think of the museum as a rectangle with a central stairway in the middle that divides right and left. Then divide each side into front and back. Look at the twin columns flanking the entrance. On the front right side of those columns is the Egyptian Collection (and the Temple of Dendur), and on the back side, the American Wing (which continues in the same position onto the second floor). To the front left side of the columns you will find Greek and Roman art and then a self-service cafeteria and restaurant. On the back left side is the Lila Atcheson Wallace Wing with 20th-century art. In between are the arts of Africa, Oceania, and the Americas.

Once you enter and pay your admission, if you walk up the grand staircase immediately in front of you, you will be on the second floor in what many consider to be the heart of this museum, its superior collection of European painting, sculpture, and decorative arts.

There you will find masterpieces by Botticelli, Brueghel, Rembrandt, Vermeer, Degas, and Rodin, plus the Petrie Sculpture Court, a delightful and contemplative place to relax. Although things will feel more complicated once you enter the museum, if you can keep in mind the rough locations of these six areas (Egyptian; American; Greek and Roman; eating; Africa, Oceania, and the Americas; and modern art) on the first floor, and, at the top of the stairs on the second floor, European paintings, you can be assured of finding them, and once you are in them, finding your way back out. As you walk up the exterior steps, notice how they level off repeatedly, allowing one to pause. So, too, it is best to take periodic breaks when sampling the collections. If you keep track of where you are, you will avoid the anxiety of getting lost.

PLANNING WHAT TO SEE

When you enter, pick up a floor plan and take time to look it over and write your choices on it and then plan where to start. If you do not want to go on your own, there are guides and recorded tours to take you through almost every part of the museum. A relaxing way to enjoy the ambience, architecture, and sheer beauty of the interior is to visit after 5 p.m. on Friday and

Metropolitan Museum of Art

www.metmuseum.org

- Map p. 133
- 1000 5th Ave. at E. 82nd St.
- 212/535-7710
- Closed Mon.
- Donation ($$$) includes admission to the Cloisters (see pp. 196–97)
- Subway: 4, 5, 6 to 86th St.

Note: Some wings are closed certain days due to funding problems. Visitors should call ahead if they are interested in a particular wing.

Opposite: The Great Hall of the Met, where visitors can orient themselves before plunging into the seemingly endless collections

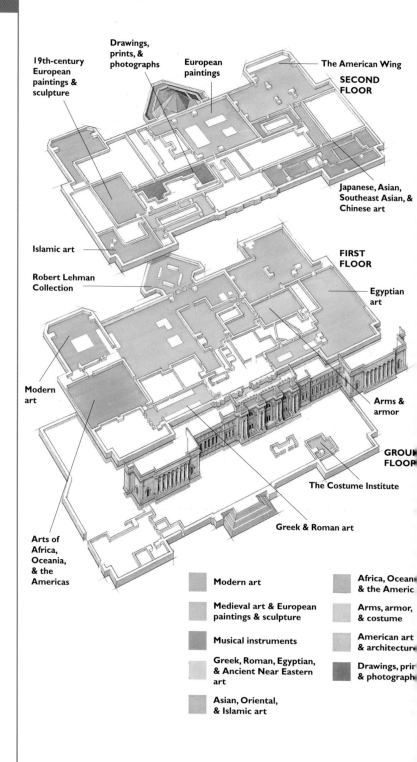

Drawings,
prints, &
photographs

European
paintings

19th-century
European
paintings &
sculpture

The American Wing

SECOND
FLOOR

Japanese, Asian,
Southeast Asian, &
Chinese art

Islamic art

FIRST
FLOOR

Robert Lehman
Collection

Egyptian
art

Modern
art

Arms &
armor

GROUND
FLOOR

The Costume Institute

Greek & Roman art

Arts of
Africa,
Oceania,
& the
Americas

Modern art

Medieval art & European
paintings & sculpture

Musical instruments

Greek, Roman, Egyptian,
& Ancient Near Eastern
art

Asian, Oriental,
& Islamic art

Africa, Oceania
& the Americas

Arms, armor,
& costume

American art
& architecture

Drawings, prints
& photographs

Saturday. Then you can take tea or have drinks on the balcony, while in the Great Hall a string quartet performs classical music, often playing on ancient instruments from the Metropolitan's own collections. Many people are drawn by blockbuster shows. Some of these—the 1978 "Treasures of Tutankhamun," for example, or the Mona Lisa's frantic visit to the Metropolitan in 1963—are major events in the cultural life of the city. But just as important to the world of art are works unveiled for the first time, such as those in the 2005 "Master Photographs from the Gilman Collection: A Landmark Acquisition."

Some visitors return again and again to the same galleries. Certain adults are drawn back to the galleries they knew as children, particularly the Egyptian tombs and medieval arms and armor. There is, in fact, something here for everybody.

There are even reasons other than art to visit the Met. In addition to lectures, concerts, and films, there is a reference facility and print study rooms. The **Uris Center** on the ground floor has its own library and classrooms and publishes educational books and films. The museum also offers an array of shopping options. The first-floor museum store is stocked to overflowing with separate boutique shops and features not just books and reproductions covering the whole history of world art, but fine jewelry, scarves, children's toys and games, recordings, three-dimensional reproductions, and more. It is a unique source of gifts for all occasions, with a mail-order catalog as well (plus ancillary city shops, including one across from the main branch of the Public Library on 42nd Street). Food options include the rooftop café

and the first-floor cafeteria and restaurant. But there is no truer New York pastime than buying food from a vendor outside and sitting on the steps, often never even venturing a foot inside.

Visitors stand back in a painting gallery.

HISTORY

In 1866 John Jay, a diplomat, lawyer, and grandson of America's first chief justice, told a group of American businessmen visiting Paris that the time had come "for the American people to lay the foundation for a national institution and gallery of art." His words so stirred them that, on their return, they put poet and newspaper editor William Cullen Bryant at the head of a committee charged with founding the Metropolitan Museum of Art. Bryant enlisted the help of other leading New Yorkers, mostly members of the Union League Club; but it was Bryant himself, wrote critic Russell Lynes, "more than any other New Yorker who nursed the concept of a museum of art from a hope into a solid stone-and-mortar reality."

In 1870 the museum opened in temporary quarters. The next year it acquired a collection of 174 European paintings and hired

Calvert Vaux and Jacob Wrey Mould to design its first building. This small, redbrick high Gothic building had a steel-and-glass roof and was situated at the edge of Central Park at 82nd Street and Fifth Avenue, the very spot that Vaux and his partner Frederick Law Olmsted, in their "Greensward plan" for Central Park, had set aside for a museum. The front entrance of the museum originally faced Central Park.

As the Metropolitan grew, the Vaux-Mould building was literally swallowed up by new wings and additions. Portions of the original building are now visible from the Lehman Wing and the European Sculpture Court. The signature Fifth Avenue facade, with its neo-classic features, and Great Hall were added in 1902, designed by Richard Morris Hunt and executed by his son. McKim, Mead & White added the north and south wings in 1911 and 1913. Roche, Dinkeloo & Associates have been in charge of recent additions, among them the Lehman Wing in 1975, the Skaler Wing added in 1979 for the Far East collection, and the Rockefeller Wing added in 1982 to house the arts of Africa, Oceania, and the Americas. The museum's new American Wing (1980) was built around the old and provides generous new space for the Americana collection, by then the largest in the country. The Lila Atcheson Wallace Wing housing modern art was added in 1987. Renovations and changes are constantly under way.

BUILDING THE COLLECTION

In 1883 the museum purchased a large collection of architectural casts. At the time, the museum assumed, wrongly, that important European masterpieces would never become available for purchase, so "casts and reproductions" were considered important parts of the collection. For years, according to a 1917 guide, "models, on a scale of one-twentieth of the original, of the Parthenon, the Pantheon, Notre-Dame, and the Hypostyle Hall of Karnac" greeted visitors in the Great Hall.

In 1887 an extraordinary loan of 37 European paintings from railroad financier Henry Gurdon Marquand instantly made the museum one of the best in the country. The works included Vermeer's "Young Woman with a Water Jug," still considered one of the finest works in the collection, as well as paintings by Van Dyck, Rembrandt, Franz Hals, Petrus Christus, Turner, and Gainsborough. In 1913 a bequest from Benjamin Altman, the department store owner, which included almost 500 Chinese porcelains and a number of Rembrandts, came with several strings attached, one being that the paintings hang "in a single line, not one above the other," as was then the custom in art museums.

After financier J. P. Morgan died in 1913, his son gave about 40 percent of his huge collection to the museum. Other important acquisitions included, in 1929, the collection of French Impressionists assembled by Louisine Havemeyer. It took the museum decades to develop an interest in American art.

In 1930 it rejected Gertrude Vanderbilt Whitney's offer of 500 modern American paintings so quickly that her representative did not have a chance to add that the offer included a new wing to house them. Since that time, the museum has welcomed many important donations and gifts.

OVERVIEW, GROUND FLOOR

Many might overlook the **Costume Institute** because of its location, but if your interest is fashion, this is an essential area to visit. Noted for its imaginative exhibits, the institute began independently in 1937 as the Museum of Costume Art and became part of the Metropolitan in 1946. The 75,000 items (dating from the 15th century to the present) include high fashion and native garb from every corner of the world. Recent shows include "Coco," about the revered Coco Chanel, and "Rara Avis: Selections from the Iris Barrel Apfel Collection," featuring fully accessorized vintage ensembles.

The popular Charles Engelhard Court of the American Wing offers views of American art and of Central Park beyond.

In the museum's unrivaled collection of paintings, George Washington by Gilbert Stuart (1755–1828)

OVERVIEW, FIRST FLOOR

The founders of the Metropolitan believed that American painting, decorative arts, and furniture had no place in a serious museum. The attitude began to change after the museum's first exhibit of American furniture and silver in 1909 proved immensely popular. American arts and crafts became a separate department in 1922 and the **American Wing** opened in 1924. In 1980, it was renovated and expanded: It now occupies galleries on three floors and is a world unto itself where one can easily spend an entire day. The collection here is indeed varied with everything from an unsurpassed assemblage of American paintings to a rare Honus Wagner baseball card to a room from the Frank Lloyd Wright Prairie House in Minnesota. Period rooms are organized chronologically, beginning with the earliest colonial ones on the third floor.

Highlights include the wing's focal point, the glass-covered **Charles Engelhard Court** on the first floor, which features fountains, Central Park views, an 1824 bank facade from Wall Street, and stained glass by Louis Comfort Tiffany. In the courtyard, flooded with natural light, the work of well-known sculptors, including Gutzon Borgum (of Mount Rushmore fame), is displayed on a rotating basis. There are many significant American paintings, including those of the Hudson River school, Winslow Homer, Childe Hassam, and Mary Cassatt. Try to see the largest painting in the Metropolitan,

"The Harvesters" (1565), an oil on wood by Pieter Bruegel the Elder, is one of a series representing the seasons.

John Vanderlyn's "Panorama of the Palace and Gardens of Versailles" (1818–19), displayed in its own oval gallery. On the second floor in the new wing there are portraits of George Washington by Charles Willson Peale and Gilbert Stuart. Emanuel Leutze's popular "Washington Crossing the Delaware" (1851) is also here.

Located on the first floor to the right of the staircase and past European and Decorative Arts, the **Arms and Armor** collection is one of the first sought out by all enamored of Camelot. Especially popular here is the Equestrian Court, whose armored knights on horseback evoke the world of King Arthur and the Knights of the Round Table. The Japanese armor is highlighted by fierce face masks worn in battle. American arms include a Kentucky rifle and a Colt revolver.

Located on a first-floor wing donated by Nelson Rockefeller, in memory of his son, Michael, who died on an expedition in New Guinea, is the **Arts of Africa, Oceania, and the Americas.** The collection incorporates Rockefeller's former Museum of Primitive Art that used to be in midtown Manhattan. Don't miss the sculptures of the Buli Master, one of the first African artists recognized as an individual.

Any tour of the museum would devote considerable attention to the extensive Egyptian Collection, even if it did not have its counterpart next door: the exquisite three-room **Temple of Dendur** (circa 23–10 B.C.). Since 1978, the temple has rested in isolated splendor in its own high-ceilinged gallery in the **Sackler Wing.** Originally the Roman emperor Augustus had the temple built as a tribute to the Nile god, Osiris. The Gateway leading to the temple is adorned with reliefs showing Augustus honoring local gods. What is most fascinating is how the temple came to rest in New York City. When it was threatened with destruction because of the Aswan High Dam, it was given to the United States, transported block by block, and then reassembled.

The **Egyptian Collection,** located in adjacent galleries, features objects and artifacts spanning more than three and a half millennia, from circa 3000 B.C. to A.D. 641. The collection is organized chronologically. The tomb of Perneb (circa 2440 B.C.), a reconstruction of the *mastaba,* or tomb, in which an official of the Old Kingdom was buried, is very impressive, with vivid reliefs of servants preparing and carrying food. Also of note are the statues from the funerary temple of Queen Hatshepsut (circa 1502–1482 B.C.), including one in which she wears masculine garb. Finally, see the remarkably detailed models of daily life in the 11th Dynasty (circa 2009–1998 B.C.).

Above: The Arms and Armor collection has been a favorite ever since the museum acquired its first pieces in the early 20th century.

Pierre-Auguste Renoir painted "The Daughters of Catulle Mendès" in oil on canvas in 1888. Mendès was a well-known writer and publisher and a friend of the artist.

Near the stairs you will find the department of **European Sculpture and Decorative arts,** which surrounds the department of medieval art. Its galleries include works from the Renaissance to the early 20th century. Be sure to visit the **European Sculpture Court.** Noteworthy is Auguste Rodin's "The Burghers of Calais" (1885–1895), depicting citizens who saved Calais from English reprisals. The **Jack and Belle Linsky Galleries,** a collection of furniture, bronzes, exquisitely detailed objects, and paintings includes Fra Bartolomeo's "Portrait of a Man" (after 1497).

This department also encompasses the **Robert Lehman Collection,** which came to the museum with the stipulation that the art be displayed in rooms re-created from the donor's home. Thus it is that one of the country's most outstanding private art collections came to reside in a modern glass pyramid-shaped pavilion,

the **Robert Lehman Wing,** in the back corner of the first floor of the museum. Among the seven re-created rooms, the **Grand Gallery** includes works by Corot, Monet, and van Gogh, but the collection covers old masters to the 20th century. Among the highlights are Gauguin's "Tahitian Woman Bathing" (1891) and El Greco's "St. Jerome as a Cardinal" (circa 1600–1610). The 15th-century Italian masterpieces in the exquisite Red Velvet Room include Giovanni de Paolo's "Expulsion from Paradise" (circa 1445), and Botticelli's "Annunciation" (circa 1490).

By the turn of the 20th century, the Metropolitan had acquired considerable **Greek and Roman art,** including Cypriot statues and artifacts donated by Louis Palma di Cesnola, director of the museum from 1879 to 1904, and the Roman and Etruscan glass from Henry Gurdon Marquand. Don't miss the Boscoreale frescoes, from a villa buried under volcanic ash by the eruption of Vesuvius in A.D. 79; the Kouros (700 B.C.), the earliest Greek marble statue in the museum; and the Euphronios vase (circa 515 B.C.), depicting detailed scenes from the Trojan War.

Originally based on the collection made by J. P. Morgan, the **Medieval art** galleries, on the first floor behind the staircase, span 12 centuries, from 300 to 1500. Included are early Christian art, the Romanesque Chapel, medieval tapestries, paintings, and sculpture, plus the **Medieval Treasury,** containing items of gold and other precious metals. Of particular importance are the Antioch Chalice, a sixth-century liturgical cup; the 15th-century "Annunciation" tapestry from Arras, France; and the glazed terra-cotta altarpiece by Andrea Della Robbia depicting the Assumption. Those interested n this period will also want to visit he Metropolitan's museum devoted o medieval art in a medieval set-ing, the Cloisters (see pp. 196–97).

Housed in the first-floor **Lila Acheson Wallace Wing** 1987), named for a founder of the *Reader's Digest* magazine, the **modern art** department is strong n an area the museum once purned—modern American paint-ngs. The wing housing it is worth a visit for its own sake: There are glass curtain walls and an attractive oof garden. This department began with Alfred Stieglitz's collec-ion of modern painting, sculpture, and drawings that his widow, Georgia O'Keeffe, gave to the museum in 1949. Important to the development of art in New York is Nasturtiums" (1912), one of the first works by Henri Matisse to be shown in this country—it debuted at the famous 1913 Armory Show see pp. 82–83). Also be sure to see the work of the New York innova-ors known as the Eight and the abstract expressionists.

OVERVIEW, SECOND FLOOR

On this floor you'll find the remaining exhibits from the **American Wing.**

Spanning 6000 B.C. to the sev-nth century A.D., the **Ancient and Near Eastern art** galleries nclude Assyrian art, Mesopot-mian art, pre-Islamic antiquities rom Iran, and Achaemenid, Parthian, and Sasanian art. Be sure o see the gypsum statue of a beard-d Sumerian worshiper (circa 2750–2600 B.C.) or, if in residence, he statue of Ur-Ningirse, whose body belongs to the Louvre, but he head to the Metropolitan; the ntire statue alternates between Paris and New York.

A highlight of the newly reno-ated **Chinese art** galleries at the top of the stairs is Dong Yuan's "The Riverbank," a monumental tenth-century hanging scroll land-scape. Also, visit the **Astor Court Garden** on the third floor, a 16th-century-style garden for medita-tion. It was constructed for the museum in 1979 by Chinese crafts-people using ancient techniques and tools.

The **drawing, painting, and photograph** collections hold some extraordinary works, includ-ing drawings by Michelangelo and Matisse, prints by Rembrandt, and photographs collected by Alfred Stieglitz. Visit the **Howard Gilman Gallery,** inaugurated in 1997. Three changing exhibits year-ly display photographs from the private 5,000-piece collection of the late Howard Gilman.

The 30 galleries devoted to **European paintings** form an especially rich part of the museum, spanning five centuries. Two of the

galleries are devoted to Italian Renaissance painting (Mantegna, Botticelli, Della Robbia) and Dutch painting (Rembrandt, Hals, Vermeer, Ruisdael). These works came from the Benjamin Altman Collection, bequeathed to the museum in 1913 by the department

Seated on the hard marble floor, a student sketches a statue by the 17th-century Italian Gianlorenzo Bernini.

store millionaire. The masterpieces in this gift made the Metropolitan one of the world's leading museums. The galleries are arranged by school: 18th-century Venetian painting (Tiepolo); 15th-century Italian painting (Filippo Lippi, Ghirlandaio, Signorelli, Perugino); 17th-century Dutch portraits (Rembrandt, Hals); English portraits (Reynolds, Gainsborough, Lawrence); and so forth. A highlight here is Rembrandt's "Aristotle with a Bust of Homer" (1653), purchased by the museum in 1961 for a record sum at the time of 2.3 million dollars.

Extensive **Far Eastern art** galleries wind through the second floor and encompass three major areas: Chinese art, Japanese art, and the art of South and Southeast Asia—the last areas comprising 18 galleries with works from India, Tibet, Nepal, Thailand, Indonesia, Cambodia, Myanmar, and Vietnam. See the collection of Chinese ceramics, which dates back to China's historical beginnings, the Shang dynasty (17th–11th centuries

B.C.); the collection of large Chinese Buddhist sculptures; a 5th-century Standing Buddha from northern India; and the **Khmer Courtyard,** featuring the Angkor period (9th–13th centuries) of Cambodia, Vietnam, and Thailand.

The **Greek and Roman art** galleries continue onto the second floor. They include a fine collection of Greek vases.

One of the jewels of the museum is the **Islamic art** collection. It starts with the reign of the four caliphs in A.D. 632, extends into the 19th century, and stretches geographically from Spain east to Southeast Asia. One gallery is devoted to the museum-sponsored excavations of Nishapur in Iran, once a great Islamic center, and a re-created early 18th-century reception room from a wealthy Ottoman home in Damascus. Highlights include art from the Mughal period in India (1526–1858)—carpets, miniature painting, jewelry, and jade carving.

The sweeping display of **Japanese art** in familiar settings

The Temple of Dendur, a gift from Egypt to the U.S., stands alone as it did on the Nile, in its own gallery.

s spread out over ten galleries. Chronological and thematic displays include some exquisitely detailed tapestries and ceremonial costumes and a re-creation of a *hoin,* or study.

If you have children, or if you ove music, turn right at the top of he stairs to the collection of rare nd fascinating **musical instru-ments.** Dating from prehistory to he present, the instruments are rom Europe, the Americas, Asia, nd Africa. Among the distin-uished objects here is the oldest urviving piano (1720) by artolomeo Cristofori, inventor of he instrument; Andres Segovia's uitars; and Native American ipes. Visitors can hear the sounds f instruments on audio. Mrs. lary Crosby Brown's donation, in 889, of 270 instruments from round the world is at the heart of e collection. Like many other onors, she continued to collect nd donate to the museum; by 906 there were 3,500 instruments.

The **19th-century Euro-ean painting and sculpture** collection is one of the greatest of its kind in the world and one of the museum's most popular. The collection is displayed in galleries that reflect the spirit of the period. Two galleries are named for the collection's great benefactors, Louisine and H. O. Havemeyer. Mrs. Havemayer's interest in European Impressionist and Postimpressionist paintings began with her friendship with the American painter Mary Cassatt. The museum's holdings include many works by such well-known artists as Courbet, Corot, Degas, Manet, Monet, Cézanne, Seurat, van Gogh, and Rodin. There are also areas devoted to Neoclassicism, Romanticism, the Barbizon school, French still lifes, pastels, and salon painting. The paintings are displayed in a loose chronological order, starting with neoclassicists David and Ingres and ending with such turn-of-the-20th-century work as Pissarro's "Garden of the Tuileries" (1899) and Rousseau's "The Repast of the Lion" (1907). ∎

The Guggenheim

WHEN YOU VISIT THE SOLOMON R. GUGGENHEIM Museum, keep in mind that it is the only building in New York by Frank Lloyd Wright, possibly America's greatest architect ever. T architects the museum is circular form in a rectilinear space. To th rest of us, it is a round building amid square ones. However you pu it, it is a presence; today, four decades after Frank Lloyd Wright concrete spiral opened on Fifth Avenue, it is impossible to visit, tall or think about the museum without considering the building. Befo the structure was renovated in the early 1990s, it was emptied of it paintings, but visitors came anyway—just to see Wright's building

**Solomon R.
Guggenheim
Museum**

www.guggenheim.org

🅰 Map p. 133

✉ 1071 5th Ave. at
E. 89th St.

☎ 212/423-3500

🕐 Closed Thurs.

💲 $$$

🚇 Subway: 4, 5, 6
to 86th St.

Note: Fri. 6–8 p.m. pay
what you wish.

The Guggenheim, as it is called, grew out of the private collection of the millionaire Solomon R. Guggenheim. He began collecting old masters but expanded into modern art under the influence of Hilla Rebay von Ehrenwiesen, a European artist and baroness, opening the Museum of Non-Objective Painting in 1939. In 1943 it was Rebay who selected and hired Wright as the architect for a new museum. In a letter that must have appealed to his considerable ego, she wrote: "I need a fighter, a lover of space, an originator, a tester and

a wise man.… I want a temple of spirit, a monument!" Nonobjective painting, as Rebay defined it, "represents no object or subject known to us on earth. It is simply a beautiful organization arranged in rhythmic order of colors and form to be enjoyed for beauty's sake."

Wright responded that he was "eager to build to objectify the non-objective point of view." That was 1943. Over the next 16 years Wright submitted six sets of plans and 749 drawings. Wright informe his clients that he was striving for "one extended expansive well-

proportioned floor space from bottom to top…gloriously lit from above." Guggenheim died in 1949 but left two million dollars to build the museum. In 1956 construction began. The museum opened to the public in October 1959. Wright had died six months before, on April 9.

TODAY'S COLLECTION

The present collection covers the history of modern art, including European art of the first half of the 20th century as well as late 19th-century and postwar European and American art. Ongoing curatorial efforts include recent acquisitions in film, photography, multimedia, and high-technology art. In the 1980s, the Guggenheim began its growth into a bicontinental entity. In addition to its Fifth Avenue site in New York, it now occupies locations in Venice, Berlin, and Bilbao. All of this expansion has made the Guggenheim an institution uniquely equipped to present the evolution of 20th-century art in the global arena.

THE ROTUNDA & THE RAMP

Immediately upon entering from Fifth Avenue you confront the daring design. To the left is the museum store and to the right, the admission desk, but ahead is the Great Rotunda, spiraling upward 92 feet to the domed skylight. The Rotunda at street level is often filled with an exhibit entitled "1900: Art at the Crossroads," featuring 250 works by more than 170 artists from 24 countries. In 1998 a cluster of gleaming machines greeted

Above and below: The Guggenheim's spiral ramp, reaching some 90 feet above the main floor, offers easy access to the collection.

visitors when "The Art of the Motorcycle" camped in the space.

You do not need to walk all the way to the top (the cantilevered ramp that circles the interior through five levels is a quarter of a mile long); instead, thankfully proceed to the elevators straight ahead.

A visitor ponders a minimalist painting at an exhibit of Russian avant-garde art.

Wright expected visitors to start at the top and work their way down. Though many find the experience unnerving, the 1992 renovation and addition of the ten-story **Gwathmey Siegel Tower** adjacent to the original building has provided the viewer relief during the descent. You may now leave the gradually pitched ramp at each level and walk into a gallery in the tower (where floors do not slope), and then return to the ramp. The alternation of sloping and level gallery experiences reduces the disconcerting effect of a single circular descent.

EXPLORING THE COLLECTION

Exhibits frequently change and not all of the permanent collection is on display at any given time. However, you can always find some examples of works by key artists. The museum's collection includes more than 200 works by Kandinsky. It also has

works by Brancusi, Calder, Delaunay, Klee, Miró, Nevelson, and Mondrian, naming but a few. Favorites include Chagall's "Paris Through the Window" (1913), Léger's "Great Parade" (1954), Modigliani's "Nude" (1917), and Picasso's "Woman Ironing" (1904).

The **Thannhauser tower galleries** (named for Justin K. Thannhauser, a dealer and collector who donated 75 Impressionist and Postimpressionist works) display both the permanent collection and contemporary changing exhibits. Levels 2, 5, and 7 contain larger works, while level 4 is low-ceilinged and holds drawings and smaller paintings, plus the **Robert Mapplethorpe Gallery** for photography. There are also four video viewing rooms and a fifth-floor sculpture terrace.

Ramp exhibits change frequently, often containing a blockbuster, such as the 2002 multimedia epic "Mathew Barney: The Cremaster Cycle," which went on tour. On ramp 3 are the **Guggenheim Family Galleries.** In 1963, Solomon's niece, Peggy Guggenheim, a gallery owner, collector, and, briefly, wife of Max Ernst, gave the museum works representing surrealism, cubism, and abstract expressionism.

Many of the special exhibits draw large crowds and often forge new artistic or curatorial ground. Jenny Holzer's "Untitled" (1989) from her "Truisms" series consisted of a strip of electronic display signboard mounted along the inside of the ramp. Messages such as "When Something Terrible Happens People Wake Up" appeared on the display, casting a neon glow over the spiral interior. Recent exhibits have featured Jeff Koons's large paintings of modern "food, fashion, and fun" and Rachel Whiteread's sculptures transformed from ordinary objects and architectural spaces. ■

National Academy of Design

LIKE THE FRICK, THIS MUSEUM GIVES THE VISITOR A TASTE of what it was like to be wealthy early in the 20th century. Since 1940 the academy has been housed in this beaux arts town house, built in 1914 for railroad heir Archer Huntington and donated by him to the academy in 1940. Archer's wife, Anna, was an academy member. So were Winslow Homer, Augustus Saint-Gaudens, and Frank Lloyd Wright. Recent members include painters Isabel Bishop, Jim Dine, Robert Rauschenberg, and Chuck Close; sculptor Louise Bourgeois; and architects I. M. Pei, Philip Johnson, and Maya Lin.

National Academy of Design and School of Fine Arts

www.nationalacademy.org

 Map p. 133

✉ 1083 5th Ave. between E. 89th & E. 90th Sts.

☎ 212/369-4880

🕐 Closed Mon.–Tues.

💲 $$

🚇 Subway: 4, 5, 6 to 86th St.

The statue of Diana in the National Academy of Design's entrance hall

The National Academy of Design was formed by Asher Durand, Samuel F. B. Morse, and others in 1825 in protest against the domination of the American Academy of Fine Arts by businessmen. With the purpose of increasing recognition of the role of art in America, the new organization helped to make New York the art capital of the nation and left a rich legacy of art treasures that continues to grow. Uniquely governed by member artists, its full name (National Academy of Design and School of Fine Arts) reflects the academy's scope and breadth—the institution encompasses a museum, school of fine arts, and honorary association of artists. Elected by their peers, members are established architects, painters, sculptors, and printmakers. All members are required to donate representative work.

The result is one of the country's largest public collections of 19th- and 20th-century American art. It comprises more than 5,000 works in almost every artistic style, and it is constantly enriched by member gifts. New acquisitions hang in the lobby, an intimate space with a gift shop where original works are for sale. Prominent in the entrance foyer is a bronze sculpture of Diana by Anna Hyatt Huntington.

Galleries on the second and fourth floors offer changing exhibits; the third floor is closed to the public. One popular show mounted from the permanent collection in 2002, for example, was "Transformations: American Paintings from Frederic E. Church to Wayne Thiebaud." For a look at the latest from the national art scene, time your visit to coincide with the month-long Annual Exhibition in late spring, held every year since 1826. ■

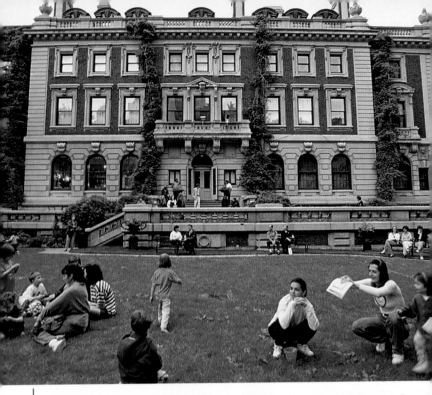

Cooper-Hewitt National Design Museum

Cooper-Hewitt National Design Museum, Smithsonian Institution

www.cooperhewitt.org

- 🅰 Map p. 133
- ✉ 2 E. 91st St.
- ☎ 212/849-8400
- 🕐 Closed Mon. & a.m. Sun.
- 💲 $$
- 🚇 Subway: 4, 5, 6 to 86th or 96th St.

Extensive grounds surround the mansion housing the Cooper-Hewitt.

THIS IS THE ONLY DESIGN MUSEUM IN THE UNITED STATES. Its fascinating collection of some quarter of a million objects from all over the world constitutes a history of design from the sixth century B.C. to the present. And a visit to its home, the former Andrew Carnegie mansion, provides a glimpse of history. It was built between 1899 and 1903 when only squatters lived in this section of Manhattan. Part of the appeal of the 64-room mansion today is its expansive garden and lawn, a reminder that there was much vacant land along Fifth Avenue when Carnegie built his house.

Founded in 1897 as the Cooper Union Museum for the Arts of Decoration, the Cooper-Hewitt has occupied its present quarters only since 1976. Though the museum was undertaken as a resource for decorators, architects, and other professionals, its appeal today is wide-ranging, and its eclectic collection remarkable. Thematic exhibits on urban architecture and graphic design change constantly, weaving material from the collection's four main areas: applied arts and industrial design; drawings and prints; textiles; and wall coverings. There is a small exhibition area on the ground floor and primary galleries on the street-level first floor and second floor. The library and archives on the third floor are open by appointment. An appointment is also needed to visit the Design Resource Center. This deluxe study facility opened in 1998 as part of a four-year, 20-million-dollar renovation.

The house itself is extraordinary, so plan to spend time looking at the interior as well as the collection. On entering the first-floor **Great Hall,** note the wood paneling throughout. Carnegie's use of Scottish oak reflects his love of his homeland. Always interested in new technology and design, Carnegie had his home equipped with the first domestic electric elevator and state-of-the-art air-conditioning and heating systems. On the west side of the hall is a gallery that was formerly his study. The low doorway is a clue to Carnegie's height, for he was only about five foot two.

Other first-floor rooms now identified only as galleries include the **Music Room,** with a bagpipe motif in the ceiling; the Garden Vestibule, with leaded Tiffany windows; the formal **Dining Room,** where guests included such luminaries of the day as Booker T. Washington, Mark Twain, and Marie Curie; and the **Breakfast Room,** overlooking the garden and leading to the skylit conservatory. A popular 1999 exhibit occupying the first floor was "The Architecture of Reassurance: Designing the Disney Theme Parks."

The museum is at its most enjoyable when it pays serious attention to everyday objects—buttons, watches, razors, wallpaper, cameras, computers—almost anything imaginable. One exhibit was devoted to the lowly doghouse—as rendered by leading architects—and another entirely devoted to kitchen utensils. "Design for Life," staged on the museum's centennial in 1997, illustrated the range of the collections. The 300 offerings included 1930s wallpaper, a 1936 cocktail shaker shaped like a penguin, a scale model of the Marmon 16—a sedan designed in 1930 to compete with the Cadillac—and a Tiffany goblet made for Andrew Carnegie in 1907.

INTERIOR DECORATION STARTED HERE

Sarah and Eleanor Hewitt, founders of the museum, were, like other wealthy young women of the time, well traveled. They were impressed by the Musée des Arts Decoratifs in Paris and the Victoria and Albert Museum in London and set out to emulate them in their museum in New York.

New York is the undisputed center of American interior design. It owes that status to the Hewitt sisters and others working to develop the field at the turn of the century. The Hewitts believed that by educating the wealthy and the decorators who worked for them, taste would filter down to the masses. Author Edith Wharton echoed the Hewitt philosophy in her influential *The Decoration of Houses:* "When the rich man demands good architecture his neighbors will get it too....Every carefully studied detail, exacted by those who can afford to indulge their taste, will in time find its way to the carpenter-built cottage" (1897).

In 1905, Elsie de Wolfe, the country's first professional interior decorator, began catering to the wealthy. That same year, Frank Alvah Parsons introduced interior decoration courses at his art school—today the Parsons School of Design. In 1913 Wanamaker's opened the first interior decorating department in a store. Three years later architect Augustus Sherrill Winton founded the New York School of Interior Decoration (today Design), now a thriving institution at 155 East 56th Street. By the 1970s, interior design was the preferred term. ■

Jewish Museum

HOUSED IN A FRENCH GOTHIC CHÂTEAU-STYLE MANSION, this esteemed institution is an important repository of Jewish culture and art. Through exhibits ranging from contemporary art to rare ethnographic material, and programs designed to engage all ages, Jews and non-Jews alike, it illuminates the remarkable scope and diversity of Jewish culture. The museum's collection holds some 28,000 items, from coins and medals to ceremonial objects, paintings, and archaeological treasures, capturing four thousand years of history.

Jewish Museum
www.thejewishmuseum.org
- Map p. 133
- 1109 5th Ave. at 92nd St.
- 212/423-3200
- Closed Sat.
- $$
- Subway: 4, 5, 6 to 86th or 96th St.

Right: A Czech Torah scroll Below: An 1803 Jewish Omer calendar from Italy depicts Samson destroying the Philistine temple.

The first and second floors of the museum are devoted to special temporary exhibits, which may be historical or contemporary in nature and which often attract very large crowds. Recent special exhibitions have included "Paris in New York: French Jewish Artists in Private Collections," featuring painters and sculptors who were influenced by key avant-garde figures such as Henri Matisse and Pablo Picasso.

First-time visitors will not want to miss the permanent exhibition "Culture and Continuity: The Jewish Journey," which begins on the fourth floor and continues throughout the third. Vibrantly installed in 17 galleries, highlights on the fourth floor are a re-creation of an ancient synagogue; a gallery devoted to the Sabbath with an audio installation; and a silver menorah collection.

On the third floor, among the more spectacular artifacts, are the 18th-century Bavarian ark and the Urbino Ark (circa 1500). On this floor, you can also view selected television and radio programs from the museum's archives or visit the delightful interactive **Children's Gallery.**

Founded in 1904, the Jewish Museum is operated by the Jewish Theological Seminary. For 40 years its collection was housed in the seminary's library. An important addition was the 1947 purchase of the **Benjamin and Rose Mintze Collection,** 500 items from Poland—kiddush cups, Torah crowns and mantles, and Hanukkah lamps. The museum opened at its present location in 1947. Originally designed by architect C. H. P. Gilbert, the mansion had been built in 1908 for Felix M. Warburg, a Polish-born banker, philanthropist, and leader of the Jewish-American community. ■

Left: A painting by Russian-born Max Weber (1881–1961)

Museum of the City of New York

Museum of the City of New York
www.mcny.org

△ Map p. 133

✉ 1220 5th Ave. at 103rd St.

☎ 212/534-1672

🕐 Closed Mon.

💲 $$

🚇 Subway: 6 to 103rd St.; 2, 3 to 110th St.

IN 1923 NEW YORK CITY DECIDED THAT, LIKE PARIS AND London and other great cities, it must have a museum to document its history. The result of this decision is the Museum of the City of New York (MCNY), a treasure-house of some 1.5 million objects from the city's storied past, from Dutch colonial times to the present. This is a place for many tastes and audiences, from those who simply want to sample the broad range of New York's history to those with a specialized interest, be it firefighting, toys, furniture, silver, theater, prints, or paintings.

This is a fascinating place where you can find such seemingly unrelated displays as the charred timbers from a 17th-century merchantman that burned off the coast of the island of Manhattan; furniture of New York cabinet-maker Duncan Phyfe; and Gypsy Rose Lee's "chaste G-string with her name embroidered in blue silk by her own hand." There is also an outstanding collection of Currier & Ives prints as well as a photo archive that includes the **Jacob Riis Collection.**

If you're lucky, perhaps you'll catch some of the museum's treasures not often displayed, including vintage Barbie dolls, a lock of George Washington's hair, and shoes belonging to Bill "Bojangles" Robinson. The museum continues to search for larger premises so that more of the large collection can be shown.

The museum left its original home in Gracie Mansion, today's Mayoral Mansion, and opened in its present neo-Georgian building in January 1932. Exhibits here spread out over five floors and change frequently. On the entry-level first floor are a gift shop and three galleries devoted to major changing exhibitions. Shows here attract large crowds. Recent ones have included "Glamour, New York Style"; "The Destruction of Lower Manhattan," Danny Lyon photographs; and "El Barrio," about East Harlem and Puerto Rican identity.

An elevator down to the ground floor brings you to the **Fire Gallery.** This unusual themed exhibition is filled with prints, paintings, artifacts, and other memorabilia related to fires, plus antique fire engines. One is the "Big Six," the 1851 fire engine belonging to the volunteer fire company that gave William Marcy "Boss" Tweed his start in city politics. A snarling tiger, the symbol of Tammany Hall, is painted on the front panel.

Also on the ground floor is the **City Partners Gallery,** where city-based organizations partner with MCNY to tell their stories. A recent exhibition was "The Mount Sinai Hospital, 1852–2002: Extraordinary People, Extraordinary Medicines."

UPPER FLOORS
On the second floor you may wish to see "Timescapes," a 25-minute multimedia experience tracing New York City's growth, narrated by Stanley Tucci. Also on this floor is an ongoing installation of cityscapes from the collection called "Painting the Town." Beyond are

the **Period Alcoves,** six rooms re-creating the unique interiors of New York houses from the late 17th to the early 20th centuries. The Flagler Drawing Room, from a 1906 Park Avenue home, was originally inspired by the Sala della Zodiaco in the Ducal Palace at Mantua, while an 18th-century colonial parlor has Chinese hand-painted wallpaper. At the other end of the hall, dioramas, artifacts, paintings, and models are devoted to New York's maritime history.

The third floor holds **New York Toy Stories,** always a popular exhibit. A highlight is its collection of dollhouses and doll furniture from 1769 to the present. Especially captivating is the dollhouse created by Carrie Stettheimer in the 1920s. Its interior includes an art gallery with miniatures of paintings by Marcel Duchamp and other artists of the first New York Avant Garde.

Exhibits here are filled with memorabilia, vintage materials, period costume, and photographs. Examples include "Richard Rodgers' Broadway" (2002) and the recent hit, "Broadway! A History of the American Theater." The fourth floor is closed to the public.

On the fifth floor visit the **Rockefeller Rooms,** an opulent 1880s master bedroom and dressing room from the West 54th Street home of John D. Rockefeller, Sr. With such details as woodwork with floral inlays, red damask chairs and chaises, and even a "Turkish corner" in the bedroom, the rooms are no more extravagant than you might expect in the private quarters of one of the city's most prominent and wealthy businessmen. ■

The sumptuous late 19th-century bedroom of John D. Rockefeller, Sr., has been reassembled in the Museum of the City of New York.

Neue Galerie New York

**Neue Galerie
New York**

www.neuegalerie.org

🅼 Map p. 133

✉ 1048 5th Ave.
(enter on 86th St.)

☎ 212/628-6200

🕐 Closed Tues.–Thurs.

💲 $$

🚇 Subway: 4, 5, 6
to 86th St.; B, C
to 86th St. at
Central Park West

Note: Children under
12 not admitted;
those 13–15 must
be accompanied
by an adult.

**The museum's
lovely Louis XIII-
style beaux arts
facade**

FOR A MUSEUM WITH A EUROPEAN FLAVOR, VISIT THIS newcomer to Fifth Avenue's Museum Mile. Housed in a splendid 1914 beaux arts limestone mansion once owned by a Vanderbilt, the Neue Galerie New York is devoted to early 20th-century German and Austrian art and design. Its works represent the pinnacle of the modernist German Expressionism and Bauhaus movements in Vienna and Berlin between 1900 and 1938, after which the Nazis banned experimental art.

The transformation of one of Fifth Avenue's most opulent landmark residences into a museum began with the dream of two collectors. Ronald Lauder, philanthropist and businessman son of cosmetics magnate Estée Lauder, and art dealer Serge Sabarsky envisioned a museum that would exhibit the best examples of the German and Austrian art they loved. Sabarsky purchased the building for the Neue Galerie in 1994. After Sabarsky's death in 1996, Lauder bought the building and made their dream a reality. Neue Galerie means "new gallery" in German and comes from the modernist wave of European galleries, especially Vienna's Neue Galerie, founded in 1923.

The collection is made up of more than 800 works from the Sabarsky Foundation, 500 from the Lauder family, and 100 purchased by the museum. Included are more than 100 paintings and graphic works by Gustav Klimt and Egon Schiele, the largest holding of works by these artists outside Vienna.

VISITING THE GALLERY

On the first floor are a bookstore, a design center selling many items exclusive to the museum, and the Viennese-style Café Sabarsky, with authentic Austrian meals and superb pastries and coffee. Expect a line, but it is well worth the wait.

On the second floor, you'll find galleries containing paintings and drawings from turn-of-the-20th-century Vienna. Signature works include Klimt's "Dancer" in oil (1916–18) and numerous Schiele self-portraits. Oskar Kokoschka, Max Beckmann, and Emil Nolde are also represented.

The third-floor galleries feature German movements and artists, from Vasily Kandinsky and Paul Klee to Laszlo Moholy-Nagy and Ludwig Mies van der Rohe.

Decorative arts from the Wiener Werkstätte and Bauhaus design movements, including sleek furniture, decorative jewelry, ceiling fixtures, and flatware, are also on display.

Lectures, music, films, and cabaret performances are offered; ask the museum for a schedule. ∎

El Museo del Barrio

EL MUSEO DEL BARRIO, AT THE NORTH END OF MUSEUM Row, is dedicated to the art and culture of Latin America, especially Puerto Rico, the homeland of so many residents of nearby East, or Spanish, Harlem. Del Barrio preserves and documents both traditional folk arts and the contemporary urban art of the barrio, the city's Spanish-speaking enclave.

El Museo del Barrio
www.elmuseo.org
Map p. 133
1230 5th Ave. at 104th St.
212/831-7272
Closed Mon.–Tues.
$
Subway: 6 to 103rd St.

The (S) Files/The Selected Files, a modern sculpture on display at the Museo del Barrio

Founded in 1969, the museum grew out of the turmoil of the 1960s, when local Puerto Rican artists began protesting their lack of representation in downtown museums. The permanent collection contains more than 8,000 objects from all over Latin America and the Caribbean: pre-Columbian ceramics and vessels from the Taino culture of Puerto Rico and the Dominican Republic; Mexican masks; santos, or carved saints; and paintings, sculptures, works on paper, and photographs by artists of Latin American descent.

The spacious white-walled museum occupies the ground floor in the Heckscher Building. This city-owned structure houses other organizations and a theater where del Barrio presents films and videos. After entering the building, turn left to access the museum through its gift shop. Works are exhibited in a number of spaces, beginning with the **Contemporanea Gallery** for recent works. An important aim of the gallery is to disseminate art of the barrio, and work by the artists of El Taller, an artist-run collective, may be seen here.

The **Borinquen Gallery** is named for the Taìno Indian word for Puerto Rico. It holds the highlight of the permanent collection of sculptural works, "Santos de Palo," an assemblage of 240 carved and painted saints. Made by artisans from Puerto Rico, Spain, Mexico, Guatemala, and the Philippines, usually for home devotions, most date from the 19th and early 20th centuries.

Major exhibitions are in the **East Gallery** and **Alegria Gallery.** Recent shows have included "Mexico: The Revolution and Beyond," photographs by Casasola from 1900–1940; "Rafael Tufino, Painter of the People"; and "Gods, Spirits, and Legends," 20th-century art from El Salvador. ■

More stops along Upper Fifth Avenue

AMERICAN IRISH HISTORICAL SOCIETY (AIHS)

Open to members and guests, this society sponsors concerts, readings, and lectures throughout the year, with such speakers as political leader Gerry Adams and poet Seamus Heaney. Its library is the most complete private collection of Irish and Irish-American history and literature in the U.S.

✉ 991 5th Ave. at E. 80th St. ☎ 212/228-2263 🚇 Subway: 4, 5, 6 to 86th St.

GOETHE INSTITUT–NEW YORK

Founded in 1957, Goethe Institut–New York (formerly Goethe House) is run by the Goethe Institut in Munich for the purpose of promoting German language study and cultural exchange. Located in a handsome 1907 beaux arts town house, the institute has a library/information service open to the public and sponsors frequent lectures and exhibits. A popular 2005 program featured Christo and Jeanne-Claude's Central Park installation, "The Gates."

✉ 1014 5th Ave., between 82nd and 83rd Sts. ☎ 212/439-8700 🕐 Closed Sun. 🚇 Subway: 4, 5, 6 to 86th St.

NEW YORK ACADEMY OF SCIENCES

Formed in 1817, the academy is housed in a Renaissance-style mansion (1920) built for William Ziegler, Jr., president of a baking powder company. The academy mounts shows on subjects combining art and science, for instance, Berenice Abbott's photographs on "The Beauty of Physics."

✉ 2 E. 63rd St. ☎ 212/838-0230 🕐 Closed Sun. 🚇 Subway: 4, 5, 6, N, R to 59th St.

UKRAINIAN INSTITUTE OF AMERICA

Housed in a regal French Renaissance mansion, the institute has a large collection of paintings, sculpture, textiles, and more. In addition to exhibits, there are lectures, conferences, films, and a popular classical music series. A Ukrainian immigrant, William Dzus (inventor of Dzus fasteners), founded the institute in 1948 and helped fund the purchase of the building in 1955.

✉ 2 E. 79th St. ☎ 212/288-8660 🕐 Closed Mon. 💲 Donation suggested 🚇 Subway: 6 to 77th St. ∎

The collection of the Ukrainian Institute of America includes *Pysanky*, painted Easter eggs.

In & around the
Upper East Side

THE UPPER EAST SIDE HAS SUCH AN ABUNDANCE OF landmark buildings that you can spot eye-pleasing architecture everywhere, much of it from a more gracious past. You can also indulge in extravagant shopping, or find a place for quiet repose.

You can find elegant designer clothing and shoppers at stores along Madison Avenue in the 60s, or wander in **Bloomingdale's** flagship store *(1000 3rd Ave., tel 212/705-2000)*, reigning over an entire city block—between 59th and 60th Streets and Lexington and 3rd Avenues. For sightseeing, try places close to the East River, such as the tiny sunken parks overlooking the river at 57th Street and Sutton Place. Here, in one of New York's most exclusive neighborhoods, you may sit on benches and enjoy the river view.

A four-minute bird's-eye view of the city can be had by taking the aerial tram at 60th Street and Second Avenue to Roosevelt Island and back *(tel 212/832-4555; $)*. Also on the East River, **Rockefeller University** *(1230 York Ave.)* is a world-renowned research institute for medicine and the physical sciences. Founded by John D. Rockefeller in 1901, the university moved here in 1906.

MOUNT VERNON HOTEL MUSEUM & GARDEN

This quiet site may seem out of place, but from 1826 to 1833, as an elegant country day retreat, it welcomed the city's burgeoning upper middle class. The museum illuminates early 19th-century hotel life. Originally the land was part of a 23-acre plot purchased in 1795 by Col. Stephen Smith and his wife, Abigail Adams (daughter of President John Adams), who christened the site Mount Vernon after President

Washington's home. Finances forced them to sell before they could build, but the name remained. An enterprising merchant opened the first Mount Vernon Hotel on the site in 1808. Fire destroyed the building in 1826, but another hotel followed when the next owner converted the surviving stone carriage house into a much finer day resort. It was sold after 1833 for a private residence.

In the 1930s the Colonial Dames of America rescued the building. Its reinterpretation was completed in 2000 and its furnished rooms reflect its heyday. Men caroused in the Tavern Room or retreated to the more sedate Gentleman's Parlor. Women enjoyed singing and needlework in the richly decorated Ladies' Double Parlors. This is a rare architectural time capsule, replete with artifacts and a sense of times past. ■

Mount Vernon Hotel Museum & Garden

www.mvhm.org

🗺 Map p. 133

✉ 421 E. 61st St. between 1st & York Aves.

☎ 212/838-6878

🕐 Closed Mon. & Aug.

💲 $$

🚇 Subway: N, R, 4, 5, 6 to 59th St.

The Mount Vernon Hotel Museum, built of Manhattan schist, offers a rare glimpse into life in a 19th-century day resort.

The Union Club, founded in 1836, is New York's oldest social club.

Silk stocking district

Zip 10021. Just another zip code to most of us, but not to demographers who know it as the wealthiest postal zone in the United States: from East 61st to East 80th Streets between Fifth Avenue and the East River. At its heart is the Upper East Side's wealthy silk stocking district. This is where the institutions of wealth, power, and social standing are located—the city's fanciest clubs, the best private schools, and architecturally distinguished churches and synagogues. The buildings that house them are often not open to the public, but many are landmarks well worth a look.

At the hub (but south of the geographic center) of the silk stocking district is the fortresslike 1880 Seventh Regiment Armory *(643 Park Ave. between E. 66th and E. 67th Sts.)*, a 19th-century architectural treasure. Today it is home to the National Guard and homeless women—as well as the city's best antiques show and a restaurant far too many know about, the 7th Regiment Mess Restaurant & Bar *(tel 212/744-4107, open Tues.–Sat. 5 p.m. to 9:30 p.m., www.seventhregi mentrestaurant.com)*. When socially prominent New Yorkers formed the unit in 1847, it was known as the Silk Stocking Regiment. The men designed their own uniforms and raised the money for the armory, which has distinguished interior rooms by Louis Comfort Tiffany and other designers. The magnificent 54,000-square-foot Drill Room is the largest unobstructed interior space in the city.

From the armory it's only a few steps to the haunts of the elite, not all of whom, by any means, are men. Literally in the armory's shadow, the Cosmopolitan Club *(122 E. 66th St., closed to the public)* is a refuge for professional women. Its counterpart for society women, the Colony Club *(564 Park Ave. at E. 62nd St., closed to the public)*, founded in 1903, is located in a 1916 building designed by Delano & Aldrich. The Lotos Club *(5 E. 66th St., closed to the public)*, the city's oldest literary society, is in a 1900 house. It was designed by Richard Howland Hunt for William Schiefflin, a well-born (great-great-grandson of John Jay) and effective political reformer.

The Union Club *(101 E. 69th St., closed to the public)*, founded in 1836, is only two blocks away in 1933 quarters designed by Delano &

Aldrich. The nearby Metropolitan Club *(1 E. 60th St., closed to the public)* was founded by Union Club members disgruntled when their friends and relatives were turned down for membership. The Metropolitan is housed in an 1893 building designed by McKim, Mead & White, who also did, in 1906, the Harmonie Club *(4 E. 60th St., closed to the public)*, founded by German Jews in 1852.

The spiritual needs of the silk stocking district are met by a variety of churches and synagogues. Within view of the armory, the neo-Gothic Central Presbyterian Church *(Park Ave. and E. 64th St.)*, built between 1920 and 1922, was originally the Baptist church where John D. Rockefeller worshiped. Socially prominent Episcopalians can still expect to be christened, confirmed, married, and eulogized at St. James Episcopal Church *(865 Madison Ave. at E. 71st St.)*. This neo-Gothic church (1884) was rebuilt in 1924 by architect Ralph Adams Cram.

Roman Catholics and Jews, once excluded from the seat of power, are today well represented in the silk stocking district. The 1929 Temple Emanu-El *(5th Ave. and E. 65th St.)*, a combination of Western and Byzantine architectural styles, was the first reformed congregation in the city. It is one of the largest synagogues in the world, seating 2,500—more than St. Patrick's Cathedral.

Well-scrubbed schoolchildren, accompanied by nannies or governesses, go to such prestigious and academically rigorous area institutions as Dalton, Chapin, and Brearley; there is also John Kennedy, Jr.'s alma mater, St. David's *(12–16 E. 89th St.)*, in a row of neo-Georgian town houses designed in 1919 by Delano & Aldrich.

It all seems so idyllic—genteel neighborhoods, beautiful people, elegant architecture—like a picture-perfect small town in the middle of a tumultuous city. But, before giving in to envy, consider the palatial 1931 limestone mansion at 56 East 93rd Street, home to impresario Billy Rose from 1955 until his death in 1966. Now it is a drug-and-alcohol rehabilitation center catering to the troubled among the privileged—proof that all is not bliss in paradise. ∎

The elegant Upper East Side

Whitney Museum of American Art

THE WHITNEY MUSEUM IS UNUSUAL IN SEVERAL RESPECTS. It is one of the few museums anywhere founded by an artist, in this case, Gertrude Vanderbilt Whitney. A member of two of New York's most prominent and wealthy families, she was also a sculptor with a taste for the avant-garde. The Whitney is still one of the few museums dedicated to American art of the 20th century, and one that energetically seeks out independent artists in fields other places overlook, such as film and video. Its invitational spring Biennial, first held in 1932, continues to stir up controversy with its exhibition of emerging American artists and trends.

Whitney Museum of American Art

www.whitney.org

- Map p. 133
- 945 Madison Ave. at 75th St.
- 212/570-3676, 800/WHITNEY
- Closed Mon.–Tues.
- $$$
- Subway: 6 to 77th St.

The Whitney's present modern home was designed by Bauhaus architect Marcel Breuer in 1966. The massive three-story granite building is cantilevered out like the steps of an inverted pyramid, with an entrance ramp above a "moat." That area holds a popular brunch spot, Sarabeth's *(tel 212/570-3670)*, accessed through the museum. On the first floor is a bookstore and gift shop and, past the turnstile, a small gallery. Here and in galleries on the next three floors, more recent holdings rotate, interspersed with temporary exhibits. Some are thematic, such as one on the Beats, while others feature contemporary artists, such as William Wegman, and African-American artist Bob Thompson (1937–1966). One whole gallery is devoted to photography, a relatively new area for the Whitney. Here the works of Diane Arbus, Weegee, and Robert Mapplethorpe are among those on display.

PERMANENT COLLECTION

The Whitney underwent a renovation and expansion in the 1990s. Completed in 1998, the project created new Permanent Collection galleries on the museum's fifth floor and mezzanine levels. The **Leonard & Evelyn Lauder Galleries** are devoted exclusively to the Whitney's collection of 20th-century American art. They feature a significant selection of works from 1900 to 1950, including such greats as Edward Hopper, Marsden

The building for the Whitney Museum is itself an example of 20th-century art. The severe rectangular block of granite-clad reinforced concrete was designed by Marcel Breuer in 1966.

Hartley, Georgia O'Keeffe, Stuart Davis, Arshile Gorky, and Alexander Calder. Favorites include Calder's playful sculpture "Circus" (1926–1931); O'Keeffe's "Flower Abstraction" (1926); and Hopper's "Early Sunday Morning" (1930).

In 2000 the museum dedicated its second-floor **Mildred & Herbert Lee Galleries** to an ongoing exhibition of the collection's key postwar and contemporary works. Willem De Kooning, Andy Warhol, Jasper Johns, Philip Guston, Alex Katz, Joseph Stella, Jackson Pollock, Louise Nevelson, and Kiki Smith are just some of the names you'll recognize here. Keep an eye out for Warhol's "Green Coca-Cola Bottles" (1962); Johns's "Three Flags" (1958); and Nevelson's "Black Majesty" (1955).

The Permanent Collection holds approximately 13,000 paintings, sculptures, prints, drawings, and photographs representing more than 2,000 artists.

A CONTINUING FORCE FOR CHANGE

Founded at a time when America did not take its own art seriously or encourage its artists, the Whitney Museum is largely responsible for changing that attitude.

In 2005 it engaged Renzo Piano, acclaimed for his work on the Morgan Library in New York, to renovate and enhance the entire museum. Piano's design includes a new structure set behind the present building and the addition of galleries, a public piazza, an auditorium, and more. ■

Edward Hopper's "Early Sunday Morning," a cornerstone of the Whitney collection

More places to visit

ASIA SOCIETY

This repository of Asian art and culture is housed in a 1981 red granite building designed by Edward Larrabee Barnes. Its permanent collection of Asian art and crafts is based on one compiled by John D. Rockefeller III, who founded the society in 1956 to promote American understanding of Asian art and culture.

✉ 725 Park Ave. at 70th St. ☎ 212/517-2742 🕐 Closed Mon. 💲 $ 🚇 Subway: 6 to 68th St.

EPISCOPAL CHURCH OF THE HOLY TRINITY, YORKVILLE

This complex of French Renaissance–style structures was built in 1896–99 to serve the quickly growing immigrant population of Yorkville. This once mainly German-Hungarian neighborhood runs from East 77th to 96th Streets. There is an interesting stretch along Second Avenue in the mid-80s with traditional German shops and delicatessens.

✉ 316–322 E. 88th St. ☎ 212/289-4100 🚇 Subway: 4, 5, 6 to 86th St.

Once a country estate, Gracie Mansion today functions as the mayor's official residence and an uptown branch of City Hall.

GRACIE MANSION, THE MAYORAL HOME

This well-preserved federal house was built in 1799 by shipping merchant Archibald Gracie on the site of a Revolutionary fort. In 1924, the house, by then city-owned, became the first home of the Museum of the City of New York, which occupied it until 1932. In 1942 it became the mayor's official residence. Guided tours, on Wednesdays only, require reservations and include the mayor's study, featuring Childe Hassam lithographs of New York street scenes and a permanent exhibit on the history of the house. Gracie Mansion is located in **Carl Schurz Park,** an uncrowded, ten-acre, riverside tract with wonderful views of the East River and Roosevelt Island.

✉ 88th St. and East End Ave. ☎ 212/570-4751 🕐 Open Wed. only; reservations required (allow 2 weeks for processing) 💲 $$ 🚇 Subway: 4, 5, 6 to 86th St.

NEW YORK SOCIETY LIBRARY

The city's oldest library is housed in a landmark town house (1917). It is open to the public, although only members can borrow books.

✉ 53 E. 79th St. ☎ 212/288-6900 🚇 Subway: 6 to 77th St.

SOCIETY OF ILLUSTRATORS: MUSEUM OF AMERICAN ILLUSTRATION

This unusual museum exhibits commercial illustration, an art form not usually displayed. Housed in an 1875 carriage house, the society, founded in 1901 to promote the art of commercial illustration, had as early members such notables as Charles Dana Gibson, William Glackens, Norman Rockwell, and Frederic Remington. The museum's collection consists of some 1,500 original works from 1838 to the present. There is an extensive bookstore.

✉ 128 E. 63rd St. between Park & Lexington Aves. ☎ 212/838-2560 🕐 Closed Sun.–Mon. 💲 Donation suggested 🚇 Subway: N, R, W to Lexington Ave./59th St.; F to Lexington Ave./63rd St. ∎

Central Park is aptly named. It is 800 or so acres of greenery located smack-dab in the middle of Manhattan. Nearly everyone in the city uses it at one time or another, be it for exercise or a rare commune with nature.

Central Park

Introduction & map 168–169
Around Central Park 170–172
Hotels & restaurants 253

At bat in Central Park

Central Park

ONE LITTLE-KNOWN FACT ABOUT CENTRAL PARK: ITS gates—at least its 18 original ones—have names, although only three are inscribed: the Inventors', Mariners', and Engineers' Gates. Unknowingly, you may be entering through the Artists' Gate (Central Park South and Sixth Avenue) or, at the opposite, northern end, the Warriors' Gate, or at some other titled entrance. There are, however, no gates named for the some 20 million people a year who use the park: joggers, skateboarders, birdwatchers, cyclists, softball players, sunbathers, chess players, lovers, Rollerbladers, model boat sailors, kite fliers, tourists, sketch artists, and others.

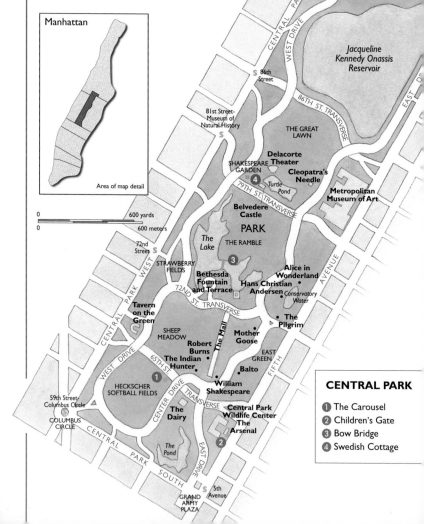

Manhattan

Area of map detail

0   600 yards
0   600 meters

CENTRAL PARK

1. The Carousel
2. Children's Gate
3. Bow Bridge
4. Swedish Cottage

Central Park, the first large public park in America, is a product of vision, revision, and compromise. Its inspiration was the great parks of London and Paris. Wealthy New Yorkers believed that a park in New York would add to the city's cachet, give them a place to drive their carriages, and provide the working classes with healthful recreation. Although the park has gone through periods of neglect and deterioration (a recent renovation ended one such cycle), it has consistently played an important role in city life. It is more than just greenery; critic Paul Goldberger has called it "the nonbuilding that could well lay claim to being New York's greatest work of architecture."

When you visit Central Park today, you will see it at its spanking best. Improvements, undertaken at the initiative of the Central Park Conservancy, a private fund-raising group that contributes substantially to the park's operating budget, have ranged from reseeding the Great Lawn to restoring the Swedish Cottage, a reproduction—recently renovated—of a typical Swedish schoolhouse of the 19th century that was shipped to this country for the 1876 Philadelphia Centennial Exposition. Other important park additions include the new nature center in the imposing, lakeside fortress known as Belvedere Castle.

GREENSWARD PLAN: AN URBAN VISION

Central Park's naturalistic landscaping successfully hides its mostly man-made origins. The area, now 843 acres, was filled with shanties and small farms when the state legislature, in 1853, authorized the city to seize a 700-acre parcel in the middle of Manhattan.

Four years later, the Central Park Commission held a contest to determine the design of the park. The winning entry, a "Greensward plan," based on romantic landscaping notions then popular in England, was submitted by Frederick Law Olmsted, who would oversee its construction as the park's superintendent, and his partner, Calvert Vaux. The plan stressed variety and contrast: open meadows, dense woods, and formal areas such as the Mall. The park's "one great purpose," Olmsted wrote, is "to supply to the hundreds of thousands of tired workers, who have no opportunity to spend their summers in the country, a specimen of God's handiwork."

It took some 20,000 laborers 20 years to construct Central Park, which opened in 1859, before work was complete. In that time, they removed almost three million cubic yards of soil, blasted the rocky outcroppings to create the picturesque rifts the Olmsted-Vaux plan called for, planted four or five million trees and 816 varieties of other plants, drained marshlands, and dug the reservoir now named for Jacqueline Kennedy Onassis, which today is circumscribed by a popular 1.6-mile jogging track.

In its early years, the park was a preserve of the wealthy and their carriages; the strict rules discouraged others by prohibiting group activities such as picnics. Over the years, these rules were relaxed, then eliminated. At the same time, there were encroachments on the park's open space: wings added to the Metropolitan Museum of Art, the Tavern on the Green restaurant, two skating rinks, playgrounds, tennis courts, and other facilities, most of which were opposed by those who objected to any alteration of the original Greensward plan. (Proposals for a horse-racing track, an airstrip, and an underground garage were defeated.) The parks commissioner, Robert Moses, once tried to pave over a playground to enlarge the parking lot for the Tavern on the Green. His scheme was defeated by mothers pushing baby carriages, who blocked his bulldozers.

It was through this sort of give and take that Central Park became what it is today: a remarkable expanse of greenery in the midst of some of the most valuable real estate on Earth. ■

Around Central Park

WHERE TO START? THE MAJOR ATTRACTIONS ARE SOUTH of 86th Street, so you might begin with a group of attractions near the Children's Gate (64th Street and Fifth Avenue) and work your way north. Descend the stairs off Fifth Avenue to the Arsenal, a redbrick fortress built in 1848 to house armaments, now the Parks Department headquarters.

Central Park information center

www.centralparknyc.org

✉ The Dairy, 65th St.

☎ 212/794-6564

🕐 Closed Mon.

Central Park Wildlife Center

✉ Children's Gate, 5th Ave. at E. 64th St.

☎ 212/439-6500

🕐 Sea lions fed at 11:30, 2, 4

💲 $

🚌 Bus: M1-4
   Subway: N, R, W
   to 5th Ave.;
   6 to 68th St.

The walkway around the building will take you to the **Central Park Wildlife Center,** which offers its 450 residents natural settings instead of cages. Feeding time for the sea lions is a favorite with children, as is the adjacent **Tisch Children's Zoo.** West of the zoo is the **Dairy,** an 1870 building designed by Calvert Vaux, now a park information center. Contact the Dairy about free walking tours of the park, offered by the Central Park Conservancy.

Beyond is the Chess and Checkers Building (secure chess pieces at the Dairy with a deposit) and the **Carousel,** the latter a Coney Island transplant and, at a dollar a ride, one of the park's most

popular attractions. Footpaths in the park meander, so do not worry if you begin to wonder where you are. There are signs, and local visitors can help with directions as well. Plus, it is fun to wander—as long as it is daytime.

Northwest of the Dairy, the **Sheep Meadow** is a huge expanse of lawn. Next to it on the east is the **Mall** (between 66th and 72nd Sts.), a formal promenade lined with American elms, which includes the sculpture-lined Literary Walk at its southern end. At the northern end are steps to the **Bethesda Fountain Terrace** (at 72nd St.). This two-level architectural space centers on the sculptured fountain "Angels in the Water," by Emma

Central Park
was not at all
"central" when
created, but has
since been
hemmed in by
the city.

Carousel
- ✉ E. 64th St.
- ☎ 212/879-0244
- 🕐 Closed weekdays
  Jan.–March
- 💲 $

Loeb Boathouse
- ☎ 212/517-3623
- 💲 $$$$ (plus
  refundable deposit)

**Central Park
Summerstage**
www.summerstage.org
- ✉ Rumsey Playfield
- ☎ 212/360-2777 or
  212/360-2756
- 🕐 Summer only

**Swedish Cottage
Marionette Theatre**
- ✉ Near West Drive
- ☎ 212/988-9093
- 🕐 Open summer only,
  call for hours
- 💲 $. Reservations
  required.

**Shakespeare in
the Park**
- ✉ Delacorte Theater
- ☎ 212/539-8750
- 🕐 Summer only
- 💲 Free, but tickets
  required

**Henry Luce
Nature
Observatory**
- ✉ Belvedere Castle
- ☎ 212/772-0210
- 🕐 Closed Mon.

Stebbins. It overlooks the serpentine 18-acre body of water known as the **Lake.** Boats and bikes can be rented at the **Loeb Boathouse** on the Lake's eastern end *(74th St.)*, and there is a delightful open-air bar/café. Closer to Fifth Avenue *(at 74th St.)* is **Conservatory Pond,** where remote-controlled boats are raced and where there is an ice-cream café.

West of Bethesda Terrace are sites that honor musician John Lennon, who was killed in front of his Dakota Apartment home nearby in 1980. His widow, Yoko Ono, funded **Strawberry Fields** (named for Lennon's song "Strawberry Fields Forever"), a 2.5-acre, tear-shaped garden just off the entrance at Central Park West and 72nd Street. Naples, Italy, donated the nearby sidewalk mosaic, with the word "Imagine" (another Lennon song) at the center.

Throughout the summer, free events—from concerts to opera to readings, all with professional performers—happen daily at **Central Park Summerstage** at Rumsey Playfield. For the action-minded, there are free Rollerblading clinics at the West 72nd Street park entrance from April through October.

The cast-iron **Bow Bridge** *(mid-park around 74th Street)* across the Lake leads to the **Ramble,** a 37-acre, hilly maze of paths and foliage, a favorite with bird-watchers. Near the park's West Drive *(around 79th St.)* is **Swedish Cottage Marionette Theatre.** Next door, the **Shakespeare Garden,** established in 1916 on the 300th anniversary of the Bard's death, contains half the plants mentioned in his plays. Shakespeare and other plays are performed at the open-air **Delacorte Theater** each summer by the New York Shakespeare Festival.

On Turtle Pond, formerly Belvedere Lake, picturesque Belvedere Castle nestles into the rock outcropping. The castle houses the **Henry Luce Nature Observatory.** The Wood and Water Discovery Room is at the center of the observatory's children's programs. **The Great**

To children especially, there is no better statue in Central Park than this bronze grouping of Alice and friends.

Sculpture in the park

The first statue in Central Park, a bronze bust of German dramatist and philosopher Johann Christoph Friedrich von Schiller, was placed in the Ramble in 1859. Other literary figures are represented on the Mall's southern end along Literary Walk, including Robert Burns and Walter Scott. The only American is Fitz-Greene Halleck, a minor but well-known poet and a member of the literary Knickerbocker Group. American sculptor John Quincy Adams Ward did the bronze statue of William Shakespeare, the realistic "Indian Hunter" (1886), located southwest of the Mall, and "The Pilgrim" (1884) on the 72nd Street transverse, just south of Conservatory Lake. Here, children climb over the bronze grouping "Alice in Wonderland" (1959), by Jose de Creeft, and sit on the lap of "Hans Christian Andersen" (1956), rendered in bronze by Georg John Lober, with a book open on his lap and a duckling at his feet. ∎

Charles A. Dana Discovery Center

✉ Northern shore, Harlem Meer

☎ 212/860-1370

🕐 Closed Mon.

Lasker Rink & Pool

✉ Between 106th & 108th Sts.

☎ 212/534-7639

💲 $. Call for rental & lesson fees.

Lawn, recently re-planted and reseeded, is where the Metropolitan Opera and the New York Philharmonic perform free summer concerts. It is behind the Metropolitan Museum of Art, where **Cleopatra's Needle,** the park's most prominent landmark, is also located. This 65-foot-tall, granite obelisk, dating from about 1475 B.C., was Egypt's gift to the U.S. in 1885.

The park north of here is wilder and less densely peopled. An exception is the jogging track, scheduled for restoration, around the 106-acre Jacqueline Kennedy Onassis Reservoir. The **Conservatory**

Garden (5th Ave. at 105th St.) is entered through the Vanderbilt Gate that once graced the Vanderbilt mansion on Fifth Avenue. The symmetrical formal garden with two sculptural fountains is noted for its seasonal plantings.

At the northern end of the park is the 11-acre Harlem Meer. On its northern shore, the **Charles A. Dana Discovery Center** offers nature programs for children and families. Here is some of the park's wildest scenery. For a wintertime activity in a splendid outdoor setting, try **Lasker Rink.** In the warmer months, the rink is used for swimming. ∎

Spread out between two of the city's best parks, this is a lively area inhabited by people who are devoted to their neighborhoods. Since the advent of Lincoln Center, the performing arts have flourished here.

Upper West Side

Introduction & map 174–175
Lincoln Center 176–178
Time Warner Center 179
Walk from park to park 180–181
New-York Historical Society 182–183
American Museum of Natural History 184–186
Central Park West 187
Some small Upper West Side museums 188
Hotels & restaurants 253–254

Tyrannosaurus rex in the American Museum of Natural History

Upper West Side

BORDERED ON THE WEST BY RIVERSIDE PARK AND THE HUDSON RIVER AND on the east by Central Park, this popular residential neighborhood extends from West 59th Street north to 110th Street. Busy thoroughfares lined with shops and historic buildings cross quiet side streets with handsome brownstones. In this community the arts, commerce, and residential life peacefully coexist. The intimacy of the area and the open-mindedness of its residents create a vibrant social dynamic. Upper West Siders also have demonstrated their respect for the past—practically everybody lives in an old building—and their willingness to battle to preserve it. Even so, tall new buildings rising here and there are changing the skyline.

The Upper West Side has attractions that draw visitors, but not so many as to overwhelm its neighborhood appeal. Technically, since Fifth Avenue divides the East Side from the West Side, all of Central Park is part of the Upper West Side, although that particular asset truly belongs to the entire city. Along with the park's many visitors, West Siders make good use of its proximity, making it especially jammed on weekends.

The multifaceted Time Warner Center at Columbus Circle (see p. 179) provides a fitting gateway to treasures farther on. The American Museum of Natural History (see pp. 184–86) is one of the great museums of its kind in the world. The New-York Historical Society (see pp. 182–83) is another wonderful institution families will enjoy. Lincoln Center is the country's foremost performing arts center, a must for those interested in live orchestral or chamber music, ballet or opera.

The surrounding area is filled with cafés, restaurants, and delightful small stores, where you will find yourself among many residents. In fact, one of the pleasures of a visit to the Upper West Side is to glimpse how most New Yorkers live—in a series of close-knit neighborhoods serviced by a wide variety of shops, stores, schools, and eateries.

THE DAKOTA LED THE WAY FOR SETTLEMENT

The major factors in developing the Upper West Side were access and transportation. Before the elevated line along Columbus Avenue, then called Ninth Avenue, was completed in 1879, the area was filled with shanties and squatters, many of them displaced by the development of Central Park. Still, the construction of the Dakota Apartments in 1884 in such an out-of-the-way wasteland was considered a rash and daring move—hence its name.

But others followed: In 1884 Isidor Straus, a merchant who would eventually take over R. H. Macy's, moved to 105th Street and West End Avenue to be near Riverside Park; William Tecumseh Sherman, the Union general famous for his rampage through the South during the Civil War, moved into a house on West 71st Street in 1886. That year the *New York Times* noted: "Thousands of carpenters and masons are engaged in rearing substantial buildings where a year ago nothing was to be seen but market gardens or barren rocky fields."

The arrival of the subway in 1904 prolonged the boom, which lasted into the late 1920s and early 1930s, years that saw the construction of the huge twin-towered apartment hotels on Central Park West.

Developers hoped that the Upper West Side would attract the city's social and business elite. Instead it tended to draw New Yorkers engaged in the arts or publishing or advertising and similar fields. One prestigious address, the Ansonia Hotel (1904), had as residents such diverse individuals as baseball star Babe Ruth, novelist Theodore Dreiser, composer Igor Stravinsky, impresario Florenz Ziegfeld, and tenor Enrico Caruso.

The Upper West Side still attracts stars and celebrities for its many amenities, the nearness of the park, the historical integrity of its buildings, and the fact that many other famous people live there as well. ■

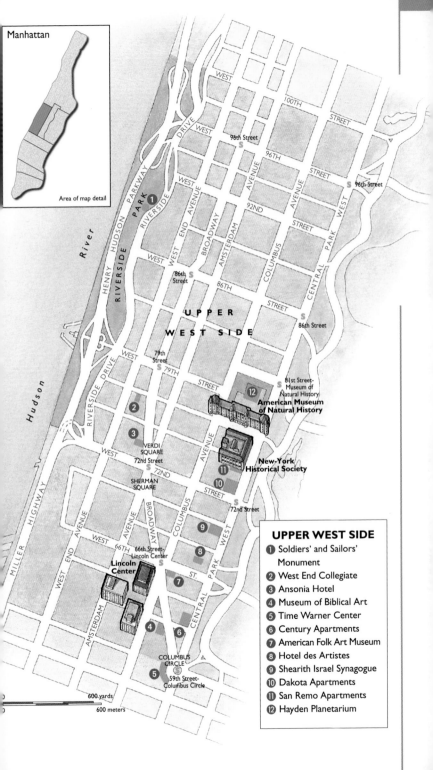

Manhattan

Area of map detail

WEST 100TH STREET

96th Street

WEST 96TH STREET

AVENUE

AVENUE

96th Street

WEST 92ND STREET

RIVERSIDE PARK

HENRY HUDSON PARKWAY

RIVERSIDE DRIVE

WEST

WEST END AVENUE

BROADWAY

AMSTERDAM

COLUMBUS

CENTRAL PARK WEST

River

86th Street

86TH

WEST STREET

86th Street

U P P E R

W E S T   S I D E

Hudson

79th Street

79TH

WEST STREET

81st Street-
Museum of
Natural History

American Museum
of Natural History

12

RIVERSIDE DRIVE

WEST

VERDI SQUARE

72nd Street

72ND

AVENUE

STREET

New-York
Historical Society

11

10

SHERMAN SQUARE

72nd Street

MILLER HIGHWAY

WEST

AMSTERDAM

AVENUE

BROADWAY

COLUMBUS AVENUE

CENTRAL PARK WEST

9

8

WEST END AVENUE

66TH

WEST

66th Street-
Lincoln Center

Lincoln
Center

ST.

7

4

6

COLUMBUS
CIRCLE

5

59th Street-
Columbus Circle

600 yards

600 meters

UPPER WEST SIDE

1 Soldiers' and Sailors'
   Monument
2 West End Collegiate
3 Ansonia Hotel
4 Museum of Biblical Art
5 Time Warner Center
6 Century Apartments
7 American Folk Art Museum
8 Hotel des Artistes
9 Shearith Israel Synagogue
10 Dakota Apartments
11 San Remo Apartments
12 Hayden Planetarium

Lincoln Center

Lincoln Center for the Performing Arts

www.lincolncenter.org

 Map p. 175

✉ 65th St. at Broadway

☎ 212/875-5000. Information & schedules: 212/546-2656. Lincoln Center tour: 212/875-5350. Metropolitan Opera House backstage tours: 212/769-7020 (reservations required).

🚇 Subway: 1 to 66th St.–Lincoln Center

NOW, MORE THAN 30 YEARS SINCE THE LINCOLN CENTER for the Performing Arts opened, there is no disputing its resounding success. As a public space, Lincoln Center, the country's largest performing arts complex, serves and pleases even those New Yorkers and visitors who have never been inside its theaters and concert halls. Some five million people a year attend performances there, but countless more simply wander through the spacious plaza, enjoy summer nights at the fountains, participate in open-air dances in the plaza, or attend free concerts and other events at the Guggenheim Bandshell in Damrosch Park on the center's southwest corner.

In addition to regular concerts and performances by the Metropolitan and New York City operas, the New York Philharmonic, and the American Ballet Theater, Lincoln Center is noted for featured events such as concerts at Alice Tully Hall, the summer Lincoln Center Festival, and the Mostly Mozart Festival.

In 1987, on the bicentenary of Mozart's death, the center's various concert stages were used to perform all of the composer's works in over 500 concerts. Concerts and operas are also televised on public television's *Live from Lincoln Center* series. Plays and musicals are staged at the Vivian Beaumont Theater. Various one-hour tours are offered.

NEW YORK PUBLIC LIBRARY OF THE PERFORMING ARTS

One of the New York Public Library's great collections—on music, dance, and theater—opened in Lincoln Center in 1965. The research library, open to the public *(tel 212/870-1630, closed Sun.–Mon.)*, has more than 200,000 books, records, tapes, compact

discs, videos, and music scores and materials suitable for children. Researchers can use the collections on the third floor. Four galleries hold rotating exhibits.

The **Dance Collection,** the world's largest archive on the subject, has more than 30,000 books as well as manuscripts, costume and set designs, and taped interviews with leaders in the field. It includes the Jerome Robbins Archive of Recorded Moving Image, a collection of videos and films of dance performances.

The **Music Division** comprises the Rodgers & Hammerstein Archives of Recorded Sound— nearly half a million recordings and videos—and the American Collection of jazz, pop, and imprints of colonial music. The **Billy Rose Theater Collection** includes thousands of clippings, programs, posters, and photos on theater, film, radio and TV, vaudeville, the circus, and magic. The **Theater of Film and Tape Archives** has more than 1,600 films and videos of live performances.

SCULPTURES

Lincoln Center has several pieces of modern sculpture, most notably Henry Moore's "Reclining Figure" (1965), a 30-foot-long, bronze abstract sculpture in two segments located in the reflecting pool in the plaza. After completing the work, Moore expressed the hope that "it will give contrast to the architecture, which, like all architecture, is rather geometric and static." Alexander Calder's spiderlike "Le Guichet" (1965), a 14-foot-high assemblage consisting of a large steel plate attached to four legs, is located in front of the library of the performing arts. In the park across from Lincoln Center formed by the crossing of Broadway and Columbus Avenue, there is a bronze bust by Milton Hebald of Richard Tucker, the Metropolitan Opera's leading tenor from 1945 until his death in 1975.

CONSTRUCTION

Robert Moses, the city's strong-willed master planner and builder, conceived of Lincoln Center as

At dusk, Lincoln Center glows with soft lighting. Below: A Chinese dancer

an urban renewal project. Construction, its costs largely underwritten by the Rockefeller family, caused the demolition of several West Side landmarks and the dislocation of the tenement dwellers who had inhabited the neighborhood for years. High-rise housing for 10,000 people was built along West End Avenue, but the construction of Lincoln Center irrevocably changed the area from a working-class to a middle-class neighborhood. Ironically, just before they were demolished, the tenements had one last moment of

Lincoln Center's production of The Nutcracker has become a traditional part of a New York Christmas.

glory—as the street setting for the film version of the musical *West Side Story*.

The first building in the complex to be completed was the 19.7-million-dollar concert hall designed by Max Abramovitz, which opened on September 23, 1962. Philharmonic Hall, as it was called then, was plagued from the beginning with acoustical problems, which were finally solved in 1976 after several major readjustments. The auditorium, seating over 2,700 people, was renamed

Avery Fisher Hall in 1973, after the philanthropic manufacturer of high-fidelity equipment, who donated ten million dollars to Lincoln Center. Some of the funds went toward the acoustics.

Architect Wallace K. Harrison, head of the Lincoln Center's board of architects, designed the **Metropolitan Opera House,** the largest (nearly 4,000 seats) and most costly (46.9 million dollars) hall in the complex. Philip Johnson was the architect of the third largest building, the **New York State Theater** (1964), the one building in the complex constructed with state and city funding. It, too, had poor acoustics, a problem that was remedied in 1982. These three principal buildings, wrote architectural critic Ada Louise Huxtable, "are lushly decorated, conservative structures that the public finds pleasing and most professionals consider a failure of nerve, imagination and talent."

The **Lincoln Center Theater,** a building housing both the Vivian Beaumont and the Mitzi E. Newhouse theaters, and the New York Public Library of the Performing Arts were both completed in 1965 in an unusual collaboration between architects: Eero Saarinen & Associates did the theater, while Skidmore, Owings & Merrill designed the library, which is cantilevered out over the theater at the plaza level. The **Juilliard School** *(144 W. 66th St.)* was completed in 1968. It houses the thousand-seat Alice Tully Hall, home to the Chamber Music Society of Lincoln Center. In 1991 the 28-story Samuel B. and David Rose Building was completed. This most recent addition to the complex houses offices, rehearsal studios, dormitories, a library branch, and a fire station. ■

Time Warner Center

SPREADING OUTWARD AND UPWARD ON 3.4 ACRES, Time Warner Center at Columbus Circle rises at the convergence of five major corridors: Central Park West, Central Park South, Broadway, 58th Street, and 60th Street. No single building complex since Rockefeller Center has offered such unrivaled possibilities for entertainment, fine dining, shopping, lodging, and public enjoyment. Topped by soaring twin towers, the 2.8-million-square-foot complex is at once New York's newest landmark and a cultural heart of the city.

Time Warner Center
www.timewarner.com
www.shopsatcolumbus
circle.com
 Map p. 175
✉ 10 Columbus Circle;
Rose Theater box
office: Corner 60th
St. & Broadway
☎ CNN: 866/426-6692;
Dizzy's Club Coca-
Cola: 212/258-9595
🕐 Retail hours vary
🚇 Subway: A, B, C, D,
1 to 59th St.—
Columbus Circle

Since its 2004 opening, the center has drawn tourists and residents equally. Its lobbies are enhanced by performance events and displays, while Whole Foods on the lower level is a delight unto itself. Among the 40 shops are family favorites, such as Borders Books & Music and J. Crew, and designer/boutique stores, from J. W. Cooper for homemade boots and Montmartre for women's fashions, to Armani Exchange and Bose. Also onsite are the Equinox Fitness Club, a bank, and restaurants helmed by world-acclaimed chefs, from Café Gray and Jean-Georges's V Steakhouse, to Thomas Keller's Per Se.

Many visitors will enjoy the 45-minute "adventure behind the scenes" at CNN's new studios. The center's most unique offering is "Jazz at Lincoln Center" (Artistic Director Wynton Marsalis), which produces more than 400 events annually here at its Rose Theater—the first education, performance, and broadcast facility devoted to jazz. Dizzy's Club Coca-Cola has jazz, drinks, great views, and a late-night menu plus "After Hours" sets. For other spectacular views seek out the sky-high public spaces of the Mandarin Oriental Hotel New York (enter on 60th St).

The center is on the site of the smaller New York Coliseum, built in 1950 by Robert Moses for city events and trade shows. The 1988 opening of the Javits Center led to the Coliseum's steady demise. The site was purchased in 1998, and construction on the current buildings began in 2000. ■

The new Time Warner Center dominates the west side of Columbus Circle.

Walk from park to park

The Upper West Side once boasted some of New York's finest hotels and residences. This walking tour visits those bygone days, beginning with grand old buildings at Central Park West and West 70th Street. It ends on the relaxing greenery of Riverside Park, with its view of the Hudson River and the Palisades and spaces for jogging, baseball, cross-country skiing, or just taking it easy. As you walk, be prepared for an area of exhilarating contrasts and tempting places to stop: One minute you can be buying a rare book at a bargain price from a street bookseller, the next peering skyward at an awesome structure. You will pass assorted shops and restaurants and may also choose to pick up some delicious gourmet takeout and picnic at Riverside Park at the end.

Begin at the **Shearith Israel Synagogue** ❶ *(W. 70th St. at Central Park W., tel 212/873-0300)*, a Spanish and Portuguese synagogue built in the classical revival style in 1897 by the oldest Jewish congregation in New York. The Sephardic Jews arrived in New York from Brazil in 1654. One block north, at 115 Central Park West, the **Majestic Apartments** were built by developer Irwin S. Chanin in 1930–31. It is one of four twin-towered apartment buildings facing the park. Go left on West 71st Street.

The area between Central Park West and Columbus Avenue has a fine selection of 1890s brownstones with high stoops and balustrades; note the cupids on the cornice of No. 24. The Roman Catholic **Church of the Blessed Sacrament** ❷ *(W. 71st St., between Columbus Ave. and Broadway)* is a neo-Gothic landmark designed in 1917 by Gustave Steinback, a prominent church architect. At No. 171 (northeast corner of Broadway), the beaux arts **Dorilton**, nine floors topped by a two-and-a-half story mansard roof, is today a landmarked apartment building. When it opened in 1902, however, a critic complained that "the sight of it makes strong men swear and weak women shrink affrighted," and it was condemned for the same multiplicity of details that are today described as handsome.

The square nearby, at the intersection of Amsterdam Avenue and Broadway at West 73rd Street, is **Verdi Square** ❸, named for a statue of Giuseppe Verdi unveiled in 1906, five years after the Italian composer/patriot's death. The statue sits on a cylindrical pedestal; figures of four of his characters surround the base—Falstaff, Aida, Otello, and Leonora. An ornate **subway kiosk**, designed in 1904, graces the island at the intersection. This area in the heart of shopping is a popular subway stop. At 2100 Broadway, the **former Central Savings Bank** building (1928) is an imposing backdrop for the Verdi statue.

Proceed north (uptown) along Broadway. The beaux arts **Ansonia Hotel,** at No. 2109 *(bet. W. 73rd and W. 74th Sts.)*, is one of New York's most acclaimed apartment buildings. Architect Paul E. M. Duboy gave the highly ornamented building its Parisian flair. Solid construction for fireproofing made its apartments soundproof, which pleased its tenants and guests, including Igor Stravinsky, Enrico Caruso, and Babe Ruth.

Turn left on West 77th Street to No. 250. The beaux arts **Hotel Belleclaire** (1901) is the first known design of apartment-house architect Emery Roth, Sr.

Continue on West 77th Street to West End Avenue, a street lined with stylish apartment houses. The **West End Collegiate Church** ❹ *(245 W. 77th St.)* is an 1893 Dutch Renaissance structure marked by stepped gables. It is a direct descendant of New Amsterdam's first church (a Dutch Reformed church built in 1628); No. 312 was for many years home to jazz musician Miles Davis. Walk west, to curving Riverside Drive, and turn right to an area lined with stunning town houses and mansions, with a historic district of 1890s row houses between West 80th and 81st Streets. Those by architect Clarence F. True are Nos. 103, 104, 105, and 107–109.

At 140 Riverside Drive (the northeast corner of West 86th Street), the 19-story

Normandy Apartments by Emery Roth combine art deco touches such as the rounded corners with details borrowed from the Italian Renaissance. One of two freestanding mansions remaining on Riverside Drive, the **Isaac L. Rice House** ⑤, at the southeast corner of 89th Street, was designed by Herts and Tallent, theatrical designers. The impressive 100-foot-tall **Soldiers' and Sailors' Monument,** honoring the Civil War dead, is opposite in **Riverside Park** ⑥, Paul E. M. Duboy collaborated on its design.

Riverside Drive and Riverside Park are both designated scenic landmarks. The land was set aside in 1865 to enhance real estate values and in 1873 Frederick Law Olmsted designed the park, which slopes down toward the Hudson River, a place to relax after your long walk. ■

- ⧉ Map inside front cover
- ▶ Shearith Israel Synagogue
- ↔ Nearly 2 miles
- ⊕ About an hour
- ▶ Riverside Park

NOT TO BE MISSED
- Church of the Blessed Sacrament
- Verdi Square
- West End Collegiate Church
- Soldiers' and Sailors' Monument

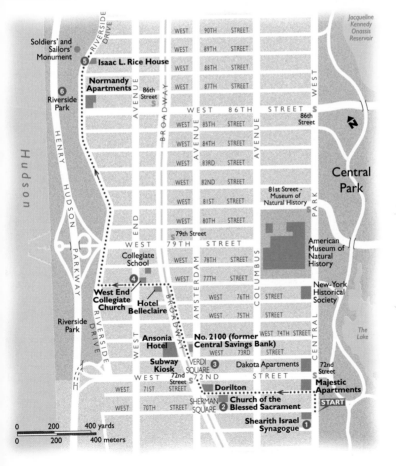

New-York Historical Society

FOUNDED IN 1804, THE NEW-YORK HISTORICAL SOCIETY IS the oldest museum in the city and the second oldest in the country. The society's name proudly retains the hyphen in New-York that was in use when the society was founded. Known for its vast and varied collection, its holdings include the country's largest collection of Tiffany lamps, John James Audubon's original watercolors for his *Birds of America,* and millions of books and manuscripts. The museum has taken a leadership role in establishing an archive of objects and information related to the events of Sept. 11, 2001.

**New-York
Historical Society**
www.nyhistory.org
- Map p. 175
- 170 Central Park W. (between 76th & 77th Sts.)
- 212/873-3400
- Closed Mon.; library closed Sat.–Mon.
- $$
- Subway: B, C to 81st St.

The museum moved to its present neoclassical building in 1908. The entrance on West 77th Street leads into an elegant hall, with several galleries and a gift shop. Pick up a brochure upon admission to see what temporary exhibits are showing. There are many: Having survived a financial crisis in the early 1990s, the society is now back on its

The granite-faced exterior of the society's austere neoclassical home

feet with a vigorous program. Recent exhibits of note have included "The Tumultuous Fifties: A View from the *New York Times* Photo Archive."

There are more galleries on the next three floors. The second floor holds the **Department of Prints and Photographs,** with rare materials such as Audubon originals (access by appointment). Also here is the recently reopened **Dexter Hall,** with 19th-century masterpieces from the society's permanent collection, some being shown for the first time in 25 years. Among the artists represented are Thomas Cole and John Trumbull. The **Henry Luce Center,** on the fourth floor, is an innovative display of nearly 40,000 objects covering 400 years of American history.

MORE HIGHLIGHTS

The **Luman Reed Gallery,** named for a 19th-century collector and patron of the arts, is a recreation of the picture gallery at Reed's 13 Greenwich Street residence, where he lived in the 1830s. Reed believed that art was important to the development of the nation and commissioned Thomas Cole, the founder of the Hudson River school of landscape painting, to create a five-part allegory. "The Course of Empire" is the focal point of the gallery here, but it also holds Dutch, Flemish, German, and Italian paintings and engravings and other treasures.

In the **Lowlight Gallery,** lights are dimmed. Here one can view rare documents, books, and correspondence, such as British Gen. John Burgoyne's articles of surrender ending the American Revolution, the authorization in 1674 from Charles II for the British takeover of New Netherland from the Dutch, or a piece of ticker tape from the day the

stock market crashed. Items are frequently rotated.

Finally, the society's library is well worth visiting, and no appointment is needed. Its scope is immense, with 600,000 volumes and more than a million manuscripts, including the first printing of Lincoln's Second Inaugural Address, and an outstanding collection of 18th-century newspapers, including the city's earliest, the *New-York Gazette* (1725–1744) and John Peter Zenger's *New-York Weekly Journal*.

SPECIALIZED COLLECTIONS

The silver collection, with objects from the colonial through Victorian periods, includes work by New York silversmith Myer Myers and flatware that belonged to such important families as the Roosevelts and the Schuylers. The **Neustadt Collection** of Tiffany lamps was compiled by a New York physician in the latter half of the 20th century.

The **Bella C. Landauer Collection of Business and Advertising Ephemera,** with over one million items, is open by appointment only.

HISTORY

The society has its roots in a collection of "everything and from whatever clime," assembled by John Pintard, one of its founders, and briefly displayed in City Hall in 1791. The historical society is also an art museum, the city's first, and the only one until the Metropolitan Museum of Art opened in 1870. In 1858 the society received the collection of Luman Reed, a wealthy grocer; when he died in 1836, friends and associates arranged for his art collection to be displayed to the public on a paying basis—an enterprise they called the New York Gallery of Fine Arts—in the Rotunda in City Hall Park. When the Rotunda closed, the collection was given to the Historical Society. ■

An 1826 oil painting by Thomas Cole depicts a scene from James Fenimore Cooper's *Last of the Mohicans.*

American Museum of Natural History

WITH ITS HUGE SKELETONS OF DINOSAURS AND DIORAMAS of cavemen, the American Museum of Natural History is a great place to take children. But, make no mistake, it is not a museum primarily for them. It is a complex scientific and educational institution and one of the largest and most important museums in the world. Sprawled out over four square blocks, the museum owns nearly 40 million specimens (including 96 percent of all known species of birds).

The facade of the American Museum of Natural History

American Museum of Natural History
www.amnh.org
- Map p. 175
- Central Park West at 79th St.
- 212/769-5100; 212/769-5200 (tickets & programs)
- $$ (donation)
- Subway: C to 81st St.; 1 to 79th St.

Opposite: Dinosaurs command the entrance to the American Museum of Natural History.

Visitors—more than three million a year—must decide what and how much to see in the museum's maze of buildings. There are guided tours of certain exhibits, but many people solve the problem by heading straight for something they know. Often this is the dinosaurs; the reproduction of the 55-foot *Barosaurus* in the first-floor Rotunda stops people in their tracks, and many more dinosaurs await on the fourth floor. Some head for the North American Indian exhibits, or the **Hall of Ocean Life,** with its giant blue whale immersed in a virtual ocean, or one of the newest areas, the **Hall of Biodiversity,** featuring an African rain forest: There is much from which to choose.

The first floor of the museum includes halls and exhibit spaces devoted to birds, invertebrates, North American mammals, fish, forests, and the environment of

New York State. The **Hall of the Northwest Coast Indians** has two imposing lines of totem poles running down the center of the room. The **Hall of Mollusks and Our World** includes items from a collection of 50,000 shells that the museum acquired in 1874, when shell collecting and decorating was a popular pastime. A 34-ton piece of a meteorite discovered in 1897 in Greenland and excavated by explorer Robert Peary is a highlight of the **Arthur Ross Hall of Meteorites. The Hall of Gems** includes the 563-carat "Star of India" sapphire that J. P. Morgan donated to the museum in 1901.

Gertrude Vanderbilt Whitney gave the second-floor **Whitney Hall of Oceanic Birds** on the death of her husband, Harry Payne Whitney, who supported the museum's ornithological research and collecting expeditions in the 1920s and 1930s.

On the third floor is the **Margaret Mead Hall of Pacific Peoples,** reflecting the studies of anthropologist Margaret Meade, who worked in the museum's Anthropology Department until her death in 1978. Other halls on the floor include ones devoted to reptiles and amphibians, eastern Woodland and Plains Indians, primates, and North American birds.

Six halls on the grandly restored fourth floor follow 500 million

years of the evolution of vertebrates—animals with backbones. The **Miriam and Ira D. Wallace Orientation Center** and the **Hall of Vertebrate Origins** introduce the story. Start by viewing "The Evolution of Vertebrates," a video presentation narrated by Meryl Streep, shown in the 200-seat theater. The **Hall of Saurishian Dinosaurs** (those that could walk upright) include mounted skeletons of *Tyrannosaurus rex* and *Apatosaurus,* the latter sporting a longer tail after a recent reinstallation. The **Hall of Ornithischian Dinosaurs** includes the armored *Stegosaurus,* discovered in Wyoming, and *Styracosaurus,* with a spiked neck and nose. Two halls in the **Lila Acheson Wallace Wing of Mammals and Their Extinct Relatives** showcase 250 fossils, among them mastodons, saber-toothed cats, and giant sloths. Highlights are a baby mammoth and a 12-million-year-old horse, *Protohippus.*

Throughout the museum are opportunities for shopping, dining, and entertainment: the Dino Store, the Junior Store, and the Main Shop; the Naturemax Theater featuring IMAX films; the Diner Saurus cafeteria; and the Garden Café.

The museum moved to its present site in 1874. President Ulysses S. Grant laid the cornerstone for the first building, a high Victorian Gothic structure designed by Vaux and Mould, which has been almost completely swallowed up by additions to the museum.

The equestrian statue at the museum's main entrance is by James Earle Fraser and shows a vigorous Theodore Roosevelt, flanked by two native guides, one African, the other American Indian.

In its beginnings, the museum consisted mostly of mounted birds and fishes; in the modern era, the museum has strived to exhibit its specimens in the most educational and compelling manner. Thus, the **Hall of Human Biology and Evolution** contains dioramas of our hominid ancestors in action that capture the drama inherent in the story of man. Similarly, the dioramas in the **Akeley Memorial Hall of African Mammals** *(second floor)* are startlingly realistic in their detail and presentation. The hall is named for Carl Akeley, one of many great scientists and taxidermists associated with the museum over the years. Constant demonstrations, talks, and special events—such as the popular "Butterfly Conservatory" (an annual event), or a "Meet the Astronauts" day, make any visit to the museum a surefire hit. This grand institution always surprises and delivers more than one could possibly expect. ∎

The Rose Center

Rose Center for Earth and Space

✉ Central Park West at 81st St.

☎ 212/769-5100; advance tickets for Hayden Planetarium 212/769-5200

💲 $$$–$$$$$ (suggested donation)

🚇 Subway: C to 81st St.

Rose Center for Earth and Space

Described as both a metaphorical tour de force and one of the city's newest architectural icons, the center provides a dramatic portal into a multisensory experience of the universe.

Its heart is a gleaming glass cube enveloping the four-million-pound Hayden Sphere. In the re-created Hayden Planetarium, visitors experience outer space via the world's largest and most powerful virtual reality simulator. Other areas include the Hall of Planet Earth (HoPE), the Hall of the Universe, the Scales of the Universe, and the dynamic Cosmic Pathway, a spiraling ramp that ushers visitors through 13 billion years of cosmic evolution. ∎

Central Park West

CENTRAL PARK WEST IS A GRAND COUNTERPART TO THE Upper East Side. The East Side has its millionaires' mansions, but the West Side is graced by the dramatic silhouette of four twin-towered apartment buildings and a fifth with three towers. These five monumental structures, the Century, the Majestic, the San Remo, the Beresford (with three towers), and the Eldorado, were constructed between 1929 and 1931. They are found at intervals between West 62nd and West 91st Streets.

Several of the buildings were either built or commissioned by the Irwin Chanin Company. Chanin first encountered art deco at the 1925 Paris Exposition and, on his return, introduced the style in his New York buildings, including the 1931 **Century Apartments** *(25 Central Park W. at 62nd to 63rd Sts.).* The **New York Society for Ethical Culture** *(2 W. 64th St., tel 212/874-5210)* is an austere art nouveau building of 1910. This humanist religious organization was instrumental in the founding of the ACLU and the NAACP. The heavily ornamental art deco brick building at 55 Central Park West *(corner of 66th St.)* was the setting for the 1984 film *Ghostbusters.*

At 1 West 67th Street, the **Hotel des Artistes** opened in 1918. Residents of the kitchenless apartments ordered their meals from the **Café des Artistes** on the ground floor. Although the apartments now have kitchens, the café has remained one of the city's most popular restaurants *(tel 212/877-3500).* Architect Henry J. Hardenbergh's **Dakota Apartments** *(1 W. 72nd St.)* were completed in 1884. The German Renaissance–style structure was named after the Dakota Territory, in response to criticism of the building's then remote location. Its many celebrity occupants have included actress Lauren Bacall, singer Roberta Flack, and Yoko Ono and John Lennon, who was shot out front in 1980. The **San Remo** (1930), between 74th and 75th Streets, features neoclassical trim and circular Roman towers. Past the beaux arts New-York Historical Society (see pp. 182–83) and the American Museum of Natural History (see pp. 184–86), the **Beresford** *(211 Central Park W. at 81st St.),* another Emery Roth

apartment building, has three baroque towers. In the 1950s, resident Alan Jay Lerner wrote the lyrics for *My Fair Lady* here. The 1931 **Eldorado** *(300 Central Park W. between 90th and 91st Sts.)* has art deco trim. Novelist Sinclair Lewis lived here in the 1940s in what he described as a "gaudy flat, a cross between Elizabeth Arden's Beauty Salon and the horse-stables at the Ringling Circus Winter Quarters." ■

The Dakota Apartments were built in 1884.

Some small Upper West Side museums

CHILDREN'S MUSEUM OF MANHATTAN

Four floors are devoted to educational activities and hands-on exhibits for children, including a room of children's books and a television studio.
✉ 212 W. 83rd St. ☎ 212/721-1234
🕐 Closed Mon.–Tues.; summer closed Mon.
💲 $$ 🚇 Subway: 1 to 86th St.; B to 81st St.

THE MUSEUM OF BIBLICAL ART

The American Bible Society, which houses the museum on its second floor, was founded in 1816 to disseminate the Bible without involving doctrine or creeds. Museum exhibits explore artistic expressions of faith from various times and in all media. Visitors can also view a full-size replica of the Gutenberg printing press and Helen Keller's Braille Bibles.
✉ 1865 Broadway at 61st St. ☎ 212/408-1500 🕐 Closed Mon. 💲 Free 🚇 Subway: A, B, C, D, 1 to 59th St./Columbus Circle

NICHOLAS ROERICH MUSEUM

This museum is dedicated to the works of Russian-born Nicholas Roerich (1874–1947), a mystic, Theosophist, philosopher, stage designer, painter, and writer. He was nominated for a Nobel Peace Prize for his proposal (passed as the Roerich Pact in 1935) that important cultural, scientific, and religious sites be protected by treaty in wartime as in peacetime. The museum contains about 200 of his paintings, examples of his writings, and art objects from his collection.
✉ 319 W. 107th St. at Riverside Drive
☎ 212/864-7752 🕐 Closed Mon. & a.m. daily 💲 $$ 🚇 Subway: 1 to 110th St. ■

Above: Learning through play at the Children's Museum
Below: The Nicholas Roerich Museum

U neven terrain here provides a dramatic setting for some of the city's greatest assets—among them a medieval cloister, a renowned university, and an immense cathedral. The area is also a melting pot of different races and ethnic groups.

The Heights & Harlem

Introduction & map 190–191
Cathedral Church of St. John
  the Divine 192
Columbia University 193
General Grant National Memorial
  194–195
Audubon Terrace 195
The Cloisters Museum & nearby
  196–197
In & around Harlem 198–199
Schomburg Center for Research
  in Black Culture 202
Restaurants 254–255

An arcade at The Cloisters

The Heights & Harlem

AS THE ISLAND OF MANHATTAN NARROWS AT ITS NORTHERN END, IT ALSO rises in an undulating and disorderly sequence of rocky outcroppings, escarpments, ridges, plateaus, and bluffs until it reaches its greatest elevation—267.75 feet—near where Fort Washington once stood. Here, during the Revolution, American troops made a last stand against the British before they were driven from the island.

Northern Manhattan, once exclusively home to the landed gentry, is made up of several historic neighborhoods. At the northernmost tip is ethnically diverse Inwood, where, some believe, Peter Minuit "bought" the island from the Indians.

To the south is Washington Heights, today home to immigrants from the Dominican Republic, since the mid-1960s the fastest growing ethnic group in the city. Here the streets teem with life, shops are called bodegas, and Spanish is the preferred language.

Farther south is Hamilton Heights, home to Ecuadoreans, Chinese, Dominicans, and African Americans, among others. Within Hamilton Heights is Sugar Hill (*W. 141st St. to W. 145th St.*), since early in the 20th century a neighborhood of well-to-do African Americans.

Finally, between 125th and 110th Streets, is Morningside Heights, where Columbia University—nearly 20,000 students enrolled in its 16 schools—and its women's affiliate, Barnard College, are at the heart of a lively, student-oriented neighborhood.

The eastern section of northern Manhattan is Harlem, world-famous in the 1920s as a vital center of African-American culture. Harlem was Jewish, German, and Irish until 1905, when an African-American realtor, Philip A. Payton, rented apartments to African Americans in a building on West 133rd Street. A few years later there were so many African Americans in Harlem that the *Harlem Home News* warned against "black hordes that stand ready to destroy homes and scatter fortunes of the whites living and doing business in the very heart of Harlem." By 1930, Harlem had a high concentration of African Americans. Today, the demographics are shifting and national chains are investing in this prime marketplace. As you exit the subway, a Starbucks awaits, along with the famed Apollo.

When northern Manhattan was truly the hinterlands, Manhattanites such as Alexander Hamilton and John James Audubon owned large tracts of land there. Today their names live on: in Hamilton Heights, where Hamilton's House still stands, and the Audubon Ballroom, remembered as the place where the African-American nationalist leader Malcolm X was assassinated in 1965. On the northern edge of Harlem is onetime Coogan's Bluff, a turn-of-the-20th-century neighborhood on the Harlem River between 155th and 160th Streets. Here the revered Polo Grounds once stood, home of the New York Giants from the 1890s until the baseball team moved to San Francisco in 1957.

Fort Tryon Park, with its splendid view of the Hudson River, is the location of the Cloisters Museum, a branch of the Metropolitan Museum of Art and the best assemblage of medieval art and architectural elements in America. Near Columbia in Morningside Heights is the Cathedral Church of St. John the Divine, the largest Gothic cathedral in the world. In Riverside Park, the General Grant National Memorial (restored in 1997) was once one of the city's premier attractions.

Audubon Terrace is an enclave of buildings housing cultural institutions, such as the American Academy and Institute of Arts and Letters, which celebrated its centennial in 1998. At 112th Street and Broadway, the Goddard Institute for Space Studies is an affiliate of the National Aeronautics and Space Administration (*tel 212/678-5500*). The Union Theological Seminary (*tel 212/662-7100*), a nondenominational institution, is located in a Gothic quadrangle north of Columbia; since its founding in 1836, it has had some of the country's most distinguished theologians on its faculty.

Even today northern Manhattan's distance from the city's center makes some reluctant to explore here. A certain caution about the area is advisable; some parts are unsafe. On the other hand, an economic revival is under way, and no one should hesitate to seek out the great treasures of the area. Many available tours make this easy to do. ■

THE HEIGHTS & HARLEM

1 Dyckman Farmhouse Museum
2 Morris-Jumel Mansion 3 Mother African Methodist Episcopal Zion Church
4 Studio Museum in Harlem

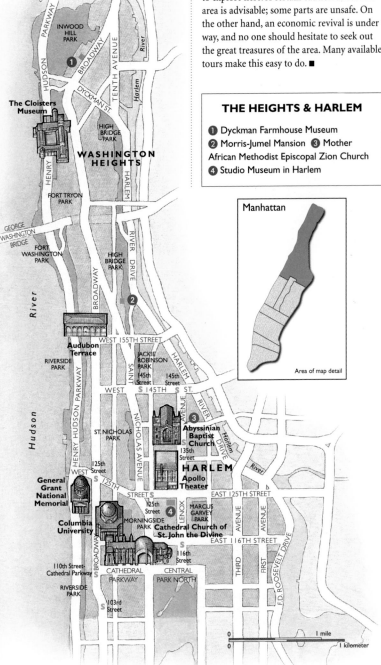

Manhattan

Area of map detail

INWOOD HILL PARK

The Cloisters Museum

WASHINGTON HEIGHTS

HIGH BRIDGE PARK

FORT TRYON PARK

GEORGE WASHINGTON BRIDGE

FORT WASHINGTON PARK

HIGH BRIDGE PARK

RIVERSIDE PARK

Hudson River

Audubon Terrace

WEST 155TH STREET

JACKIE ROBINSON PARK

145th Street   145th Street

WEST 145TH ST.

ST. NICHOLAS PARK

Abyssinian Baptist Church

135th Street

HARLEM

Apollo Theater

General Grant National Memorial

WEST 125th Street

125th Street

EAST 125TH STREET

MARCUS GARVEY PARK

Columbia University

MORNINGSIDE PARK

Cathedral Church of St. John the Divine

116th Street

EAST 116TH STREET

110th Street-Cathedral Parkway

CATHEDRAL PARKWAY

CENTRAL PARK NORTH

RIVERSIDE PARK

103rd Street

0   1 mile
0   1 kilometer

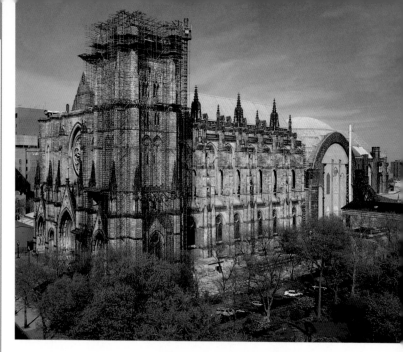

Begun in 1892,
St. John the
Divine remains
unfinished.

Cathedral Church of St. John the Divine

BECAUSE IT HAS TAKEN MORE THAN A CENTURY TO BUILD, the Cathedral Church of St. John the Divine in Morningside Heights has had, for many years, the distinction of being both a historic landmark (not an official one) and a work in progress.

Cathedral Church of St. John the Divine (Episcopal)

www.stjohndivine.org

- Map p. 191
- Amsterdam Ave. at W. 112th St.
- 212/316-7540
- Donation
- Subway: 1 to Cathedral Parkway (110th St.)

The cornerstone was laid on St. John's Day, December 27, 1892. The construction of the choir and crossing was begun in the Byzantine-Romanesque style. In 1911, architect Ralph Adam Crams took over; his nave and west front were in French Gothic style. Construction ceased during World War II, resuming in 1979. Although damaged by fire in 2001, the cathedral continues to evolve and extend its social activism mission.

A CHURCH FOR ALL

The Episcopal bishop at the time construction began was Henry Codman Potter, the "people's bishop," who believed the cathedral should serve all creeds, nations, and levels of society. St. John's today lives up to this philosophy, engaging in community service and work among the poor, even making it a priority over the completion of the cathedral. The church also reaches out to the larger population through its many events, from concerts to art exhibits, lectures, theater, and special holiday offerings. The main attraction, however, remains the incredible structure itself. You can marvel at the beauteous interior—the nave alone is 248 feet long and 124 feet high; more than 10,000 pieces of glass are in the 40-foot-diameter Great Rose Window. ∎

Columbia University

AS A LEADING MEMBER OF THE ELITE BAND OF EAST COAST universities known as the Ivy League, Columbia University, located in upper Manhattan's Morningside Heights, is both an integral part of New York City and its history and apart from it.

But Columbia is no ivory tower isolated from the general population. While there is a large distinct quad, there are many places in its seven-block campus (between Amsterdam Avenue and Broadway) where you can pass between the campus and the city streets without knowing it. The **Wallach Art Gallery** has changing exhibits, curated by faculty and students, in the fields of art history and visual arts. Visitors enjoy the adjacent streets, especially the secondhand bookstores and the coffeehouses along Broadway and Amsterdam, including the West End *(2911 Broadway).*

FROM DOWNTOWN TO UPTOWN

Chartered in 1754 as King's College, the school first met in the schoolhouse of Trinity Church in Lower Manhattan. Colonial-era graduates included Alexander Hamilton, John Jay, and DeWitt Clinton. Renamed Columbia after the American Revolution, it moved to Madison Avenue and 49th Street in 1857, to land it had received in 1814 as a windfall from the legislature. Formerly the Elgin Botanical Gardens, this tract of land on Fifth Avenue between 47th and 51st Streets (which Columbia owned until 1985) eventually became home to Rockefeller Center. The school moved to its Morningside Heights campus in 1897.

At its heart was domed **Low Library,** modeled on the Roman Pantheon, which sits at the head of an expanse of stairs. It is named for Seth Low, donor of the library,

Columbia's president from 1890 to 1901, and a key figure in Columbia's development. He moved the university to Morningside Heights, added the School of Nursing and Teachers' College, and strengthened ties with Barnard, the women's college affiliated with Columbia. In 1934, Low Library was turned into administrative offices. However, it remains—together with Daniel Chester French's larger-than-life bronze statue, "Alma Mater" (1903),

Columbia University
www.columbia.edu
🗺 Map p. 191
✉ Broadway & W. 116th St.
☎ 212/854-1754; visitor center and tours: 212/854-4900
🕐 Closed Sat.–Sun.
🚇 Subway: 1 to 116th St.

Wallach Art Gallery
✉ Schermerhorn Hall
☎ 212/854-7288
🕐 Closed Sun.–Tues. & a.m. daily

at the foot of the library's steps—a symbol of a great university.

Among other campus buildings, **St. Paul's Chapel** on the main quad, and McKim, Mead & White's 1927 **Casa Italiana** on Amsterdam Avenue, stand out. ∎

Daniel Chester French sculptured the "Alma Mater" on the steps of Columbia University's Low Library.

General Grant National Memorial

General Grant National Memorial

www.nps.gov/gegr

🏔 Map p. 191

✉ Riverside Dr. & W. 122nd St.

☎ 212/666-1640

🕐 Daily 9 a.m.–5 p.m.

🚇 Subway: 1 to 116th St.–Broadway

The tomb of Ulysses S. Grant, the only U.S. President buried in New York City, overlooks the Hudson River.

General Grant National Memorial

GRANT'S TOMB, THE LARGEST MAUSOLEUM IN THE UNITED States, was until World War I one of the most popular sights in New York City. A former President of the United States, a native of the Midwest, and victorious commander of Union forces in the Civil War, Ulysses S. Grant (1822–1885) moved to New York in 1884.

Grant was immensely popular when he died. One million people observed his funeral procession in 1885. Mayor William R. Grace donated the land for the tomb, and the Grant Memorial Association raised $600,000 (from about 90,000 contributors) to build it. President Benjamin Harrison laid the cornerstone in 1892, and President William McKinley attended the dedication on April 27, 1897.

Architect John H. Duncan, designer of the Brooklyn Soldiers' and Sailors' Memorial Arch, won the competition to design Grant's Tomb, which he based on such classical models as the Mausoleum at Halicarnassus. The 150-foot-tall granite tomb consists of a domed

rotunda ringed by Ionic columns atop a square base. Over the entrance, carved figures representing Victory and Peace flank a plaque inscribed with Grant's famous words, "Let Us Have Peace."

The interior of the tomb, a cruciform in Carrara marble, is based on Napoleon's Tomb in Paris. Grant's military victories and Lee's surrender at Appomattox are the subjects of mosaics above the windows. A double staircase leads down to the crypt where Grant and his wife, Julia Dent Grant, are interred. Bronze busts along the wall depict Grant's generals, among them William Tecumseh Sherman and

Philip Sheridan. The tomb was taken over by the National Park Service in 1959 and restored in 1997. Grant is the only U.S. President buried in New York City. ■

The tombs of Ulysses Grant and his wife, Julia Dent Grant, who died in 1902.

Audubon Terrace

This distinguished beaux arts complex was built beginning in 1904, on farm land that once belonged to painter and naturalist John James Audubon. Railroad magnate Archer Milton Huntington developed the site as a museum complex, with Spanish Renaissance buildings around a long plaza adorned by monumental statuary. Today these house the American Academy of Arts and Letters and the Hispanic Society of America, which Huntington founded in 1904. The American Geographic Society, the Museum of the American Indian–Heye Foundation, and the American Numismatic Society, once occupants here, have all since moved.

Also on the site, entered only via 156th Street, is the exquisite **Church of Our Lady of Esperanza.** Señora Doña Manuela de Laverrerie de Barril, wife of the Spanish consul-general in New York, founded it as a church for Spanish-speaking people. After her untimely death, Huntington saw the church through to com-

pletion in 1911. In 1912, Spain's King Alfonso III donated the stained-glass windows, skylight, and lamp.

The **American Academy of Arts and Letters,** an organization of artists and writers, limited to 250 living members, is housed in two buildings designed by McKim, Mead & White, and Cass Gilbert. These house the North and South Galleries, where annual exhibitions in March and May are open to the public. Original members included Henry Adams, William and Henry James, Theodore Roosevelt, Augustus Saint-Gaudens, John La Farge, and Mark Twain.

The **Hispanic Society of America** welcomes the public. Its free museum and reference library with more than 200,000 books and manuscripts are an outstanding resource for the study of the arts and cultures of Spain, Portugal, and Latin America. The surrounding neighborhood offers an extensive selection of Spanish and Latin American restaurants. ■

Audubon Terrace
 Map p. 191
Broadway, between
155th & 156th Sts.
Subway: 1 to
157th St.

American Academy of Arts and Letters
☎ 212/368-5900
🕐 Library by appt. only

Hispanic Society of America
☎ 212/926-2234
🕐 Closed Mon.

Church of Our Lady of Esperanza
 624 W. 156th St.
☎ 212/283-4340

Note: The American
Numismatic Society
moved in 2004 to
96 Fulton Street.
Tel. 212/571-4470.

The Cloisters Museum & nearby

WHAT BETTER LOCATION FOR A MEDIEVAL CLOISTER THAN a high and wooded point of land. In just such a place, on the far northern end of Manhattan, stands the Cloisters, devoted to art of the Middle Ages. Looking remarkably authentic, the building is actually from the 20th century, designed in a style evocative of medieval architecture and incorporating columns and stonework from French medieval abbeys. It opened to the public in 1938 as a branch museum of the Metropolitan Museum of Art. Many find a visit to the Cloisters a uniquely contemplative experience.

The Cloisters Museum

 Map p. 191

✉ Fort Tryon Park, W. 190th St. at Fort Washington Ave.

☎ 212/923-3700

🕐 Closed Mon.

💲 $$$ (donation)

🚇 Subway: A to 190th St.—Overlook Terrace

The arcades of four different medieval cloisters have been integrated into the modern Cloisters to create a sympathetic context for the exhibition of sculpture, tapestry, stained glass, metalwork, paintings, and manuscripts. "Cloister" denotes a covered walkway surrounding a large open courtyard with access to other monastic buildings. In similar manner, the museum's cloisters are passageways to galleries.

The nucleus of the Cloisters' collection, including large sections of the medieval buildings, was gathered by American sculptor George Grey Barnard (1863–1938) while living in France. In 1925, John D. Rockefeller, Jr., purchased the collection for the Metropolitan Museum of Art. He also provided the building and its Fort Tryon setting and donated works from his own collection.

FOUR CLOISTERS

The main level, where one enters, contains a number of gallery areas enclosing two cloisters. The capitals of the 12th-century **Cuxa**

Cloister have robust Romanesque carvings of double-bodied animals with a single head, a design that fits corners well. In the **St. Guilhem Cloister,** built about 804 by a peer of Charlemagne's court, drill holes in a honeycomb pattern embellish the capitals. On the lower level, **Tri Cloister** is from a 16th-century convent destroyed by Huguenots. And encompassing a medieval herb garden, the **Bonnefont Cloister** is from the late 13th or early 14th century. Its naturalistic floral decorations were a reaction to grotesque Romanesque carvings.

The museum is organized in roughly chronological manner, beginning with art from the Romanesque period, continuing through the Gothic era, and ending with the flowering of medieval art around 1520. Although every space contains superb art, especially popular on the main floor are the 15th-century stained-glass panels in the **Boppard Room;** the idealized funerary monument in the **Gothic Chapel** of a crusader knight portrayed as young man, eyes open and hands joined in prayer; and the **Unicorn Tapestries Room,** where six woven tapestries (circa 16th century, Brussels) tell an allegorical story of the Incarnation of Christ. Downstairs, the **Treasury** displays small objects, such as a 12th-century walrus ivory cross, while the **Glass Gallery** contains glass, sculpture, and tapestries.

You will also want to visit the excellent gift shop and bookstore, try out the café, and take advantage of the spectacular views of the Hudson River from the grounds. Be forewarned: Some bus tours leave you at the base of the hill, so expect a walk.

NEARBY SITES

Built in 1765 by a British military officer, Roger Morris, the **Morris-** **Jumel Mansion** was George Washington's headquarters for a month in 1776 before the British took it over. A French merchant, Stephen Jumel, and his American wife, Eliza Bowen, restored it in 1810. After Jumel's death, the former prostitute was married briefly to Aaron Burr, formerly vice president. The house, a museum since 1904, is noted for its Palladian portico, an octagon room, and Georgian interiors.

The **Dyckman Farmhouse Museum,** a Dutch colonial house, with gambrel roof and overhanging eaves, belonged until 1871 to the Dyckman family. They were owners of Manhattan's largest farm in colonial times, some 300 acres

surrounding the house. The house was rebuilt in 1783 after the British destroyed it before evacuating the city. Early in the 20th century two Dyckman descendants purchased the house, furnished it in period style, and then donated it to the city. Manhattan's only remaining farmhouse, it opened as a museum in 1916. There is a formal garden in the rear. ■

Morris-Jumel Mansion

www.morrisjumel.org

- Map p. 191
- 65 Jumel Terrace
- 212/923-8008
- Closed Mon.–Tues.
- $
- Subway: C to 163rd St.

Visitors resting in a cloistered walkway

Dyckman Farmhouse Museum

www.dyckmanfarmhouse.org

- Map p. 191
- 4881 Broadway at W. 204th St.
- 212/304-9422
- Closed Mon.–Tues.
- $
- Subway: A to 207th St.

In & around Harlem

Abyssinian Baptist Church

www.abyssinian.org

 Map p. 191

✉ 132 Odell Clark Pl. W. at 138th St.

☎ 212/862-7474

🚇 Subway: 2, 3 to 135th St.

Harlem Heritage Tours

www.harlemheritage.com

☎ 212/280-7888

🕐 Tours daily

💲 $–$$$. Reservation required.

125th Street is a thriving business corridor in the heart of Harlem.

STRETCHING FROM 110TH TO 168TH STREET, HARLEM IS one of the city's most vibrant neighborhoods. New York City's nickname "The Big Apple" came from a jazz club here, and many know Harlem as home to the Apollo Theater and the Harlem Renaissance (see pp. 200–201). Of great excitement now is a second renaissance under way, in commerce, culture, property redevelopment, and tourism. Former residents are returning, and new ones—even a former U.S. President, Bill Clinton—are moving in. There are plans for both the National Jazz Museum and the National Black Sports & Entertainment Hall of Fame.

The **St. Nicholas Historic District,** a late 19th-century development of four blockfronts along West 138th and 139th Streets, is the work of three prominent architects—James Brown Lord, Bruce Price, and Stanford White. During the 1920s the development, known as Striver's Row, was home to many prominent blacks, including surgeon Louis T. Wright, architect Vertner Tandy, and bandleader Fletcher Henderson. Redevelopment between 134th and 136th Streets is introducing boutiques, restaurants, and jazz clubs.

Close by is the **Abyssinian Baptist Church,** known for its prominent minister, Adam Clayton Powell, Jr. (1908–1972), the first black congressman from New York City. Founded in 1808, its church building dates from 1923. **Mother African Methodist Episcopal Zion Church** (140 W. 137th St.) is the oldest black congregation in New York. George W. Foster, Jr., one of the country's first black architects, designed the neo-Gothic building, completed in 1925. Foster collaborated with Vertner Tandy on the 1911 neo-Gothic

St. Philip's Episcopal Church *(214 W. 134th St.).*

Hamilton Heights Historic District, on Harlem's western edge, includes the fine collection of row houses known as Sugar Hill, built in 1886–1906 on land once belonging to Alexander Hamilton. To the south is the **North Campus of City College** *(Convent Ave. between W. 138th and W. 140th Sts.),* a collection of Gothic buildings constructed in the early 20th century.

The **Mount Morris Park Historic District,** which contains a number of landmark churches and some of the city's finest brownstones, received government and private rehabilitation funding in the late 1990s. The neighborhood takes its name from the park in its center (renamed Marcus Garvey Park in 1973, after the black nationalist leader), which has the city's only remaining fire watchtower. The 1888 **St. Martin's Episcopal Church & Rectory** has been called the finest Romanesque Revival religious complex in the city; it also possesses the smaller (42 bells) of the city's two carillons (the other is at Riverside Church in Morningside Heights). The **Greater Metropolitan Baptist Church** *(147 W. 123rd St.)* was built in the late 19th century.

New businesses and revitalization efforts are enriching Harlem's main east–west thoroughfare, 125th Street (Martin Luther King Boulevard). Upscale stores, multiplex cinemas, and a rejuvenated **Apollo Theater** attract droves of visitors. Built in 1914, the Apollo began featuring black entertainers, such as Bill "Bojangles" Robinson, in the 1930s. Since then, virtually every top black performer has appeared here. Whoopi Goldberg recently drew raves.

Also on 125th Street—at Adam Clayton Powell, Jr., Boulevard (Seventh Avenue)—**Hotel Theresa,** known in its heyday as the Waldorf of Harlem, still stands, although it is now an office building called Theresa Towers. Built in 1913 when 125th Street was a white area, the Theresa did not admit blacks until 1940; by 1946, it was celebrated as "social headquarters for Negro America." Heavyweight champion Joe Louis and musicians and singers Duke Ellington, Lena Horne, and Paul Robeson were among its celebrity guests. From 1948 to 1953, the hotel was the childhood home of late Secretary of Commerce Ron Brown, whose father was manager. By the mid-1950s the Theresa's popularity was declining. In the early 1960s the hotel housed Malcolm X's Organization of Afro-American Unity.

Though Harlem's main street changes, its authenticity remains—in historic sites, sidewalk vendors, and proprietor-run shops, clubs, and restaurants. ■

A colorful mural on a building side

St. Martin's Episcopal Church & Rectory

- Map p. 191
- 230 Lenox Ave.
- 212/534-4531
- Bells are still played on Sundays and for special occasions such as weddings
- Subway: 2, 3 to 135th St.

Apollo Theater

- Map p. 191
- 253 W. 125th St.
- Info: 212/531-5305; tours: 212/531-5337 ($$); tickets: 212/307-7171 (Ticketmaster)
- Subway: A, B, C to 125th St.

Harlem Renaissance

The cultural flowering of black New York, a period known as the Harlem Renaissance, took place in the liberating years of the 1920s. The black artists, writers, and musicians who gathered in Harlem shared the belief that black culture had the power to improve the status of their race. It was also the first time that black intellectuals looked to Africa, folk culture, and black heroes as a source of racial pride.

The roots of the renaissance have been traced back to *The Souls of Black Folks* (1903), a collection of essays by writer and civil rights leader W. E. B. Du Bois. In it he wrote the oft-quoted: "The problem of the twentieth century is the problem of the color-line." Du Bois was also editor of *The Crisis: A Record of the Darker Races*, a magazine published in 1910 by the National Association for the Advancement of Colored People (NAACP). In its pages, he encouraged blacks to relate to their common African heritage—a philosophy known as Pan-Africanism. Du Bois was an elitist, who pinned his hopes for blacks on what he called the "New Negro" and the "Talented Tenth," the privileged group that "rises and pulls all that are worthy of saving up to their vantage ground."

An all-black musical revue, *Shuffle Along*, which opened on Broadway in 1921, giving, in the words of African-American poet Langston Hughes (1902–1967), "a scintillating sendoff to that Negro Vogue in Manhattan," is often cited as the beginning of the Harlem Renaissance. The revue was written by songwriters Eubie Blake and Noble Sissle. Although the production, which starred Florence Mills, was not much more than a sophisticated minstrel show, it paved the way for other black shows on Broadway and made black entertainers the rage with whites, who flocked to Harlem to hear the likes of Fletcher Henderson, Cab Calloway, and Duke Ellington at the Cotton Club and other nightspots.

It was in literature that the spirit of the Harlem Renaissance was best expressed. An early work was "If We Must Die," a sonnet written in 1919 by Claude McKay, a Jamaican

Author Zora Neale Hurston

immigrant who has been called the Harlem Renaissance's first celebrity. A response to violence against blacks, the poem ended: "Like men we'll face the murderous, cowardly pack / Pressed to the wall, dying, but fighting back!" Other literary highlights included the mid-decade publication of poetry by Countee Cullen and Langston Hughes by mainstream publishing houses.

Zora Neale Hurston published her first short story in 1925, in *Opportunity, a Journal of Negro Life*, a publication edited by African-American sociologist Charles Johnson. Johnson, a literary mentor to many young African Americans, organized a dinner in 1924 to introduce the cream of the Harlem writers to the white publishing establishment. As a result of the dinner, the editors of a white magazine, *Graphic Survey*, invited Alain Locke, a Phi Beta Kappa graduate of Harvard (1907) and the first African-American Rhodes Scholar, to put together a special issue on "the progressive spirit of contemporary Negro life." The issue became a landmark book, *The New Negro*.

In 1926 white author Carl Van Vechten (a "Negrotarian," as whites attracted to Harlem were called) published a best-selling novel about Harlem. His book increased interest in Harlem among whites, although it was controversial among blacks.

Harlem's Cotton Club in its heyday

Artists are probably the least remembered from the decade, with the exception of photographer James VanDerZee, who documented the movement and whose work is well represented at the Studio Museum in Harlem (see p. 202). Illustrator Aaron Douglas did covers for the journal *Opportunity*. Painter William H. Johnson specialized in primitive-style paintings of religious themes. Augusta Savage was the Harlem Renaissance's best-known sculptor and ran the Savage Studio of Arts and Crafts, which reached out to younger artists.

The crash of 1929 and the ensuing Depression effectively killed the Harlem Renaissance. During the 1930s, unemployment in Harlem was five times that of the rest of the city. Looking back on that time, most participants realized that cultural ferment in Harlem had failed to benefit blacks as a whole.

As Langston Hughes succinctly put it: "The ordinary Negroes hadn't heard of the Negro Renaissance. And if they had, it hadn't raised their wages any." ■

Langston Hughes (1902–1967)

Duke Ellington (1899–1974)

Schomburg Center for Research in Black Culture

Schomburg Center for Research in Black Culture
www.schomburg.org

🅰 Map p. 191
✉ 515 Lenox Ave.
   at 135th St.
☎ 212/491-2200
🕐 Closed Sun.–Mon.
🚇 Subway: 2, 3
   to 135th St.

Studio Museum in Harlem
www.studiomuseum.org

✉ 144 W. 125th St.
☎ 212/864-4500
🕐 Closed Mon.–Tues.
💲 $
🚇 Subway: 2, 3
   to 125th St.

"Midsummer Night in Harlem," a painting by Palma Hayden (1883–1973), at the Schomburg Center

NAMED FOR ARTHUR A. SCHOMBURG (1874–1938), A BLACK Puerto Rican bibliophile, collector, and scholar, the center is one of the best research facilities in the world for the study of the black experience. Among more than five million items in the collection are 125,000 books, 400 black newspapers, and 1,000 periodicals. Rare books include early editions of the poetry of Phyllis Wheatley, an American slave, and Richard Wright's *Native Son*, in the original manuscript. Its facilities include a theater, art galleries, and a well-stocked bookstore/gift shop.

The center's collection is based on material Schomburg compiled after moving to New York from Puerto Rico in 1891. In 1911 he cofounded the Negro Society for Historical Research. In 1926, the Carnegie Foundation purchased his collection—described as "the most extensive collection of Afro-American history and culture in America" (5,000 books, 3,000 manuscripts, 2,000 etchings, and several thousand pamphlets)—for $10,000 and gave it to the New York Public Library. Shortly afterward, the library moved the collection to Harlem to the 135th Street Branch Division of Negro Literature, where Schomburg served as its curator from 1932 until his death in 1938. The branch library was housed in a 1905 building where renaissance writers often met. In 1980, the collection was moved to a new adjacent building; the original building was redone as gallery space for exhibits. ■

STUDIO MUSEUM IN HARLEM

Founded in 1967 to provide studio space for Harlem artists, the Studio Museum soon developed into a leading museum of black culture housed, since 1982, in its present spacious quarters. Its permanent collection includes paintings by Romare Bearden, Jacob Lawrence, and Faith Ringgold and photography by James VanDerZee (1886–1983) and Gordon Parks. In the late 1970s the museum merged with the James VanDerZee Institute—named for the well-known Harlem photographer and founded to promote the photography of young blacks—and acquired a large collection of his work. The museum sponsors workshops, lectures, artists-in-residence, and films and has a shop selling books and African crafts. ■

Nw York's four vast
outer boroughs—
Brooklyn, Staten Island, the
Bronx, and Queens—offer
museums, parks, and open
space, along with rich ethnic
communities and some of the
oldest buildings in the city.

The Outer Boroughs

Introduction & map **204–205**
Brooklyn 206–214
Brooklyn Heights walk **206–207**
Prospect Park & environs **208**
Park Slope Historic District **209**
Brooklyn Museum of Art
210–212
Brooklyn Botanic Garden **213**
Coney Island **214**
Staten Island 215–218
In & around Staten Island **215**
Alice Austen House **216**
Historic Richmond Town **217**
More Staten Island sites **218**
The Bronx 219–222
In & around the Bronx **219**
New York Botanical Garden **220**
Bronx Zoo **221**
More sites in the Bronx **222**
Queens 223–226
In & around Queens **223–224**
Museum of Modern Art Queens
204
Museum of the Moving Image **225**
Isamu Noguchi Garden
Museum **226**
Nearby sites **226**
Restaurants **255**

Brooklyn Bridge detail

The Outer Boroughs

GONE ARE THE DAYS WHEN A VISIT TO THE OUTER BOROUGHS WAS a maybe on the list of things to do in New York. Today your top ten destinations will likely include at least one borough. There is something for everyone, from the "Artloop" of museums in Queens; to Arthur Avenue, the Little Italy of the Bronx; to Brooklyn's historic Prospect Park. For those drawn to water, nothing can beat the Staten Island Ferry.

Leading the list of family attractions is the Bronx Zoo, free on Wednesdays. If you are interested in gardening, plan a trip to the equally renowned Bronx Botanical Garden.

Brooklyn also has outstanding cultural institutions. The Brooklyn Academy of Music, known as BAM, is a preeminent performing arts center, housed in a neo-Italianate building and known for its avant-garde programming. The Brooklyn Museum of Art (see pp. 210–212) is an institution that would be the pride of any city.

Some people believe Staten Island is the city's undiscovered treasure; Staten Islanders know this, and many have wanted to secede from the city for decades. It offers unique museums and more colonial-era buildings than anywhere else in the city.

Queens, the largest borough, is a rich cultural tapestry. Its immigrant populations give it a vital, ethnic flavor, especially in its restaurants. But it is the influx of cultural organizations that has caused a spike in tourism. P.S.1 Contemporary Art Center broke new ground when it opened its vast exhibit space in 1997, and in 2000 when it formalized its affiliation with MoMA. MoMA's 2002–2005 temporary relocation of their Manhattan programs to MoMA Queens further boosted the borough's profile in the arts. MoMA Queens is now used for offices and collection storage. The Queens Council of the Arts (tel 718/647-3377) offers free illustrated maps to the Artloop in western Queens and other attractions.

For sports and outdoor recreation, the boroughs are a paradise. Baseball fans

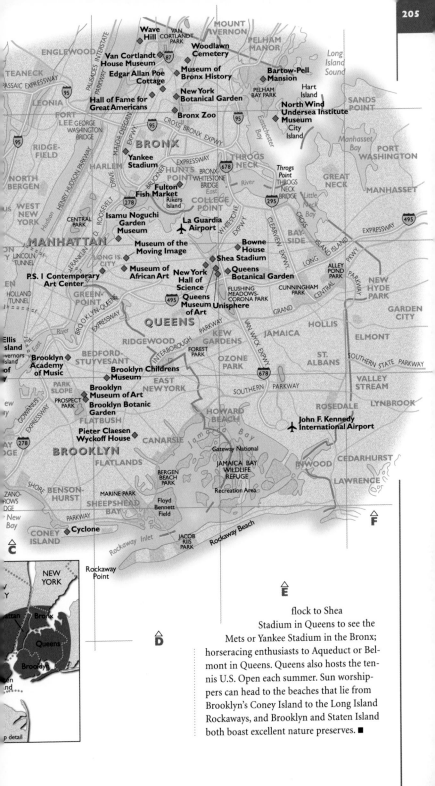

flock to Shea Stadium in Queens to see the Mets or Yankee Stadium in the Bronx; horseracing enthusiasts to Aqueduct or Belmont in Queens. Queens also hosts the tennis U.S. Open each summer. Sun worshippers can head to the beaches that lie from Brooklyn's Coney Island to the Long Island Rockaways, and Brooklyn and Staten Island both boast excellent nature preserves. ■

Brooklyn Heights walk

Brooklyn Heights was developed in the early 1800s as the city's first suburb; many of its streets—Pierrepont, Hicks, Middagh, Remsen, Joralemon—are named for early landowners. Today it is a living museum of residential architecture, and the city's first historic district. Just a brief distance from Wall Street by subway, or a quick walk across the Brooklyn Bridge, this is a cohesive, well-kept neighborhood, where such well-known writers as Walt Whitman and Truman Capote lived and where many prominent people still reside. Go there to escape busy Manhattan, to enjoy views from the Brooklyn Promenade, and to absorb the atmosphere of 19th-century privilege and contentment its tranquil streets exude.

Start at **Borough Hall** ❶ (*209 Joralemon St.*)—a subway stop—a highly regarded marble Greek Revival building constructed between 1845 and 1848 as the Brooklyn City Hall and renamed Borough Hall after the 1898 consolidation with Manhattan and the other boroughs. Continue west on Joralemon Street to No. 170. The colleges of Oxford and Cambridge were the model for Minard Lafever's Gothic Revival **Packer Collegiate Institute** (1856), among the city's oldest private schools.

Turn right onto Henry Street and head north toward Remsen Street. The (Congregational) Church of the Pilgrims (1846) here was designed by Richard Upjohn in the Romanesque Revival style with typical rounded arches. A Victorian addition was made in 1869. In 1994, the church merged with Plymouth Church (see p. 207), and the building was sold to **Our Lady of Lebanon Cathedral** ❷. Continue on Henry Street to Montague Street and turn right to the Holy Trinity Church (Episcopal), on Clinton at Montague Street. Now **St. Ann and the Holy Trinity Episcopal Church** ❸ (*tel 718/875-6960*), this church was also designed by Lafever. When built in 1844–47, it was the largest church in Brooklyn. The red sandstone exterior and the stained-glass windows by William and John Bolton have been restored.

Turn left on Clinton Street and left again on Pierrepont Street to No. 128, the **Brooklyn Historical Society** ❹ (*tel 718/222-4111, closed Sun.–Tues.*), where many unusual Brooklyn artifacts are exhibited. The Renaissance-style exterior has terra-cotta ornamentation, and its interior is a designated landmark. (The society's building has been undergoing extensive renovations since 1999, and construction is ongoing.) Built between 1842 and 1844 at Pierrepont Street and Monroe Place, the **First Unitarian Congregational Society** ❺ (*tel 718/624-5466*) is widely considered to be one of Lafever's masterpieces.

Continue on Pierrepont to Willow Street and turn right. This pleasant street has fine examples of residential architecture. Note Nos. 108, 110, and 112 on the west side, whose bay windows, dormers, towers, and doorways make them examples of the 1880s shingle style. Across the street, an earlier stable at 151 and 155–159 Willow Street was, according to legend, linked to a tunnel used for the Underground Railroad.

Turn left on Clark, and then right, which places you on the romantic **Brooklyn Promenade** ❻ or Esplanade, a parklike, cantilevered walkway completed in 1950 over the Brooklyn Queens Expressway. Running between Remsen and Orange Streets, it has incomparable views of the harbor, the Brooklyn Bridge, and Lower Manhattan and is a frequent film location. You may remember it from the film *Saturday Night Fever*.

With the water on your left, pass Pineapple Street, turning right onto Orange Street, left on Willow, and then right onto Middagh to **24 Middagh Street** ❼. The beautifully proportioned, federal-style, clapboard house at the corner of Willow is the former Eugene Boisselet residence. Built in 1829, it is one of Brooklyn Heights' oldest and most cherished houses. **No. 30 Middagh Street** is even older, dating from 1824, though it is not as well preserved.

Continue to Hicks Street and turn right, then left on Orange Street. If you get a bit lost on any of these turns, just wander. Between Hicks and Henry Streets, the famous Plymouth Church, now **Plymouth Church of the Pilgrims 8** (*tel 718/624-4743*), is a simple, barnlike brick structure designed by Joseph C.

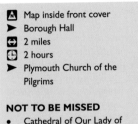

🅰	Map inside front cover
▶	Borough Hall
↔	2 miles
🕐	2 hours
▶	Plymouth Church of the Pilgrims

NOT TO BE MISSED
- Cathedral of Our Lady of Lebanon
- Brooklyn Historical Society
- Brooklyn Promenade
- Plymouth Church of the Pilgrims

Wells and completed in 1849. The parish house and connecting arcade at 75 Hicks Street are 1914 additions. From 1847 to 1887, Henry Ward Beecher (brother of Harriet Beecher Stowe, the author of *Uncle Tom's Cabin*) was the church's pastor. Beecher was a spellbinding preacher and an ardent abolitionist. To demonstrate the horrors of the slave trade, he once auctioned off a slave girl from the pulpit and then used the proceeds to buy her freedom. Beecher was later publicly accused of improper relations with a married woman. Although exonerated, the widely publicized scandal was damaging to his career.

The tour ends here, and you can stroll to the corner of Henry, turn right, and wander down to **Montague Street.** This is the heart of the Heights, with many appealing shops and restaurants. ■

The well-kept row houses of Brooklyn Heights make the neighborhood one of the most desirable in the city.

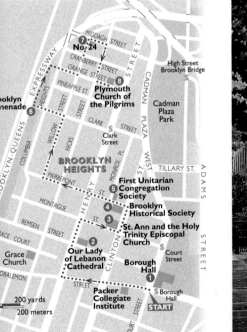

Prospect Park & environs

LANDSCAPE ARCHITECTS CALVERT VAUX AND FREDERICK Law Olmsted thought that Prospect Park (1867) was their best effort; today many agree, including some Manhattanites who consider it their favorite park. Unlike Central Park, which is confined in a rectangular box, Prospect Park's 526-acre area is irregularly shaped, a configuration that makes it seem more a natural part of the urban landscape.

Prospect Park
www.prospectpark.org
🅰 205 C2
✉ Boathouse Visitor Center, Lincoln Rd. entrance, Brooklyn
☎ 718/965-8999
🚇 Subway: 2, 3 to Grand Army Plaza

Victory in a chariot drawn by four horses streaks across the top of the triumphal arch at Grand Army Plaza.

A short distance from the Brooklyn Public Library is the northern entrance to the park, **Grand Army Plaza.** Designed by Olmsted and Vaux in 1870, the statuary here makes this indeed grand and memorable. Take a look at the plaza. It is centered on the Soldiers' and Sailors' Memorial Arch, erected in 1892 to honor the Union dead in the Civil War. The 80-foot-high arch is topped by a bronze group done by sculptor Frederick W. MacMonnies at the turn of the 20th century. Since 1981 there has been a small art gallery inside the arch that shows changing exhibits.

By the park entrance is a detailed standing park map for orientation. First, you enter the enormous 75-acre **Long Meadow,** usually filled with clusters of people—barbecuing, playing catch, sunning, drumming, playing guitars—having a good

time. From here, the park unfolds in a succession of open spaces alternating with intimate ones.

Olmsted and Vaux also designed **Eastern Parkway,** today a designated scenic landmark, running between Grand Army Plaza and Ralph Avenue. The partners envisioned it as a first link in a tree-lined boulevard that would connect Prospect and Central Parks. Later in the century, architects McKim, Mead & White added more formal elements to the park, such as gates, pavilions, and the Corinthian templelike **Croquet Shelter** at Parkside Avenue on the park's southern end near Prospect Lake.

One of the favorite park attractions is the **Prospect Park Carousel,** a reminder of the days when Brooklyn was a center of carousel manufacturing, from 1875 to 1918. Nearby, located in an 18th-century structure, **Lefferts Historic House** (Flatbush Ave., tel 718/789-2822) offers period rooms, workshops, and crafts demonstrations. Another popular children's destination is the 14-acre **Prospect Park Zoo** (450 Flatbush Ave., tel 718/399-7339). Throughout the year, the park is used by joggers, skaters, and hikers, plus there are sponsored celebrations and musical and performing arts events; many are held at the Prospect Park Bandshell (Prospect Park W. at 9th St., tel 718/965-8999 for weekly performance schedules). ∎

Park Slope Historic District

The classic
row houses
of Park Slope

PROSPECT PARK IS BORDERED TO THE NORTHWEST BY THE
Park Slope Historic District, a residential area developed after
the opening of the Brooklyn Bridge in 1883, which facilitated the
commute to downtown Manhattan.

The row houses in the district are
outstanding, especially those
designed by C. H. P. Gilbert on
Carroll Street and Montgomery
Place. The **Montauk Club** *(25
7th Ave. and Lincoln Pl., closed to
the public)* has terra-cotta detailing
that mixes Venetian style with
sculptural representations of the
Montauk Indians. At St. John's Place
and Seventh Avenue await three
exceptional Gothic-style churches:
St. John's Episcopal (1889),
Grace United Methodist
(1883), and **Memorial
Presbyterian** (1883).

Southwest of the park, the 478-
acre **Greenwood Cemetery,**
which opened in 1840, became
popular when Gov. DeWitt
Clinton's body was moved there in
1844. Twenty miles of paths wind
about wooded glades, streams,
lakes, and hills. "Boss" Tweed and
Horace Greeley are among the
notables who have chosen this spot
for their last resting place.

The **Pieter Claesen
Wyckoff House Museum** is
the oldest building in New York
City and one of the oldest wooden
houses in the country. It was built
in 1652—with additions in 1740
and 1819—by a Dutch indentured
servant who became a wealthy
farmer. The one-story, shingled
house has overhanging eaves typical of Dutch vernacular architecture. It remained in the Wyckoff
family until 1902. The city restored
it using period materials and
building techniques in 1982. After
exploring here, go to **Seventh
Avenue,** one of the main thoroughfares in the area for shopping
and places to eat. ■

**St. John's Episcopal
Church**
✉ 139 St. John's Place
☎ 718/783-3928

**Grace United
Methodist Church**
✉ 33 7th Ave.
☎ 718/230-3473

**Memorial
Presbyterian
Church**
☎ 718/638-5541

**Pieter Claesen
Wyckoff House
Museum**
www.wyckoffassociation.org
✉ 5816 Clarendon Rd.
☎ 718/629-5400
🕐 Open Tues.–Sun.,
by appt. only
💲 $

Brooklyn Museum of Art

Brooklyn Museum of Art

www.brooklynmuseum.org

🅰 205 C2

✉ 200 Eastern Parkway, Brooklyn

☎ 718/638-5000

🕐 Closed Mon.–Tues.; "First Saturdays" have free adm. & special events

💲 $$

🚇 Subway: 2, 3 to Eastern Parkway; B, Q, S to Prospect Park

JUST PAST THE BROOKLYN BOTANIC GARDEN ON EASTERN Parkway stands the Brooklyn Museum of Art. Housed in a 19th century beaux arts landmark, it is New York's second-largest museum and one of the country's most prestigious. Its permanent collection holds more then one million objects, from ancient, time-honored masterpieces to contemporary works charting new ground. Works on display frequently change, and modern installation methods and special events enhance ways for audiences to enjoy the museum's treasures.

Contemporized front grounds blend handsomely with the museum's original architecture and statuary, while a sweeping entryway opens onto an information area, coat check, and gift shop. Farther along is the **Blum Gallery** for changing exhibits, where "Monet's London" was a 2005 hit. Also on this floor is a café and outdoor **Sculpture Garden,** with a Coney Island lion from Steeplechase Park and a monumental 19th-century replica of the Statue of Liberty.

MUSEUM HIGHLIGHTS

On the first floor, visitors can wander among the African, Central American, and Native American collections. In 1923 the Brooklyn Museum was the first to exhibit African objects as art—one masterpiece here is the brass figure of a hornblower, made for the Nigerian king of Benin in the 16th century. Nearby, the arts of Central and South America include the exquisite 2,000-year-old "Paracas Textile." The Native American collection features freestanding 19th-century totem poles from British Columbia. On the second floor are the Asian and Islamic collections. The grouping of later Persian art from the Qajar period (1779–1924) is one of the finest to be found outside Iran.

On the third floor, don't miss the fascinating Egyptian collection (see p. 212). European paintings are also here, with works by 19th-century French artists—Cezanne, Degas, Matisse, and others—splendidly installed in the skylit Beaux-Arts Court. Breton's pastoral oil painting "The End of the Working Day" (1886–87), offers a majestic image of peasantry in the artist's native Artois. The fourth floor (temporarily closed) will house Judy Chicago's iconic work "The Dinner Party" in the **Sackler Center for Feminist Art** (opens 2007). On the fifth floor, the **Cantor Gallery** features 58 Rodin sculptures.

LUCE CENTER FOR AMERICAN ART

Also on the fifth floor is the **Luce Center for American Art,** established by a $10 million grant from the Henry Luce Foundation. Here the innovative **Visible Storage/Study Center** lets the public view some 1,500 objects from the museum's collection of American painting and sculpture, as well as material from the Decorative Arts, Native American, and Print, Drawing and Photography collections. These are organized by type and medium on rolling racks and shelves in glass-walled storage. The Luce Center's second component is the installation "American Identities." Taking up several themed galleries, it draws from the museum's 2,500 oil paintings, sculptures, watercolors, and pastels from 1720 to the late 20th century. Contemporary photographs and short period films enrich each exhibit. The scope is immense, from objects such as a basket made by the last Brooklyn Canarsie Indian and a 1930s RCA Victor portable phonograph to paintings by Winslow Homer,

George Caleb Bingham's "Shooting for the Beef" (1850)

Thomas Eakins, and Georgia O'Keeffe. Edward Hicks's "The Peaceable Kingdom" is here, along with many other favorites.

EGYPTIAN COLLECTION

Covering four millennia, and displayed in the renovated west wing, this collection is based on the bequest of Charles Edwin Wilbour (1833–1896). A journalist turned Egyptologist, Wilbour conducted extensive excavations in the Nile Valley. His widow gave his library and collection to the museum, and in 1932 their children provided an endowment to establish the Department of Egyptology. In 2003, the museum completed the reinstallation of its world-famous Egyptian collection. In seven galleries, three of them new, "Egypt Reborn" tells the story of Egyptian art through more than 1,200 objects—sculpture, relief, paintings, pottery, and papyri—from Egypt's earliest known origins (circa 3500 B.C.) until the period of Roman rule (30 B.C.–A.D. 395). This spectacular long-term installation is replete with treasures, including one of Wilbour's more famous finds: a plaque depicting King Akhenaten, who became pharaoh in 1352 B.C., and his wife Nefertiti. Be sure also to see the material from the reign of King Tutankhamun (circa 1336–1327 B.C.); the extraordinary "Coffin for an Ibis," made for a mummified bird believed to be a manifestation of the god Thoth; and 30 limestone blocks with finely carved reliefs, some still in progress, from the tomb of Nespeqashuty (664–610 B.C.).

DEVELOPMENT OF THE MUSEUM

Walt Whitman was among the early directors of the Brooklyn Apprentices Library, founded in 1823 to aid youths "in learning the mechanic arts and…becoming useful and respectable members of society." The library grew to become the Brooklyn Institute of Arts and Sciences—later renamed the Brooklyn Museum.

In 1893 architects McKim, Mead & White won the competition to design a new building. Their plan would have made the Brooklyn Museum the world's largest, surpassing the Louvre, but only the west wing and one court were ever finished.

Today, modernization is ongoing. The new front entrance (2005), with its stepped glass pavilion, creates an exhilarating gateway, while the adjacent public plaza offers pleasant seating amidst dramatic water features. Even the nearby subway entrance was re-oriented, and its interior renovated. ∎

Brooklyn Childrens Museum

✉ 145 Brooklyn Ave., Brooklyn
☎ 718/735-4400
🕐 Closed Mon.–Tues.
💲 Donation
🚇 Subway: 2 to Kingston Ave.

Brooklyn Children's Museum

This museum, several blocks west of the Brooklyn Museum, is entered under a 1907 trolley kiosk, located below ground in Brower Park. Founded in 1899, the museum is the world's oldest children's museum. It moved to its new underground facility in 1976. Its interior, approached through a culvert, is an intriguing maze of passageways on different levels.

The museum led the way in creating interactive exhibits for children. One permanent exhibit, "Night Journeys," offers children the opportunity to stretch out on beds from different cultures. The museum also has a popular large doll collection. ∎

Brooklyn Botanic Garden

FROM THE AROMATIC FRAGRANCE GARDEN TO THE winding Japanese Garden, the Brooklyn Botanic Garden is a triumph of the garden designer's art. With a seemingly endless succession of formal and informal landscapes and different specialized areas, the garden seems much larger than its mere 52 acres.

The Brooklyn Institute of Arts and Sciences founded the Botanic Garden, next to the museum, in 1910. Architects McKim, Mead & White designed the **Victorian Palm Conservatory** and the administration building, and landscape architect Harold Caparn did the layout of the grounds.

Important additions in 1914 were the **children's garden,** the first of its kind in the world—where schoolchildren are able to learn techniques of vegetable and flower gardening—and the **Japanese Hill and Pond Garden,** north of the main entrance. Designed by a Japanese artist living in New York, the garden borders an irregularly shaped pond overlooked by a shrine to the Shinto god of the harvest. Nearby is the rectangular **Cherry Esplanade,** planted with double rows of Kwanzan cherry trees, a gift from Japan. Cherry blossom season in May draws large crowds.

The garden's latest addition is the 1988 **Steinhardt Conservatory,** housing the Bonsai Museum, with over 750 species of bonsai, and an exhibit called the "Trail of Evolution," illustrating four billion years of plant development. The conservatory also includes the Aquatic House, with displays of water lilies and other water plants. On the lower level, visit the Conservatory Gallery, with changing art exhibits. ∎

Brooklyn Botanic Garden

www.bbg.org

🅐 205 C2

✉ 1000 Washington Ave., Brooklyn

☎ 718/623-7200

🕐 Closed Mon.

💲 $

🚇 Subway: 2, 3 to Eastern Parkway; B, Q to Prospect Park (no B on wknds.)

Coney Island

BROOKLYN'S CONEY ISLAND IS AN ETHNICALLY DIVERSE
and complex neighborhood of some 50,000 people—and home to its
claim to fame today, the historic and world-famous amusement park,
Coney Island. The park flourished early in the 20th century, then
declined after World War II, but the glamour and fantasy of it all
seized the American imagination and has hung on to this day. In fact,
revitalization plans are on the drawing board.

Coney Island
www.coneyisland.com
205 CI
718/372-5159
Subway: D to Coney
Island/Stillwell Ave.

NY Aquarium
718/265-3474

The original **Famous Nathan's,** a
hot dog stand opened in 1916, is still
a fixture on Stillwell Avenue to welcome you. Whether you start with
exotica at the museum or just wander and gape, there is enough left in
the way of history and thrills to
make your trip (an hour by subway)
worthwhile. Three attractions have

Ferris wheel, opened on Memorial
Day in 1920. It has 24 passenger cars
that both rock and slide along tracks
as the wheel turns. The **Parachute
Jump,** near the Coney Island
Boardwalk, came to Coney Island
from the New York World's Fair of
1939–1940. Although long closed,
the steel tower remains a beckoning
landmark. The **New York
Aquarium** and Brighton Beach, a
fascinating Russian neighborhood
(on the Q subway line), are nearby
and also worth a visit.

CONEY ISLAND'S THREE PARKS

Coney Island was actually
three amusement parks that have
blended into one in memory.
George Tilyou opened Steeplechase
Park at West 17th Street in 1897;
here patrons could race on mechan-
ical horses attached to iron rails or
try to hold on to a fast-spinning
wooden disk called the Human
Roulette Wheel. Luna Park (1903)
was a fantasyland of minaret towers,
its buildings outlined by more than
a million lightbulbs. The third park,
Dreamland, quieter and more
tasteful, featured reproductions of
the Tower of Seville and Venetian
canals. Of the three, it was the least
successful. Fire ended it in 1911.
Luna Park burned in 1944, and
Steeplechase Park closed in 1964.

Nostalgia seekers: Visit Coney
Island while you can, before it
becomes Las Vegas East with new
themed attractions. ■

**Still an attraction
after nearly
80 years—the
Wonder Wheel
at Coney Island**

landmark status. The legendary
Cyclone, one of the few gravity-
ride, wooden track roller coasters
left in the world, is the most famous.
Built in 1927, it hits speeds of
68 miles an hour as it races through
nine drops and six curves. The
Wonder Wheel, a 150-foot-high

In & around Staten Island

A FERRY RIDE FROM MANHATTAN TO THE ISLAND LEAVES you at the St. George Ferry Terminal, reopened in 2005 after a sparkling renovation. You can explore the area by foot or hop a bus right at the terminal to take you directly to nearby attractions, including the Snug Harbor Cultural Center, the Alice Austen House, Fort Wadsworth, and the zoo. For more distant attractions, a car is recommended, for public transportation involves many connections.

Leaving the terminal on Richmond Terrace, you'll find **Borough Hall,** which has historical exhibits. Behind the police station, the **Staten Island Institute of Arts and Sciences** (75 Stuyvesant Place, tel 718/727-1135, closed Mon.) dates from 1881. It has more than two million items, including 55,000 photos and a collection of 19th-century painting, sculpture, and decorative arts.

On the island's northern end (but just a few minutes from the terminal by bus), the **Snug Harbor Cultural Center** is located in the impressive Greek Revival buildings founded in 1831 as a retirement home for "aged, decrepit, and worn out sailors." The former Administration Building (also called Building C) houses the **Newhouse Center for Contemporary Art** (tel 718/448-2500, closed Mon.–Thurs.), a community gallery. Other organizations in the center include the **Staten Island Children's Museum** (tel 718/273-2060, closed Mon.), with interactive, hands-on exhibits, and the **Staten Island Botanical Garden** (tel 718/273-8200), which maintains specialized gardens and collections.

Farther inland, the eight-acre **Staten Island Zoo,** founded in 1936, is known for its Serpentarium with its many North American rattlesnakes. ■

The Staten Island Ferry's five-mile, 25-minute ride provides unforgettable views.

Snug Harbor Cultural Center
- 204 B2
- 1000 Richmond Terrace
- 718/448-2500
- Closed Mon.
- $
- Bus: S40 from the ferry terminal

Staten Island Zoo
- 204 B2
- 614 Broadway
- 718/442-3100
- $ (free Wed.)

Staten Island Ferry (still free)
www.siferry.com
- From Manhattan

Alice Austen House

Alice Austen House

www.aliceausten.org

 205 C2

✉ 2 Hylan Blvd.,
Staten Island

☎ 718/816-4506

🕐 Closed Mon.–Wed.,
& Jan.–Feb.

💲 $

🚌 Bus: S51 from
the ferry terminal

THIS UNIQUE MUSEUM IS LOCATED AT THE VERY EDGE OF Staten Island, overlooking the Narrows. The onetime home of Alice Austen (1866–1952), the museum is dedicated to the life and work of one of America's finest early women photographers. The Austen house was originally built as a cottage in the early 18th century. Austen's grandfather purchased it in 1844 and enlarged and remodeled it in the Gothic Revival style, naming it Clear Comfort. A visit here provides an opportunity not only to view some of Austen's work, but to savor the lifestyle of Staten Island's middle class at the turn of the 20th century, when travel was as much by water as by foot—hence the waterfront location of the better homes.

Much of Austen's extant work consists of scenes from the photographer's pleasant surroundings and lifestyle—picnics, the interiors of friends' homes, motor racing, and parties. One sequence done for a woman's "how-to" book on bicycling illustrated the art of mounting, pedaling, and dismounting in a long skirt. More daring, and difficult to achieve, given the size and weight of the large-format equipment she used, was her street photography. Austen ventured into the midst of New York City to photograph such subjects as immigrants arriving at the Battery and at the Quarantine Station on Staten Island. Her work on the

Photographer Alice Austen lived at Clear Comfort on Staten Island until 1945.

Lower East Side includes the well-known 1896 photograph of an egg peddler on Hester Street. In this body of work, Austen has been cited alongside photographers Jacob Riis and Lewis Hine, who focused on social issues of the time.

An inheritance from her father enabled Austen to live comfortably for most of her life, until losses in the 1929 stock market crash forced her to mortgage the house, which she lost in 1945. By the time a researcher for *Life* magazine came across some of her photographs in 1951, she was an indigent resident at the Staten Island Farm Colony. *Life* did an article on her that gave her the funds to spend the last six months of her life in a private nursing home. The article also spurred the Staten Island Historical Society to acquire what remained of her work—some 4,800 negatives, many of them glass. The Friends of Alice Austen House are gradually restoring the residence, which was declared a city landmark in 1971. Although Austen's rediscovery came too late to do her much good, today the Alice Austen House preserves her home, her place in the history of American photography, and, most importantly, her work, a fascinating female perspective on the New York of a century ago. ∎

Historic Richmond Town

HISTORIC RICHMOND TOWN IS PROOF THAT NEW YORK City has everything—even a restored rural village. In this Staten Island complex, you can browse through a late 19th-century general store (in the Stephens-Black House) or watch craftsmen make wood-splint baskets in the Basketmaker's House (1810) or throw pots in the basement of the Guyon-Lake-Tysen House, an exquisite Dutch Colonial–style house built about 1740 (with later additions).

The site has some of the oldest restored buildings in the city. The wood-and-stone Britton Cottage (central section, circa 1670) predates the founding of the settlement in 1690. The house was moved to Richmond Town in 1967. Because Richmond Town was located at the center of the island, it became the seat of government about 1730.

Eleven of the 27 buildings in the restoration are original to the site, including the circa 1695 Voorleezer House—also the oldest surviving elementary school in the country. The settlers, members of the Dutch Reformed Church, built the house for their lay reader, or *voorleezer,* who was also the schoolteacher. More than a century and a half later, in 1855, the congregation built the Parsonage for the Dutch Reformed minister, but by then their church was in decline.

The Greek Revival Third County Courthouse (1837) is now the Visitor Center and the first stop on a tour of the restoration to see craftsmen and costumed staff re-enacting life in the 17th century. The historical museum is also located in a government building: the Richmond County Clerk's and Surrogate's Office (1848). The museum's permanent exhibit examines the economy and history of the island. ∎

Historic Richmond Town
www.historicrichmondtown.org

🅰 204 B1
✉ 441 Clarke Ave., Staten Island
☎ 718/351-1611
🕐 Closed Mon.–Tues.; hours vary with season
🅢 $
🚌 Bus: S74 from the ferry terminal

The 1848 County Clerk's and Surrogate's Office is one of nearly 30 historic buildings found within the 100-acre site at Richmond Town.

More Staten Island sites

CONFERENCE HOUSE

One of the oldest houses in the city, the two-and-a-half-story Billop House, named for Christopher Billop who built it about 1680, is located in a park on the southern tip of Staten Island. Its current name refers to an unsuccessful peace conference that took place in the early days of the American Revolution—on September 11, 1776—between American patriots Benjamin Franklin, John Adams, and Edward Rutledge and British Vice Admiral Lord Richard Howe. The house is open for guided tours and the grounds are a pleasant spot to picnic. 🅰 204 A1 ✉ 7455 Hylan Blvd. ☎ 718/984-2086 🕐 Closed winter (call for details) & Mon.–Tues. 💲 $ 🚌 Bus: S78 to Craig Ave., walk one block south into the park

GARIBALDI-MEUCCI MUSEUM

Inland from the Alice Austen House, this is a circa 1845 farmhouse known for its two famous residents. One of them, Antonio Meucci (1808–1889) was an Italian-born immigrant with a plausible claim to having invented the telephone several years before Alexander Graham Bell; the other was the Italian hero Giuseppe Garibaldi (1807–1882). Meucci moved to Staten Island in 1850. His attempts to take out a patent on his invention failed because of his poverty and poor English. When Garibaldi fled to New York after the defeat of the republican forces in Italy, Meucci took him in. Garibaldi lived there for almost a year until becoming a sea captain, his original occupation, and finally returned to Italy in 1853 to resume his struggle. Throughout the house are exhibits on the men's lives, including a prototype of Meucci's telephone and his death mask. 🅰 204 B2 ✉ 420 Tompkins Ave. ☎ 718/442-1608 🕐 Closed Mon. 💲 $ 🚌 Bus: S52, S78 to Tompkins Ave.

JACQUES MARCHAIS MUSEUM OF TIBETAN ART

Not far from the Richmond Town restoration, built in the style of Tibetan monasteries, this

An example of the beautiful items of Tibetan art exhibited in the Jacques Marchais Museum

museum houses the art collection of a Madison Avenue art dealer, Edna Coblentz, who devoted her life to studying and collecting Tibetan art. 🅰 204 B2 ✉ 338 Lighthouse Ave. ☎ 718/987-3500 🕐 Closed Mon.–Tues. 💲 $ 🚌 Bus: S74 to Lighthouse Ave.

PIERRE BILLIOU HOUSE (BILLIOU-STILLWELL-PERINE HOUSE)

This is the oldest building surviving on Staten Island and also one of the oldest house museums, having been opened to the public in 1919. The original stone farmhouse was built in the 1660s; additions extended the house in every direction over the next century and a half. 🅰 204 B1 ✉ 1476 Richmond Rd., Dongan Hills ☎ 718/351-1611 🕐 Open by appointment, call caretaker ∎

In & around the Bronx

NAMED AN "ALL-AMERICAN CITY" IN 1997, THE BRONX IS best known as home of the Bronx Bombers, the New York Yankees. However, it has other grand attractions that are equally worth exploring.

Ever popular attractions include the Bronx Zoo (see p. 221) and Botanical Garden (see p. 220), but a tour with the Bronx County Historical Society *(tel 718/881-8900)* offers a more intimate experience. The choices are varied, covering neighborhoods, ethnic areas, and historic sites, from Riverdale, with its views of the Hudson, to the seaside area of City Island, to the art deco homes along the Grand Concourse. Tours by bicycle and horse are also possible.

The **Museum of Bronx History** *(3266 Bainbridge Ave., tel 718/881-8900)* offers unique artifacts relating to the borough's past and a research library. It is housed in the Valentine-Varian House, a circa 1758 fieldstone residence built by blacksmith Isaac Valentine.

The Bronx Community College campus boasts two architectural treasures designed by Stanford White: Gould Memorial Library (1887–1899) and the **Hall of Fame for Great Americans** *(University Ave. and W. 181st St., tel 718/289-5161)*. The latter, a 630-foot-long neoclassical open-air colonnade, holds portrait busts of 98 famous Americans, from Eli Whitney to Franklin D. Roosevelt.

Among the 300,000 interred in the 400 acres of the pastoral 1863 **Woodlawn Cemetery** *(Jerome Ave. at Webster Ave. & E. 233rd, tel 718/920-0500)* are such luminaries as Herman Melville, Miles Davis, and F. W. Woolworth, in an Egyptian Revival mausoleum.

A rickety wooden bridge connects the mainland to two-mile-long **City Island,** a picturesque fishing village rich in nautical history. Its

blend of boatyards, seafood restaurants, galleries, and antique shops overlook Eastchester Bay and Long Island Sound—to some it resembles a New England fishing village. Boatmakers here have built five America's Cup winners. Don't miss the quaint Victorian architecture along Schofield Street.

Yankee Stadium, home to the New York Yankees and soon to be replaced by the new Yankee Stadium *(River Ave. at 161st St., tel 718/293-6000; 212/307-1212 Ticketmaster),* was the first ballpark called a "stadium." On the arena's opening day in 1923, the legendary Babe Ruth hit a game-winning home run. In time, the place was known as "the house that Ruth built." In 1972 George Steinbrenner bought the team, and the city bought the stadium. After its 1976 renovation, some called it "the house that Steinbrenner rebuilt." ■

On Opening Day for the New York Yankees, Yankee Stadium is filled to capacity.

New York Botanical Garden

New York Botanical Garden
www.nybg.org

🅰 205 D5

✉ 200th St. & Kazimiroff Blvd., Bronx

☎ 718/817-8700

🕐 Closed Mon.

💲 $$

🚇 Subway: 4, D to Bedford Park Blvd. Bus: Shuttle from Manhattan (tel 718/817-8700) Train: Metro North from Grand Central Terminal (tel 212/532-4900)

The graceful Enid Haupt Conservatory is an architectural highlight of the New York Botanical Garden.

UNLIKELY AS IT MAY SEEM, NEW YORK CITY IS A MECCA FOR garden lovers; all four outlying boroughs have outstanding botanic gardens. Anyone here on a garden tour, however, must make the New York Botanical Garden in the Bronx a priority.

The Bronx garden is distinguished architecturally by the **Enid A. Haupt Conservatory** (1902), based on London's Crystal Palace of 1851. The palm court, 100 feet in diameter, is located under the 90-foot-high glass dome; there are ten other galleries in the wings, including two rain forest displays that can be viewed from various heights on an elevated catwalk. When the conservatory was renovated in 1978, 17,000 glass panes were replaced by hand. It has been renamed for the philanthropist who gave five million dollars for the restoration.

Some of the newer additions to the grounds include the **Jane Watson Perennial Garden** and the **Peggy Rockefeller Rose Garden,** installed in 1988. The rose garden is based on plans that the well-known garden designer Beatrix Farrand drew up in 1916. A unique garden for children, the nine-million-dollar, 12-acre **Everett Children's Adventure Garden,** opened in 1998. Here, among many different activities, children can look for frogs in a pond, explore the "kids only" meadow path, and examine their findings through a microscope in a laboratory located inside an Adirondack-style cottage.

The Royal Botanical Gardens at Kew outside London were the original inspiration for the Bronx garden, which opened in 1891 on an estate that the city had purchased. The three-and-a-half-story, fieldstone **Snuff Mill** (circa 1840) from the Lorillard estate has been restored and is now the garden's restaurant. ■

Bronx Zoo

WHATEVER NAME YOU CHOOSE TO CALL IT—BRONX ZOO (official), New York Zoological Park (earlier), or Wildlife Conservation Society (parent organization)—it is, for viewing wild animals in natural surroundings, unsurpassed in the country. Situated on 265 acres, with some 4,500 animals representing more than 500 species, it is also the country's largest urban zoo.

From JungleWorld to Himalayan Highlands to World of Darkness, you can visit habitats of all seven continents, each filled with native animals. What the zoo has been most famous for since its inception in 1899, however, is its innovative approaches to zookeeping. The use of natural settings surrounded by moats rather than cages, and a dedicated breeding center for endangered species are two such innovations. The designs of both **Himalayan Highlands** (1986) for snow leopards and the **Congo Gorilla Forest** (1999), a 6.5-acre African rain forest habitat with 23 lowland gorillas, incorporate habitats in which the animals can roam, explore, and play.

Tiger Mountain features endangered Siberian tigers in a re-created environment where visitors can observe the big cats' natural behavior (including swimming underwater). The indoor **Butterfly Garden,** filled with more than 1,000 butterflies (including the Monarch), is especially magical.

Consult the zoo map and strategize your visit—there's much to see! Several transportation options are available for an additional fee, including a zoo shuttle, the Safari Train, and the Skyfari aerial tramway. The 40-acre, large-scale outdoor exhibit **Wild Asia** is visible only from the Bengali Express, a 25-minute monorail tour. ■

Bronx Zoo
www.bronxzoo.com
🅰 205 D5
✉ Fordham Rd. & Bronx River Parkway, Bronx
☎ 718/367-1010
💲 $$ (free Wed.)
🚇 Subway: 2 to Pelham Parkway
Bus: Liberty Lines (private bus service) from Madison Ave. (tel 718/652-8400)
Train: Metro North from Grand Central Terminal

Tiger Mountain re-creates a corner of the Amur Valley, between China and Russia, for Siberian tigers.

More sites in the Bronx

BARTOW-PELL MANSION

Thomas Pell purchased land on Long Island Sound from Indians in 1654, but this mansion was not built until 1842. Ten rooms of the classical revival mansion are filled with period furniture, much of it on loan from city museums. The spiral staircase has been attributed to Minard Lafever, a friend of the family. The city purchased the house and the stone carriage house (1840) in 1888; it opened as a museum in 1915.

🗺 205 E5 ✉ 895 Shore Rd. N., Pelham Bay Park ☎ 718/885-1461 🕐 Open p.m. Wed. & Sat.–Sun. 💲 $

EDGAR ALLAN POE COTTAGE

Shortly after he moved to the Bronx in 1846, Edgar Allan Poe described his home as "a snug little cottage." He wrote *Ulalume* and *The Bells* here. The house became a museum in 1917. Three downstairs rooms have been restored to the period Poe lived here; upstairs is an exhibit on his life and an audio-visual presentation.

🗺 205 D5 ✉ E. Kingsbridge Rd. & Grand Concourse ☎ 718/881-8900 🕐 Closed weekdays 💲 $ 🚇 Subway: D to Kingsbridge Rd. or 4 to Kingsbridge

VAN CORTLANDT HOUSE MUSEUM

Built in 1748, this elegant Georgian-style manor house was briefly used by George Washington during the Revolution. Today it is filled with antiques that span the history of this remarkable family, which lived in the house until 1889. Included are a painted cupboard made in the Hudson Valley in the early 18th century and a Gilbert Stuart portrait of John Jacob Astor, who was related to the Van Cortlandts by marriage.

🗺 205 D5 ✉ Van Cortlandt Park, W. 246th St. & Broadway ☎ 718/543-3344 🕐 Closed Mon. 💲 $ 🚇 Subway: 1 to 242nd St.

WAVE HILL

The two mansions on this 28-acre estate were built in the mid-19th and early 20th centuries. Theodore Roosevelt, Mark Twain, and Arturo Toscanini lived here at different times. Today, Wave Hill is a cultural center, but most visitors come to tour the stunning gardens overlooking the Hudson River and New Jersey Palisades.

🗺 205 D5 ✉ West 249th St. ☎ 718/549-3200 🕐 Closed Mon. 💲 $ (free during winter months) 🚇 Subway: A to 207th Street and then No. 7 bus northbound. ∎

Sunshine highlights the fall beauty of Wave Hill.

In & around Queens

THINK OF DIVERSITY AND A WEALTH OF ATTRACTIONS when you envision Queens. Known since its Dutch colonial heritage as a place of religious freedom, it still draws new immigrant populations, giving the number 7 subway line its identity as the International Express. New York's second-largest Chinatown, a Little India, and terrific options for eating and shopping (including stores galore on 74th Street in Jackson Heights selling 22k gold jewelry) are just a few reasons to sample Queens. Its outstanding art scene is led by the internationally renowned P.S.1 Contemporary Art Center in Long Island City.

In addition to its thriving arts scene, Queens offers many unique places great for families. Thanks to its hosting of two World's Fairs, in 1939–40 and 1964–65, the **Flushing Meadows–Corona Park** area is today the site of many of the borough's leading attractions. With 1,255 acres, it is the city's second largest park. Several fair structures remain, most prominently the **Unisphere,** the largest globe in the world, built by U.S.

Steel as the symbol of the 1964–65 World's Fair. Another refurbished structure, the New York City Building (used for fairs in both 1939–40 and 1964–65), is now the **Queens Museum of Art** (tel 718/592-5555, closed Mon.). It houses contemporary art and the world's largest architectural scale model, a 9,335-square-foot panorama of New York City.

Also in the park, the 1964–65 World's Fair Space Center was

Note: The Louis K. Armstrong House, in a working-class neighborhood in Corona, Queens, opened to the public in 2003. It offers an intimate look into the life of the world's legendary jazz giant. With his wife, Lucille, "Satchmo" lived here from 1943 until his death in 1971 (tel 718/478-8274, www.satchmo.net).

The Unisphere, a colossal legacy of the 1964–65 World's Fair

The Bowne House, the oldest in Queens, is also a monument to the colonial struggle for religious tolerance.

converted into the **New York Hall of Science** *(tel 718/699-0005)* in 1986. It features more than 400 interactive displays on physics, biology, and technology, including one titled "Hidden Kingdoms–The World of Microbes," a 14-foot sewing needle on which scale models of microbes are displayed.

Even **Shea Stadium** *(tel 718/507-8499)*, Queen's major league baseball park, and home of the New York Mets, was a project related to the 1964–65 fair.

MORE QUEENS SITES

East of the park, the 1661 **Bowne House** *(37–01 Bowne St. at 37th Ave., tel 718/359-0528)* is the oldest in Queens; it was built by John Bowne, a convert to Quakerism, whom Peter Stuyvesant arrested in 1662 for holding Quaker meetings in the house. By ordering Stuyvesant to free him, the Dutch West India Company established the principle of religious tolerance in the colony (see p. 20). The house was occupied through 1945 by nine generations of Bownes, when it became a museum.

Close by, the **Friends Meeting House** *(tel 718/358-9636)* was built by Bowne and other Quakers in 1694. It has been used for Quaker services almost continuously since.

Another Quaker, Charles Doughty, built the nearby Kingsland Homestead about 1785. It is now the **Queens Historical Society** *(143–35 37th Ave., tel 718/939-0647)*, which exhibits memorabilia from the residents, including its second owner, Joseph King, Doughty's son-in-law. There is a Victorian parlor and changing exhibits on Queens history.

The 38 acres of the **Queens Botanical Gardens** *(43–50 Main St., tel 718/886-3800, closed Mon.)* in Flushing include the 4,000-plant rose garden donated by Oregon-based Jackson and Perkins, which started in Queens. There is also a Wedding Garden for marriage ceremonies' photographs, and an ethnic garden, with plants from various countries represented in an ethnically diverse community.

P.S.1 CONTEMPORARY ART CENTER

Located in what was an abandoned public school (P.S. 1), **P.S.1** *(22–25 Jackson Ave., tel 718/784-2084)* reopened in late 1997 after a three-year, 8.5-million-dollar renovation. With 125,000 square feet of exhibit space, it is the world's largest museum for contemporary art and a Museum of Modern Art (MoMA) affiliate. ■

Museum of the Moving Image

Nearly a century of multimedia memorabilia and technology are presented at MMI.

THE MUSEUM OF THE MOVING IMAGE (MMI) IS AMERICA'S only museum devoted exclusively to the study of film, television, and digital media and their impact on American culture and society. It's located in one of 13 buildings that comprise the 14-acre studio where production first began in the Silent Era and, after a hiatus, is now back in full swing. The museum houses over 150,000 moving-image artifacts—a dazzling array covering art, history, techniques, and technology, from which it draws for exhibits, screenings, and other programs.

Famous Players–Lasky (later Paramount Pictures) was the first to film at Astoria Studios, in 1920. The property transferred to the U.S. Army in 1942, which used it for its own productions until 1971. Falling into disrepair, the studio was saved by the Astoria Motion Picture and Television Foundation in 1977; it obtained landmark status soon after. In 1982, wanting to return the studio to its feature-film production abilities, the city awarded its redevelopment to George Kaufman, who renamed it Kaufman-Astoria Studios. The city also set aside one building, which opened as MMI in 1988. A major museum expansion is now underway.

Nostalgia buffs will gravitate to the stunning memorabilia, from a chariot from *Ben-Hur,* to the Yoda puppets from *The Empire Strikes Back,* to razzle-dazzle costumes from the 2002 movie *Chicago.* Interactive programs let you become part of moviemaking: Graft your voice onto famous film scenes, insert sound effects into film clips, and piece together moving images in a digital scrapbook.

A permanent exhibit, "Behind the Screen," surveys the history of making, marketing, and exhibiting motion pictures, from 19th-century optical devices to computer animation. Vintage serials play in the whimsical re-creation of a 1920s Egyptian Revival–style movie palace.

Retrospectives, screenings, and special events are offered year-round in the museum's Riklis Theater. ■

Museum of the Moving Image

www.movingimage.us

🅰 205 D3

✉ 35th Ave. at 36th St., Queens

☎ 718/784-0077

🕐 Closed Mon.–Tues.

💲 $$

🚇 Subway: R, V (R, G weekends) to Steinway St.; N, W to 36th Ave.

Note:
The museum has embarked upon a visionary expansion/renovation to nearly double its size, including an addition, a garden for outdoor events, new galleries, and cutting-edge moving-image displays.

Noguchi's indoor/outdoor Garden

Isamu Noguchi Garden Museum

Isamu Noguchi Garden Museum

www.noguchi.org

- 205 D4
- 32–7 Vernon Blvd. (at 33rd Rd.)
- 718/204-7088
- Closed Mon.–Tues.
- $
- Subway: N, W to Broadway in Queens

There is something stoic about sculpture that neutralizes or at least calms the restless energy of a big city. The works of world-renowned sculptor Isamu Noguchi (1904–1988) have that affect on New York. His specialty is sculpture for public places, and this indoor/outdoor museum displays it to perfection (he himself designed the space).

The museum reopened in 2004 after a renovation that added an education center, a new café, and a gallery devoted to Noguchi's interior design work. The permanent collection includes 250 stone, bronze, and wood sculptures, dance sets for choreographer Martha Graham, models for public projects, and Noguchi's Akari light sculptures, derived from traditional Japanese paper lanterns.

Noguchi was born in Los Angeles, his father a Japanese poet and his mother an American writer. He moved to New York in 1923 to study medicine, but turned instead to art. In 1968 the Whitney Museum mounted a retrospective of his work. The permanent Noguchi museum and garden grew from the artist's studio, which he established in the Queens neighborhood in the 1960s. ■

Nearby sites

The **Museum for African Art** (*36–01 43rd Ave., Long Island City, tel 718/784-7700, closed Tues.–Wed.*) has produced more than 40 shows in its 20-year history, with objects loaned from collections around the globe. "Facing the Mask" provided a family-friendly introduction to African art and culture. Performances and workshops complement the exhibits. A move to its permanent new home in Manhattan (*119 Fifth Ave at E. 110th St*) is currently in the works.

The **Socrates Sculpture Park** (*Broadway at Vernon Blvd., tel 718/956-1819*) is on a four-acre site facing the East River, with a Manhattan skyline view. Here you can see changing exhibits of large-scale sculpture by established and emerging artists. ■

You do not have to go far to escape the city. Nearby western Long Island is easy for day trips. The Hudson River Valley—offering military sites, riverside estates, and scenery of incomparable grandeur—is another destination. It can take several days to see it all.

Excursions

Introduction & map **228–229**
Hudson River Valley **230–232**
Long Island **233–234**

**Bear Mountain Bridge,
Hudson River Valley**

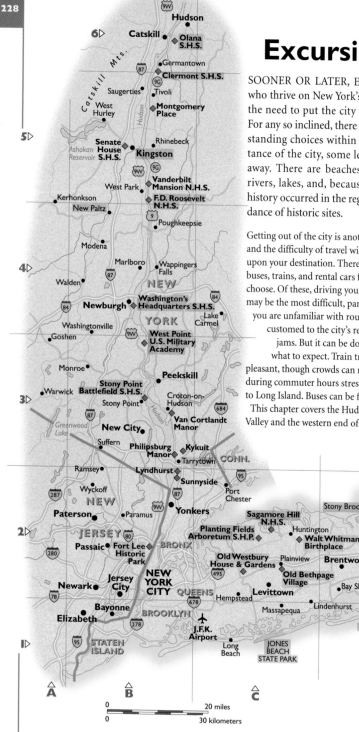

Excursions

SOONER OR LATER, EVEN THOSE who thrive on New York's intensity feel the need to put the city behind them. For any so inclined, there are many outstanding choices within shouting distance of the city, some less than a day away. There are beaches, mountains, rivers, lakes, and, because much early history occurred in the region, an abundance of historic sites.

Getting out of the city is another matter, and the difficulty of travel will depend upon your destination. There are subways, buses, trains, and rental cars from which to choose. Of these, driving your own vehicle may be the most difficult, particularly if you are unfamiliar with routes and unaccustomed to the city's renowned traffic jams. But it can be done—just know what to expect. Train travel can be pleasant, though crowds can make traveling during commuter hours stressful, especially to Long Island. Buses can be fast.

This chapter covers the Hudson River Valley and the western end of Long Island,

0   20 miles

0   30 kilometers

two nearby regions rich in attractions and quite different in topography, scenery, and character. The Hudson River Valley was home to Rip Van Winkle, Washington Irving's famous character; Long Island lives eternally in literature as the land of F. Scott Fitzgerald's Gatsby. The robber barons of the Gilded Age constructed their ostentatious mansions and gardens on the exclusive North Shore of Long Island. In colonial times, patroons built their magnificent estates along the Hudson. The descendants of Cornelius Vanderbilt constructed houses in both places.

HUDSON RIVER VALLEY

In 1807 inventor Robert Fulton built a steam-powered boat, the *Clermont*. Its inaugural run—along the Hudson River, from New York to Albany in 32 hours—signaled the first profitable venture in steam navigation and ushered in a whole new era in commercial transportation. But it was the 1825 opening of the Erie Canal, from Albany to Buffalo, that made the

Hudson River even more important commercially to Manhattan, as a link between the city and the Great Lakes via the canal. More than Long Island, the Hudson River Valley has retained its historic flavor. There are also stretches, particularly where the mountains descend to the water, that are, to the eye, as unspoiled as they were in the early 19th century, when the Hudson River artists created a school of landscape painting based on the river's incomparable scenery.

LONG ISLAND

One hundred and twenty miles long and 23 miles across at its widest point, Long Island is mostly flat. Its North Shore is graced by picturesque harbors and inlets. On its southern side, the Atlantic Ocean rolls into its beaches and barrier islands. Farms once covered the entire island; today they are found only on its eastern end. During the Revolution, General Howe drove off Washington and his troops in the Battle of Long Island, August 26–31, 1776, and the island remained in British hands for the rest of the war. Industries that rose there— whaling, shipbuilding, and shipping—are completely gone. Long Island waters are now used more for sport than for commerce. America's newly rich industrialists began building their mansions on Long Island's North Shore—the Gold Coast— at the turn of the 20th century. During the roaring 1920s, Long Island became notorious as a playground for the wealthy, who indulged themselves in fast cars, illegal liquor, polo ponies, and lavish parties. F. Scott Fitzgerald perfectly portrayed the era in *The Great Gatsby*. After World War II, developers turned large tracts into housing developments and shopping malls (the eventual fate of Roosevelt Field). Today, heavily populated western Long Island blends seamlessly into New York City. But there are places where you can step back into the past—into a horticultural paradise of the very rich at Old Westbury Gardens, for example, or into the simple life of an earlier farm at Old Bethpage Village. ■

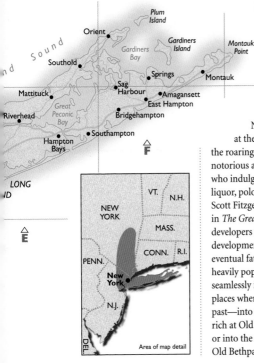

Hudson River Valley

THIS VISIT TO THE HUDSON RIVER VALLEY PROCEEDS north along the west bank, crosses the river at Catskill, and returns down the east side. Although it covers only some 200 miles, it would take several days to thoroughly see and do everything along the way. However, any combination of sites would make an interesting trip. Those wanting a shorter journey can use any of the several bridges across the Hudson River to return to New York.

Antique artillery pieces guard the Hudson River on heights overlooking West Point.

Start in New Jersey at **Fort Lee Historic Park** *(Hudson Terrace, Palisades Interstate Park)*, south of the George Washington Bridge, a reconstruction of a Revolutionary War artillery post. On November 16, 1776, from this vantage point, George Washington watched Fort Washington in northern Manhattan fall to the British.

Proceeding north, enter New York State and detour to the **Stony Point Battlefield State Historic Site (SHS)** *(Park Road off US 9W)*. Here, Gen. Anthony Wayne vanquished the British in a surprise attack on July 16, 1779. There is a small museum *(tel 845/786-2521, call for hours)* and tours of the battlefield.

West Point Museum has an extensive collection of weapons, military art, uniforms, and dioramas explaining historic battles. The **Old Cadet Chapel** (1836) is in the post cemetery; inside, battle flags line the walls. Bertram Grosvenor Goodhue designed the 1910 **Cadet Chapel** in the neo-Gothic style. Near the parade ground rises a monument to Kosciuszko.

After leaving West Point on US 9W, stop in Newburgh at **Washington's Headquarters SHS.** George Washington spent more than a year, 1782–83, in the Hasbrouck House, a small stone dwelling furnished as when he stayed there. There is also a museum of Revolutionary War artifacts on the grounds. The next stop going north is the town of **New Paltz,** founded by French Huguenots in 1677. Six stone houses (1692–1717) remain on Huguenot Street. Tours are conducted Tues.–Sun. from the Historical Society *(Deyo Hall, 18 Broadhead Ave., tel 845/255-1889).*

From New Paltz continue north on US 9W to **Kingston,** the Revolutionary War capital of New York. The first state constitution was adopted in 1777 at the **Senate House SHS** *(296 Fair St., tel 845/ 338-2786).* Here are exhibits on early state government and paintings by the Hudson River school's John Vanderlyn. Maps of walking tours through Kingston's Stockade Historic District are available at the Urban Cultural Park Visitor Center *(20 Broadway, tel 845/331-7517).*

Leaving Kingston, cross the Hudson at Catskill on the Rip Van Winkle Bridge. Take N.Y. 9G south a mile to **Olana SHS,** a villa overlooking the Hudson River. Its owner, painter Frederic Church (1826–1900), designed it in a style he called "personal Persian." Church belonged to the Hudson River school of painting.

Continue on US 9W to **West Point,** where the United States Military Academy overlooks a spectacular and unsullied bend in the Hudson River. Try to visit in the spring or fall when the cadets parade. West Point has trained Army officers since 1802; its four-year course is famous for its rigor and discipline. Before it was a school, West Point was a fortification, designed and built in 1778 by Thaddeus Kosciuszko, the Polish officer who fought for the Americans during the Revolution. Most famous American generals graduated from West Point, but not all excelled. Ulysses S. Grant finished in the bottom half of his class; Dwight Eisenhower was also a mediocre student.

West Point
www.usma.edu
228 B4
Visitor information
Building 2110, West Point
845/938-2638

Washington's Headquarters SHS
228 B4
Liberty & Washington Sts., Newburgh
845/562-1195
Closed Oct.–April
$

Olana SHS
228 B6
N.Y. 9G, Hudson
518/828-0135
Closed Nov.–March
$

Clermont SHS

- 228 B5
- 1 Clermont Ave., Germantown
- 518/537-4240
- Closed Mon. April–Oct., & Mon.–Fri. Nov.–mid-Dec.
- $

Montgomery Place

- 228 B5
- North of Kingston-Rhinecliff Bridge
- 845/758-5461
- Closed Tues. April–Oct.
- $$

Philipsburg Manor and a reconstructed mill

Vanderbilt Mansion NHS

- 228 B5
- 4097 Albany Post Rd., Hyde Park
- 845/229-7770
- Nov.–March. Call for hours.
- $

Continue south on N.Y. 9G to the **Clermont SHS** in Germantown. Clermont was the home of Robert R. Livingston, a member of the Continental Congress and chancellor of New York who administered the first presidential oath of office to George Washington. The house (named after the steam-powered boat of his partner, Robert Fulton) was burned by the British in 1777 and rebuilt after independence. A short distance off N.Y. 9G, in Annandale-on-Hudson, is **Montgomery Place,** a mansion on a river estate. It was built in 1805 by Janet Montgomery, the widow of Gen. Richard Montgomery.

For a great family outing, visit the **Old Rhinebeck Aerodrome** (*Off N.Y. 9 on Stone Church Rd., tel 845/758-8610 or 845/752-3200 for information about tours, rides, and airshows*).

North of Poughkeepsie on N.Y. 9 you will find the lavish two-million-dollar **Vanderbilt Mansion,** built for Frederick W. Vanderbilt in 1899 by McKim, Mead & White.

Continuing south, US 9 will bring you to the **Franklin D. Roosevelt National Historic Site (NHS)** (*tel 845/229-9115*) in Hyde Park, an 1826 house that remains much as it was when Roosevelt died in 1945. Roosevelt and his wife, Eleanor, are buried in the rose garden. Also on the grounds is the Franklin D. Roosevelt Museum and Library, probably the first presidential library. Two miles east is the **Eleanor Roosevelt NHS.** After her husband died, Eleanor lived in the cottage, Val-Kill, until her death in 1962. The **Culinary Institute of America** (*tel 845/471-6608*) is also located in Hyde Park. Advance reservations are needed for its four excellent student-run restaurants.

Off US 9 in Croton-on-Hudson, is the **Van Cortlandt Manor,** the home (until 1945) of the Van Cortlandt family, once patrons of an 86,000-acre domain. Van Cortlandt Manor is operated by Historic Hudson Valley (*tel 914/631-8200*), as is **Philipsburg Manor,** an early 18th-century manor house, a working farm, and mill in Sleepy Hollow.

Kykuit (*tel 914/631-9491*), a 40-room mansion built by John D. Rockefeller, with Rockefeller's collection of modern art, is open to the public (reservations are necessary) and reachable by shuttle bus from Philipsburg Manor.

In Tarrytown, **Lyndhurst** (*US 9, tel 914/631-4481*) was the summer home of railroad baron Jay Gould. Designed by Alexander Jackson Davis, it is one of the best Gothic Revival–style mansions in the country. Also in Tarrytown is **Sunnyside** (*Historic Hudson Valley, tel 914/631-8200*). Author Washington Irving purchased the stone cottage in 1836 and rebuilt it as a cozy but eccentric house.

From here you can continue to explore or head toward Long Island to visit its sights. ∎

Long Island

LONG ISLAND IS FOR MANY THE UNDISCOVERED ISLAND. IT consists of four counties: Brooklyn and Queens (boroughs of New York City) and Nassau and Suffolk. Millionaires' estates dot the North Shore, while the Hamptons have become celebrity central in the summer.

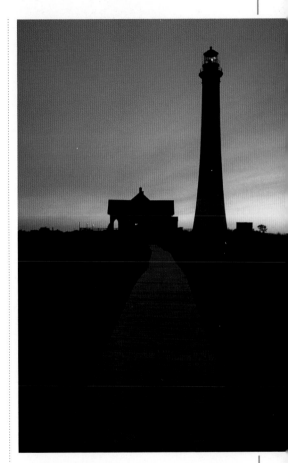

On Long Island's Fire Island, a lighthouse and keeper's cottage stand out against a darkening sky.

Having promised his English bride that he would create an estate for her similar to her childhood home, John Jay Phipps, son of Andrew Carnegie's partner, built **Old Westbury House and Gardens** (*71 Old Westbury Rd., Old Westbury, tel 516/333-0048, closed Tues.*), a 105-acre manor house and estate in 1907. The manor house contains antique furniture and paintings by Reynolds, Gainsborough, and Sargent.

The landscaped gardens that surround the mansion include a two-acre, brick Walled Garden with flower borders in bloom from spring to fall. The grounds also include a demonstration garden, rose and boxwood gardens, an allée of European lindens and hemlock hedge, and a Primrose Walk. In May the 2,000 tulips are the attraction; in June it's the arrangement of 300 giant pink and blue delphinia.

The 409-acre **Planting Fields Arboretum State Historic Park** (*Planting Fields Rd., Oyster Bay, tel 516/922-9200, ext. 13 for assistance*) was once the estate of English-born William Coe, an insurance executive who completed his Elizabethan-style manor house in 1921.

The gardens contain more than 600 species of plants, including an ever growing collection of rhododendrons and azaleas and more than 300 camellias grown in a small conservatory. Planting Fields is the translation of the Indian name for the once agricultural North Shore of Long Island.

After he graduated from Harvard, Theodore Roosevelt helped to design **Sagamore Hill National Historic Site** (*20 Sagamore Hill Rd., Oyster Bay, tel 516/922-4788, by guided tour only, house closed Mon.–Tues. in winter*). A rambling 23-room mansion, this was a place he considered home—and used as the summer White

The simple parlor in the house where Walt Whitman, perhaps America's greatest poet, began life.

House while he was President—and where he indulged himself in "hard work and the joy of life." The interior, decorated with hunting trophies and mementoes of his travels, reflects Roosevelt's vigorous lifestyle. In 1938 his son built the Old Orchard House next door, now a museum with exhibits on Roosevelt and an introductory film.

In the early 19th century, Long Island was agricultural, and the 50 buildings in the **Old Bethpage Village** *(Round Swamp Rd., Old Bethpage, tel 516/572-8400, closed Mon.–Tues.)* restoration re-create a village of this era. The Powell Farmhouse is on its original site, but the others, including a church, country store, tavern, and houses, were moved here from elsewhere on Long Island. The restoration is also a working farm with interpreters in period costume demonstrating agricultural techniques and crafts.

Walt Whitman (1819–1892) spent the first four years of his life in the early 1800s farmhouse that is now the **Walt Whitman Birthplace** *(246 Old Walt Whitman Rd., South Huntington, tel 631/427-5240, closed Tues.).* Nineteenth-century furnishings in the newly restored home and an

interpretive center with 130 Whitman portraits, Whitman's voice on tape, manuscripts, and artifacts illume the life of America's greatest poet.

Founded in 1939, **Museums at Stony Brook** *(1208 N.Y. 25A, Stony Brook, tel 516/751-0066)* is a historical complex noted for its Carriage Museum. There are more than 300 horse-drawn vehicles, including a 23-foot-long omnibus painted with still lifes, people, and animals. The Art Museum owns many works by genre painter William Sydney Mount, born in nearby Setauket in 1807, who did scenes of rural Long Island. Mount's family home, the Hawkins Mount House (1725), is on the museum grounds.

The South Shore on the Atlantic is known for its remarkable barrier beaches: **Fire Island National Seashore** *(tel 631/289-4810)* and the 2,413-acre **Jones Beach State Park** *(tel 516/785-1600)* with undeveloped areas for nature lovers and an outdoor concert stadium. The Hamptons and Montauk are at the eastern tip. For something different try a ferry ride or whale-watching cruise *(Long Island Visitors Bureau, tel 800/441-4601; www.web scope.com/li).* ■

Travelwise

**Travelwise information
232–233**
Planning your trip **232**
Getting around **232–233**
Practical advice **233**
Hotels & restaurants 234–251
Shopping 252–257
Entertainment 258–262

**Ever busy New York
taxicabs**

TRAVELWISE INFORMATION

There is really no bad time to visit New York, and although the weather is usually nicest in spring or fall, special events take place year-round. During summer's high heat and humidity, there are many outdoor festivals, often free, as well as indoor events in museums and galleries (always air-conditioned). Conventions often block-book hotels, so always check room availability before making travel reservations.

PLANNING YOUR TRIP

There are several key sources of information to help you. New York City's Official Visitor Information Center (tel 212/484-1222) or any of the theater and entertainment hotlines listed in the entertainment section of this book (see pp. 261–264) will yield useful information. For a personalized introduction to a neighborhood, contact Big Apple Greeter (tel 212/669-8159). This nonprofit volunteer group matches know-ledgeable New Yorkers with visitors, based upon visitor request applications.

USEFUL WEBSITES

Internet websites can provide up-to-date information, right down to giving street maps and finding addresses. The New York Public Library (tel 212/930-0747) offers Internet access.

www.nycvisit.com
    New York Convention & Visitors Bureau
www.bigapplegreeter.org
    Big Apple Greeter, available in several languages
www.panix.com/clay/nyc
    New York City reference index
digitalcity.com
    Manhattan User's Guide

NOTABLE EVENTS & FESTIVALS

JANUARY
Winter Antiques Show, Seventh Regiment Armory, tel 718-292-7392.
FEBRUARY
AIPAD, Photography Art Dealers Show, Seventh Regiment Armory, tel 212/986-0105.
Westminster Kennel Club
Dog Show, Madison Square Garden, tel 212/465-6741.
MARCH
St. Patrick's Day Parade, along Fifth Avenue.
Macy's Flower Show, tel 212/695-4400.
New Directors/New Films, Museum of Modern Art, tel 212/708-9400.
APRIL
Easter Parade, along Fifth Ave. (main area at 49th St.).
Baseball season opening day, Yankee Stadium, tel 718/293-6000; Shea Stadium, tel 718/507-8499.
New York International Auto Show, Jacob Javits Center, tel 212/216-2000.
MAY
Bike New York, The Great Five Borough Bike Tour (42-mile recreational bike ride), tel 212/932-0778.
New York Armory Antiques Show, Seventh Regiment Armory, tel 212-879-9713.
Ninth Avenue Food Festival, from 37th to 57th Streets.
Washington Square Outdoor Art Exhibition, tel 212/982-6255.
JUNE
Lesbian and Gay Pride Week (parade on Fifth Ave).
JULY
Fourth of July (tall ships in New York Harbor and fireworks on the East River), tel 212/695-4400.
Rockefeller Center Flower and Garden Show, tel 212/632-3975.
Midsummer Night's Swing, Lincoln Center (outdoor dance lessons, bands), tel 212/875-5766.
AUGUST
U.S. Open, Flushing Meadows Park, Queens, tel 718/760-6200.
SEPTEMBER
West Indian Labor Day Parade, Crown Heights,

Brooklyn (a Mardi Gras–like celebration), tel 718-467-1797.
New York Film Festival, Lincoln Center, tel 212/875-5610.
OCTOBER
Next Wave Festival, Brooklyn Academy of Music, tel 718/636-4100.
Greenwich Village Halloween Parade.
NOVEMBER
New York City Marathon, tel 212/860-4455.
Macy's Thanksgiving Parade, along Central Park West and Broadway, tel 212/695-4400.
Big Apple Circus, in a tent, Damrosch Park, Lincoln Center, tel 212/268-2500.
DECEMBER
Tree-lighting, Rockefeller Center, tel 212/632-3975.
New Year's Eve, Times Square (see the ball drop to bring in the New Year, live).

GETTING AROUND

FROM THE AIRPORTS

Air-Ride provides recorded information on transportation to and from all airports, tel 800/247-7433.

Buses New York Airport Service has regular buses to/from JFK, LaGuardia, and Newark airports to/from Grand Central Terminal and the Port Authority, tel 212/564-8484. SuperShuttle for JFK and LaGuardia to/from most hotels, 1-800-258-3826; online res: www.supershuttle.com. Olympia Trails between Newark and three New York City destinations, tel 212/964-6233.
Car services Try to book 24 hours in advance or earlier. Basic sedans are reliable and at reasonable rates. Carmel, tel 212/666-6666 or 800-9CARMEL; Airlink (hotel pickup), tel 877/599-8200, up to 11 passengers; Allstate, tel 212/741-7440 or 800/453-4099.
Taxis JFK: Fixed rate of $45 excluding tolls and tip to Manhattan. LaGuardia: By the

meter, $25–$30. Newark: Dispatcher-determined flat rate of $45–$65, depending on destination, excluding tolls and tip.

NYC TRANSPORTATION
If you can, walk, and as you stroll through a neighborhood or to your destination, enjoy a new food experience along the way. If you drive, park your car in a garage ($20–$40 and up per day), because traffic is always heavy and on-street parking hard to find.

MASS TRANSIT
Information: tel 718/330-1234, www.mta.info
Buses & subways These cover most of the city and cost $2.00 per ride (half price for seniors and disabled, free for children under 3'8"), including a transfer. Subways are generally safe and the most efficient way to get around. They are a good choice for long distances and during rush hour. Buses can be scenic and relaxing but unbearably slow. They stop every two blocks, except "limited" ones (ask). A free map, showing all bus and subway routes, is usually available in subway stations, and one is posted on the wall and in each subway car and bus.
Lost & Found Buses and subways, tel 212/712-4500; taxis, tel (in NYC) 311; or 212/NEWYORK.
MetroCards Available at many stores and newsstands and at all subway stations; cards can be purchased in whatever amount you choose (you get a free ride if you purchase $10 or more) and are debited each time you enter the subways or ride a bus. They allow for a free transfer from the subway to/from a connecting bus within a two-hour period. Subways require MetroCards; buses take MetroCards or exact change ($2.00).

TAXIS
Widely available and fairly reasonable, taxis can get you wherever you wish. Hail them from anywhere, though you may have better luck finding one on major avenues. Take only yellow cabs with the medallion numbers on the roof and the rates on the door. They are available if the medallion number is lit (and not the off-duty sign). The base fare is $2.50, with a 50-cent 8 p.m.–6 a.m. surcharge, and then 40 cents for every fifth-mile (4 blocks) and 20 cents for every minute in stopped or slow traffic. There is no charge for other passengers (taxis can take four) or luggage, but unusually large items are extra. Tips are expected to be 15 percent. There is also NY Water Taxi, tel 212/742-1969.

OTHER
Rollerblading and biking are a fun way of getting around in parks and traffic-free places. Many bike/skate shops rent: For bikes, try the Loeb Boathouse in Central Park, tel 212/517-3623.

PRACTICAL ADVICE

Although New York City's crime rate has steadily declined in the past few years and the most trafficked areas and subways are well-patrolled by police, one should be alert and exercise caution. The following personal safety tips should help you to have an incident-free trip:
•Do not give your bags to anyone in an airport or train/bus station other than authorized personnel or your yellow-taxi driver while loading the trunk.
•Avoid abandoned or badly lit streets.
•Know where you're going in areas of Manhattan north of 96th St., west of 8th Ave., east of Ave. A, the financial district at night, and in all of the other boroughs.
•Avoid all parks after dark, except for crowded special events.
•Do not make eye contact or get drawn into conversation with suspicious characters.
•Do not use cash machines when there's no one around, and do not count cash on the street.
•Carry your wallet in an inaccessible place and keep your handbag securely across your body, clasp facing in.
•Avoid the subway after 11 p.m. (buses are fine) and stay with the crowd.
•If you are robbed, hand over your wallet and whatever else is requested without resistance and call 911 from the nearest phone (free call).

TRAVELERS WITH DISABILITIES
Airport Travelers' Aid, tel 718/656-4870.
Asser Levy Park has a playground for disabled children and a free outdoor pool (E. 23rd at Asser Levy Place near the East River, tel 212/447-2020).
Big Apple Greeters is a clearinghouse for information for disabled travelers and offers neighborhood visits led by volunteers; reserve three days in advance. Tel 212/669-8159; TTY 669-8273.
HAI (Hospital Audiences Inc.) offers a guide to access in New York's cultural institutions and provides services for the blind for theater performances. Tel 212/575-7676.
Lighthouse International has events by and for the visually impaired and Braille subway maps (111 E. 59th St., tel 800/334-5497 or 212/821-9200).

EMERGENCIES
Any emergencies, tel 911.
•Crime Victims Hotline, tel 212/577-7777.
•Poison Control Center, tel 800/221-1222.
•Medical emergencies: Proceed to the nearest hospital emergency room (call 411 or check Yellow Pages for the nearest hospital) or call 911 for an ambulance.
•New York Healthcare Immediate Care, 55 E. 34th St., tel 212/252-6001, walk-in clinic.
•Dental Referral Service, tel 800/917-6453.
•Towed cars, tel 212/971-0770.

HOTELS & RESTAURANTS

HOTELS & RESTAURANTS

The variety and price range of places to stay in the city is remarkably varied, with options sure to meet every taste and budget. In fact, one will find that there are as many bargains available in New York as in any other place—if not more—with low-cost options that include comfortable bed-and-breakfasts and small older hotels in some of the city's most interesting neighborhoods. One might also opt to spend a few days in an inexpensive accommodation and then splurge on something exquisitely fine, the kind of metropolitan luxury one finds only in New York. When it comes to food, one can eat well in a historic Lower East Side deli, an ornate Chinese banquet hall, or a cozy French bistro that seats only 12, or savor delectable fare by a world-class chef in the most extravagant of settings. While roaming the streets sight-seeing or shopping, there is nothing more satisfying than sampling the offerings of sidewalk vendors or noshing the entire length of an avenue during one of the city's many food festivals.

HOTELS

Once you determine your total room budget, decide what neighborhood or area appeals to you and then research in depth. From Lower Manhattan to the Upper East and West Sides, the city teems with shopping, sight-seeing, cultural, and historic attractions. If you are drawn more to Broadway or other West Side attractions, then a place in the Times Square or Lincoln Center area may be best. Taxis are usually available, but a ride from the West Village to the Upper East Side, for example, can be quite expensive and also—depending on traffic—slow. Be sure to calculate transportation in your budgets of money and time. Choosing lodging for its convenience and accessibility is usually best for those with limited time to spend exploring the Big Apple. Once you pick your location, then you can explore the many options.

For disabled access, it is recommended you check with the hotel to establish the extent of their facilities. Also verify parking or access to parking spaces. All hotels are air-conditioned.

RESTAURANTS

New York may well be the world's best fed city. The variety of restaurants—from the hautest French to the simplest Asian, and absolutely everything in between—is unsurpassed. At all levels, value is generally good because everyone wants to take a bite of the Big Apple. The challenge is getting a reservation.

Included in the listings below are restaurant closings, though you should always check times when making a reservation, which is recommended when possible. Verify access for those with disabilities; facilities vary, depending on how old the restaurant is as well as its size. If you can't get through to a place by phone, it is likely to be so popular that reservations are impossible to come by. Prices at lunch can be expected to be lower than at dinner at the more upscale establishments, and many of these restaurants offer a special prix-fixe menu that can be a real bargain. All restaurants are air-conditioned unless otherwise noted, and all establishments have nonsmoking areas.

ORGANIZATION

Hotels and restaurants listed here have been grouped first according to neighborhood, then listed alphabetically by price range.

ABBREVIATIONS

L = lunch
D = dinner
Credit card abbreviations are: AE (American Express); DC (Diner's Club); MC (Mastercard); and V (Visa).

LOWER MANHATTAN

HOTELS

🏨 **MILLENNIUM HILTON**
$$$$$
55 CHURCH ST.
TEL 212/693-2001
FAX 212/571-2317
Top-end corporate destination. High-tech style with a fax in each room, and some beautiful views of New York Harbor. Lower rates available weekends.
ⓘ 561 🚇 1 to Cortlandt St.; C to World Trade Center
🚇 🍽 💳 All major cards

🏨 **SOHO GRAND**
$$$$$
310 W. BROADWAY
(BET. GRAND & CANAL STS.)
TEL 212/965-3000 or
800/965-3000
FAX 212/965-3200
Striking design and a fashionable destination for those who enjoy the downtown vantage point. Endless interesting stores and galleries are within walking distance.
ⓘ 367 + 4 suites 🚇 A, C, E to Canal St. 🍽 💳 All major cards

🏨 HOTEL ON RIVINGTON

$$$$–$$$$$

107 RIVINGTON STREET
(BET. LUDLOW & ESSEX STS.)
TEL 212/475-2600
FAX 212/475-5959

This gleaming 21-story glass tower in the historic Lower East Side offers terrific city views from the floor-to-ceiling glass windows in every room. Cutting-edge designers injected creativity into all aspects of the hotel's concept and look, making it both chic and pleasurable. Many of the rooms have balconies, and unusual amenities include Japanese soaking tubs and in-room spa services. For food, drink, and socializing, try Thor, the first-floor restaurant, bar, and lounge.

🛏 94 rooms, 16 suites 🚇 F to Delancey, J to Essex St. 💳 All major cards

---

RESTAURANTS

🍴 BAYARD'S

$$$$

1 HANOVER SQ.
(BET. PEARL & STONE STS.)
TEL 212/514-9454

Featuring a French cuisine–based menu that includes seasonal dishes such as celery root soup and rack of lamb.

🍽 80 🚇 4, 5 to Wall St. 🕐 Closed Sun. and L 💳 All major cards

🍴 CHANTERELLE

$$$$

2 HARRISON ST.
(AT HUDSON ST.)
TEL 212/966-6960

Lovely, formal dining room with TriBeCa flavor. Here you will find impeccable service, wines, and cheeses.

🍽 17 tables 🚇 1 to Franklin St. 🕐 Closed all day Sun., Mon. L 💳 All major cards

🍴 THE GRILL ROOM

$$$$

2 WORLD FINANCIAL CENTER, 225 LIBERTY ST.
(AT WEST ST.)

TEL 212-414-0295

Visit great American chef Larry Forgione's downtown outpost with a view. House specialties are roast lobster and lamb chops.

🍽 200 🚇 1 to Cortlandt St.; N, R to World Trade Center 🕐 Closed Sat., Sun. 💳 All major cards

🍴 MONTRACHET

$$$$

239 W. BROADWAY
(BET. WALKER & WHITE STS.)
TEL 212/219-2777

Superb food and award-winning wine list in sedate French bistro setting. Good service, fine roasted vegetable terrine, truffle-crusted salmon, foie gras dishes. Lunch Friday only.

🍽 85 🚇 1, 9 to Franklin St. 🕐 Closed Sun.–Thurs. L 💳 All major cards

🍴 NOBU

$$$$

105 HUDSON ST.
(AT FRANKLIN ST.)
TEL 212/219-0500

A deservedly popular Nobu Matsuhisa–Drew Nieporent venture with exciting Japanese cuisine and dramatic design. Specialties include black cod with miso and *tiradito*. Reservations almost impossible, but there's always the sushi bar.

🍽 100 🚇 1 to Franklin St. 🕐 Closed Sat. & Sun. L 💳 All major cards

🍴 BALTHAZAR

$$$

80 SPRING ST.
(AT CROSBY ST.)
TEL 212/965-1414

A beautiful SoHo brasserie with matching menu, upbeat tempo, breakfast, lunch, and dinner, late nights and weekend brunch. The oysters and cold seafood platter are particularly impressive.

🍽 160 🚇 6 to Spring St. 💳 All major cards

🍴 BLUE RIBBON

$$$

97 SULLIVAN ST.
(BET. PRINCE & SPRING STS.)
TEL 212/274-0404

Minimalist setting with excellent raw bar (ask for Alonso's sauce) and eclectic menu. They even have fondue and *pupu* platters. Evenings only.

🍽 45 🚇 C, E to Spring St. 💳 All major cards

🍴 DELMONICO'S

$$$

56 BEAVER ST.
(NEAR WILLIAM ST.)
TEL 212/509-1144

A classic dating from 1827, birthplace of eggs Benedict and lobster Newburg.

🍽 140 🚇 2, 3, 4, 5 to Wall St. 🕐 Closed weekends 💳 All major cards

🍴 ECCO

$$$

124 CHAMBERS ST.
(BET. CHURCH ST. & W. BROADWAY)
TEL 212/227-7074

Savory Italian cooking well worth the steep price. Try the veal scallopine with artichokes, penne *arrabiata*, or assorted grilled fish.

🍽 75 🚇 A, C, 1, 2, 3 to Chambers St. 🕐 Closed L Sat. & all day Sun. 💳 All major cards

🍴 14 WALL STREET RESTAURANT

$$$

14 WALL ST., 31ST FL.
(BET. BROADWAY & BROAD STS.)
TEL 212/233-2780

Dine on French cuisine in J. P. Morgan's former penthouse, overlooking the financial district. Specialties include citrus-marinated salmon baked on an oak plank and sea scallops in porcini broth.

🍽 150 🚇 2, 3, 4, 5 to Wall Street 🕐 Closed Sat. & Sun. 💳 All major cards

HOTELS & RESTAURANTS

HONMURA AN
$$$
170 MERCER ST.
(BET. PRINCE & HOUSTON STS.)
TEL 212/334-5253
Zenlike soba noodle experience. Pricey but exquisite.
🔲 50 🚇 R, W to Prince St. 🕐 Closed Mon.–Tues. L 💳 All major cards

HQ
$$$
90 THOMPSON ST.
(BET. PRINCE & SPRING STS.)
TEL 212/226-0602
Well-priced quintessential New York bistro serving eclectic American cuisine— something for everyone.
🔲 50 🚇 C, E to Spring St.-6th Ave. 💳 All major cards

LES HALLES
$$$
15 JOHN STREET.
(BET. BROADWAY & NASSAU ST.)
TEL 212/285-8585
A French brasserie offering steak and seafood; home to chef-at-large Anthony Bourdain.
🔲 210 🚇 2, 3, A, C to Fulton, Nassau St. 💳 All major cards

ODEON
$$$
145 W. BROADWAY
(AT THOMAS ST.)
TEL 212/233-0507
Hip downtown eatery with reliable French and American food, good late-night scene. Recommended dishes are steak au poivre, steak frites, and other classic bistro fare.
🔲 140 🚇 I to Chambers St. 💳 All major cards

RAOUL'S
$$$
180 PRINCE ST.
(BET. SULLIVAN & THOMPSON STS.)
TEL 212/966-3518
Always happening, lively French bistro/bar, garden in season, good late at night. The steak au poivre and foie gras terrine are recommended.
🔲 200 🚇 I to Houston St.; C, E to Spring St. 🕐 Closed L 💳 All major cards

ROY'S NEW YORK
$$$
130 WASHINGTON ST.
(BET. ALBANY & CARLISLE STS.)
TEL 212/266-6262
Skewered coconut shrimp and individual pizzas in an upbeat and cheerful setting. A refreshing change of pace in the stately Wall Street neighborhood.
🔲 195 🚇 I, N, R to Rector St. 🕐 Closed L Sat.–Sun. 💳 All major cards

SAMMY'S ROUMANIAN STEAKHOUSE
$$$
157 CHRYSTIE ST.
(AT DELANCEY ST.)
TEL 212/673-0330
Unbelievable only-in-New York option for schmaltz-laden Jewish meal in old-fashioned Lower East Side location. Go for the classics: brisket, chopped liver, along with a bottle of vodka in an ice block.
🔲 110 🚇 F to Second Ave., D to Grand Street 🕐 Closed L & some Jewish holidays 💳 All major cards

SAVOY
$$$
70 PRINCE ST.
(AT CROSBY ST.)
TEL 212/219-8570
Cozy setting with inventive, well-executed menu. New upstairs dining with rotating prix-fixe menus, fireplace cooking. A house specialty is salt-crusted baked duck.
🔲 65 🚇 R, W to Prince St.; B, D, F, V to Broadway/ Lafayette 🕐 Closed Sun. L 💳 All major cards

BOULEY BAKERY & MARKET
$$–$$$
130 WEST BROADWAY
(AT DUANE ST.)
TEL 212/608-5829
David Bouley's affordable spin-off has a basement take-out & street-level patisserie (daily 7:30 to 7:30) and upstairs bistro (Tue.–Sat. 6 p.m.–11 p.m.).
🔲 35 🚇 1, 2, 3, A, C to Chambers St. 💳 All major cards

BRIDGE CAFE
$$
279 WATER ST.
(AT DOVER ST.)
TEL 212/227-3344
Casual, charming spot next to Brooklyn Bridge. Sautéed soft-shell crabs and pan-roasted chicken are specialties.
🔲 63 🚇 A, 2, 3 to Fulton St.; 4, 5, 6 to Brooklyn Bridge 🕐 Closed Sat. L 💳 All major cards

JOE'S SHANGHAI
$$
9 PELL ST.
(BET. BOWERY & MOTT STS.)
TEL 212/233-8888
Often a wait but worth it for broth-filled crab or pork dumplings and a large selection of other Shanghai savories. The eggplant with garlic sauce and bean curd wrapped in spinach are very good.
🔲 85 🚇 6, N, R to Canal St. 💳 Not accepted

NEW YORK NOODLE TOWN
$$
28 BOWERY
(AT BAYARD ST.)
TEL 212/349-0923
No-frills Chinatown setting with great dishes: salt-baked seafood, duck with flowering chives, noodles with ginger scallion sauce.
🔲 60 🚇 6, N, R to Canal St. 💳 Not accepted

THAILAND RESTAURANT
$$
106 BAYARD ST.
(AT BAXTER ST.)
TEL 212/349-3132

Low-key spot for good Thai food. The grilled beef salad and green curry are delicious.
🏠 55–60 🚇 6, N, R to Canal St. 💳 All major cards

SOMETHING SPECIAL

🍴 COWGIRL HALL OF FAME

A theme restaurant that rings absolutely authentic, with Western decor, lots of wood, antlers, barbed wire, cowboy trappings, and a re-created 1950s-era motel room where you can wait to be seated. Definitely casual and for those with hearty appetites. Good for families too: There is a special children's menu. A small gift shop sells collectibles and Western items.
$
519 HUDSON ST.
TEL 212/633-1133
🏠 283 🚇 1 to Christopher St. 💳 AE, MC, V

🍴 BO-KY
$
80 BAYARD ST.
(BET. MOTT & MULBERRY STS.)
TEL 212/406-2292
Dozens of inexpensive Vietnamese soups served in a plain Chinatown setting with communal tables. The favorite is curried chicken, and they do a decent roast duck.
🏠 100 🚇 6 to Canal St. 💳 Not accepted

🍴 BUBBY'S
$
120 HUDSON ST.
(AT N. MOORE ST.)
TEL 212/219-0666
Casual but popular spot for all meals. Weekend breakfasts, brunch, and homemade baked goods.
🏠 120 🚇 1 to Franklin St. 💳 DC, MC, V

🍴 JING FONG
$
20 ELIZABETH ST.
(BET. BAYARD & CANAL STS.)
TEL 212/964-5256

Overwhelming and unforgettable dim sum paradise in the late morning/lunchtime hours. Don't miss the Chinese chive dumplings and the taro leaf–wrapped packages of sticky rice, chicken, and sausage. Huge and bustling.
🏠 1,000 🚇 6 to Canal St. 💳 AE, MC, V

🍴 KATZ'S DELICATESSEN
$
205 E. HOUSTON ST.
(AT LUDLOW ST.)
TEL 212/254-2246
Classic Lower East Side destination for hot dogs, the best pastrami, corned beef, pickles, and Dr. Brown's soda.
🏠 340 🚇 F to Second Ave. 💳 AE, MC, V

🍴 LOMBARDI'S
$
32 SPRING ST.
(BET. MOTT & MULBERRY STS.)
TEL 212/941-7994
Try one of the city's best pizzas in the first New York City pizza-parlor location.
🏠 100 🚇 6 to Spring St. 💳 Not accepted

🍴 NHA TRANG
$
87 BAXTER ST.
(BET. BAYARD & CANAL STS.)
TEL 212/233-5948
No-nonsense setting for Vietnamese fare. Try pork chops and hot and sour shrimp soup, then sweet Vietnamese coffee for dessert.
🏠 80 🚇 6 to Canal St. 💳 MC, V

🍴 PITA EXPRESS
$
15 ANN ST. #4
(AT BROADWAY)
TEL 212/571-2999
Not-too-spicy Middle Eastern menu serving hummus, baba gannouj, and tabbouleh.
🏠 30 🚇 4, 5, A, C to Bwy/Nassau 💳 All major cards

THE VILLAGES

HOTELS

🏨 ABINGDON GUEST HOUSE
$$$
13 8TH AVE.
(BET. 12TH ST. & JANE ST.)
TEL 212/243-5384
FAX 212/807-7473
Gracious B&B with nicely decorated rooms, two of which share a bathroom.
🛏 9 rooms 🚇 A, C, E to 14th St. 💳 All major cards

🏨 LARCHMONT
$$$
27 W. 11TH ST.
(BET. 5TH & 6TH AVES.)
TEL 212/989-9333
FAX 212/989-9496
Tiny but pleasant rooms in excellent location, quaint touches. Shared bathrooms.
🛏 50 🚇 F to 14th St. 💳 AE, MC, V

🏨 WASHINGTON SQUARE HOTEL
$$$
103 WAVERLY PLACE
(AT MACDOUGAL ST.)
TEL 212/777-9515 or 800/222-0418
FAX 212/979-8373
Good location in the heart of Greenwich Village, off park. Functional but well-furnished rooms.
🛏 180 🚇 A, B, C, D, E, F to W. 4th St. 🏋 💳 All major cards

RESTAURANTS

🍴 BABBO
$$$$
110 WAVERLY PL.
TEL 212/777-0303
Mario Batali's excellent, adventurous Italian restaurant has been a sensation since opening day. Getting reservations can be challenging.
🏠 126 🚇 A, B, C, D, E, F to W. 4th St. 🚫 Closed L 💳 All major cards

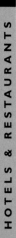

GOTHAM BAR & GRILL

In this spacious multilevel Gramercy-area eatery, the architecture, as well as the food, stands out: One reviewer called this award-winning, postmodern warehouse conversion "an awesome dining temple." Chef Alfred Portale serves up specialties such as grilled rack of lamb and seared yellowfin tuna, and whimsical creative desserts. Gotham is consistently voted a favorite.

$$$$
12 E. 12TH ST.
(BET. 5TH AVE. & UNIVERSITY PLACE)
TEL 212/620-4020
150 4, 5, 6 to Union Sq. Closed Sat. & Sun. L
All major cards

DA SILVANO

$$$$
260 6TH AVE.
(AT HOUSTON ST.)
TEL 212/982-2343
Since opening in 1975, this cozy trattoria, with a sidewalk café, has transformed into a popular celebrity haunt. Ever changing pastas, entrées such as osso buco, and owner Silvano Marchetto's hospitality are the reasons behind all the fuss.
190 A, C, E, B, D, F to W. 4th St. All major cards

JAMES BEARD HOUSE

$$$$
167 W. 12TH ST.
(BET. 6TH & 7TH AVES.)
TEL 212/627-2308
Gastronomic Carnegie Hall featuring the world's best chefs, a different one preparing meals nightly. Call for calendar. Advance reservations only.
90 1, 2, 3 to 14th St.
All major cards

LUCKY CHENG'S

$$$
24 1ST AVE.
(BET. 1ST & 2ND STS.)

TEL 212/473-0516
A veritable transvestite sideshow with passable pan-Asian food; go for the fun and late-night cocktails.
200–350 F to 2nd Ave. Closed L All major cards

MI COCINA

$$$
57 JANE ST.
(AT HUDSON ST.)
TEL 212/627-8273
Rich and varied authentic Mexican regional cuisine. A specialty is *conchinita pibil*, shredded pork in a banana leaf. Unlike the rest.
42 A, C, E to 14th St. Closed Mon.–Fri. L; Sat–Sun. brunch at 11 a.m. All major cards

PÒ

$$$
31 CORNELIA ST.
(BET. BLEECKER & W. 4TH STS.)
TEL 212/645-2189
Well-priced Northern Italian & Mediterranean food. The tasting menu is a delicious deal.
12 tables A, B, C, D, E, F to W. 4th St. Closed all Mon. & Tues. L AE

DANAL

$$
90 E. 10TH ST.
(BET. 3RD & 4TH AVES.)
TEL 212/982-6930
Eclectic cuisine in charming storefront setting. Garden seating available. Serves afternoon tea (reservations only) and brunch. Wine bar.
50 6 to Astor Place; N, R to 8th St. Closed Mon. a.m. All major cards

FLORENT

$$
69 GANSEVOORT ST.
(BET. GREENWICH & WASHINGTON STS.)
TEL 212/989-5779
Open 24 hours. Amazingly diverse clientele. Burgers, mussels, steak frites, and gratins are favorites.

70 A, C, E to 14th St. Not accepted

JAPONICA

$$
100 UNIVERSITY PL.
TEL 212/243-7752
Sushi and Japanese fare; popular for lunch and dinner.
84 4, 5, 6 to Union Sq. AE, MC, V

FIAMMA OSTERIA

Fiamma means "flame" in Italian, and this contemporary town house is ideal for fanning the flames of your romance or that special occasion meant to impress, while dining on deliciously inventive modern Italian food. Owner Steve Hanson ("the P. T. Barnum of restaurants") outfits his attentive waitstaff in ninjalike Nicole Miller and provides wondrous specialty drinks (try the cappuccino martini, with floating coffee beans). All pastas are made in-house: the signature dish is *garganelli*—quill-shaped pasta with sweet peas, truffle butter, parmigiano, and prosciutto. You'll enjoy the glass elevator too.

$$$$
206 SPRING ST. (BET. 6TH AVE. & SULLIVAN ST.)
TEL 212/653-0100
130 (plus third floor for special events, seats 55)
C, E to Spring St. Closed Sat. & Sun. L
All major cards

JOHN'S PIZZERIA

$$
278 BLEECKER ST.
(BET. 6TH AVE. & 7TH AVE. S.)
TEL 212/243-1680
Brick-oven pizza and '50s decor in a perennially favorite spot for locals, celebs, and tourists. ATM on premises.
100 A, B, C, D, E, F to W. 4th St. Not accepted

🍴 SECOND AVENUE DELI
$$
156 2ND AVE. (AT 10TH ST.)
TEL 212/677-0606
One of New York's finest and best-known, with chopped liver and matzoh ball soup to write home about, along with delicious sandwiches and other classic deli fare.
🛈 175 🚇 6 to Astor Place
🕐 Closed some Jewish holidays 🅑 All major cards

🍴 TEA & SYMPATHY
$$
108 GREENWICH AVE.
(BET. 12TH & 13TH STS.)
TEL 212/807-8329
Tiny storefront serving delicious, hearty British fare, like Welsh rarebit, and bangers and mash. Takeout available; small shop.
🍽 22 🚇 A, C, E to 14th St.
🅑 MC, V

SOMETHING SPECIAL

🍴 ONE IF BY LAND, TWO IF BY SEA
Located in a 1786 landmark stone carriage house that was once the home of Aaron Burr, this elegant restaurant on two levels overlooks a private garden with festive lights. Inside, candles, live piano music, flowers, and four fireplaces create an ambience perfect for a romantic, intimate meal or a large celebration. Menu favorites are beef Wellington, American specialties, and contemporary interpretations of classic dishes. And, if you are one of the lucky, you may dine there on a night when the ghost of Aaron Burr, victorious after his duel with Alexander Hamilton, appears.
$$$$
17 BARROW ST.
TEL 212/255-8649
🍽 150 🚇 A, B, C, D, E, F to W. 4th St.
🅑 All major cards

🍴 CORNER BISTRO
$
331 W. 4TH ST.
(AT 14TH ST.)
TEL 212/242-9502
Bar for burgers and fries on paper plates. Get the Bistro burger, with cheese, bacon, lettuce, and tomato, all for $5. Open late.
🍽 34 🚇 A, C, E to 14th St.
🅑 Not accepted

🍴 HOLY BASIL
$
149 SECOND AVE.
(BET. 9TH &10TH STS.)
TEL 212/460-5557
Thai food in the East Village with wonderful-tasting and -looking food.
🚇 6 to Astor Pl.; N, R to 8th St. 🅑 All credit cards

🍴 POMMES FRITES
$
123 2ND AVE.
(BET. 7TH ST. & ST, MARKS PL.)
TEL 212/674-1234
Not quite a meal, but a nice, big snack of Belgian-style fries in a paper cone and even a bench to sit on. Try the *especia* sauce for dipping, and the malt vinegar.
🍽 3 tables 🚇 6 to Astor Place 🅑 Not accepted

🍴 TAQUERIA DI MEXICO
$
93 GREENWICH AVE.
(BET. BANK & 12TH STS.)
TEL 212/255-5212
Authentic casual Mexican food. Good tortilla soup and *taquitos al pastor.*
🍽 14 tables 🚇 A, C, E to 14th St. 🅑 Not accepted

🍴 VESELKA
$
144 2ND AVE. (AT 9TH ST.)
TEL 212/228-9682
Casual neighborhood hangout with Ukrainian specialties, especially soups, and timeless murals. Try buckwheat pancakes or challah French toast.
🍽 60 🚇 6 to Astor Place 🅑 All major cards

MIDTOWN SOUTH

HOTELS

🏨 INN AT IRVING PLACE
$$$$$
56 IRVING PLACE
(BET. 17TH & 18TH STS.)
TEL 212/533-4600 or 800/685-1447
FAX 212/533-4611
Romantic, Victorian-style hotel with four-poster beds. Try high tea at Lady Mendl's Tea Salon (on the premises).
🛈 11 suites 🚇 4, 5, 6 to Union Sq. 🅑 All major cards.

🏨 W NEW YORK– THE TUSCANY
$$$$
120 E. 39TH ST.
TEL 212/686-1600 or 877/946-8357
FAX 212/779-7822
Large rooms with Italian marble bathrooms.
🛈 110 + 12 suites 🚇 4, 5, 6 to Grand Central 🔫
🅑 All major cards

🏨 THE GERSHWIN HOTEL
$$$–$$$$
7 E. 27TH ST.
(BET. 5TH & MADISON AVES.)
TEL 212/545-8000
This 100-year-old location, in an area where pop music was penned in the 1930s & 40s, caters to budget-conscious and creative global travelers. Rooms range from shared-bathroom dorms to private rooms and suites. Pop culture and art are still the Muses here.
🛈 140 + 10 dorm rooms 🚇 6, N, R, W to 28th St.
🅑 AE, MC, V

🏨 CHELSEA HOTEL
$$$
222 W. 23RD ST.
(BET. 7TH & 8TH AVES.)
TEL 212/243-3700
Historic home of famous artists and writers, with a

cozy lobby filled with art. Definitely worth a look even if no rooms are available.

[i] 400　[subway] 1 to 23rd St.; C, E to 23rd St.　[nearby] Nearby
[cards] All major cards

🏨 HOTEL METRO
$$$
45 W. 35TH ST.
(BET. 5TH & 6TH AVES.)
TEL 212/947-2500 or
800/356-3870
FAX 212/279-1310
Stylish, art deco rooms and a roof terrace with views of the Empire State Building.
[i] 155 + 20 suites　[subway] 1, 2, 3 to 34th St.　[nearby]　[cards] All major cards

---

SOMETHING SPECIAL

🏨 MORGANS
🍴

There's no sign out front and design is minimalist in this hotel, its colors subdued grays, black, and white. But this peaceful retreat, opened in 1984 by Studio 54 creators Ian Schrager and Steve Rubell, now packs a punch: Asia de Cuba, the first-floor restaurant. Designed in the 1990s by Phillipe Starck, it is pristine white but flashy, its focus a long share-table in the center, with a picture of a waterfall above. When you get closer, the water reveals itself as a hologram. Entertainment and sports celebrities flock here.
$$$$$
237 MADISON AVE.
TEL 212/686-0300 or
800-606-6090
FAX 212/554-6511
[i] 113　[subway] 4, 5, 6 to Grand Central　[nearby] Nearby　[cards] All major cards

---

RESTAURANTS

🍴 CHELSEA BISTRO & BAR
$$$$
358 W. 23RD ST.
(BET. 8TH & 9TH AVES.)
TEL 212/727-2026
Sophisicated, contemporary French food in attractive setting. Try hot-smoked salmon and escargots.
[seats] 110　[subway] C, E to 23rd St.
[closed] Closed L
[cards] All major cards

🍴 GRAMERCY TAVERN
$$$$
42 E. 20TH ST.
(BET. BROADWAY & PARK AVE. S.)
TEL 212/477-0777
Well-executed, contemporary cuisine, fine wines, clubby atmosphere, with Tavern Room as a more casual option. Try the tuna tartare with sea urchin vinaigrette.
[seats] 140 + 40 tavern area
[subway] 6 to 23rd St.　[cards] All major cards

🍴 LES HALLES
$$$$
411 PARK AVE. S.
(BET. 28TH & 29TH STS.)
TEL 212/679-4111
French bistro with great frisée salad, *boudins, merguez,* filet mignon, tableside steak tartare, and *côte de boeuf* for two.
[seats] 150　[subway] 6 to 28th St.
[cards] All major cards

🍴 HANGAWI
$$$$
12 E. 32ND ST.
(BET. 5TH & MADISON AVES.)
TEL 212/213-0077
An otherworldly Korean vegetarian experience. Dishes are prepared with unusual but memorable roots and greens.
[seats] 60　[subway] 6 to 33rd St; N, R to 34th St.　[cards] All major cards

🍴 LA LUNCHEONETTE
$$$$
130 10TH AVE.
(AT 18TH ST.)
TEL 212/675-0342
Classic French bistro food in a hideaway. Cassoulet, rabbit stew, and skate are house specialties.
[seats] 18 tables　[subway] 1 to 18th St.; A, C, E to 14th St.
[closed] Closed Sat. L　[cards] All major cards

🍴 MESA GRILL
$$$$
102 5TH AVE.
(BET. 15TH & 16TH STS.)
TEL 212/807-7400
Chef Bobby Flay's upbeat Southern inventions in charged atmosphere. Try the grilled salmon; spice-rubbed port; or shrimp & roasted garlic corn tamale.
[seats] 140　[subway] 4, 5, 6, N, R, Q, W to Union Sq.　[cards] All major cards

🍴 I TRULLI (& ENOTECA)
$$$$
122 E. 27TH ST.
(BET. LEXINGTON AVE. & PARK AVE. S.)
TEL 212/481-7372
The foods and wines of Italy's Apulia region, with excellent homemade pastas, especially *bavette a funghi,* rotisserie chicken, and wood-roasted fish. Next door Enoteca is a wine bar serving casual food.
[seats] 150　[subway] 6 to 28th St.
[closed] Closed Sat. & Sun. L
[cards] All major cards

🍴 PERIYALI
$$$$
35 W. 20TH ST.
(BET. 5TH & 6TH AVES.)
TEL 212/463-7890

Established destination for home-style Greek food, with exquisitely simple fish and authentic dishes. Try *pikantikes salates* to start, then grilled octopus or lamb.
🔧 100 🚇 F to 23rd St. 🕐 Closed Sat. L & all day Sun. 💳 All major cards

UNION SQUARE CAFÉ
$$$$
21 E. 16TH ST.
(BET. 5TH AVE. & UNION SQ. W.)
TEL 212/243-4020
Award-winning and eternally successful formula of chef Michael Romano's eclectic, well-executed cuisine, great wines, and attentive service. Signature dishes include fried calamari with spicy anchovy sauce and filet mignon of tuna.
🔧 125 🚇 4, 5, 6 to Union Sq. 💳 All major cards

ADA
$$$
208 E. 58TH ST.
(BET. 2ND & 3RD AVES.)
TEL 212/371-6060
Chef Rajender Rana specializes in Indian cuisine, including Garam Marsala quails and Cochin prawns. Waiters anticipate your every need. Reservations recommended.
🔧 100 🚇 R, W, 4, 5, 6 to 59th St. & Lexington Ave. 🕐 Closed L Sat.–Sun. 💳 All major cards

BRIGHT FOOD SHOP
$$
216 8TH AVE.
(BET. 21ST & 22ND STS.)
TEL 212/243-4433
Odd-sounding but good casual fare. For take-out food, try its cousin Kitchen, two doors up.
🔧 42 🚇 C, E to 23rd St. 💳 All major cards

EL CID
$$
322 W. 15TH ST.
(BET. 8TH & 9TH AVES.)
TEL 212/929-9332

Excellent tapas in jovial setting. Baby squid is best, also the shrimp in garlic sauce, and the white Sangria.
🔧 12 tables 🚇 A, C, E to 14th St. 🕐 Closed L & all day Mon. 💳 AE

PONGAL
$$
110 LEXINGTON AVE.
(BET. 27TH & 28TH STS.)
TEL 212/696-9458
Fragrant south Indian vegetarian (kosher) menu with exceptional *thalis* and *dosai*.
🔧 45–50 🚇 6 to 28th St. 💳 Not accepted

ZEN PALATE
$$
34 UNION SQUARE E.
(PARK AVENUE AT 16TH ST.)
TEL 212/614-9291
A pan-Asian favorite with unusual vegetarian dishes (that even carnivores will like) and great ambience.
🔧 80 🚇 Union Sq.

EISENBERG'S SANDWICH SHOP
$
174 5TH AVE.
(BET. 22ND & 23RD STS.)
TEL 212/675-5096
Landmark Jewish diner in Chelsea. Great Reubens and tuna salad on rye.
🔧 34 🚇 N, R to 23rd St. 🕐 Closed after 5 p.m. 💳 Not accepted

ESS-A-BAGEL
$
359 1ST AVE.
(AT 21ST ST.)
TEL 212/260-2252
New York's finest bagels, boiled and baked, and a mighty good whitefish salad. Who needs atmosphere? (Also in Midtown North.)
🔧 8 tables 🚇 6 to 23rd St. 🕐 Closed Sun. D 💳 All major cards

HOTELS

ALGONQUIN
$$$$$
59 W. 44TH ST.
(BET. 5TH & 6TH AVES.)
TEL 212/840-6800 or
888-304-2047
FAX 212/944-1419
New York's literary landmark since the 1920s. Charming, traditional rooms, nice lobby for cocktails, nice locale.
🛏 175 🚇 B, D, F to 42nd St. 💳 All major cards

FOUR SEASONS
$$$$$
57 E. 57TH ST.
(BET. PARK & MADISON AVES.)
TEL 212/758-5700
FAX 212/758-5711
This 52-story art deco–style monument designed by I. M. Pei and completed in 1993 has received top ratings and boasts the largest rooms in the city, with accompanying big views. Expect modernistic furniture, giant Florentine marble bathrooms, and elaborate bedside push-button systems.
🛏 370 🚇 4, 5, 6, N, R to 59th St. 🏋 💳 All major cards

NEW YORK PALACE
$$$$$
455 MADISON AVE.
(AT 50TH ST.)
TEL 212/888-7000 or
800/697-2522
FAX 212/303-6000
Located in what was originally the 1882 Stanford White–designed Villard Houses, this landmark site has retained its opulence through its various incarnations. Its elegantly furnished 55-story tower overlooks St. Patrick's Cathedral. Fine places for food and drink on-site include Istana Restaurant and the Villard Bar.
🛏 600 🚇 E, F to 5th Ave.; B, D, F to Rockefeller Center 🏋 💳 All major cards

HOTELS & RESTAURANTS

🏨 PENINSULA
$$$$$

700 5TH AVE.
(AT 55TH ST.)
TEL 212/956-2888 or
800/262-9467
FAX 212/903-3949

Turn-of-the-20th-century beaux arts landmark, with views down Fifth Avenue. Art nouveau furnishings and oversized beds and bathrooms create a grand environment. More luxurious trappings at the rooftop spa and outdoor rooftop Pen-Top Bar and Terrace, excellent for summertime cocktails and city views.

(i) 250 🚇 E, V to 5th Ave./53rd St.; F to 57th St. 🍽 🏊 🅰 All major cards

🏨 PLAZA HOTEL
$$$$$

CENTRAL PARK SOUTH
768 5TH AVE.
(AT 59TH ST.)
TEL 212/759-3000
FAX 212/759-3167

Although this city icon was sold in 2005, its landmark status and the public outcry saved it from being completely turned into residential condominiums. Its 18-month, 350-million-dollar makeover, begun late 2005, will keep 348 of its 805 rooms as hotel rooms, with the rest converted to 150 condos. The Grand Ballroom, Palm Court (with Tiffany ceiling), Oak Room, and Oak Bar will be retained, and some historic features restored for the first time. Oh yes, the suite where the beloved character Eloise has been a guest since 1955 remains hers, for guests to book at the revamped hotel. Strolling the exterior grounds is a requisite.

(i) 348 🚇 N, R, W to 5th Ave./59th St. 🍽 🅰 All major cards

🏨 ROYALTON
$$$$$

44 W. 44TH ST.
(BET. 5TH & 6TH AVES.)
TEL 212/869-4400 or
800/635-9013

FAX 212/869-8965

Phillipe Starck interiors with high-tech modern lobby, restaurant, bar, and lovely rooms with slate fireplaces and round bathtubs.

(i) 137 + 31 suites 🚇 1, 2, 3, 7 to Times Sq. 🍽 🅰 All major cards

🏨 ST. REGIS
🍽 $$$$$

2 E. 55TH ST.
(BET. 5TH & MADISON AVES.)
TEL 212/753-4500
FAX 212/787-3447

Elaborately restored beaux arts gem, with elegant yet accessible public rooms and the finest service and amenities. Enjoy the riches of Lespinasse, one of New York's top restaurants, and of the great King Cole Bar, dominated by the engaging Maxfield Parrish mural of the king, himself.

(i) 322 🚇 E, V, to 5th Ave./53rd St.; N, R, W to 5th Ave./59th St. 🍽 🅰 All major cards

🏨 WALDORF-ASTORIA & WALDORF TOWERS
$$$$$

301 PARK AVE.
(AT 50TH ST.)
TEL 212/355-3000
FAX 212/872-7272

The great Waldorf-Astoria is one of the quintessential New York hotels. The art deco lobby is magnificent and the exclusive, elaborately appointed Waldorf Towers (floors 28–42) provide quarters for visiting presidents, among others. The French restaurant, Peacock Alley, is lavishly praised.

(i) 1410 🚇 6 to 51st St. or E, V to Lexington Ave./53rd St. 🍽 🅰 All major cards

🏨 CARNEGIE
$$$$

229 W. 58TH ST.
(BET. BROADWAY & 7TH AVE.)
TEL 212/245-4000
FAX 212/245-6199

Nicely decorated, quiet spot with big kitchenettes,

great location.

(i) 20 suites 🚇 1, A, B, C, D to Columbus Circle 🅰 All major cards

🏨 CASABLANCA HOTEL
$$$$

147 W. 43RD ST.
(BET. 6TH AVE. & BROADWAY)
TEL 212/869-1212 or
888/922-7225
FAX 212/391-7585

Moroccan-style ambience.

(i) 40 + 8 suites 🚇 1, 2, 3, 7 to Times Sq.–42nd St. 🍽 🅰 All major cards

🏨 HOTEL ELYSÉE
$$$$

60 E. 54TH ST.
(BET. MADISON & PARK AVES.)
TEL 212/753-1066 or
800/535-9733
FAX 212/980-9278

Thirties' decor, charming rooms with antiques; small roof terrace.

(i) 88 + 11 suites 🚇 E, V to Lexington Ave.; 6 to 51st St. 🍽 🅰 All major cards

🏨 THE MANSFIELD
$$$$

12 W. 44TH ST.
(BET. 5TH & 6TH AVES.)
TEL 212/944-6050 or
877/847-4444
FAX 212/764-4477

Former bachelors' residence with nicely designed modern rooms, stainless-steel sinks. Welcoming library with concerts and cappuccino.

(i) 103 + 26 suites 🚇 B, D, F to 42nd St.; 1, 2, 3, 7 to Times Sq. 🍽 Nearby 🅰 All major cards

🏨 MILLENNIUM U.N. HOTEL

Staying here puts you in the midst of global drama, as diplomats and staff rush to their seats at the United Nations, or their offices on the first 27 floors of the Plaza. The award-winning twin-towered modern building rises high above the East Side.

KEY

🏨 Hotel 🍽 Restaurant (i) No. of guest rooms 🪑 No. of seats 🚇 Subway 🚫 Closed

Hotel rooms—all with stunning views—start at the 28th floor. Artworks from New York City and various nations are found throughout the hotel. You will want to use the excellent sports facilities, including indoor tennis courts, a pool, and an onsite reflexologist. Shuttle service to other areas of the city and the airport is available.

$$$$
1 UNITED NATIONS PLAZA 44TH ST.
(BET. 1ST & 2ND AVES.)
TEL 212/758-1234 or
866-866-8086
FAX 212/702-5051
🛏 428 🚇 4, 5, 6, 7 to 42nd St. 🏊 ⛱ 🏋 🅰 All major cards

🏨 THE PARAMOUNT
$$$$
235 W. 46TH ST.
(BET. BROADWAY & 8TH AVE.)
TEL 212/764-5500 or
888/741-5600
FAX 212/575-4892
Phillipe Starck–designed lobby and playful, attractive decor.
🛏 601 + 12 suites 🚇 1, 2, 3, 7 to 42nd St.–Times Sq. 🏋 🅰 All major cards

🏨 THE SHOREHAM
$$$$
33 W. 55TH ST.
(BET. 5TH & 6TH AVES.)
TEL 212/247-6700 or
800/553-3347
FAX 212/765-9741
Attractive art deco interior with aluminum furniture and many nice touches.
🛏 47 + 37 suites 🚇 E, V to 5th Ave./53rd St.; N, Q, R W to 57th St./7th Ave. 🏋 Nearby 🅰 All major cards

🏨 ROGER SMITH
$$$–$$$$
501 LEXINGTON AVE.
(BET. 47TH AND 48TH STS.)
TEL 212/755-1400
Casual, urban 1929 boutique hotel on the fashionable East Side. Continental breakfast is included.

🛏 130 🚇 E, V to Lexington Ave./53rd St.; 6 to 51st St. 🅰 All major cards

🏨 BROADWAY BED & BREAKFAST INN
$$
264 W. 46TH ST.
(AT 8TH AVE.)
TEL 212/921-1824 or
800/826-6300
FAX 212/768-2807
Simply designed rooms in the heart of the theater district.
🛏 41 🚇 A, C, E to 42nd St./Port Authority 🅰 All major cards

RESTAURANTS

🍴 LE BERNARDIN
$$$$$
155 W. 51ST ST.
(BET. 6TH & 7TH AVES.)
TEL 212/489-1762
Outstanding French seafood cuisine, elegant, nearly flawless service. Outstanding black bass seviche, tuna tartare, prix-fixe menus.
🍽 38 tables 🚇 1 to 50th St. 🕐 Closed Sat. L & all day Sun. 🅰 All major cards

🍴 LA CÔTE BASQUE
$$$$$
60 W. 55TH ST.
(BET. 5TH & 6TH AVES.)
TEL 212/688-6525
One of the city's nicest French restaurants in a lovely setting. Specialties are cassoulet and roast duck. Order frozen raspberry soufflé when you arrive.
🍽 160 🚇 E, V to 5th Ave.; F to 57th St 🕐 Closed Sun. L 🅰 All major cards

🍴 FELIDIA
$$$$$
243 E. 58TH ST.
(BET. 2ND & 3RD AVES.)
TEL 212/758-1479
Supreme Northern Italian cuisine by Lidia Bastianich. Wonderful pasta and risottos, and the specialties of Trieste.
🍽 90 🚇 4, 5, 6 to 59th St. 🕐 Closed Sat. L & all day Sun. 🅰 All major cards

🍴 FOUR SEASONS
$$$$$
99 E. 52ND ST.
(BET. LEXINGTON & PARK AVES.)
TEL 212/754-9494
Timeless design by Philip Johnson with the most professional service and classic Continental cuisine. Try the crab cakes or steak tartare.
🍽 100 🚇 6 to 51st St.; E, F to Lexington Ave. 🕐 Closed Sun. 🅰 All major cards

🍴 LA GRENOUILLE
$$$$$
3 E. 52ND ST.
(BET. 5TH & MADISON AVES.)
TEL 212/752-1495
Haute French cuisine in flower-filled splendor.
🍽 80 🚇 E, V to 5th Ave. 🕐 Closed Sun.–Mon. 🅰 All major cards

🍴 LE PÉRIGORD
$$$$$
405 E. 52ND ST.
(BET. 1ST AVE. & FDR DR.)
TEL 212/755-6244
Classic destination serving traditional French cuisine. Jacket and tie required.
🍽 120 🚇 6 to 51st St. 🕐 Closed Sat. L & all day Sun. 🅰 All major cards

🍴 MARCH
$$$$$
405 E. 58TH ST.
(AT SUTTON PL.)
TEL 212/754-6272
The ultimate for romance and excellent New American cuisine, in a delightful tri-level 19th-century townhouse setting. Design-your-own tasting menu and foie gras are house specialties. The chic lounge and rooftop terrace are also worth a visit.
🍽 80 🚇 N, R, to Lexington Ave./59th St.; 4, 5, 6 to 59th St. 🅰 All major cards

NOBU 57
$$$$$
40 W. 57TH ST.
(BET. 5TH & 6TH AVES.)
TEL 212/757-3000
This bi-level spin-off offers Nobu Japanese-fusion favorites such as sweet miso black cod, plus new delights. Call about dinner hours. Reservations are recommended.
🚇 200 🚊 F to 57th St.; N, R, W to 5th Ave/59th St.
🕐 Closed Sun. 💳 All major cards

SOMETHING SPECIAL

CHINA GRILL

You know you are in New York City here: The dress code appears business or casually stylish. The atmosphere almost vibrates, it's so filled with Midtown movers and shakers, especially during weekday lunch. Film, media, and stage personalities also abound. It's an ideal spot for lunch or before or after the theater. Dining is on several levels with an attractive central kitchen and two side bars. Stylishly designed, from the flower displays to the Marco Polo quotes on the floors. So is the food, a contemporary-American/European-Asian fusion. Nearly all of the food is prepared on grills or in woks. The inventive menu features such items as grilled pork tenderloin in plum sauce and cranberry coulis. Everything is served family style and in plentiful portions. It's a feast for all the senses.
$$$$
60 W. 53RD ST.
(BET. 5TH & 6TH AVES.)
TEL 212/333-7788
🚇 248 🚊 B, D, F to Rockefeller Center; E, F to 5th Ave. 🕐 Closed Sat. & Sun. L 💳 All major cards

PETROSSIAN
$$$$$
182 W. 58TH ST.
(AT 7TH AVE.)
TEL 212/245-2214
Fancy spot for the specialties that made them famous: caviar, smoked fish, and champagne.
🚇 70 🚊 N, Q, R, W to 57th St./7th Ave. 💳 All major cards

RAINBOW ROOM
$$$$$
30 ROCKEFELLER PLAZA, 65TH FLOOR
(BET. 49TH & 50TH STS.)
TEL 212/632-5000
Art deco setting, with amazing views and fine Northern Italian cuisine. Try the *carpaccio alla cipriani* or the *ossobuco* with risotto *alla Milanese*. Public hours are limited but the Grill is open nightly.
🚇 250 🚊 B, D, F, V to Rockefeller Center 🕐 Call for hours 💳 All major cards

AQUAVIT
$$$$
13 W. 54TH ST.
(BET. 5TH & 6TH AVES.)
TEL 212/307-7311
Fancy and fine Scandinavian fare. House specialties are gravlax, baked salmon, and Swedish meatballs.
🚇 180 🚊 E, V, to 5th Ave./53rd St. 💳 All major cards

FIREBIRD
$$$$
365 W. 46TH ST.
(BET. 8TH & 9TH AVES.)
TEL 212/586-0244
Old World, over-the-top decor presents fine backdrop for haute Russian cuisine, lounging, and exceptional caviar.
🚇 200 🚊 A, C, E to 42nd St. 🕐 Closed Sun. L & all day Mon. 💳 All major cards

PRICES

HOTELS
An indication of the cost of a double room without breakfast is given by $ signs.

$$$$$	Over $325
$$$$	$260–$325
$$$	$200–$260
$$	$140–$200
$	$140 or less

RESTAURANTS
An indication of the cost of a three-course dinner without drinks is given by $ signs.

$$$$$	Over $80
$$$$	$50–$80
$$$	$35–$50
$$	$20–$35
$	Under $20

OCEANA
$$$$
55 E. 54TH ST.
(BET. MADISON & PARK AVES.)
TEL 212/759-5941
Chef Neil Gallagher does wonders with seafood. House specialties include lobster salad.
🚇 100 🚊 6 to 51st St. 🕐 Closed Sat. L & all day Sun. 💳 All major cards

OSTERIA DEL CIRCO
$$$$
120 W. 55TH ST.
(BET. 6TH & 7TH AVES.)
TEL 212/265-3636
Run by the sons of Le Cirque's Sirio Maccioni, and with a menu devised by their mother, this dazzling room features some fine Tuscan dishes. Don't miss the *bombolini* (fresh donuts) for dessert.
🚇 120 🚊 N, Q, R, W to 57th St./7th Ave. 🕐 Closed Sun. L 💳 All major cards

PALM
$$$$
837 2ND AVE.
(BET. 44TH & 45TH STS.)
TEL 212/687-2953
Sawdust on the floor, giant lobsters and steaks.

🛏 120 🚇 4, 5, 6 to 42nd St.
🕐 Closed Sat. L & all day
Sun. 💳 All major cards

🍴 PARK AVENUE CAFÉ
$$$$
100 E. 63RD ST.
(BET. LEXINGTON & PARK
AVES.)
TEL 212/644-1900
Chef Neil Murphy wows
clientele with innovative
cuisine and zany presentations.
Famed for homemade
pastrami salmon.
🛏 220 🚇 4, 5, 6 to 59th St.
💳 All major cards

🍴 PIANO DUE
$$$$
151 W. 51ST ST.
(BET. 6TH AND 7TH AVES.)
TEL 212/399-9400
Northern Italian cuisine from
chef Michael Cetrulo. Try the
shelled langoustino in cream
or the veal chop. Portions
are large, service is black
tie. Located in the former
Palio space, the Palio Bar
and ceiling mural remain
downstairs, while the
revamped upstairs is con-
temporary Italian in style.
🛏 120 🚇 1 to 50th St.; N,
R, W to 49th St. 🕐 Closed
Sun. 💳 All major cards

🍴 SMITH & WOLLENSKY
$$$$
797 3RD AVE.
(AT 49TH ST.)
TEL 212/753-1530
One of the city's finest
steakhouses.
🛏 300 🚇 6 to 51st St.
🕐 Closed Sat. L & all day
Sun. 💳 All major cards

🍴 SUSHISAY
$$$$
38 E. 51ST ST.
(BET. MADISON & PARK AVES.)
TEL 212/755-1780
Fabulous sushi. Put yourself in
the hands of the chef if you
can afford it.
🛏 80 🚇 6 to 51st St.
🕐 Closed Sat. L & all day
Sun. 💳 All major cards

🍴 "21"
$$$$
21 W. 52ND ST.
(BET. 5TH & 6TH AVES.)
TEL 212/582-7200
A New York institution,
with both inventive and
classic American cuisine,
famous dishes of chicken
hash and burgers, and great
Bloody Marys.
🛏 150 🚇 B, D, F, V to
Rockefeller Center
🕐 Closed Sun. 💳 All major
cards

🍴 VONG
$$$$
200 E. 54TH ST.
(AT 3RD AVE.)
TEL 212/486-9592
Wonderful setting and exotic
Thai-French fare by Jean-
Georges Vongerichten. Try
house-infused liquors in
cocktails.
🛏 150 🚇 6 to 51st St.; E, F
to Lexington Ave. 🕐 Closed
Sat. L & all day Sun. 💳 All
major cards

🍴 BECCO
$$$
355 W. 46TH ST.
(BET. 8TH & 9TH AVES.)
TEL 212/397-7597
Lively spot with pastas from
the pan and a large selection
of Italian wines to enjoy.
🛏 150 🚇 A, C, E to 42nd
St. 💳 All major cards

SOMETHING SPECIAL

🍴 BEN BENSON'S STEAK HOUSE
If you have a lusty appetite
and love a rollicking
steakhouse atmosphere and
enthusiastic beef-eaters, this is
the place to go. Opened in
1982, it is one of America's top
100 independent restaurants.
Here, celebrities, politicians,
sports stars, and business
executives, along with visitors
and residents in the know,
consume massive juicy steaks,
huge lobsters, crab cakes, veal,
and large portions of French

fries and vegetables meant to be
shared. Dining is on two floors,
in large rooms where the
feeling is warm and familiar,
partly because of the colorful
collection of Americana all
around you. If it is for drinks
only, stop in at the bar and
cocktail lounge, where you
might well find yourself amid
faces you recognize from
television and the media.
$$$
123 W. 52ND ST.
TEL 212/581-8888
🛏 175 🚇 1, C to 50th St.
🕐 Closed Sat. & Sun. L
💳 All major cards

🍴 LE COLONIAL
$$$
149 E. 57TH ST.
(BET. LEXINGTON AND 3RD
AVES.)
TEL 212/752-0808
Vietnamese fare—an intimate
setting in velvet and teak.
Luscious specialty drinks.
🛏 195 🚇 N, R to
Lexington Ave./59th St.; 4, 5,
6 to 59th St. 🕐 Closed Sat.
& Sun. L 💳 All major cards

🍴 DAWAT
$$$
210 E. 58TH ST.
(BET. 2ND & 3RD AVES.)
TEL 212/355-7555
Haute Indian cuisine. Try
bhindi masala, okra with
onions and mangos.
🛏 130 🚇 4, 5, 6 to 59th St.
🕐 Closed Sun. L 💳 All
major cards

🍴 ESTIATORIO MILOS
$$$
125 W. 55TH ST.
(BET. 6TH & 7TH AVES.)
TEL 212/245-7400
Elegant Greek seafood spot
with fish by the pound,
excellent crabs.
🛏 250 🚇 N, Q R, W to
57th St./7th Ave. 💳 All
major cards

🏊 Indoor swimming pool 🏊 Outdoor swimming pool 🏋 Health club 💳 Credit cards **KEY**

HOTELS & RESTAURANTS

🍴 HANAMI
$$$
213 E. 45TH ST.
(BET. 2ND & 3RD AVES.)
TEL 212/687-0127
High-quality Japanese beef
and sushi.
🪑 85 🚇 4, 5, 6 to Grand
Central 🔒 Closed Sat. L &
all Sun. 💳 All major cards

🍴 JEZEBEL
$$$
630 9TH AVE. (AT 45TH ST.)
TEL 212/582-1045
Quasi-haute soul food like
smothered pork chops, sides
of okra and black-eyed peas,
in grand satin-and-lace setting.
🪑 125 🚇 A, C, E to 42nd
St. 💳 AE

🍴 OYSTER BAR AT GRAND CENTRAL
$$$
GRAND CENTRAL TERMINAL,
LOWER LEVEL
(42ND ST. & VANDERBILT AVE.)
TEL 212/490-6650
Classic setting in the historic
train station, with pan roasts
and raw oysters. Make sure to
ask for the lunch menu.
🪑 500 🚇 4, 5, 6, S to
42nd St.–Grand Central
🔒 Closed Sun. 💳 All major
cards

🍴 ROSA MEXICANO
$$$
1063 1ST AVE.
(AT 58TH ST.)
TEL 212/753-7407
Haute Mexican cuisine, authentic
dishes. Tableside guacamole,
pomegranate margaritas, and
mixiote (lamb shanks with
chilies steamed in beer) are
house specialties.
🪑 90 🚇 4, 5, 6 to 59th St.
🔒 Closed L 💳 All major
cards

🍴 SHUN LEE PALACE
$$$
155 E. 55TH ST.
(BET. LEXINGTON & 3RD AVES.)
TEL 212/371-8844
Finest upscale Chinese cuisine.
🪑 350 🚇 4, 5, 6 to 59th St.
💳 All major cards

🍴 SOLERA
$$$
216 E. 53RD ST.
(BET. 2ND & 3RD AVES.)
TEL 212/644-1166
Top Spanish cuisine and
outstanding service. Paella,
calamari, Serrano ham, and
Spanish cheeses are specialties.
🪑 100 🚇 6 to 51st St.; E, V
to Lexington Ave./53rd St.
🔒 Closed Sat. L & all day
Sun. 💳 All major cards

🍴 BAR VETRO
$$
222 E. 58TH ST.
(BET. 2ND & 3RD AVES.)
TEL 212/308-0112
Hot spot for contemporary
Italian food. Try the tasting
dishes. Also popular for
afternoon drinks & appetizers.
🪑 170 🚇 4, 5, 6 to 59th St.
🔒 Closed L Sat. & all day
Sun. 💳 All major cards

🍴 GARDEN CAFÉ
$$
147 E. 60TH ST.
(BET. LEXINGTON & 3RD AVE.)
TEL 212/832-8972
Charming spot good for both
business and romantic dining;
try the bistro beef, meatloaf,
or chicken steak.
🪑 57 🚇 4, 5, 6, N, R, W to
60th St. 💳 All major cards

🍴 JOE ALLEN
$$
326 W. 46TH ST.
(BET. 8TH & 9TH AVES.)
TEL 212/581-6464
Things like burgers and chef's
salads make this theater-
district hangout reliable for
audience and cast.
🪑 150 🚇 A, C, E to 42nd
St. 💳 MC, V

🍴 PIGALLE
$$
DAYS HOTEL
790 8TH AVE.
(AT 48TH ST.)
TEL 212/489-2233
Large portions of Parisian
food.
🪑 85 🚇 1, C, E to 50th St.
💳 All major cards

🍴 TRATTORIA DELL'ARTE
$$
900 7TH AVE.
(AT 57TH ST.)
TEL 212/245-9800
Terrific antipasto and pizzas
are part of Italian menu at
this popular restaurant.
🪑 75 🚇 N, Q, R, W to 57th
St. 💳 All major cards

🍴 UN DELEGATES' DINING ROOM
$$
UNITED NATIONS PLAZA
TEL 212/963-7626
Sample world menus at daily
lunch buffet 11:30 to 2:30.
Jackets required.
🪑 350 🚇 4, 5, 6 to 42nd St.
🔒 Closed Sat. & Sun. 💳 All
major cards

🍴 WHEELTAPPER
$$
141 E. 44TH ST.
(IN THE FITZPATRICK HOTEL)
TEL 212/351-6560
Old World Irish pub with a
railroad theme. Quality pub
grub, plus an authentic Irish
breakfast served all day.
🪑 100 🚇 4, 5, 6, 7, S to
42nd St.–Grand Central
💳 All major cards

🍴 CARNEGIE DELI
$
854 7TH AVE.
(AT 55TH ST.)
TEL 212/757-2245
New York City original with
gigantic corned beef sand-
wiches and alternately colorful
or curt service. This should be
the place where you try
smoked tongue.
🪑 150 🚇 N, Q, R, W to
57th St./7thAve. 💳 Not
accepted

🍴 COSÍ SANDWICH BARS
$
1) 498 7TH AVE.
(BET. 36TH & 37TH STS.)
TEL 212/947-1005
🚇 1, 2, 3 to 34th St.
2) 38 E. 45TH ST.
(BET. MADISON &
VANDERBILT AVES.)
TEL 212/949-7400

4, 5, 6 to 42nd St.
3) 61 W. 48TH ST.
(BET. 5TH & 6TH AVES.)
TEL 212/265-7579
4, 5, 6 to 59th St.
Try the delicious wood-fired
flatbread sandwiches. Open
for breakfast weekdays.
40–55 Closed Sat. D
& all day Sun. All major
cards

ESS-A-BAGEL
$
831 3RD AVE.
(BET. 50TH & 51ST STS.)
TEL 212/980-1010
New York's finest bagels,
cheerfully served. Also can
be found in Midtown South.
25 tables 6 to 51st St;
E, V to Lexington Ave. All
major cards

GRAND SICHUAN INTERNATIONAL MIDTOWN
$
745 9TH AVE.
(BET. 50TH & 51ST STS.)
TEL 212/582-2288
Emphasis on Sichuan (spicy)
cuisine, plus full menu of
Americanized Chinese dishes,
and some Shanghai and
Canton-style dishes. Must-tries
include the spicy double-
cooked pork and Sichuan
pickled cabbage with red oil.
125 C, E to 50th St.;
N, R, W to 49th St. All
major cards

MENCHANKO-TEI
$
43-45 W. 55TH ST.
(BET. 5TH & 6TH AVES.)
TEL 212/247-1585
Casual Japanese noodle
joint—a Midtown oasis.
15 tables N, Q, R, W
to 57th St.; E, V to 5th Ave.
 All major cards

SOUP KITCHEN INTERNATIONAL
$
259-A W. 55TH ST. (BET. 8TH
AVE. & BROADWAY)
TEL 212/757-7730
Famous takeout soup spot

with long lines but cult
following.
 No seats 1, A, B, C, D
to Columbus Circle–59th St.
 Closed D summer
 Not accepted

UPPER EAST SIDE (MUSEUM ROW)

HOTELS

SOMETHING SPECIAL

THE CARLYLE
Since 1931 this gemlike hotel
has welcomed the world's elite
in a grand European style. Rooms
have antiques, Audubon prints,
marble bathrooms with
whirlpools, and state-of-the-art
electronics. Nancy Reagan and the
late President Kennedy were
counted among the regular
guests. Those who do not check
in may partake of romantic
dining in the Carlyle Restaurant,
bistro entertainment in the Café
Carlyle, humorous murals in the
Bemelmans Bar, or tea in the
Gallery, modeled after Turkey's
Topkapi Palace.
$$$$$
35 E. 76TH ST.
TEL 212/744-1600 or
800-227-5737
FAX 212/717-4682
 190 + 65 residential
apartments 6 to 77th St.
 All major cards

GRACIE INN
$$$$$
502 E. 81ST ST.
(BET. YORK & EAST END AVES.)
TEL 212/628-1700
FAX 212/628-6420
Rustic-style rooms in various
sizes. Good, quiet location.
 12 4, 5, 6 to 86th St.
 All major cards

THE LOWELL
$$$$$
28 E. 63RD ST.
(BET. PARK & MADISON AVES.)
TEL 212/838-1400 or
800/221-4444
FAX 212/319-4230

A 1920s historic landmark
on a quiet street, providing
tasteful, Old World charm
in an intimate setting. All
rooms are suites, many with
working fireplaces, kitchens,
and libraries.
 61 4, 5, 6 to 59th St.
  All major cards

THE MARK
$$$$$
25 E. 77TH ST.
(BET. 5TH & MADISON AVES.)
TEL 212/744-4300 or
800/843-6275
FAX 212/744-2749
An elegant location with
formal contemporary decor,
large rooms with marble or
Italian ceramic baths, high-
quality artwork, and luxurious
amenities. Popular are the
Mark's Bar, and the wood-
paneled Mark Restaurant—
perfect for indulgent
afternoon teas.
 180 6 to 77th St.
 All major cards

PLAZA ATHENÉE
$$$$$
37 E. 64TH ST.
(BET. PARK & MADISON AVES.)
TEL 212/734-9100
FAX 212/772-0958
Old World charm and Louis
XVI decor star at this New
York version of the Paris
original, distinguished by its
smaller size and location on a
quiet residential block.
 149 6 to 68th St.
 All major cards

THE REGENCY
$$$$$
540 PARK AVE.
(AT 61ST ST.)
TEL 212/759-4100 or
800/233-2356
FAX 212/826-5674
Named for its Regency decor,
this hotel has both understated
elegance and every amenity,
including TVs and phones by
the marble bathtubs.
 288 + 74 suites
 4, 5, 6 to 59th St.
 All major cards

HOTELS & RESTAURANTS

🏨 THE WESTBURY
$$$$$
15 E. 69TH ST.
(AT MADISON AVE.)
TEL 212/535-2000 or
800/321-1569
FAX 212/535-5058
A departure from others in its English style and decor, these gracious quarters come with personalized service and direct access to shopping at neighboring Madison Ave. boutiques.
🛏 231 🚇 6 to 68th St. 🔶 🔷 All major cards

🏨 THE FRANKLIN
$$$
164 E. 87TH ST.
(BET. LEXINGTON & 3RD AVES.)
TEL 212/369-1000 or
800/607-4009
FAX 212/369-8000
Nicely decorated rooms with canopy beds, custom furniture, and photos of the city.
🛏 53 🚇 4, 5, 6 to 86th St. 🔷 AE, MC, V

🏨 HOTEL WALES
$$$
1295 MADISON AVE.
(AT 92ND ST.)
TEL 212/876-6000 or
877/847-4444
FAX 212/860-7000
Turn-of-the-20th-century haven with spacious suites.
🛏 45 + 47 suites 🚇 6 to 96th St. 🔷 AE, MC, V

RESTAURANTS

🍴 AUREOLE
$$$$$
34 E. 61ST ST.
(BET. MADISON & PARK AVES.)
TEL 212/319-1660
Charlie Palmer's famous contemporary American cuisine. Seasonal prix-fixe menu is recommended.
🍽 37 tables 🚇 4, 5, 6 to 59th St. 🚫 Closed Sat. L & all day Sun. 🔷 All major cards

---

🍴 DANIEL

This gastronomic palace opened in the Mayflower Hotel (now private condominiums) in early 1999, with a reported price tag of 10 million dollars. Chef and proprietor Daniel Boulud turned his former Restaurant Daniel at 20 East 76th Street into Café Boulud so he could open this larger, "Venetian-Byzantine-Deco fantasy." Boulud is New York's longest-reigning four-star chef, known also for his days at the old Le Cirque. Although his restaurant decor is not French, his food is—founded on ancient French farmhouse recipes that he re-creates with flair. Roasted saddle of lamb with black-truffle gnocchi, root vegetables with a satiny au jus, and other delights await those fortunate enough to get a table here.
$$$$$
60 E. 65TH ST.
(BET. MADISON & PARK AVES.)
TEL 212/288-0033
🍽 100 🚇 6 to 68th St. 🔷 All major cards

🍴 JO JO
$$$$
160 E. 64TH ST.
(BET. LEXINGTON & 3RD AVES.)
TEL 212/223-5656
Outstanding bistro fare by Jean-Georges Vongerichten. The lobster and the Vahlrona chocolate cake come recommended.
🛏 150 🚇 4, 5, 6 to 59th St. 🔷 All major cards

🍴 PEARSON'S TEXAS BARBEQUE
$$$$
170 E. 81ST ST.
(BET. LEXINGTON & 3RD AVES.)
TEL 212/288-2700
Standard barbeque fare as well as unusual dishes—wild boar and alligator—slow-cooked in a wood-fired pit.
🍽 60 🚇 6 to 77th St. 🚫 Closed L 🔷 All major cards

🍴 PAOLA'S
$$$
245 E. 84TH ST.
(BET. 2ND & 3RD AVES.)
TEL 212/794-1890
An Upper East Side find, with lovely Italian cuisine, including homemade pastas.
🍽 70 + 30 outdoors 🚇 4, 5, 6 to 86th St. 🔷 All major cards

🍴 AFGHAN KABAB HOUSE II
$$
1345 2ND AVE.
(BET. 70TH & 71ST STS.)
TEL 212/517-2776
Nicely flavored, reasonably priced foods, also good for vegetarians. Best value: the Combo Plate.
🍽 45 🚇 6 to 86th St. 🔷 All major cards

🍴 HEIDELBERG
$$
1648 2ND AVE.
(BET. 85TH & 86TH STS.)
TEL 212/628-2332
Old World haven for oompah food: wursts and beers.
🍽 80–85 🚇 4, 5, 6 to 86th St. 🔷 All major cards

🍴 SERENDIPITY 3
$$
225 E. 60TH ST.
(BET. 2ND & 3RD AVES.)
TEL 212/838-3531
Over-the-top ice-cream sundaes and casual fare. Famous for frozen hot chocolate.
🍽 165 🚇 4, 5, 6 to 59th St. 🔷 All major cards

🍴 EL POLLO
$
1746 1ST AVE.
(BET. 90TH & 91ST STS.)
TEL 212/996-7810
Outstanding Peruvian rotisserie chicken, especially for take-out meals (also in SoHo).
🍽 40 🚇 4, 5, 6 to 86th St. 🔷 All major cards

CENTRAL PARK

HOTELS

🏨 ESSEX HOUSE HOTEL
$$$$$
160 CENTRAL PARK S.
(BET. 6TH & 7TH AVES.)
TEL 212/247-0300 or
888/645-5697
FAX 212/315-1839
Dramatic art deco setting with tasteful rooms and stunning views of Central Park stretching to the north. A great location near the new Time Warner Center.
ℹ 516 + 81 suites 🚇 1, A, C, B, D to Columbus Circle–59th St.; N, R, Q, W to 57th St. 🔲 🅾 All major cards

🏨 THE PIERRE
$$$$$
2 E. 61ST ST. (AT 5TH AVE.)
TEL 212/838-8000 or
800/743-7734
FAX 212/940-8109
Elegance, antiques, and opulent decor characterize this hotel and luxury co-op building overlooking Central Park to the west. Public rooms include the gorgeous Rotunda, where afternoon tea is served.
ℹ 206 🚇 N, R to 5th Ave. 🔲 🅾 All major cards

🏨 THE RITZ-CARLTON NEW YORK, CENTRAL PARK
$$$$$
50 CENTRAL PARK S.
(AT 6TH AVE.)
TEL 212/308-9100 or
800/241-3333
Formerly the St. Moritz, this 33-story luxury hotel offers glamour, a great location (with some of the city's best views), special value in complimentary Bentley service within Midtown, technology butlers, and fabulous lounges. Atelier restaurant serves innovative French cuisine.
ℹ 261 🚇 F to 57th St. 🅾 All major cards

SOMETHING SPECIAL

🏨 SHERRY-NETHERLAND HOTEL
This landmark 1927 Romanesque boutique hotel promises an experience of timeless elegance. Attention to detail and service are everywhere, from the crystal chandeliers and lobby modeled on the Vatican library, to the white-gloved attendants running the guest elevators that once graced the Vanderbilt Mansion. All rooms are spacious and individually decorated, with fresh in-room flowers and complimentary mineral water and soft drinks. A welcoming box of Belgian chocolates greets you, the marble baths are divine, and the complimentary continental breakfast opens each day with a flourish. Suites include a separate living room and kitchenette. There is a state-of-the-art fitness center, and 2006 renovations gave the legendary restaurant, Harry Cipriani, a new look. This intimate, extraordinary hotel at the edge of Central Park is one of the city's true grande dames: Experience it while you can.
$$$$$
781 5TH AVE
(AT 59TH ST.)
TEL 212/355-2800 or
877-743-7710
www.sherrynetherland.com
ℹ 53 🚇 N, R, W to 5th Ave/59th St. 🅾 All major cards

RESTAURANT

🍴 TAVERN ON THE GREEN
$$$$
CENTRAL PARK W.
(AT 67TH ST.)
TEL 212/873-3200
Unique setting in the park, huge, splendid decor. Mixed food reviews. Try going for jazz on Saturday nights.
🍴 1,000+ 🚇 1 to 66th St.; A, C to 59th & Columbus 🅾 All major cards

UPPER WEST SIDE

HOTELS

🏨 TRUMP INTERNATIONAL HOTEL & TOWERS
$$$$$
1 CENTRAL PARK W.
(AT COLUMBUS CIRCLE)
TEL 212/299-1000 or
888/448-7867
FAX 212/299-1150
Donald Trump's megaventure at the tip of Central Park, featuring floor-to-ceiling windows and personal attachés assigned to guests to coordinate their lives in New York. Dine downstairs at Nougatine or Jean Georges (see p. 254), the excellent first-class restaurant, or have one of the chefs cook in your suite, if you prefer.
ℹ 176 suites 🚇 1, A, B, C, D to Columbus Circle–59th St. 🔲 🅾 All major cards

🏨 BEACON HOTEL
$$$
2130 BROADWAY
(AT 75TH ST.)
TEL 212/787-1100 or
800/572-4969
FAX 212/724-0839
Generously sized rooms, newly renovated, and family friendly are the buzz words for this hotel.
ℹ 248 suites 🚇 1, 2, 3 to 72nd St. 🔲 Nearby 🅾 All major cards

🏨 COUNTRY INN
$$$
W. 77TH ST.
(BET. BROADWAY & WEST END AVE.)
TEL 212/580-4183
Nicely restored landmark town house with lovely suites. No elevator.
ℹ 4 🚇 1 to 79th St.

🏨 EXCELSIOR
$$$
45 W. 81ST ST. (BET. COLUMBUS AVE. & CENTRAL PARK W.)
TEL 212/362-9200 or

800/368-4575
FAX 212/721-2994
Large, comfortable rooms
with traditional decor,
some views.
🛏 200 🚇 1 to 79th St.; C, B
to 81st St. 💳 AE, MC, V

🏨 LUCERNE
$$$
201 W. 79TH ST.
(AT AMSTERDAM AVE.)
TEL 212/875-1000
FAX 212/362-7251
Simple, clean rooms.
🛏 184 🚇 1 to 79th St.
💳 AE, MC, V

RESTAURANTS

🍴 JEAN GEORGES
$$$$$
TRUMP INTERNATIONAL
HOTEL, 1 CENTRAL PARK W.
(BET. 60TH & 61ST STS.)
TEL 212/299-3900
Top-class contemporary
French-American cuisine by
Jean-Georges Vongerichten.
Try the tasting menu.
🪑 60 🚇 1, A, B, C, D to
Columbus Circle–59th St.
🕐 Closed Sat. L & all day
Sun. 💳 All major cards

🍴 CAFÉ DES ARTISTES
$$$$
1 W. 67TH ST.
(BET. COLUMBUS AVE. &
CENTRAL PARK W.)
TEL 212/877-3500
French cuisine with specialties
of pot-au-feu and steak
tartare, amid lovely murals
and an Old World motif.
🪑 100 🚇 1 to 66th St.
💳 All major cards

🍴 CAFÉ LUXEMBOURG
$$$$
200 W. 70TH ST.
(BET. AMSTERDAM & WEST
END AVES.)
TEL 212/873-7411
A classic hip destination with
bistro fare.
🪑 107 🚇 1, 2, 3 to 72nd St.
💳 All major cards

🍴 NOUGATINE
$$$$
TRUMP INTERNATIONAL
HOTEL, 1 CENTRAL PARK W.
(BET. 60TH & 61ST STS.)
TEL 212/299-3900
A more casual part of Jean-
Georges restaurant. Open
for breakfast except Sundays.
🪑 65–80 🚇 1, A, B, C, D to
Columbus Circle–59th St.
💳 All major cards

🍴 PICHOLINE
$$$$
35 W. 64TH ST.
(BET. BROADWAY & CENTRAL
PARK W.)
TEL 212/724-8585
Fine Mediterranean cuisine and
outstanding service, with the
city's best cheese cart. Try the
salmon with horseradish crust.
🪑 200 🚇 1 to 66th St.
🕐 L Sat. only 💳 All major
cards

🍴 SHUN LEE CAFÈ
$$$$
43 W. 65TH ST.
(BET. COLUMBUS AVE. &
CENTRAL PARK W.)
TEL 212/769-3888
First-rate Chinese dining,
some of New York's finest.
🪑 300 🚇 1 to 66th St.
💳 All major cards

🍴 OUEST
$$$
2315 BROADWAY
(AT 84TH ST.)
TEL 212/580-8700
See-and-be-seen at this
intimate foodie's paradise,
popular among celebrities,
featuring Chef Tom Valenti's
distinctive boldly layered style.
Don't miss his signature lamb
shanks. Sunday brunch.
🪑 135 🚇 1 to 86th St.
🕐 Closed L 💳 All major
cards

🍴 BARNEY GREENGRASS
$$
541 AMSTERDAM AVE.
(BET. 86TH & 87TH STS.)
TEL 212/724-4707
Visit the "Sturgeon King" for a
classic meal of smoked fish

delights. Salmon and eggs and
scallion cream cheese are
recommended.
🪑 55 🚇 1 to 86th St.
🕐 Closed Mon. 💳 Not
accepted

🍴 SARABETH'S KITCHEN
$$
1295 MADISON AVE.
(AT 92ND ST.)
TEL 212/410-7335
Baked goods and popular
brunches. Open for breakfast.
🪑 90 🚇 6 to 96th St.
💳 All major cards

HEIGHTS & HARLEM

RESTAURANTS

🍴 LONDEL'S OF STRIVERS' ROW
$$
2620 8TH AVE..
(BET. 139TH & 140TH STS.)
TEL 212/234-6114
Great Southern cooking with
classic fried chicken and greens.
🪑 150 🚇 B, C, 2, 3 to 135th
St. 🕐 Closed Sun. D & all
day Mon. 💳 All major cards

🍴 SYLVIA'S
$$
328 LENOX AVE.

HOTELS & RESTAURANTS

(BET. 126TH & 127TH STS.)
TEL 212/996-0660
Famous soul food; brunch
Sun., and jazz 1–4 Sat. Try the
barbequed ribs, ham, and
collard greens.
🍴 300 🚇 2, 3 to 125th St.
💳 All major cards

OUTER BOROUGHS

BROOKLYN

🍴 PETER LUGER'S STEAKHOUSE
$$$$
178 BROADWAY
(AT DRIGGS AVE.)
TEL 718/387-7400
One of the city's finest
steakhouses. No frills, just
great porterhouse and
creamed spinach.
🍴 150 🚇 J, M, Z to Marcy
Ave. 💳 Not accepted

🍴 RIVER CAFÉ
$$$$
I WATER ST.
(UNDER BROOKLYN BRIDGE)
TEL 718/522-5200
Spectacular view of
Manhattan in elegant setting—
sit outdoors in summer.
Lobster, lamb, and soft shells
are recommended.
🍴 110 🚇 A to High
St.–Brooklyn; 2, 3 to Clark St.
💳 All major cards

🍴 BAMCAFÉ
$$
BROOKLYN ACADEMY OF
MUSIC, 30 LAFAYETTE AVE.
TEL 718/636-4111
International cuisine at a
cultural landmark that
opens two hours before
performances.
🍴 300 🚇 2, 3, 4, 5 to
Atlantic Ave. 💳 All major
cards

🍴 CAFÉ TATIANA
$$
3145 4TH ST.
(ON THE BRIGHTON BEACH
BOARDWALK)
TEL 718/646-7630
Fine setting in Brooklyn for

Russian cuisine. Especially
good are the soups and
dumplings. Open for breakfast.
🍴 100 🚇 B, Q to Brighton
Ave. 💳 Not accepted

🍴 PRIMORSKI
$$
282 BRIGHTON BEACH AVE.
(BET. 2ND & 3RD STS.)
TEL 718/891-3111
First-choice Russian
restaurant, with fine casual
dining or prix-fixe banquet
dinners and a show. Don't
miss *lavash* (bread), *pelmeni*,
or *sashlik*.
🍴 194 🚇 B, Q to Brighton
Beach 💳 All major cards

🍴 PATSY GRIMALDI'S
$
19 OLD FULTON ST.
TEL 718/858-4300
Traditional New York–style
pizza place, with juke box
and red-checkered
tablecloths.
🍴 50 🚇 C to High St.
💳 Not accepted

QUEENS

🏨 SHERATON LAGUARDIA EAST HOTEL
$$$–$$$$
135-20 39TH AVE.
TEL 718/460-6666
Modern airport hotel near
the U.S. Open Tennis Center
and Shea Stadium. Restaurant.
🛏 173 rooms & suites 🚇 7
to Main St., Flushing 🏋
💳 All major cards

🏨 BEST WESTERN CITY VIEW MOTOR INN
$$$
33-17 GREENPOINT AVE.,
LONG ISLAND CITY
TEL 718/392-8400 or
800/248-9843
Converted 19th-century
public school near Shea
Stadium and U.S. Open
Tennis Center. Free shuttle
to and from LaGuardia.
🛏 72 rooms 🚇 7 to 40th
St. 💳 All major cards

🍴 ELIAS CORNER
$$
24-02 31ST ST.
(AT 24TH AVE.)
TEL 718/932-1510
Authentic Greek seafood
joint.
🍴 100 🚇 N to Astoria
Boulevard 🚫 Closed L
💳 Not accepted

🍴 JACKSON DINER
$$
37-47 74TH ST.
(BET. ROOSEVELT & 37TH
AVES.)
TEL 718/672-1232
Fine Indian food.
🍴 65 🚇 7 to 74th St.-
Broadway 💳 Not accepted

🍴 JOE'S SHANGHAI
$$
136-21 37TH AVE.
(BET. MAIN & UNION STS.)
TEL 718/539-3838
Fantastic broth-filled
dumplings and other specials
(also in Chinatown).
🍴 70 🚇 7 to Main St.
💳 Not accepted

🍴 LA BOINA ROJA
$
80-22 37TH AVE.
JACKSON HEIGHTS
TEL 718/424-6711
Small Colombian steakhouse,
with 23 different sauces for
your beef (including one
made from coffee). Chilean
and Argentinian wines.
🍴 100 🚇 7 to 82nd St.
💳 All major cards

🍴 TOURNESOL, BISTRO FRANÇAIS
$
50-12 VERNON BLVD.
LONG ISLAND CITY
TEL 718/472-4355
www.tournesolny.com
A taste of France, including
mussels in white wine, salad of
lardons with poached egg, and
rabbit terrine with a red
onion compote. Brunch
features perfect omelets.
🍴 65 🚇 7 to Vernon
Blvd.–Jackson Ave.
🚫 Closed Mon. 💳 AE

🏊 Indoor swimming pool 🏊 Outdoor swimming pool 🏋 Health club 💳 Credit cards   KEY

SHOPPING IN NEW YORK

Everything is available in New York at both the highest and the lowest prices. Many natives spend a good portion of their lives trying to stay on one end of the spectrum by doing their homework and shopping around. Department stores are best visited weekdays mid-morning or early afternoon, some are open well into the evening. Many specialty stores do not open early in the morning. It may be worth calling specific destinations to verify hours, which can change seasonally (some places stay open later in the summer).

Although Lower Manhattan is primarily a financial district, there are also many diversified shops in all price ranges. Nearly all of the chain stores are represented at the South Street Seaport, not included in these listings. TriBeCa is an up-and-coming shopping district, especially around Franklin St. and lower West Broadway. The Lower East Side is a fascinating area, originally Jewish but now multiethnic. Shopping there is a treat for the adventurous who will find a fascinating mixture of old and new. It's a great Sunday destination, since everything is open (stores are closed Saturday for the Sabbath).

The area dubbed "NoLita" (North of Little Italy) unofficially stretches from Houston to Spring Sts. and from Lafayette to Elizabeth Sts., and is the home to many cute boutiques. Lafayette St. contains a number of "modern vintage" furniture sources. SoHo offers a sea of shopping opportunity, but if you can go during the week, the crowds of browsers will be decidedly thinner.

In the West Village little places are tucked away here and there, and Bleecker St. and Christopher St. are good shopping locations. The East Village is the most unique neighborhood, multiethnic and ever changing. Ninth St. between Second Ave. and Ave. A is a treasure trove. Bond St., between Lafayette St. and Bowery, is a new strip of interesting old furniture stores, and the antiques zone is on 10th and 11th Sts., from University Pl. to Broadway. While Fifth Ave. is the acknowl-edged shopping center of New York, Madison Ave. is a strip of many of the ritziest stores around. Columbus Circle's Time Warner Center is loaded with shops and attractions, and both Columbus and Amsterdam Aves. offer good shopping. Broadway is always booming uptown and down, and don't forget midtown around Macy's; Chelsea's Seventh Ave.; and Harlem uptown.

ACCESSORIES & SHOES

Billy Martins, 220 E. 60th St., bet. 2nd & 3rd Aves., tel 212/861-3100. Subway: 4, 5, 6 to 59th St.
Western apparel and cowboy boots.
Dö Kham, 51 Prince St., tel 212/966-2404. Subway: N, R to Prince St.
Tibetan hats and crafts.
Harry's Shoes, 2299 Broadway, tel 212/874-2035. Subway: 1 to 86th St. Closed Sun. July/Aug.
Great family store.
The Hat Shop, 120 Thompson St., tel 212/219-1445. Subway: C, E to Spring St. Closed a.m.
Stylish hats.
Hermès, 691 Madison Ave., at E. 62nd St, tel 212/751-3181. Subway: N, R, W to 5th Ave., 4, 5, 6 to 59th and Lexington Ave. Closed Sun.
Unique silk scarves, neckties, handbags.
Kiehl's, 109 3rd Ave. (at 13th St.), tel 212/677-3171. Subway: N, R, W, 4, 5, 6 to Union Sq.; L to 3rd Ave.
High-end beauty porducts.
Otto Tootsi Plohound, 413 W. Broadway, tel 212/925-8931. Subway: C, E to Spring St.; 1 to Houston St.
The hippest shoes, with a mind-boggling selection.
Shoofly, 465 Amsterdam Ave., tel 212/580-4390. Subway: 1 to 86th St. Closed a.m. Sun.
Children's shoes.
T. O. Dey, 9 E. 38th St., tel 212/683-6300. Subway: 4, 5, 6, 7 to 42nd St. Call for hours.
Custom shoes.

ANTIQUES

Gill & Lagodich, 108 Reade St., tel 212/619-0631. Subway: 1, 2, 3 to Chambers St. Call for hours.
Antique frames.
Manhattan Art & Antiques Center, 1050 2nd Ave. (bet. 55th & 56th Sts.), tel 212/355-4400. Subway: E, V to 53rd/Lexington Ave.
More than 100 galleries.
Pageant Print Shop, 69 E. 4th St., tel 212/674-5296. Subway: 6 to Bleeker St., F to 2nd Ave. Closed a.m. & Sun.
Superior antique maps and prints.

ARTS & CRAFTS

Ceramica, 59 Thompson St., tel 212/941-1307. Subway: A, C, or E to Canal St.
Hand-painted Italian ceramics.
Jerry Ohlinger's, 253 W. 35th St. (bet. 7th & 8th Aves.), tel 212/989-0869. Mon.–Sat. 11 a.m–7 p.m. Subway: C, E to 34th St.
Classic and new movie stills and posters.
TriBeCa Potters, 313 W. 37th St. (bet. 8th and 9th Aves.), tel 212/431-7631. Subway: A, C, E to 34th St. Call for hours.
Ceramics for sale.
Triton Gallery, 323 W. 45th St. (bet. 8th & 9th Aves.), tel 212/765-2472. Subway: A, C, E to 42nd St.
Broadway show posters.
Urban Archeology, 143 Franklin St., tel 212/431-4646, Subway: 1 to Franklin St. Closed Sun.
Amazing array of architectural elements as well as new fixtures.

BAGS & HANDBAGS

Altman Luggage, 135 Orchard St., tel 212/254-7275. Subway: F to Delancey St. Closed Sat.
Well-priced bags, backpacks, and pens.

Big Drop, 174 Spring St., tel 212/966-4299. Subway: C or E to Spring St.
Bags, caps, & trendy clothing.

Gucci, 685 5th Ave., tel 212/826-2600. Subway: E, F to 5th Ave. Closed a.m. Sun.
Expensive designer goods.

Il Bisonte, 120 Sullivan St., tel 212/966-8773. Subway: C, E to Spring St.; A, C, E to Canal St. Closed a.m.
Leather goods and bags.

Jutta Neumann, 158 Allen St., tel 212/982-7048. Subway: F to 2nd Ave. Closed a.m. and Sun.
Leather accessories.

Kate Spade, 454 Broom St., tel 212/274-1991. Subway: C, E to Spring St.
Chic handbags.

BOOKS

Biography Bookshop, 400 Bleecker St., tel 212/807-8655. Subway: C, E to 14th St. Opens 11 a.m., Mon.–Sat.
Many lives.

Gotham, 16 E. 46th St., tel 212/719-4448. Subway: B, D, F to Rockefeller Center. Closed Sun.
Out-of-print books and first editions.

Housing Works Used Book Café, 126 Crosby St., tel 212/334-3324. Subway: B, D, F to Broadway–Lafayette St.
Comfortable shop for book lovers, cafe lounging, and talks.

Kitchen Arts & Letters, 1435 Lexington Ave., tel 212/876-5550. Subway: 4, 5, 6 to 86th St.; 6 to 96th St. Closed Sun. & a.m. Mon.
Outstanding cookbook collection.

Rizzoli, 31 W. 57th St. (bet. 5th & 6th Aves.), tel 212/759-2424. Subway: N, R to 57th St.
Books and magazines in a distinguished environment.

Strand, 828 Broadway, tel 212/473-1452. Subway: 4, 5, 6 to 14th St.-Union Sq. Closed early a.m. Sun.
Ultimate new & used bookstore with "8 miles of books." Other locations: **Central Park Kiosk,** 60th St. & 5th Ave., daily 10am to dusk, April–Oct.; **Strand Annex,** 95 Fulton St. (near the Seaport), tel 212/732-6070; Subway 4, 5, A, C, 1, 2 to Fulton St.

Weitz Weitz & Coleman, 1377 Lexington Ave., tel 212/831-2213. Subway: 4, 5, 6 to 86th St.; 6 to 96th St. Closed a.m. Sat. & Sun.
Rare & used books; custom bookbinding & leather albums.

West Sider, 2246 Broadway (bet. 80th & 81st Sts.), tel 212/362-0706. Subway: 1 to 79th St.
A variety-filled space including rare art and fiction books.

CLOTHES

Agnès B., 103 Greene St. (bet. Prince & Spring Sts.), tel 212/925-4649. Subway: N or R to Prince St.
Designer clothing.

Anna Sui, 113 Greene St., tel 212/941-8406. Subway: N, R to Prince St.
Women's designer clothing.

April Cornell, 487 Columbus Ave., tel 212/799-4342. Subway: 1 to 86th St.
Indian fabrics used in clothes and linens.

Atomic Passion, 430 E. 9th St. (bet. 1st Ave. & Ave. A), tel 212/533-0718. Subway: 6 to Astor Place. Closed until 2 p.m.
Vintage clothing and objets d'art.

A/X: Armani Exchange, 568 Broadway (at Prince St.), tel 212/431-6000. Subway: N, R to Prince St.
The Armani name at an affordable price: T-shirts, jeans, jackets, and more.

Bebe, 100 5th Ave., tel 212/675-2323. Subway: 4, 5, 6 to 14th St.–Union Sq.
Well-priced knock-offs of trendy clothing.

Ben Freedman, 137 Orchard St., tel 212/674-0854. Subway: F to Delancey.
"Gents' furnishings" with discounted London Fog coats.

Brooks Brothers, 346 Madison Ave., tel 212/682-8800. Subway: 6 to 33rd St.
Menswear and furnishings.

Calvin Klein, 654 Madison Ave., tel 212/292-9000. Subway: N, R, W to 5th Ave./59th St.; 4, 5, 6, to 59th St. Closed a.m. Sun.
American chic for men, women, and home.

Canal Jean Co., 718 Broadway, tel 212/226-3663. Subway: N, R to 8th St.; 6 to Astor Place.
New and used street clothes.

Century 21, 22 Cortlandt St., tel 212/227-9092. Subway: C, E to World Trade Center; 1, N, R to Cortlandt St.
Discount clothing.

Chanel, 5 E. 57th St., tel 212/355-5050. Subway: N, R, W to 5th Ave./59th St. Closed Sun.
Designer wear.

Comme des Garçons, 520 W. 22nd St., tel 212/604-9200. Subway: C, E to 23rd St.
Designer clothing.

Diesel, 770 Lexington Ave., tel 212/308-0055. Subway: 4, 5, 6 to 59th St.
Hip Italian fashion.

DKNY, 655 Madison Ave. (at E. 60th St.), tel 212/223-3569. Subway: M, R, W to 5th Ave.
Wearables and nonwearables ensuring a very unique look.

Gucci, 685 5th Ave. (bet. 53rd & 54th Sts.), tel 212/826-2600. Subway: E, V to 53rd St.
Hot and cool styles for every occasion.

INA, 101 Thompson St., tel 212/941-4757. Subway: C, E to Spring St. Closed a.m.
Resale designer clothing.

Infinity, 1116 Madison Ave., tel 212/517-4232. Subway: 4, 5, 6 to 86th St. Closed Sun.
Girls' and juniors' clothes and accessories paradise.

Lilliput, 265 Lafayette St., tel 212/965-9567. Subway: B, D, F to Broadway–Lafayette St.; 6 to Bleecker St.
Children's clothes.
Also: 240 Lafayette, clothes for teens.

SHOPPING

NY Fire Store, 263 Lafayette St., tel 212/226-3142. www. nyfirestore.com. Subway: 6 to Spring St.
Clothes and toys.
Original Levi's Store, 750 Lexington Ave., tel 212/826-5957. Subway: 4, 5, 6 to 59th St. Closed a.m. Sun.
Flagship store with all models of jeans (even custom).
Patricia Field, 382 W. Broadway, tel 212/254-1699. Subway: 6 to Astor Pl.
Established destination for wild clothing and accessories.
Paul Smith, 108 5th Ave., tel 212/627-9770. Subway: N, Q, R, 4, 5, 6 to Union Sq. Closed a.m. Sun.
Tasteful menswear.
Peanut Butter & Jane, 617 Hudson St., tel 212/620-7952. Subway: C, E to 14th St. Closed a.m. Sun.
Toys, vintage and new children's clothes.
Resurrection, 217 Mott St., tel 212/625-1374. Subway: 6 to Spring St. Opens 11 a.m.
Antique and vintage clothing.
TG-170, 170 Ludlow St., tel 212/995-8660. Subway: F to 2nd Ave. Closed a.m.
Women's clothing.
Trash & Vaudeville, 4 St. Mark's Pl., tel 212/982-3590. Subway: 6 to Astor Pl., N, R to 8th St.
Vaudeville upstairs and Trash down, loaded with vintage goods.
Versace, 815 Madison Ave., tel 212/744-6868, closed Sun. Subway: 6 to 68th St.
Italian glitz.
Yohji Yamamoto, 103 Grand St., tel 212/966-9066. Subway: A, C, E to Canal St. Closed a.m. Sun.
Designer clothing abounds.
Yu, 151 Ludlow St., tel 212/979-9370. Subway: F to Delancey. Closed a.m.
Designer consignment.

DEPARTMENT STORES

Barney's, 660 Madison at 61st St., tel 212/826-8900. Subway: N, R to 5th Ave.; 4, 5, 6 to 59th St.

Closed a.m. Sun.
Upscale department store with fashions, cosmetics, housewares. Popular with the trendy crowd. Also, try **Barney's Co-ops** for sportswear and casual clothes: 116 Wooster, tel 212/965-9964; 236 W. 18th St., tel 212/593-7800; 2151 Broadway at 75th St., tel 646/335-0978.
Bergdorf Goodman, 754 5th Ave. at 57th St., tel 212/753-7300. Subway: E, F, N, R to 5th Ave.
Elegant fashions.
Bergdorf Goodman Men, 745 5th Ave., tel 212/753-7300. Subway: E, F, N, R to 5th Ave.
High-end men's fashion.
Bloomingdale's: (two entrances) 1000 3rd Ave. or 59th & Lexington, tel 212/705-2000. Subway: 4, 5, 6 to 59th St.
Flagship department store.
Henri Bendel, 712 5th Ave., tel 212/247-1100. Subway: E, V to 5th Ave.
Boutique department store.
Lord & Taylor's, 424 5th Ave., tel 212/391-3344. Subway: B, D, F to 42nd St.; 7 to 5th Ave.
Classic department store specializing in women's wear.
Macy's, 151 W. 34th St., tel 212/695-4400. Subway: 1, 2, 3 to 34th St.
NYC's biggest, with everything.
Saks Fifth Avenue, 611 5th Ave., tel 212/753-4000. Subway: B, D, F to Rockefeller Center; E, F to 5th Ave. Closed a.m. Sun.
Flagship store of fashion.
Shanghai Tang, 714 Madison Ave., tel 212/888-0111. Subway: N, R to 5th Ave.; 4, 5, 6 to 59th St. Closed a.m. Sun.
Chinese luxury department store.
Takashimaya, 693 5th Ave., tel 212/350-0100. Subway: B, D, F to Rockefeller Center; E, F to 5th Ave. Closed Sun.
Fabulous Japanese department store with new and old.

FOOD STORES

Angelica's Herb & School, 147 1st Ave., tel 212/677-1549. Subway: F to 2nd Ave. Closed all day Sat. & a.m. Sun.
Herbal remedies and herbs.

Balducci's, 155 W. 66th St., tel 212/226-6800. Subway: 1 to 66th. Also on Union Sq.
Lovely gourmet food and house-brand pastas.
Dean & Deluca, 560 Broadway, tel 212/226-6800. Subway: N, R to Prince St.
Where food is fashion.
Economy Candy, 108 Rivington St., tel 212/254-1531. Subway: F to Delancey St.
Chocolates, candies, nuts.
International Grocery and Meat, 543 9th Ave. (at 40th St.), tel 212/279-5514. Subway: A, C, E to 42nd St. Closed Sun.
Amazing spice and dried goods selection, Greek dips and cheeses.
Kalustyan's, 123 Lexington Ave., tel 212/685-3451. Subway: 6 to 28th St.
The best spices, Indian foods.
Kam Man Food, 200 Canal St. (at Mott St.), tel 212-571-0330. Subway: J, M, Q, R, 6 to Canal St. Daily 9 a.m.–5 p.m.
Ocean edibles (including dried squid and shark fins) serving the Asian community
Li-lac, 40 8th Ave. (at Jane St.), tel 212/242-7374. Subway: A, C, E to 14th St. Closed a.m. Sun.
Handmade chocolates.
McNulty's, 109 Christopher St., tel 212/242-5351. Subway: 1 to Christopher St.
Teas and coffees.
Murray's Cheese Shop, 257 Bleecker St., tel 212/243-3289. Subway: A, B, C, D, E, F to W. 4th St.
Great selection served by a knowledgeable staff.
Myer's of Keswick, 634 Hudson St., tel 212/691-4194. Subway: A, C, E, L to 14th St. Closed a.m. Sun.
British foods.
Payard, 1032 Lexington Ave (bet. 73rd & 74th Sts.), tel 212/717-5252. Closed Sun. Subway: 6 to 68th St.
Bistro with delectable pastries and celebrated chocolates.
Russ & Daughters, 179 E. Houston St., tel 212/475-4880. Subway: F to Houston St.
Some of NYC's best smoked fish and caviar.

Sullivan St. Bakery, 73 Sullivan St., tel 212/334-9435. Subway: C, E to Spring St. Great breads and snacks. Also in Hell's Kitchen, 533 W. 47th St. (bet. 10th and 11th Aves.)

T Salon & Emporium, 11 E. 20th St., tel 212/358-0506. Subway: 6, N, R to 23rd St. 400 varieties of tea and accessories.

Veniero's Pasticceria & Cafe, 342 E. 11th St., tel 212/674 7264. Subway: L to 1st Ave.; 6 to Astor Pl. Italian pastries.

Vinegar Factory, 431 E. 91st St. (bet. York & 1st Aves.), tel 212/987-0885. Subway: 4, 5, 6 to 86th or 96th Sts. Vast selection of vinegar and oils, produce and cheese, and weekend brunch.

Zabar's, 2245 Broadway (at 80th St.), tel 212/787-2000. Subway: 1 to 79th St. Famous for its gourmet foods and housewares.

FURNITURE: ANTIQUE & MODERN

The Antiques Garage, 112 W. 25th St. (bet. 6th & 7th Aves.). Subway: F, V to 23rd St. Sat & Sun, 6:30 a.m.–5 p.m. This bi-level parking garage is loaded with vendors selling eclectic mechandise, including antique rugs and furniture.

Art & Industry, 50 Great Jones (at Lafayette St.), tel 212/477-0116. Subway: B, D, F to Broadway–Lafayette St. Closed Sun. Vintage 20th-century furniture.

Cathers & Dembrosky, 43 E. 10th St., tel 212/353-1244. Subway: 6 to Astor Pl. Mission furniture. By appt. only.

Crate & Barrel, 650 Madison Ave. (at E. 59th St.), tel 212/308-0011. Subway: 4, 5, 6, N, R to 59th St. Simple furniture to kitchen essentials.

Wyeth's, 315 Spring St., tel 212/243-3661. Subway: 1 to Franklin St. Closed Sat. & Sun. Modern and refurbished furniture, lighting, ceramics. By appt.

HOUSEHOLD

ABC Carpet & Home, 888 Broadway, tel 212/473-3000. Subway: 6 to 23rd St.; N, Q, R, 4, 5, 6 to Union Sq. Unbelievable emporium of absolutely everything for the home, gifts, antiques, etc.

Bridge Kitchenware, 711 3rd Ave. (enter on 45th St.), tel 212/688-4220. Subway: 4, 5, 6 to Grand Central. Closed Sun. Very NYC, funky kitchenware store. Also at 828 Madison (at 69th St.)

Felissimo, 10 W. 56th St., tel 212/247-5656. Subway: N, R to 5th Ave. Closed Sun. Unique goods for the table.

JB Prince, 36 E. 31st St., 11th floor, tel 212/683-3553. Subway: 33rd St. Closed Sat.–Sun. Knives and kitchen gadgets.

Kam Man Food, 200 Canal St., tel 212/571-0330. Subway: J, M, R, Q, 6 to Canal St. Daily 9 a.m.–5 p.m. Chinese food and housewares emporium.

Le Fanion, 299 W. 4th St., tel 212/463-8760. Subway: 1 to Christopher St. Closed a.m. & Sun. French ceramics old and new.

Mxyplyzyk, 125 Greenwich Ave., tel 212/989-4300. Subway: C, E to 14th St. Closed a.m. Sun. Housewares and gadgets of the most modern design.

Porthault, 18 E. 69th St. (bet. Madison & 5th Aves.), tel 212/688-1660. Subway: 6 to 68th St. Closed Sun. French luxury linens.

Pratesi, 829 Madison Ave. (at 69th St.), tel 212/288-2315. Subway: 6 to 68th St. Closed Sun. Italian linens.

Shabby Chic, 83 Wooster St. (bet. Spring & Broome Sts.), tel 212/274-9842. Subway: N, R to Prince St.; F to Bwy./Lafayette. Furnishings with multifaceted fabrics.

Waterworks, 225 E. 57th St. (bet. 2nd & 3rd Aves.), tel 212/371-9266, closed Sun. Subway: 4, 5, 6, N, R to 59th St. More than just a faucet shop.

Woodrow-Greenstein, 506 E. 74th St. (bet. York Ave. & FDR Dr), tel 212/988-2906. Subway: 6 to 77th St. Sat. by appt. only; closed Sun. Painted American country antiques, quilts.

JEWELRY

Cartier, 653 5th Ave. (near 52nd St.), tel 212/753-0111. Subway: E, V to 53rd St. Closed Sun. Old favorites to new design jewelry.

David Baruch, 36 W. 47th St., tel 212/719-2884. Subway: B, D, F to Rockefeller Center. Closed Fri.–Sun. Brand name silver.

Fortunoff, 681 5th Ave., tel 212/758-6660. Subway: B, D, F to Rockefeller Center. Closed Sun. a.m. Gold and silver jewelry, both new and antique.

Fred Leighton, 773 Madison Ave., tel 212/288-1872. Subway: 6 to 68th St. Closed Sun. Antique jewelry.

Gold Standard, 21 W. 47th St., tel 212/719-5656. Subway: B, D, F to Rockefeller Center. Closed Sat.–Sun. Gold jewelry and objets d'art.

Jean's Silversmiths, 16 W. 45th St. (bet. 5th & 6th Aves.), tel 212/575-0723. Subway: 4, 5, 6 to Grand Central. Closed Sat.–Sun. Antique silverware and objects. The place for those seeking value.

Jewelry Exchange, 15 W. 47th St., Subway: B, D, F to Rockefeller Center. Dizzying array of 30–40 retail jewelers' booths and shops.

M. M. Global, 32 W. 47th St., tel 212/391-4279. Subway: B, D, F to Rockefeller Center. Closed Sat.–Sun. Silver jewelry wholesaler.

Robert Lee Morris, 400 W. Broadway, tel 212/431-3630. Subway: C, E to 6th Ave.; 1 to

Houston St.; N, R to Prince St. Closed Sun. a.m.
Original gold and silver jewelry.
Tiffany, 727 5th Ave., tel 212/755-8000. Subway: N, R to 5th Ave. Closed Sun.
Jewelry, tabletop, and other fancy items. No breakfast.

TOYS: BIG KIDS, LITTLE KIDS

Chess Forum, 219 Thompson St., tel 212/475-2369. Subway: A, B, C, D, E, F to W. 4th St. Open daily 11 a.m. to midnight. www.chessforum.com.
Long-established, in the heart of the West Village—with an unparalleled collection of chess sets; playing room two doors away.
Dinosaur Hill, 306 E. 9th St. (bet. 1st & 2nd Aves.), tel 212/473-5850. Subway: 6 to Astor Pl.
Precious classics, from marionettes to craft kits. Wonderful and eclectic.
Enchanted Forest, 85 Mercer St., tel 212/925-6677. Subway: N, R to Prince St. Closed Sun a.m.
Fantasy toy store.
FAO Schwartz, 767 5th Ave. (at 58th St.), tel 212/644-9400. Subway: N, R to 5th Ave. Open since the mid-19th century. Toys, toys, toys.
Forbidden Planet, 840 Broadway, tel 212/475-6161. Subway: 4, 5, 6, N, R, L, Q to 14th St.–Union Sq.
The self-proclaimed sci-fi megastore, with everything from comics and graphic novels to apparel, games, and toys. Some material will be too adult for the younger set, so parents stay close.
Geppetto's Toy Box, 10 Christopher St. (at Greenwich Ave.), tel 212/620-7511. Subway: 1 to Christopher St.; A, C, E, B, D, F to W. 4th St.
Dolls to rubber duckies— most are handmade.
Pokémon Center, 10 Rockefeller Plaza (at 48th St.), tel 212/307-0900. Subway: B, D,

F, V to Rockefeller Center.
Go animated with trading cards or in the video game room.

MARKETS

The Annex/Hell's Kitchen Flea Market, 39th St. (bet. 9th & 10th Ave.). Subway: A, C, E to Port Authority/42nd St. Sat & Sun.
More than 100 vendors selling antiques, clothing, books, and rare and unusual things.
Flea Market, corner of Broadway and Grand St. Subway: 6 to Canal St.-Broadway. Sat & Sun.
Flea Market at P.S. 183, 419 E. 67th St. Subway: 6 to 68th St. Sat. only.
Union Square Greenmarket, uptown side of Union Sq. Subway: 4, 5, 6 to Union Sq. Mon., Wed., Fri., and Sat.
Local farmers sell their produce and flowers, cheeses, and ciders. Amazing selection with lots of unusual items and special events.

RECORDS, CDS

Academy Records & CDs, 12 W. 18th St., tel 212/242-3000. Subway: 1 to 18th St.
Used items, specializing in classical music.

PHOTOGRAPHY

Adorama Camera, 42 W. 18th St., tel 212/627-8487; 800/223-2500. Subway: 1 to 18th St.; 4, 5, Q to Union Sq. Closed Fri. at 1:15, all Sat.
B & H, 420 9th Ave., tel 212/444-6615 or 800/606-6969. Subway: A, C, E to 34th St. Closed Fri. 2 p.m., all Sat.
Well-priced photo/video supplies and equipment at this very large store.
K & M Camera, 377 E. 23rd St. (bet. 1st & 2nd Aves.), tel 212/532-1106. Subway: 6 to 23rd St. Mon.–Fri. 8:30 a.m.–7 p.m., Sat. 10 a.m.–6 p.m. **Also in Tribeca:** 385 Broadway (bet.

Walker & White). Subway: J, N, Q, 6, R to Canal St. Mon.–Fri. 9 a.m.–7 p.m., Sat. 11 a.m.–6 p.m.

THIS & THAT

The Art of Shaving, 141 E. 62nd St., tel 212/317-8436. Subway: 4, 5, 6 to 59th St. Closed Sun.
Supplies or a shave.
E.A.T., 1064 Madison Ave., tel 212/772-0022. Subway: 6 to 77th St. Closed a.m. Sun.
Gifts for all ages.
Fountain Pen Hospital, 10 Warren St., tel 212/964-0580. Subway: A, C to Chambers St. Closed Sat.–Sun.
Well-priced vintage and new pens. For a treat, call this place to hear the recording.
Kate's Paperie, 561 Broadway, tel 212/941-9816. Subway: N, R to Prince St.
Lovely paper and stationery.
Leo Kaplan Ltd., 114 E. 57th St. (bet. Park & Lexington Aves.), tel 212/355-7212. Subway: 6 to 59th St. Closed Sun.
Impressive antique and new paperweight collection.
Museums, museums, throughout the city. If you are stuck on what to bring home as a gift or are trying to find a unique memento for yourself, try any of the many excellent museum/institutional shops, including that of the New York Public Library. They offer a surprisingly wide selection of gift items in all price ranges, from the very inexpensive to fine textiles and exotic jewelry from throughout the world, as well as both art reproductions and fine art works. You are guaranteed to find items in these places you will see nowhere else. Plus, a shop visit is a fascinating way to glimpse some of what the institution itself offers, even if you do not have time to tour. Most places let visitors into the gift shop without paying admission.

ENTERTAINMENT

Oh, can you be entertained in New York City! The questions are how, and for how much? Just as with eating and shopping, there are options across the spectrum. Perhaps the most interesting time can be had by carefully scheduling anything you really have your heart set on doing, then leaving the rest to last-minute inspirations and serendipity. The real magic of the city often presents itself right on the street and out of the blue, and it is that element of exquisite randomness that native New Yorkers most enjoy talking about at the end of the day.

GENERAL ENTERTAINMENT INFORMATION
New York Convention & Visitors Bureau, 229 W. 42nd St. (bet. 7th–8th Aves.), tel 800/NYC-VISIT.
Literature on various forms of entertainment mailed to you, or speak to an agent (tel 212/484-1222 or website: www.nycvisit.com). Free tickets to concerts and TV tapings sometimes offered in person.
NYC/On Stage,
Theater Development Fund, 1501 Broadway (bet. 43rd–44th Sts.), tel 212/221-0885.

USEFUL PUBLICATIONS
Check out the *New York Times,* particularly Friday's Weekend section and Sunday's Arts and Leisure section; *The New Yorker, New York Magazine,* the *New York Observer,* the *Village Voice, Time Out New York,* and *Paper* (monthly).

USEFUL WEBSITES
www.nytimes.com The *New York Times,* strong on cultural events.
www.newyorkmag.com *New York Magazine* site with Cue section.
www.timeout.com/newyork *Time Out* listings and city guide.

THEATER

Theater, like other forms of entertainment in New York, runs the gamut from Broadway blockbusters to the most experimental skits in an East Village cellar. No one can say which you will find most appealing, but neither should be

written off. Off-off Broadway is inexpensive but can still be soul-nurturing, while wily ticket buyers can end up spending the same to see world-class productions. There are officially 38 Broadway theaters, about 20 Off Broadway (most under 500 seats), and about 300 Off-off Broadway venues (most under 100 seats).

SOURCES OF INFORMATION
It's always worth checking with the box office of the theater showing what you'd like to see. There may be house or single seats available, or cancellations. They are generally open from 10 a.m. until after the performance begins, and you can call them.

TKTS booths For 25–50% savings on Broadway and Off Broadway tickets, try your luck here. The Lower Manhattan Center is located at the South Street Seaport, 199 Water St. For evening and next-day matinee tickets only. Hours are 11 a.m.–6 p.m. Mon.–Sat. and 11 a.m.–3:30 p.m. Sun. The main branch is in the heart of the Theater District at 47th St. and Broadway, Duffy Sq. It is open daily (for same-day tickets), 3 p.m.–8 p.m. for evening performances, 10 a.m.–2 p.m. Wednesday and Saturday for matinees, and 11 a.m.–7 p.m. Sunday for all performances. They accept cash or travelers' checks only. Bring your theater-review magazines to help you decide. It is unusual to get your first choice.
Association for a Better New York, tel 212/370-5800.
Good information on smaller productions, and for investigating by venue versus show title.

Broadway Line, tel 212/563-2929 or 888/BROADWAY.
Current show information; you can be transferred to buy tickets.
New York Shakespeare Festival, tel 212/539-8500.
Free summer festival put on by the Public Theater, held at the Delacorte Theater, Central Park (at 81st St.). Two tickets per person are given out Tues.–Sun. at 1 p.m. (must line up at 10 a.m.) at the Public Theater (425 Lafayette St. bet. 4th St. and Astor Pl.) or at the Delacorte.
Prestige Entertainment, tel 212/697-7788.
Independent agent who may be able to find that seat.
Telecharge, tel 212/239-6200 or 800/432-7250.
Ticket agency to reserve seats for Broadway and Off Broadway by credit card for a small handling fee.
Ticketmaster, tel 212/307-4100 or 800/755-4000.
Same as above. Buy tickets on their website, www.ticketmaster.com.

BROADWAY VENUES
See pp. 114–115 for listings.
New Amsterdam, 214 W. 42nd St. (bet. 7th & 8th Aves.), tel 212/282-2900. Subway: 1, N, R to Times Square.
Acclaimed performances and outstanding productions. Tours available.

OFF BROADWAY VENUES
Astor Place Theater, 434 Lafayette St., tel 212/254-4370. Home of long-running Blue Man Group's *Tubes.*
Brooklyn Academy of Music, 30 Lafayette Ave., Brooklyn, tel 718/636-4100.
Established destination for innovative works.
Classic Stage Company, 136 E. 13th St. (bet. 3rd & 4th Aves.), tel 212/677-4210. Subway: L, N. R, 4, 5, 6 to 14th St.
Past works find influence again in today's audiences.
The Culture Project, 45 Bleecker St., tel 212/253-9983. Subway: 6 to Bleecker St.
Excellent short-run drama &

ENTERTAINMENT

performance with a socio-political edge. Meryl Streep and others have co-produced here.
La Mama E.T.C., 74A E. 4th St., tel 212/475-7710.
The mama of Off Broadway groundbreakers.
Lincoln Center Theater, 150 W. 65th St., tel 212/239-6200.
Top productions on two stages.
Manhattan Theatre Club, 131 W. 55th St., tel 212/581-1212.
Two theaters, one for new and established playwrights, the other for readings, workshops.
New York Theater Workshop, 79 E. 4th St., tel 212/780-9037.
New plays by young directors, including *Rent*.
The Public Theater, 425 Lafayette St., tel 212/260-2400.
One of the finest theaters in New York, founded by Joseph Papp.

OFF-OFF BROADWAY VENUES & COMPANIES
Bowerie Lane Theater, 330 Bowery at Bond St., tel 212/677-0060.
Home of Jean Cocteau Theater Company, retakes of classics.
Irish Repertory Theater, 132 W. 22nd St., tel 212/727-2737.
Classic and contemporary Irish playwrights.

DANCE

At the Music and Dance Booth in Bryant Park, half-price, day-of-performance tickets can be available to certain dance events. Also try TKTS (see p. 261).

BALLET
The American Ballet Theater, Metropolitan Opera House, 19th and Broadway, tel 212/477-3030.
Classics and works created in traditional style by founder Michael Mordkin. Large theater, so top tiers are far from stage. Also visiting foreign ballet companies.
New York City Ballet, New York State Theater, Columbus Ave. at 63rd St., tel 212/870-5570.

World-famous company, highlights works by founder George Balanchine, Jerome Robbins, Peter Martins, and other choreographers. Two seasons: just before Thanksgiving to the beginning of March, then beginning late April/May for 8 weeks. Its summer home is at the Saratoga Performing Arts Center—if you're looking for an overnight visit upstate, it is directly on the Amtrak line (tel 518/ 587-3330).

CONTEMPORARY DANCE
Brooklyn Academy of Music, 30 Lafayette Ave., Brooklyn, tel 718/636-4100.
Excellent modern dance companies, lovely stage, Next Wave festival every autumn featuring renowned artists and experimental dance, and other festivals featuring many dance forms.
Joyce, 175 8th Ave. (at 19th St.), tel 212/242-0800.
One of the best dance destinations with great variety and an emphasis on newer artists.
New York City Center, 131 W. 55th St., tel 212/581-1212.
Regular performances by famous, lesser known, and visiting troupes.

OTHER TROUPES & VENUES
Dance Theater of Harlem, 466 W. 152nd St., tel 212/690-2800.
Rarely in town, catch them if you can.
Dance Theater Workshop, 219 W. 19th St., tel 212/924-0077.
Relaxing atmosphere for alternative dance performances.
Julliard Theater, 155 W. 65th St, tel 212/769-7406 or 212/721-6500.
The Juilliard School performs at the Julliard Theater.
The Kitchen, 512 W. 19th St., tel 212/255-5793.
Experimental works.
Merce Cunningham Studio, 55 Bethune St., tel 212/691-9751. Various works.
Movement Research, 537

Broadway, tel 212/539-2611.
Free Monday night dance series since the 1960s.
P.S. 122, 150 1st Ave., tel 212/477-5288.
Unconventional works.

OUTDOOR SUMMER DANCE EVENTS
Central Park Summerstage, Rumsey Playfield at 72nd St., tel 212/360-2777.
Free dance program Fridays in July and the beginning of August.
Out of Doors Lincoln Center, 70 Lincoln Plaza, 212/875-5766.
Free dance events on plaza.

MUSIC

Tickets are available directly from venues, or can be booked through Ticketmaster for a fee, (tel 212/307-4100).
Another option, for discounted same day tickets, is TKTS (see p. 261).

CLASSICAL MUSIC
Alice Tully Hall, tel 212/721-6500. Home of Chamber Music Society.
Avery Fisher Hall, tel 212/875-5030. Home of the New York Philharmonic.
Bargemusic, Fulton Ferry Landing, Brooklyn, tel 718/636-6944.
Chamber music Thurs. to Sun. on a barge with an awesome view of Manhattan.
Brooklyn Academy of Music, 30 Lafayette Ave., Brooklyn, tel 718/636-4100.
Home of Brooklyn Philharmonic Orchestra, specializing in contemporary classical composers.
Carnegie Hall, 881 7th Ave., 154 W. 57th St., tel 212/247-7800.
One of the world's greatest.
Damrosch Park, tel 212/875-5500.
Free outdoor concerts in summer.
Julliard School of Music, tel 212/799-5000.
Many free recitals.

Kaufmann Concert Hall,
92nd St. YMCA, 1395 Lexington
Ave., tel 212/415-5440.
Great acoustics and interesting
series.
Lincoln Center, 55 W. 65th St.,
tel 212/875-5000. Hotline
212/LINCOLN.
**Metropolitan Museum of
Art,** 5th Ave. at 82nd St.,
tel 212/535-7710.
Chamber music in various
locations.

OTHER CLASSICAL MUSIC VENUES
**Cathedral of St. John the
Divine,** Amsterdam Ave. at
112th St., tel 212/316-7540.
Central Park Summerstage,
tel 212/360-2777.
Summertime concerts—many
are free.
**Church of St. Ignatius
Loyola,** 980 Park Ave.,
tel 212/288-2520.
Church of the Ascension,
5th Ave. (at W. 10th St.), tel
212/254-8620. Subway: N, R
to 5th Ave.
The Cloisters, Fort Tryon
Park, Inwood, tel 212/650-2290.
Subway: A to 190th St.
World Financial Center,
West St. (enter on Vesey St.),
tel 212/945-0505.

OPERA
Amato Opera Theater
Intimate, 319 Bowery at 2nd
St., tel 212/228-8200.
Julliard Opera Center,
Lincoln Center, tel 212/769-
7406. Students' productions.
Metropolitan Opera House,
Lincoln Center, tel 212/
362-6000.
Has its own company and
visiting performers, world-class
productions.
New York City Center,
131 W. 55th St., tel 212/581-
1212. Subway: N, R, Q, W to
57th St.
New York State Theater,
Lincoln Center, tel 212/ 870-
5570.
Variety of productions.

MUSIC VENUES
Many of these venues do not
accept credit cards.
Apollo Theater, 253 W. 125th
St., tel 212/531-5305 or
212/531-5337.
Variety of African-American
musical acts, especially on
amateur night (Wednesday).
Beacon Theater, 2124
Broadway (at 74th St.), tel
212/496-7070.
Mainstream and unusual groups.
Bitter End, 147 Bleecker St.,
tel 212/673-7030.
Small singer-songwriter joint.
Central Park Summerstage,
tel 212/360-2777.
Variety of acts.
Irving Plaza, 17 Irving Pl.,
tel 212/777-6800.
Mid-level nearly big-time acts.
Joe's Pub, 425 Lafayette St.,
tel 212/239-6200. Subway: 6
to Astor Place. Wide range of
music and a hip scene.
Jones Beach, Long Island,
tel 516/221-1000.
Summertime open amphitheater
for top performances.
Knitting Factory, 74 Leonard
St., tel 212/219-3132.
Progressive rock, experimental
music, etc.
Madison Square Garden,
7th Ave. at 33rd St.,
tel 212/465-6741.
Biggest rock acts.
Meadowlands, 50 Route 120,
East Rutherford, N.J.,
tel 201/935-3900.
Huge complex for big, big acts.
Mercury Lounge, 217 E.
Houston St., tel 212/260-4700.
Hip spot for new bands.
Nassau Coliseum, 1255
Hempstead Turnpike, Uniondale,
N.Y., tel 516/794-9303.
Biggest rock acts.
Paddy Reilly's, 519 2nd Ave.,
tel 212/686-1210.
Irish rock.
Radio City Music Hall, 50th
St. (at 6th Ave.), tel 212/465-
6100.
Art deco hall with huge acts.
Roseland, 239 W. 52nd St., tel
212/247-0200.
Major acts.
Shea Stadium, 126th St. at
Roosevelt Ave., Queens,
tel 718/507-8499.
The biggest rock concerts.

Sin'e, 148 Attorney St.,
tel 212/388-0077.
Modern Irish folk.
S.O.B's, 204 Varick St.,
tel 212/243-4940.
Premier world music venue.
Webster Hall, 125 E. 11th St.,
tel 212/353-1600.
Big downtown dance bar.

JAZZ & BLUES
Birdland, 315 W. 44th St.,
tel 212/581-3080.
A classier spot for top jazz.
Blue Note, 131 W. 3rd St.,
tel 212/475-8592.
Big names.
Dizzy's Club Coca-Cola,
Time Warner Center, 5th fl.,
Broadway at 60th St., tel 212/
258-9800.
Hottest new place for jazz; soul
food menu, affordable, amazing
Central Park views.
Iridium, 1650 Broadway at 51st
St., tel 212/582-2121.
Top performers.
Jazz Standard, 116 E. 27th St.,
tel 212/576-2232.
Restaurant/jazz club combo.
Knickerbocker, 74 Leonard St.
(bet. Broadway & Church St.),
tel 212/219-3055. Subway: N, R
to Astor Pl.
Good lineups of blues players.
Lenox Lounge, 288 Malcolm X
Blvd. (bet. W. 124th & W. 125th
Sts.), tel 212/427-0253. Subway:
2, 3 to 125th St.
Historic 1939 Art Deco
nightclub with good music and
good food.
Manny's Carwash, 1558 3rd
Ave. (bet. 87th–88th Sts.), tel
212/369-2583.
Local and national blues acts.
Smalls, 183 W. 10th St.,
tel 212/675-7369.
Emerging artists in a casual all-
night spot.
Village Vanguard, 178 7th Ave
South (at 11th St.), tel 212/255-
4037.
A basement club—the best.
Zinc Bar, 90 W. Houston St.
(corner of LaGuardia Pl.), tel
212/477-8337. Subway: 1 to
Houston St.
Preeminent spot for jazz &
Latin & Brazilian sounds.
Micro stage.

ENTERTAINMENT

CABARET

Bemelmans Bar, Carlyle Hotel, 35 E. 76th St., tel 212/744-1600.
Great ambience with fine pianists.
Café Carlyle, 35 E. 76th St., tel 212/744-1600.
Classic shows by Eartha Kitt and others (Woody Allen Ensemble plays Dixieland Mondays).
Danny's Skylight Room, 346 W. 46th St. (bet. 8th & 9th Aves.), tel 212/265-8130.
Subway: L to 8th Ave.
A variety of musical performances including jazz.
Don't Tell Mama, 343 W. 46th St., tel 212/757-0788.
Cabaret, emerging acts, revues.
Joe's Pub, 425 Lafayette St. (bet. E. 4th St. & Astor Pl.), tel 212/539-8770. Subway: 6 to Astor Pl.
Italian menu available at night.
The Oak Room, Algonquin Hotel, 59 W. 44th St., tel 212/419-9331.
Newly renovated & great performers.
Supper Club, 240 W. 47th St., tel 212/921-1940.
Ballroom with big bands and dancing; hot spot for salsa, Fri.–Sat.

COMEDY

Caroline's Comedy Club, 1626 Broadway at 49th St., tel 212/757-4100.
Comedy Cellar, 117 MacDougal St., tel 212/254-3480.
Comic Strip, 1568 2nd Ave. (bet. 81st and 82nd Sts.), tel 212/861-9386.
Dangerfield's, 1118 1st Ave. (at 61st St.), tel 212/593-1650.
Gotham Comedy Club, 34 W. 22nd St., tel 212/367-9000.
Top performers.
Improv Comedy Club, 318 W. 53rd (bet. 8th and 9th Aves.), tel 212/757-2323.
New & established acts.
New York Comedy Club, 241 E. 24th St., tel 212/696-5233.
Stand Up NY, 236 W. 78th St.,

tel 212/595-0850.
Small venue for up-and-coming as well as established acts.

FILM

In addition to regular Hollywood fare, the city offers unparalleled film selections unavailable in other locales, from small independent premieres to outdoor movies in Bryant Park in the summer. Many museums sponsor film festivals and there are fine collections open to the public in libraries and museums. Some of the world's best film-making programs and schools are here as well.

MovieFone, tel 212/777-FILM, www.moviefone.com, is a ticket-buying system ($1.50 surcharge) with recorded information on all films showing and their nearest locations.
The New York Film Festival, tel 212/875-5166, www.film linc.com, presented by the Film Society of Lincoln Center, begins in late September and consists of two weeks of new American and foreign films.
Tribeca Film Festival, www.tribecafilm.com. Premieres, screenings, panels, events throughout the city, and a Tribeca Family Street Fair. Focus on independent films. April–May for two weeks.

FOREIGN & INDEPENDENT FILM HOUSES
Angelika Film Center, 18 W. Houston St., tel 212/995-2000.
Asia Society 725 Park Ave., tel 212/517-2742.
IFC Center, 323 6th Ave. (at W. 3rd St.), tel 212/924-7771.
Lavishly renovated 3-screen movie theater run by the Independent Film channel.
Cinema Village, 22 E. 12th St., tel 212/924-3363.
Film Forum, 209 W. Houston St., tel 212/727-8110.
French Institute, 55 E. 59th St., tel 212/355-6160.
Lincoln Plaza Cinema,

Broadway (bet. 62nd & 63rd Sts.), tel 212/757-2280.
Paris Theater, 4 W. 58th St., tel 212/688-3800.
Quad Cinema, 34 W. 13th St., tel 212/255-8800.
68th St. Playhouse, 3rd Ave. (at 68th St.), tel 212/734-0302.
Walter Reade Theater, 165 W. 65th St. (bet. Broadway & Amsterdam), tel 212/875-5600.
Home of the Film Society of Lincoln Center.

CLASSIC FILM VENUES
Anthology Film Archives, 32 2nd Ave., tel 212/505-5181.
Film Forum, 209 W. Houston St., tel 212/727-8110.
Museum of Modern Art, 11 W. 53rd St., tel 212/708-9480.
Year round.
Museum of Television and Radio, 25 W. 52nd St., tel 212/621-6800.
Museum of the Moving Image, 35th Ave. at 36th St., Astoria, Queens, tel 718/784-0077.
Public Theater, 425 Lafayette St., tel 212/539-8500.
Whitney Museum of Art, 945 Madison Ave. (at 75th St.), tel 212/570-3600.

ULTRA MOVIE EXPERIENCES
The Ziegfeld, 141 W. 54th St., tel 212/765-7600.
1,400-seat, velvet-seated palace. A throwback and a classic venue, no matter what's playing.
Sony Theater, 1998 Broadway (at 68th St.), tel 212/336-5000.
Multistory screen with 3-D offerings. Short subjects.

CHILDREN'S CINEMA
IMAX Theater, at the American Museum of Natural History, Central Park W. at 79th St., tel 212/769-5200.
Nature movies on a huge screen.
Walter Reade Theater/Film Society of Lincoln Center, 165 W. 65th St. (bet. Broadway and Amsterdam Ave.), tel 212/875-5600.
Saturday morning children's series.

INDEX

Bold page numbers
indicate illustrations.

A

Abyssinian Baptist Church
198
Actors Studio 114
Adler Gallery 132
African Burial Ground 63
Airports and air services
46, **236**
Algonquin Hotel 111
Alice Austen House 216,
216
Alice Tully Hall 176, 178
Allen, Woody 14, 37, 81
American Academy and
Institute of Arts and
Letters 190, 195
American Bible Society 188
American Folk Art Museum
128
American Museum of
Natural History 174,
184–6, **184, 185, 186**
American Numismatic
Society 195
American Radiator Building
100
Angelika 73
Ansonia Hotel 174, 180
Apollo Theater 199
Appellate Division of the
Supreme Court 94
Architecture 38
Armory Show (1913) 82, **83**
Arnold Constable Dry
Goods Store 94
Arts, the 30–43
Asia Society 166
Astor Library 85
Astor Place 85
Audubon Terrace 190, 195
AXA Gallery 129

B

Bank of Manhattan Building
106
Bank of New York 25
Bar Association of the City
of New York Building 111
Barnard College 190
Barrymore Theater 114
Bartholdi, Frédéric 50
Bartow-Pell Mansion 222
Battery Park **42–3**, 53, 55
Castle Clinton 24, 53, **53**
Beekman Place 102
Belasco Theater 114
Bella C. Landauer
Collection of Business
and Advertising Ephemera
183
Beresford 187
Bialystoker Synagogue 69
Bike rental 237
Billiou-Stillwell-Perine
House 218

Bitter End 81
Bloomingdale's 161
Bobst Library, Washington
Square South 84
Borough Hall Brooklyn 206
Bowery Savings Bank 66
Bowling Green 54, 55
Bowne & Co 65
Brill Building 108
Broadhurst 114
Broadway 32–4, **34–5**,
60–61, 114–5, **114, 115**
884 Broadway 94
889–891 Broadway 94
901 Broadway 94
Bronx 204, 219–22
Bronx-Whitestone Bridge
44
Bronx Zoo 204, 221, **221**
Brooklyn 204, 206–14
Brooklyn Academy of Music
(BAM) 204
Brooklyn-Battery Tunnel
44
Brooklyn Botanic Garden
213, **213**
Brooklyn Bridge 44, **45**,
203
Brooklyn Children's
Museum 212
Brooklyn Heights 206–207,
207
Brooklyn Historical Society
206
Brooklyn Museum of Art
205, 210–12, **210–11**
Brooklyn Promenade 206
Bryant Park 100
Buses 236, 237

C

Cabaret 264
Café des Artistes 187
Capa, Robert 156
Carl Schurz Park 166
Carnegie, Andrew 128,
153
Carnegie Hall 128
Castello plan 158
Cathedral Church of
St. John the Divine 190,
192, **192**
CBGB's 77
Central Park 82, 33,
167–72, **167, 170–71**, 174
hotels 253
Central Park South 102,
130
Central Park West 187
Central Presbyterian
Church 163
Central Synagogue 116
Century Apartments 187
Century Association 111
Century Building 94
Chanin Building 105
Chelsea 90–91
Chelsea Art Museum 90
Chelsea Hotel 91, **91**

Chelsea Piers 46
Cherry Lane Theater 81
Children's Museum of
Manhattan 188, **188**
Chinatown 66, **67**
Chrysler Building 29, 38,
39, 106, **106**
Chumley's 81
**Churches, synagogues,
& temples**
Abyssinian Baptist Church
198
Bialystocker Synagogue
69
Cathedral Church of St.
John the Divine 190,
192
Central Synagogue 116
Church of our Lady of
Pompeii 81
Church of the Blessed
Sacrament 180
Church of the Holy
Apostles 91
Church of the Holy
Communion 91
Church of Our Lady of
Esperanza 195
Church of the Incarnation
and the Rectory 99
Church of the Most
Precious Blood 68
Church of the
Transfiguration 66
Eastern States Buddhist
Temple 66
Eldridge Street Synagogue
69
Episcopal Church of the
Holy Trinity 166
First Unitarian
Congregational Society
in Brooklyn 206
Friends Meeting House
224
Grace Church 86
Grace United Methodist
Church 209
Greater Metropolitan
Baptist Church 199
Holy Cross Church 104
John Street United
Methodist Church 60
Marble Collegiate Church
20
Mother African Methodist
Episcopal Zion Church
198
Our Lady of Lebanon
Cathedral 206
Plymouth Church of the
Pilgrims 207
St. Ann and the Holy
Trinity Episcopal Church
206
St. Bartholomew's Church
116
St. James Roman Catholic
Church 66

St. Luke in the Fields 81
St. Mark's-in-the-Bowery
86
St. Martin's Episcopal
Church & Rectory 199
St. Patrick's Cathedral
120
St. Patrick's Old Cathedral
68
St. Paul's Chapel 60
St. Peter's Episcopal
Church 91
St. Philip's Episcopal
Church 199
Shearith Israel Synagogue
180
Trinity Church 57
West End Collegiate
Church 180
Church of the Ascension
79
Church of the Blessed
Sacrament 180
Church of the Holy
Apostles 91
Church of the Holy
Communion 91
Church of the Incarnation
and the Rectory 99
Church of the Most
Precious Blood 68
Church of the
Transfiguration 66
Citicorp Center **40**,
116
City Hall 61, **61**, 62
City Hall Park 62–3, **63**
City Island 219
Civil War 26–28
Classical music 32
Clermont SHS 232
Cloisters **189**, 190, 196–97,
196, 197
Colony Club 162
Colony Records 110
Columbia University 190,
193, **193**
Low Library 193, **193**
Wallach Art Gallery 193
Columbus, Christopher
100
Columbus Circle **40**, 179,
179
Comedy venues 264
Commissioners' Plan
(1811) 26
Coney Island 214, **214**
Conference House 218
Coogan's Bluff 190
Cooper-Hewitt National
Design Museum 152–53,
152
Cooper Union 85
Cort Theater 114
Cosmopolitan Club 162,
162
Costume Institute 141
Crime and personal safety
237

Cunard Building 60
Cushman Row 91

D

Daily News Building 105
Dakota Apartments 38, 187, **187**
Davis, Miles 180
De Lamar Mansion 99
Delicatessens 15–16, **15–16**
Dental treatment 237
Dia Center for the Arts 90
Disabilities, travelers with 237
Dorilton 180
Doyers Street 66
Drawing Center 74
Duffy, Father Francis P. 104, 108
Duffy Square 104, 108
Dyckman Farmhouse Museum 197

E

East Village 76, 77, 86
Eastern States Buddhist Temple 66
Eating out 14–17, 238–55
Edgar Allan Poe Cottage 222
Edgar Rice Mansion 42
Educational Alliance 70
Edward Mooney House 66
El Barrio 132
El Museo del Barrio 132, 159, **159**
Eldorado 187
Eldridge Street Synagogue 69
Eleanor Roosevelt National Historic Site 232
Ellis Island National Monument 52, **52**
Elmhurst 204
Embassy Theater 108
Emergencies 237
Emergency phone numbers 237
Empire State Building 29, 38, 96, **96**
Entertainment 261
Episcopal Church of the Holy Trinity 166
Equitable Building 38, 60
Essex Street Market 70
Eva & Morris Feld Gallery 128
Events and festivals 236
Excursions 227–34
  Hudson River Valley 229, 230–32, **230–31**
  Long Island 229, 233–34
  map 228–29

F

F.A.O. Schwartz 121
Fashion Institute of Technology 88–89

Father Demo Square 81
Federal Hall 59, **59**
Federal Reserve Bank 60
Fifth Avenue 121, **121**, 132
Fillmore East 86
Film screenings 264
Film and television 37
Fire Island National Seashore **233**, 234
First Presbyterian Church 79
First Unitarian Congregational Society in Brooklyn 206
560 Broadway 73
Flatiron Building 29, 38, **87**, 94, **95**
Ford Foundation Building 105
Fort Lee Historic Park 230
Fort Tryon Park 190, 196
42nd Street 104
43nd Street 111
44th Street 111
Forward Building 70
Franklin D. Roosevelt National Historic Site 232
Fraunces Tavern **22**, 23, 55
Fred F. French Building 121
Freedom Tower 10, 49
Frick Collection 134–35, **134**, **135**
Fuller Building 116
Fulton, Robert 30, 57, 65
Fulton Fish Market 65

G

Garibaldi-Meucci Museum 218
Garment District 88–89
Gay Street 80
General Electric (GE) Building 116, 118
General Grant NM 190, 194–95, 194
General Post Office 97
General Theological Seminary 90
George Washington Bridge 44
Goddard Institute for Space Studies 191
Goethe Institut-New York 160
Grace Church 86
Grace United Methodist Church 209
Gracie Mansion 166, **166**
Gramercy Park 92–93, **93**
Gramercy Park Historic District 93
Grand Central Terminal 10, 104, **104–105**
Great White Way 103, 112–13, **112–13**
Greater Metropolitan Baptist Church 199
Green Market 94–95
Greenwood Cemetery 209

Greenwich Village 36, 76–77, 80–81, **80**, 82
  see also The Villages
Grey Art Gallery 84
Ground Zero 60
Guggenheim Museum **31**, **131**, 148–50, **148–49**, **150**
Guinness Exhibition of World Records 96

H

Hagop Kevorkian Center for Near Eastern Studies 84
Hall of Fame for Great Americans 219
Hamilton, Alexander **23**, 25, 57, 190, 193
Hamilton Heights 190
Hamilton Heights Historic District 199
Hamilton's House 190
Harlem 10, 190, 198–202, **198**, **199**
Harlem Renaissance 36, 200–201
Harmonie Club 163
Harrison Street Houses 71
Haughwout Building 72
Hayden Planetarium 186, **186**
Heights and Harlem 189–202
  Audubon Terrace 195
  Cathedral Church of St. John the Divine 190, 192, **192**
  Cloisters **189**, 190, 196–97, **196**, **197**
  Columbia University 190, 193, **193**
  General Grant National Memorial 190, 194–95, **194**
  Harlem 190, 198–202, **198**
  Heights 192–97
  map 191
  restaurants 255
  Schomburg Center for Research in Black Culture 202
Hell's Kitchen 102, 259
Helmsley Building 116
Helmsley Palace Hotel 116
Henderson Place Historic District 132
Henry Street Settlement 69
Herald Square 97
High Line 10
Hirschl Gallery 132
Hispanic Society of America 195
Historic preservation movement 41–3
Historic Richmond Town 217, **217**
History of New York 18–29
Holland Tunnel 44

Holy Cross Church 104
Hotel des Artistes 187
Hotel Belleclair 180
Hotel Theresa 199
Hotels and restaurants 238–55
Housing Works Used Book Café 73
Hudson River Valley 229, 230–32, **230–231**
  Clermont SHS 232
  Eleanor Roosevelt National Historic Site 232
  Fort Lee Historic Park 230
  Franklin D. Roosevelt National Historic Site 232
  Kingston 231
  Kykuit 232
  Montgomery Place 232
  New Paltz 231
  Olana S.H.S. 231
  Old Rhinebeck Aerodrome 232
  Philipsburg Manor 232
  Senate House S.H.S. 231
  Stony Point Battlefield S.H.S. 230
  Tarrytown 232
  Van Cortlandt Manor 232
  Vanderbilt Mansion 232
  Washington's Headquarters SHS 231
  West Point 230–231

I

IBM Building 116
Immigration 10
International Center of Photography 129
Wildlife Conservation Society (Bronx Zoo) 204, 221, **221**
Intrepid Sea, Air, Space Museum 129
Inwood 190
Irving, Washington 36, 60, 93
Isaac L. Rice House 181
Isamu Noguchi Garden Museum 226, **226**

J

Jacob K. Javits Convention Center 97, 179
Jacques Marchais Center of Tibetan Art 218, **218**
James N. Wells Row 91
James Watson House 49
Japan Society Gallery 129
Jazz at Lincoln Center 179
Jefferson Market Courthouse Library 80
Jewish Museum 154–55, **154–55**
John Street United Methodist Church 60

Johnson, Philip 38, 116, 123, 127, 128, 178
Jones Beach State Park 234
Judson Memorial Church 79
Julliard School of Music 178

K
Katz's 71
King of Greene Street 72
Kingston 231
Knickerbocker Hotel 105
Knoedler Gallery 132
Kykuit 232

L
La Guardia, Fiorello H. 46
Ladies' Mile 94–5
Lever House 41, 116
Lincoln Center 174, 176–78, **176–77, 178**
Lincoln Tunnel 44
Literature 35–37
Little Italy 66, 68
Little Singer Building 72–73
Long Island 229, 233–34
  Fire Island NS 234, **233**
  Jones Beach State Park 234
  Museums at Stony Brook 234
  Old Bethpage Village 234
  Old Westbury House and Gardens 233
  Planting Fields Arboretum State Historic Park 233
  Sagamore Hill NHS 233
  Walt Whitman Birthplace SHS 234, **234**
Lotos Club 162
Louis K Armstrong House 223
Lower East Side Tenement Museum 38, 69
Lower Manhattan 48–74
  Chinatown 66, **67**
  City Hall Park 62–63, **63**
  Ellis Island NM 52, **52**
  Federal Hall 59, **59**
  hotels and restaurants 238–41
  Little Italy 66, 68
  Lower East Side 68–70, **68, 69**
  map 48–49
  National Museum of the American Indian 56, **56**
  Neighborhoods 66–73
  New York Stock Exchange 25, 58, **58**
  SoHo and TriBeCa 70–71, **70–71**
  South Street Seaport 46, 61, 64–65, **64, 65**
  Statue of Liberty NM 10, **11, 47, 50–51, 50, 51**
  Trinity Church 57, **57**
  walk 60–61

Lyceum 114
Lyndhurst 232

M
McGraw-Hill Building 104
McSorley's Old Ale House 77
Macy's 97
Madison Avenue 132
Madison Square 94
Madison Square Garden 88, 97
Majestic 114, **114**
Majestic Apartments 180
Malcolm X 190
Manhattan 10, 18-19, **18-19, 190**
  see also Lower Manhattan
Marine Midland Building 60
Markets 260
Martin Beck Theater 114
Medical treatment 237
Memorial Presbyterian Church 209
Mercantile Exchange 130
Metropolitan Club 163
Metropolitan Life Insurance Company Building 94
Metropolitan Museum of Art 136–47, **136, 139, 140–47**
Metropolitan Opera House 178
Meyer Physics Hall 84
Middagh Street 206
Midtown North 101–130
  Broadway theaters 114–15
  Central Park South 102, 130
  Chrysler Building 29, 38, **39,** 106, **106**
  Fifth Avenue 121, **121,** 132
  42nd Street 104
  43rd and 44th Streets 111
  Grand Central Terminal 104–105, **105**
  hotels and restaurants 245–51
  map 102–103
  Museum of Modern Art 40, 122–27, **122–23, 124, 125, 126–27,** 204
  Rockefeller Center **101,** 102, 118–19, **119**
  St. Patrick's Cathedral 102–103, 120, **120**
  skyscraper walking tour 116–17
  Times Square 29, 34, 102, 103, 108–113, **109, 110, 112–13**
  United Nations Plaza 107, **107**
Midtown South 87–100
  Chelsea 90–91
  Empire State Building 29, 38, 96, **96**
  Gramercy Park 92–93, **93**

Herald Square 97
  hotels and restaurants 243–45
  map 88–89
  New York Public Library 40, 41, 88, 100, **100**
  walk 94–95
Millay, Edna St. Vincent 81
Mitzi E. Newhouse Theater 178
Monroe, Marilyn 114, 130
Montague Street 207
Montauk Club 209
Montgomery Place 232
Monuments
  Castle Clinton 53
  Ellis Island NM 52
  Federal Hall 59
  General Grant NM 194–95
  Statue of Liberty NM 50–51
Morgan House 99
Morgan Library and Murray Hill 98–99, **98**
Morningside Heights 190
Morris-Jumel Mansion 197
Mossman Collection of Locks 111
Mother African Methodist Episcopal Zion Church 198
Mount Morris Park Historic District 199
Mount Vernon Hotel Museum & Garden 161, **161**
Municipal Art Society 116
Municipal Building 62–63
Murray Hill 99
Museum of the Moving Image 225, **225**
Museums
  American Folk Art Museum 128
  American Irish Historical Society 160
  American Museum of Natural History 184–186
  American Numismatic Society 195
  Asia Society 166
  Bartow-Pell Museum 222
  Bowne House 224
  Brooklyn Children's Museum 212
  Brooklyn Historical Society 206
  Brooklyn Museum of Art 210–212
  Chelsea Art Museum 90
  Children's Museum of Manhattan 188
  The Cloisters Museum 196–197
  Conference House 218

Cooper-Hewitt National Design Museum 152–153
Edgar Allan Poe Cottage 222
Frick Collection, 134–35,
Garibaldi-Meucci Museum 226
Goethe Institut-New York 160
Gracie Mansion 166
The Guggenheim 148–150
Hispanic Society of America 195
International Center of Photography 129
Intrepid Sea-Air-Space Museum 129
Isamu Noguchi Garden Museum 226
Jacques Marchais Museum of Tibetan Art 218
Japan Society Gallery 128
Jewish Museum 154–55
Lower East Side Tenement Museum 69
Merchant's House Museum 86
Metropolitan Museum of Art 136–147
Morgan Library 98-99, **98**
Mount Vernon Hotel Museum & Garden 161, **161**
El Museo del Barrio 159
Museum for African Art 226
Museum of American Financial History 60, 74
Museum of Arts & Design 128, 129
Museum of Biblical Art 188
Museum of Bronx History 219
Museum of Chinese in the Americas 66
Museum of the City of New York 156–57
Museum of Jewish Heritage 74
Museum of Modern Art 122–27
Museum of the Moving Image 225, **225**
Museum of Sex 90
Museum of Television & Radio 130
National Academy of Design 151
National Museum of the American Indian 54, 56,
Neue Galerie New York 158
New York Academy of Sciences 160
New York City Fire Museum 74

New York Hall of Science 223
New-York Historical Society 182–83
New York Unearthed 74
Nicholas Roerich Museum 188
Pierre Billiou House 218
Queens Historical Society 224
Queens Museum of Art 223
P.S. 1 Contemporary Art Center 224
Rose Museum at Carnegie Hall 130
Rubin Museum 90
Schomburg Center for Research in Black Culture 202
Snug Harbor Cultural Center 215
Society of Illustrators: Museum of American Illustration 166
Socrates Sculpture Park 226
Staten Island Institute of Arts and Sciences 215
Studio Museum in Harlem 202
Ukrainian Institute of America 160
Ukrainian Museum 86
Van Cortlandt House Museum 222
Wallach Art Gallery, Columbia Univ. 193
Wave Hill 222
Whitney Museum of American Art 164–65
Whitney Museum of American Art at Altria 105, 164
Museum for African Art 226, **226**
Museum of American Financial History 60, 74
Museum of Arts & Design 128, **129**
Museum of Biblical Art 188
Museum of Bronx History 219
Museum of Chinese in the Americas 66
Museum of the City of New York 156–57, **156**, **157**
Museum of Jewish Heritage 74, **74**
Museum of Modern Art (MoMA) 40, 122–27, **122-23,124–25, 126, 204**
Museum of Sex 90
Museum of Television and Radio 130

Museum of the Moving Image 225, **225**
Museums at Stony Brook 234
Music venues 262–63

N
National Academy of Design 151, **151**
National Museum of the American Indian 56, **56**
Neighborhoods 66–71
Neue Galerie New York, 158, **158**
Neustadt Collection of Tiffany Lamps 183
New Amsterdam (theater) 114, 115
New Museum of Contemporary Art 73
New Paltz 231
New York Academy of Sciences 160
New York Botanical Garden 220, **220**
New York City Fire Museum 74
New York City Heritage Tourism Center 62
New York Hall of Science 223
New York Harbor 46
New-York Historical Society 174, 182–83
New York Life Insurance Company Building 94
New York Public Library 40, **41**, 88, 100, **100**
New York Public Library of the Performing Arts 176–77
New York Society for Ethical Culture 187
New York Society Library 166
New York State Theater 178
New York Stock Exchange 25, 58, **58**
New York Tea Party 21
New York Times 103
New York Times Building 29
New York Unearthed 74
New York University 84
New York Vietnam Veterans Memorial 55
New York Yacht Club 111
Newhouse Center for Contemporary Art 215
Nicholas Roerich Museum 188
Normandy Apartments 181
Norris, Frank 79
North Campus of City College 199
Northern Dispensary 81

O
Olana S.H.S. 231
Old Bethpage Village 234

Old Merchant's House 86
Old Rhinebeck Aerodrome 232
Old St. Patrick's Cathedral 68
Old Westbury House and Gardens 233
Orchard Street 69, **68–69**
Our Lady of Pompeii Church 81
Outer Boroughs 203–26
Bronx 204, 219–22
Brooklyn 204, 206–13
Coney Island 214
map 204–205
Queens 204, 223–26
restaurants 254–55
Staten Island 204, 215–18
Oyster Bar 14, **14–15**

P
Packer Collegiate Institute 206
Paramount Building 110
Paramount Hotel 110
Park Avenue 103, 132
Park Row 62
Park Slope Historic District 209, **209**
Parks
Bryant Park 100
Central Park 167–72
Flushing Meadows-Corona Park 223
Gramercy Park 92
Madison Square Park 94
Ralph Bunche Park 107
Riverside Park 181
Socrates Sculpture Park 226
Patchin Place 80
Paterson Strike Pageant 82, **83**
Pearl Paint 72
Peninsula New York 121
Pennsylvania Station 40, 41, 43
Performing Garage 72
Pharmacies 237
Philipsburg Manor 232
Photography District 89
Pieter Claesen Wyckoff House Museum 209
Planning your trip 236
Planting Fields Arboretum State Historic Park 233
Plaza Hotel 130, 246
Plymouth Church of the Pilgrims 207
Prospect Park 208
Grand Army Plaza 208, **208**
Lefferts Homestead 208
Prospect Park Zoo 208
Provincetown Playhouse 79
P.S. 1 Contemporary Art Center 224

Public transport 237
Puerto Rican Workshop 1 60

Q
Queen of Greene Street 72
Queens 204, 223–26
Bowne House 224, **224**
Friends Meeting House 224
Isamu Noguchi Garden Museum 226, **226**
Museum of the Moving Image 225, **225**
New York Hall of Science 223
P.S. 1 Contemporary Art Center 224
Queens Botanical Gardens 224
Queens Historical Society 224
Queens Museum of Art 223
Queens Wildlife Center 224
Unisphere 223, **223**
Shea Stadium 204, 224
Queens-Midtown Tunnel 44, **45**
Queensboro Bridge 44, 46

R
Racquet and Tennis Club 116
Radio City Music Hall 118
Rainbow Room 118
Ralph Bunche Park 107
Revolution 23
Riverside Park 181, 190
Rockefeller Center **101**, 102, 118–9, **119**
21 Club 118
Radio City Music Hall 118
Rainbow Room 118
Rockefeller University 161
Rollerblading 237
Rose Center for Earth & Space 186
Rose Museum at Carnegie Hall 130
Royalton Hotel 111, **111**
Rubin Museum 90

S
Sagamore Hill NHS 233
St. Ann and the Holy Trinity Episcopal Church 206
St. Bartholomew's Church 116
St. James 114
St. James Episcopal Church 163
St. James Roman Catholic Church 66
St. John's Episcopal Church 209

St. Luke's in the Fields 81
St-Mark's-in-the-Bowery 86
St. Martin's Episcopal Church and Rectory 1 99
St. Nicholas Historic District 198
St. Patrick's Cathedral 102–103, 120, **120**
St. Paul's Chapel 60
St. Peter's Episcopal Church **90**, 91
St. Peter's Lutheran Church 116
St. Philip's Episcopal Church 198
St. Regis Hotel 121
San Remo 187
Sardi's 110
Schermerhorn Row 64
Schomburg Center for Research in Black Culture 202
Seagram Building 116
Senate House SHS. 231
Seton, Blessed Elizabeth Ann 49
Shea Stadium 204, 224
Shearith Israel Graveyard 66
Shearith Israel Synagogue 180
Sheridan Square 81
Shopping 256–60
Silk Stocking District 162–63
Singer Tower 41
Skyride 96
Skyscrapers 38, 116–17
walking tour 116–17
Sniffen Court 99
Society of Illustrators: Museum of American Illustration 166
SoHo 49
Soldiers' and Sailors' Monument 181
Solomon R. Guggenheim Museum see Guggenheim Museum
Sony Building 116
Sony Wonder Technology Lab 116
South Street Seaport 46, 61, 64–5, **64**, **65**
Spanish Harlem 132
Staten Island 204, 215–18, **215**
Alice Austen House 216, **216**
Billiou-Stillwell-Perine House 218
Conference House 218
Garibaldi-Meucci Museum 218
Jacques Marchais Center of Tibetan Art 218, **218**

Newhouse Center for Contemporary Art 215
Snug Harbor Cultural Center 215
Staten Island Botanical Garden 215
Staten Island Children's Museum 215
Staten Island Institute of Arts & Sciences 215
Staten Island Zoological Park 215
Statue of Liberty 10, **11**, **47**, 50–51, **50**, **51**
Stephen Van Rensselaer House 215
Stonewall Inn 81
Stony Brook 234
Stony Point Battlefield S.H.S. 230
Strand Book Store 86, 257
Strasberg, Lee 114
Streit's Matzoh Company 70
Studio Museum in Harlem 202
Stuyvesant-Fish House 86
Subways 237
Sugar Hill 190, 199
Surrogates' Court or Hall of Records 62
Sutton Place 102

T
Tarrytown
Lyndhurst 232
Sunnyside 232
Temple Emanu-El 163
Theater 32–35, 261–62
The National Arts Club 93
The Public Theater 85
Theodore Roosevelt Birthplace N.H.S. 93
Throgs Neck Bridge **44**
Ticker-tape parades **26**, 62
Tiffany's 121
Time Warner Center 10, 17, 40, 179, **179**
Times Square 29, 34, 102, 103, 108–113, **109**, **110**, **112–13**
Times Tower 103, 110
Tisch Hall 84
TKTS 108
Tompkins Square 77
TriBeCa 49, 71
TriBeCa Film Center 71
TriBeCa Film Festival 264
Triborough Bridge 44
Trinity Church 57, **57**
Trinity Church Museum 57
Trump Building 59
Trump Tower 121
Tunnels 44

Turtle Bay Gardens Historic District 130
Tweed Courthouse 63

U
UBS Art Gallery 129
Ukrainian Institute of America 160, **160**
Ukrainian Museum 86
Union Club 162
Union Square 94
Union Theological Seminary 190
Unisphere 223, **223**
United Nations Plaza 107, **107**
Conference Building 107
General Assembly 107
Secretariat Building 38, 107
Upper East Side 131–66
Cooper Hewitt National Design Museum 152–53, **152**
El Museo del Barrio 160, **160**
Frick Collection 134–35, **134**, **135**
Guggenheim Museum **31**, **131**, 148–50, **148–49**, **150**
hotels and restaurants 251–53
Jewish Museum 154–55, **154–5**
map 132–33
Metropolitan Museum of Art 136–47, **136**, **139**, **140–47**
Museum of the City of New York 158–9, **158**, **159**
Whitney Museum of American Art 164–65, **164–65**
Upper West Side 173–88
American Museum of Natural History 174, 184–86, **184**, **185**
Central Park West 187
hotels and restaurants 253–54
Lincoln Center 174, 176–78, **176–77**, **178**
map 175
Museum of American Folk Art 128, **128**
New-York Historical Society 174, 182–83
walk 180–81
Urban Center Galleries 116
Urban rejuvenation 28–29
U.S. Custom House 54

V
Van Corlandt House Museum 222
Van Cortlandt Manor 232

Vanderbilt Mansion 232
Verdi Square 180
Verrazano Narrows Bridge 44
The Villages 75–86
Astor Place 85
East Village 76, 77, 86
hotels and restaurants 241–43
map 76–77
New York University 84
walk 80–81
Washington Square Park 78–9, **78–79**
Villard Houses 116
Vivian Beaumont Theater 176, 178

W
Waldorf-Astoria Hotel 116
Walking tours
Broadway 60–61
Brooklyn Heights 206–207
Greenwich Village 80–81
Ladies' Mile 94–95
skyscrapers 116–17
SoHo 70–71
Upper West Side 180–81
Wall Street 55
Walt Whitman Birthplace S.H.S. 234, **234**
Washington Heights 190
Washington Square 77
Washington Square Park 78–79, **78–79**
Washington's Headquarters S.H.S. 231
Wave Hill 222
Websites 236
West End Collegiate Church 180
West Point 230–31
West Village 76, 77
White Horse Tavern 77
Whitney Museum of American Art at Altria 105
Whitney Museum of American Art 82, 164–65, **164–65**
Wildlife Conservation Society (Bronx Zoo) 204, 221, **221**
Woodlawn Cemetery 219
Woolworth Building 29, 60–61
Worldwide Plaza 130
W.R. Grace Building 105

Y
Yankee Stadium 204, 219
Yorkville 132

Z
Zeigfeld Follies 115

ILLUSTRATIONS CREDITS

Abbreviations for terms appearing below: (t) top; (b) bottom; (l) left; (r) right.

Cover, (l), Image Bank. (c), Kelly/Mooney Photography. (r), Tony Stone Images.
Back cover, Royalty-Free/CORBIS.

1, Steve Allen/Getty Images. 2-3, Dallas & John Heaton/CORBIS. 4, Nathan Benn/CORBIS. 9, Setboun Michel/CORBIS SYGMA. 11, Kelly/Mooney Photography. 12-13, Cosmo Condina/Getty Images. 14-15, Mark Peterson/CORBIS. 16-17, Steve McCurry. 18-19, akg-images. 21, Bridgeman Art Library. 22, Fraunces Tavern Museum/Sons of the Revolution in the State of NY, Inc. 23, Art Resource. 24-25, The Metropolitan Museum of Art. 26, NASA. 27, Kelly/Mooney Photography. 28-29, Karen Kasmauski. 31, The Worlds of Nam June Paik, February 11-April 26, 2000. Solomon R. Guggenheim Museum, New York. Ellen Labenski/The Solomon R. Guggenheim Foundation, New York. 33, Kelly/Mooney Photography. 34-35, Jeff Christensen/Reuters/CORBIS. 36, FPG. 39, Nathan Benn. 40, Martha Cooper/Peter Arnold, Inc. 41, Michael S. Yamashita/CORBIS. 42-43, Andrew Gordon/Panoramic Images/National Geographic Image Collection. 45(t), Royalty-Free/CORBIS. 45(b), Reuters NewMedia Inc./CORBIS. 47, Clive Sawyer/AA Photo Library. 50, Photo Researchers Inc. 51(t), Royalty-Free/CORBIS. 51(b), art-work Matlings. 52, Kelly/Mooney Photography. 53, Douglas Corrance/AA Photo Library. 54-55, Kelly/Mooney Photography. 56(t), Katherine Fogden/National Museum of the American Indian, Smithsonian Institution. 56(b), Walter Larrimore/National Museum of the American Indian, Smithsonian Institution. 57, Photo Researchers Inc. 58, Kelly/Mooney Photography. 59, Kelly/Mooney Photography. 61, R. Elliott/AA Photo Library. 62, Kelly/Mooney Photography. 63, Royalty-Free/CORBIS. 64, Kelly/Mooney Photography. 65, Omni Photo Communications Inc./PictureQuest. 67, Photo Researchers Inc. 68-69, Mary Ann Lynch. 69, Mary Ann Lynch. 70-71, Steve McCurry. 73, Mary Ann Lynch. 74, Lee Snider/Photo Images/CORBIS. 75, Bernard Grilly/Getty Images. 78-79, Mitchell Funk/Getty Images. 80, Mary Ann Lynch. 81, Ellen Rooney/AA Photo Library. 83(t), Tamiment Institute Library, New York University. 83(bl), Tamiment Institute Library, New York University. 83(br), Image is courtesy of the Walt Kuhn, Kuhn family papers, and Armory Show records, 1882-1966 in the archives of American Art, Smithsonian Institution. 84, Paul Hawthorne/Getty Images. 85, Allan Montaine/Lonelyplanetimages.com. 86, Stephen Chernin/Getty Images. 87, Todd Gipstein/National Geographic Image Collection. 90, Mario Tama/Getty Images. 91(t), Steve McCurry. 91(b), Peter Bennett/New York Stock Photo. 92, Farrell Grehan/CORBIS. 95, Kelly/Mooney Photography. 96, Kelly/Mooney Photography. 97, Seth Wenig/Reuters/CORBIS. 98, Joe McNally. 100, Mike Segar/Reuters/CORBIS. 101, Todd Gipstein/National Geographic Image Collection. 104-105, Francesco Ruggeri/Getty Images. 106, Richard Berenholtz/CORBIS. 107, Photo Researchers Inc. 109, Grant Faint/Getty Images. 110, Photo Researchers Inc. 111, Royalton. 112-113, Macduff Everton/Getty Images. 114, Rick Shupper /New York Stock Photo. 115, The Image Bank, Getty Images. 116, Richard T. Nowitz/CORBIS. 117, Alan Schein Photography/CORBIS. 119, David James/Getty Images. 120, Chris Hondros/Getty Images. 121(t), Superstock. 121(b), Douglas Corrance/AA Photo Library. 122-123, Mary Altaffer, AP/Wide World Photos. 124, Zack Seckler, AP/Wide World Photos. 125, Amy Jicha. 126, Zack Seckler, AP/Wide World Photos. 127, Amy Jicha. 128, Michael Moran/American Folk Art Museum. 130, Photo Researchers Inc. 131, Roger Wood/CORBIS. 134, The Frick Collection, New York. 135, The Frick Collection, New York. 136, Richard Elliott/AA Photo Library. 138, artwork Maltings. 139, Douglas Corrance/AA Photo Library. 140-141, Joe McNally. 142(t), Bridgeman Art Library. 142(b), Pieter Bruegel the Elder. The Harvesters, 1565. Oil on wood. The Metropolitan Museum of Art. 143, Photo Researchers Inc. 144, Pierre-Auguste Renoir. The Daughters of Catulle Mendès, Hughette (1871–1964), Claudine (1876–1937), and Helyonne (1879–1955). 1888. Oil on canvas. The Metropolitan Museum of Art. 145, Joe McNally. 146-147, Joe McNally. 148-149, Joe McNally. 149, Catherine Karnow/CORBIS. 150, Joe McNally. 151, Courtesy of the National Academy Museum. 152, Michael S. Yamashita/CORBIS. 154, Art Resource. 154-155, Jeffrey Greenberg /New York Stock Photo. 155, Art Resource. 157, Bridgeman Art Library. 158, Neue Galerie New York/Courtesy Museum of the City of New York. 159, El Museo del Barrio. 160, Pysanky by Sofika/photo by L.Zielyk/www.sofika.com 161, The Mount Vernon Hotel Museum. 162, nyc-architecture.com. 163, Richard Elliott/AA Photo Library. 164, Whitney Museum of American Art. 164-5, Whitney Museum of American Art. 166, Phillip Schoultz, AP/Wide World Photos. 167, José Azel. 170-171, Photo Researchers Inc. 172, Craig Lovell/CORBIS. 173, Louie Psihoyos/CORBIS. 176-177, Photo Researchers Inc. 177, Kelly/Mooney Photography. 178, Kelly/Mooney Photography. 179, Mary Ann Lynch. 182, New York Historical Society. 183, Bridgeman Art Library. 184, D.Finnin/American Museum of Natural History. 185, D.Finnin/American Museum of Natural History. 186, D.Finnin/American Museum of Natural History. 187, Douglas Corrance/AA Photo Library. 188(t), Rebekka Kunh/Children's Museum of Manhattan. 188 (b), Nicholas Roerich Museum. 189, Philip Gould/CORBIS. 192, Photo Researchers Inc. 193, Photo Researchers Inc. 194, Photo Researchers Inc. 195, James Leynse/CORBIS. 196, Photo Researchers Inc. 197, Kelly/Mooney Photography. 198, Mary Ann Lynch. 199, Mary Ann Lynch. 200, Library of Congress/CORBIS. 201(t), Culver Pictures. 201(bl), Bettmann/CORBIS. 201(br), Culver Pictures. 202, Bridgeman Art Library. 203, National Geographic Society. 207, SuperStock. 208, Lee Snider/Photo Images/CORBIS. 209, Kathrine Novak. 210-211, Bridgeman Art Library. 213, Mario Tama/Getty Images. 214, AA Photo Library/Richard Elliott. 215, Chip East/Reuters/CORBIS. 216, Courtesy of Friends of Alice Austen House. 217, Tony Perrottet /New York Stock Photo. 218, The Jacques Marchais Museum of Tibetan Art. 219, Steve Crandall/ProAm Sports.

220, Lee Snider/Photo Images/CORBIS. 221, D. DeMello/Wildlife Conservation Society. 222, Wave Hill. 223, Joshua Sheldon/Getty Images. 224, Richard Elliott/AA Photo Library. 225, Museum of the Moving Image. 226, Tony Perrottet /New York Stock Photo. 227, Richard Elliott/AA Photo Library. 230-231, SuperStock. 232, SuperStock. 233, SuperStock. 234, SuperStock. 235, Andrew Shennan/Getty Images.

The world's largest nonprofit scientific and educational organization, the National Geographic Society was founded in 1888 "for the increase and diffusion of geographic knowledge." Since then it has supported scientific exploration and spread information to its more than nine million members worldwide.

The National Geographic Society educates and inspires millions every day through magazines, books, television programs, videos, maps and atlases, research grants, the National Geographic Bee, teacher workshops, and innovative classroom materials.

The Society is supported through membership dues, charitable gifts, and income from the sale of its educational products. Members receive NATIONAL GEOGRAPHIC magazine—the Society's official journal—discounts on Society products, and other benefits.

For more information about the National Geographic Society, its educational programs, publications, or how to support its work, call 1-800-NGS-LINE (647-5463), or write to: National Geographic Society, 1145 17th Street, N.W., Washington, D.C. 20036 U.S.A.

Printed in Spain

Published by the National Geographic Society

John M. Fahey, Jr., *President and Chief Executive Officer*
Gilbert M. Grosvenor, *Chairman of the Board*
Nina D. Hoffman, *Executive Vice President,*
    President, Books and School Publishing
Kevin Mulroy, *Senior Vice President and Publisher*
Marianne Koszorus, *Design Director*
Kristin Hanneman, *Illustrations Director*
Elizabeth L. Newhouse, *Director of Travel Publishing*
Barbara A. Noe, *Senior Editor and Series Editor*
Lawrence M. Porges, *Project Manager for 2006 edition*
Cinda Rose, *Art Director*
Carl Mehler, *Director of Maps*
Nicholas P. Rosenbach, *Map Coordinator*
R. Gary Colbert, *Production Director*
Richard S. Wain, *Production Project Manager*
Rebecca Hinds, *Managing Editor*
Mary Ann Lynch, *Contributing Editor and author of New York Today*
Jack Brostrom, Jennifer Davis, Steven D. Gardner, Caroline Hickey, Rebecca Gross, Teresa Neva Tate, Ruth Thompson, John Wagley, and Mapping Specialists, *Contributors to 2006 edition*

First edition: Edited and designed by AA Publishing (a trading name of Automobile Association Developments Limited, whose registered office is Norfolk House, Priestley Road, Basingstoke, Hampshire, England RG24 9NY. Registered number: 1878835).
Betty Sheldrick, *Project Manager*
David Austin, *Senior Art Editor*
Marilynne Lanng, *Editor;* Phil Barfoot, Nick Otway, *Designers*
Simon Mumford, *Senior Cartographic Editor*
Nicky Barker-Dix, Helen Beever, *Cartographers*
Richard Firth, *Production Director*
Picture Research by Poppy Owen, Image Select International Limited
Map art by Chris Orr Associates, Southampton, England
Cutaway illustrations drawn by Maltings Partnership, Derby, England

Second Edition 2006
ISBN: 0-7922-5370-1

Library of Congress Cataloging-in-Publication Data
The National geographic traveler. New York.
    p. cm.
    Includes index.
    ISBN 0-7922-7430-X (alk. paper)
    1. New York (N.Y.)—Guidebooks. 1. National Geographic Society
(U.S.) 11. Title: New York.
F128.18.N28   1999
917.47'10443—dc21   99-11701
                                      CIP

Printed and bound by Cayfosa Quebecor, Barcelona, Spain. Color separations by Leo Reprographic Ltd., Hong Kong. Cover separations by L.C. Repro, Aldermaston, U.K.

Visit the society's Web site at http://www.nationalgeographic.com